Routledge Questions & Answers

Commercial

2013–2014

Routledge Q&A series
Each Routledge Q&A contains approximately 50 questions on topics commonly found on exam papers, with comprehensive suggested answers. The titles are written by lecturers who are also examiners, so the student gains an important insight into exactly what examiners are looking for in an answer. This makes them excellent revision and practice guides. With over 500,000 copies of the Routledge Q&As sold to date, accept no other substitute.

New editions publishing in 2013:

Civil Liberties & Human Rights
Company Law
Commercial Law
Constitutional & Administrative Law
Contract Law
Criminal Law
Employment Law
English Legal System
Equity & Trusts
European Union Law

Evidence
Family Law
Jurisprudence
Land Law
Medical Law
Torts

Published in 2012:

Business Law 2012–2013
Intellectual Property Law 2012–2013

For a full listing, visit http://cw.routledge.com/textbooks/revision

Routledge Questions & Answers Series

Commercial Law

2013–2014

Jo Reddy, LLB, LLM
Barrister

AND

Howard Johnson, LLB (BIRM)
Part-time LL.M Tutor, Cardiff Law School

Additional content supplied by:
Kathrin Kühnel-Fitchen
Northumbria University

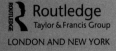
Routledge
Taylor & Francis Group

LONDON AND NEW YORK

Seventh edition published 2013
by Routledge
2 Park Square, Milton Park, Abingdon, Oxon OX14 4RN

Simultaneously published in the USA and Canada
by Routledge
711 Third Avenue, New York, NY 10017

Routledge is an imprint of the Taylor & Francis Group, an informa business

First edition published by Cavendish Publishing 1994
Sixth edition published by Routledge 2011

British Library Cataloguing in Publication Data
A catalogue record for this book is available from the British Library

Library of Congress Cataloging in Publication Data
Reddy, Jothi.
 Q & A commercial law / Jo Reddy and Howard Johnson. — 7th ed.
  p. cm.
 ISBN 978–0–415–69684–5 (pbk)—ISBN 978–0–203–08395–6 (ebk)
 1. Commercial law—England. I. Johnson, Howard (Howard Allun), 1948– II. Title. III. Title: Q and A
 commercial law. IV. Title: Commercial law.
 KD1554.Z9R43 2012
 346.4207076—dc22

                                                          2012029827

ISBN: 978–0–415–69684–5 (pbk)
ISBN: 978–0–203–08395–6 (ebk)

Typeset in TheSans
by RefineCatch Limited, Bungay, Suffolk

MIX
Paper from
responsible sources
FSC
FSC® 0004035

Printed and bound in Great Britain by the MPG Books Group

Contents

Table of Cases

Table of Legislation

EU LEGISLATION

SECONDARY LEGISLATION

Guide to the Companion Website

http://cw.routledge.com/textbooks/revision

Visit the Routledge Q&A website to discover even more study tips and advice on getting those top marks.

On the Routledge revision website you will find the following resources designed to enhance your revision on all areas of undergraduate law.

The Good, The Fair, & The Ugly

Good essays are the gateway to top marks. This interactive tutorial provides sample essays together with voice-over commentary and tips for successful exam essays, written by our Q&A authors themselves.

Multiple Choice Questions

Knowledge is the foundation of every good essay. Focusing on key examination themes, these MCQs have been written to test your knowledge and understanding of each subject in the book.

Bonus Q&As

Having studied our exam advice, put your revision into practice and test your essay writing skills with our additional online questions and answers.

Don't forget to check out even more revision guides and exam tools from Routledge!

Lawcards

Lawcards are your complete, pocket-sized guides to key examinable areas of the undergraduate law.

Routledge Student Statutes

Comprehensive selections; clear, easy-to-use layout; alphabetical, chronological, and thematic indexes; and a competitive price make *Routledge Student Statutes* the statute book of choice for the serious law student.

Introduction

This book is intended to be of help to students studying commercial law who feel that they have acquired a body of knowledge, but do not feel confident about using it effectively in exams. This book sets out to demonstrate how to apply the knowledge to the question and how to structure the answer. Students, especially first-year students, often find the technique of answering problem questions particularly hard to grasp, so this book contains a large number of answers to such questions. This technique is rarely taught in law schools and the student who comes from studying science or maths A levels may find it particularly tricky. Equally, a student who has studied English literature may find it difficult to adapt to the impersonal, logical, concise style that problem answers demand. A student who has done largely project work will often find a 3 hour unseen paper written examination very daunting. It is hoped that this book will be particularly useful at exam time, but may also prove useful throughout the year. The book provides examples of the kind of questions that are usually asked in end-of-year examinations, along with suggested solutions. Each chapter deals with one of the main topics covered in commercial law courses and contains typical questions on that area. The aim is not to include questions covering every aspect of a course, but to pick out the areas that tend to be examined because they are particularly contentious or topical. Many courses contain a certain amount of material that is not examined, although it is important as providing background knowledge. It cannot be over emphasised enough that it will help students to have an awareness of the general context of the subject and what issues are currently topical or controversial. Examiners are always impressed if an answer alludes to a current issue to illustrate an argument, particularly if it is not one the lecturer has raised.

PROBLEM AND ESSAY QUESTIONS

Some areas tend to be examined only by essays, some mainly – although not invariably – by problems, and some by either. The questions chosen reflect this mix, and the introductions at the beginning of each chapter discuss the type of question usually asked. It is important not to choose a topic and then assume that it will appear on the exam paper in a particular form unless it is in an area where, for example, a problem question is never set. If it might appear as an essay or a problem, revision should be geared to either possibility: a very thorough knowledge of the area should be acquired, but also an awareness of critical opinion in relation to it. In most cases, unless there has been a change of personnel or revision of the syllabus past exam papers should always be looked at carefully. Reading the rubric and understanding it is absolutely essential. Students should not assume that all questions will be confined to a single area of the subject – commonly in Commercial Law there may well be an issue about exemption clauses or damages alongside for example an issue about the application and scope of the implied terms in **ss 12–15** of the **Sale of Goods Act 1979**.

LENGTH OF ANSWERS

The answers in this book are about the length of an essay that a good student would expect to write in an exam. Some are somewhat longer and these will also provide useful guidance for students writing assessed essays, which typically are between 2,000 and 3,000 words. In relation to exam questions, there are a number of reasons for including lengthy answers: some students can write long answers – about 1,800 words – under exam conditions; some students who cannot nevertheless write two very good and lengthy essays and two reasonable but shorter ones. Such students tend to do very well, although it must be emphasised that it is always better to aim to spread the time evenly between all four essays. Therefore, some answers indicate what might be done if very thorough coverage of a topic were to be undertaken.

THE ENDNOTES

Some of the questions also provide footnotes exploring some areas of the answer in more depth, which should be of value to the student who wants to do more than cover the main points. Some answers provide a number of footnotes; it would not be expected that any one student would be able to make all of the points they contain, but they demonstrate that it is possible to choose to explore, say, two interesting areas in more depth in an answer once the main points have been covered. It cannot be emphasised enough that the main points have to be covered before interesting, but less obvious, issues can be explored. These are distinct from the marker commentary, which are marked numerically in the footnotes

EXPRESSING A POINT OF VIEW

Students sometimes ask, especially in an area such as say the imposition of bank changes for unauthorised overdrafts, which can be quite topical and politically controversial, whether they should argue for any particular point of view in an essay. It will be noticed that the essays in this book tend to do this. In general, the good student does argue for one side but he or she always uses sound arguments to support his or her view. Further, a good student does not ignore the opposing arguments; they are considered and, if possible, their weaknesses are exposed. Of course, it would not be appropriate to do this in a problem question or in some essay questions but, where an invitation to do so is held out, it is a good idea to accept it rather than sit on the fence. Individual expression is not something to be avoided but should be based on reasoned and rationale arguments.

EXAM PAPERS

Commercial law exam papers vary in relation to the number of substantive topics included in the syllabus e.g. some will deal with agency but others not, however normally will include one question on each of the main areas of the syllabus. For example, a typical paper might include problem questions on the implied terms (ss 12–15 of the Sale of Goods Act 1979), passing of property and risk (ss 16–20 of the Sale of Goods Act 1979), the nemo dat rule and its exceptions (ss 21–25 of the Sale of Goods Act 1979, s 2 of the Factors Act 1889, Pt III of the Hire-Purchase Act 1964), if dealt with retention of title (Romalpa Clauses), and some aspect of remedies. As said subsidiary issues such as the validity of an exclusion clause in a business to business contract will probably appear. If agency has been dealt with then a question on the authority of an agent and the scope and application of the Commercial Agents Directive are favourites. Some courses will deal with Consumer Credit law others will not or will treat it as part of a separate consumer law module, so do not be surprised to find in the book answers to questions on areas you will not have dealt with in the module offered by your Law School. Therefore, the questions have to be fairly wide-ranging in order to cover a reasonable amount of ground on each topic. Some answers in this book therefore have to cover some of the same material, especially where it is particularly central to the topic in question e.g the scope and application of the implied term as to satisfactory quality in s 14(2) of the Sale of Goods Act 1979.

SUGGESTIONS FOR EXAM TECHNIQUE

Below are some suggestions that might improve exam technique; some failings are pointed out that are very commonly found on exam scripts. A pre-question plan is a very useful idea particularly in a problem question – as many marks are lost by bad technique – particularly in a problem question – as are lost by lack of knowledge. A very good example of this is a question of tracking a series of transactions to determine whether the buyer at the end of a line of sub-sales has obtained a good title, involving the nemo dat rule and its exceptions – it is all too easy to miss a transaction or leave a party out if a proper structure plan is not prepared indicating the main points and cases to discuss.

(1)   When tackling a problem question, do not write out the facts in the answer. Quite a number of students write out chunks of the facts as they answer the question – perhaps to help themselves to pick out the important issues. It is better to avoid this and merely to refer to the significant facts.

(2)   Use an impersonal style in both problem and essay answers. In an essay, you should rarely need to use the word 'I' and, in our view, it should not be used at all in a problem answer. (Of course, examiners may differ in their views on this point.) Instead, you could say 'it is therefore submitted that' or 'it is arguable that'; avoid saying 'I believe that' or 'I feel that'.

(3)   In answers to problem questions, try to explain at the beginning of each section of your answer what point you are trying to establish. You might say, for example: 'In order to show that liability under s 1 will arise, three tests must be satisfied.' You

should then consider all three, come to a conclusion on each, and then come to a final conclusion as to whether or not liability will arise. If you are really unsure whether or not it will arise (which will often be the case – there is not much point in asking a question to which there is one very clear and obvious answer), then consider what you have written in relation to the three tests. Perhaps one of them is clearly satisfied, one is probably satisfied and the other (arising under, for example, s 1(8)) probably is not. You might then say: 'As the facts give little support to an argument that s 1(8) is satisfied, it is concluded that liability is unlikely to be established.'

(4) You do not get double the marks for saying the same thing twice – you waste time and may not complete the paper – say what you have to say and move on to the next question – if a little unsure about whether you wish to say more leave some space and come back to the question – try and avoid tacking on bits to a question at the end of the paper these can obviously be overlooked. Equally avoid contradicting yourself – it is surprising the number of students who change their mind in the course of an answer and do not correct an earlier statement so initially say 'A obviously has a good claim' but then on the next page 'It is clear A cannot succeed'!

(5) Remember essays and exam papers are also an exercise in writing the English language – try and avoid over long complex sentences. Use paragraphs and break up the work – have a structure – in simple terms a beginning, middle and end. Avoid overly pretentious language wherever possible use simple English. Avoid what can be called the 'stream of consciousness approach' just pouring out material in a more or less continuous fashion with few no paragraph brakes and very long sentences – if an examiner can read and follow your answer easily it may well reflect in a better mark.

(6) Particularly in essays a good strong conclusion is helpful – you need not come down on one side or the other but you want to leave the examiner in no doubt that you are aware of the issues involved – again in essays proposals for changes or reform will usually gain extra marks. Do not leave things in the air – if the question has asked you to critically evaluate you want to show you have done so and not be simply descriptive or just let the essay tail off into nowhere.

(7) Answer the question set and not the one you would have liked to be set e.g. if the question asks you to discuss the issues of 'satisfactory quality' in s 14(2) of the **Sale of Goods Act 1979** and you have learnt a lot about 'sales by description' in s 13 of the **Sale of Goods Act 1979** and this has not come up elsewhere on the paper, you waste time and will fail the question, probably, if you spend a lot of time talking about s 13 and little or no time discussing s 14(2) however happy you feel that you have shown the examiner that you are fully on top of s 13!

(8) A statement of the obvious but often overlooked – use a good writing implement. If you have very small writing using a pale blue biro with a thin nib does not help!

Common Pitfalls

The most common mistake made when using Questions & Answers
books for revision is to memorise the model answers provided and try to
reproduce them in exams. This approach is a sure-fire pitfall, likely to result
in a poor overall mark because your answer will not be specific enough to
the particular question on your exam paper, and there is also a danger that
reproducing an answer in this way would be treated as plagiarism. You must
instead be sure to read the question carefully, to identify the issues and
problems it is asking you to address and to answer it directly in your exam.
If you take our examiners' advice and use your Q&A to focus on your
question-answering skills and understanding of the law applied, you will
be ready for whatever your exam paper has to offer!

General Questions

INTRODUCTION

This chapter contains four questions which are not confined to one particular part of the syllabus but are broader. Such questions are often included in examinations in order to test your knowledge of recent developments in the subject or simply to give you an opportunity, which most questions in law papers do not, to demonstrate a wider knowledge of the syllabus. The first question poses an important general question: 'Does commercial law exist?' Question 2 is of a general type often found in examinations, inviting the student to take an overview of commercial law and its function in the business world. The third question requires a good knowledge of the whole area of sale of goods and related law. Question 4 is centred around the UN Convention on Contracts for the International Sale of Goods (the Vienna Convention 1980) which now plays, and will play, a very important role in regulating contracts for the international sale of goods.

QUESTION 1

Does Commercial Law exist?

▶ Discuss.

How to Answer this Question

This is a challenging question and one to which there can be no definitive answer. This is because commercial law means different things to different people. You may wish to consider some often quoted definitions. Goode: 'the totality of the law's response to the needs and practices of the mercantile community'. Bradgate: 'the law relating to commercial activity, especially transactions concerned with the supply of goods and services and financing thereof'. But neither absolutely defines commercial law.

The problem we face is that England does not have a self-contained body of principles and rules specific to commercial transactions. English commercial law has been developed by common law, and its principles are all over the place in case reports. It is almost impossible to rely on law reports alone. We depend on academic textbooks, practitioner texts and journals but such materials do not form a commercial code. Authors do not create law; they merely explain it. Students need to set their own boundaries in answering this question and the challenge is to engage in the discussion rather than striving to a conclusion as to its definition.

Answer Structure

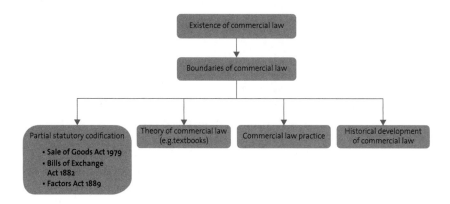

ANSWER

It is difficult to know what commercial law is but yes it does exist.[1] The boundaries of commercial law are not easily defined. That is because the UK does not have a code. It does not have a self-contained integrated body of principles and rules specific to commercial transactions (unlike the American Uniform Commercial Code). It certainly goes beyond regulation of relationships between merchants and traders. It is the absence of anything resembling either a commercial code or the commercial part of a civil code which makes defining the boundaries of commercial law difficult. In the UK, commercial law has traditionally been treated as an aggregation of specific subjects, for example sale, agency and financing. Each is self-contained and governed by its own distinctive rules. But commercial law is much more than this. Professor Goode[2] defines commercial law as: 'the **totality of the law's response to the needs and practices of the mercantile community'**. In other words, commercial law represents everything relating to mercantile disputes; all the principals, rules and statutory provisions. Anything to do with rights and obligations of parties to commercial transactions.[3] This is true whether the commercial transactions are between merchants themselves or between merchants and individuals. Commercial law draws on all areas of law that make up the English legal system.

1 It is essential that your essay has a structure. By outlining the issues to be discussed in your introduction you take the first important step towards ensuring that you achieve this aim.
2 The inclusion of academic references rather than the 'mere' consideration of case law shows not only that you have researched and read more widely but also adds to the criticality of your analysis.
3 Placing the essay question into its wider, practical context is a good way to demonstrate knowledge and understanding.

At the heart of commercial law is the law of contract, with its doctrines of freedom of contract and contracts are to be observed.[4] Freedom of contract allows parties to define their own rights and remedies, and organise their relationships in whatever way they consider best suited to their needs. This gives foreign traders in the UK a sense of stability and predictability that is vital to commerce. The courts' approach is to enforce parties' bargains as long as they not cross the line between acceptable and unacceptable behaviour.

Commercial law is rooted in the recognition of trade usage as a source of contractual rights[a]. Commercial law has developed to give binding force to letters of credit despite there being no consideration moving from the seller of goods to the issuing bank. There is no privity of contract between the parties, yet the law recognises the practice.[b]

As commercial transactions become more sophisticated, commercial law itself expands and becomes more sophisticated. The main feature which distinguishes English commercial law from civil law jurisdictions is the relative absence of mandatory law. Much of our commercial law is judge-made. Not statute. The legislation we have are largely codifying in character, eg Sale of Goods Act 1979. But the argument is that there is no need for too much mandatory law. If entrepreneurs are to be encouraged, the legal system must be flexible and responsive. Statute sets out rights and obligations which apply unless parties between them agree otherwise.[c]

English Commercial Law seeks to maintain a fair balance between protecting the interests of the parties to a transaction and protecting the interests of third parties, who are not directly involved in that transaction but who may be affected by it.[d] Although the boundaries of commercial law is not easily defined, it is possible to look at different ways to try and find some answers.

(1) COMMERCIAL LAW TEXTBOOKS

The simplest (and possibly the least instructive) approach is to take the lead from commercial law textbooks.[5] The content of commercial law textbooks determines or reinforces ideas about what commercial law is. The obvious problem with defining commercial law in this way is that we do not know *why* some topics are included while others are not dealt with or are categorised as being only 'ancillary' to commercial law.

---

4   After placing the issues raised by the question into their wider context, it is a good idea to then consider a few more specific incidents, thus demonstrating your knowledge.

5   In the middle section of your answer you should develop the issues outlined in your introduction, i.e. discuss and evaluate the arguments which are relevant to the question set.

The various topics however reveal an enduring theme. In all aspects of commercial law, the focus is on transactions. Some commercial law (for example, sale of goods) regulates transactions directly. Other areas (for example, banking and insurance law) concern mechanisms necessarily ancillary to such transactions. Others (for example, product liability) stem from the consequences of transactions even where the party seeking the help of the law is not a direct party in the transaction.

Commercial law textbooks perhaps reinforces ideas about what commercial law is; textbooks also represent authors' perceptions of commercial law as it is practised, that is, commercial law is what commercial lawyers do. This leads to the second approach to answering the question.

(2) COMMERCIAL LAWYERS

Commercial law is what commercial lawyers do. But what does 'commercial lawyer' mean? It does not really tell us very much, other than a commercial lawyer can be distinguished from, for example, a family lawyer or an international lawyer. Even these distinctions are debatable.

The work of a commercial lawyer may involve any aspect of law as it relates to business clients, and the role of a lawyer is to facilitate business clients' commercial transactions with third parties. A commercial lawyer may be asked to advise a client on both non-contentious and contentious work. Non-contentious work involves advising clients on drafting of contracts, whereas contentious work involves consequences of breach of contract.

From this perspective, commercial law is pragmatic in its approach. Commercial law is about getting things done; it is about problem-solving. Commercial law has been developed in response to the needs of commerce. Without trading, there would be no commercial law. The fundamental purpose of commercial law is the facilitation of commercial activity.

It is pertinent to note that the Civil Procedure Rules provide that the Commercial Court has jurisdiction in 'any case arising out of trade and commerce in general'. This includes (but is not limited to) any case relating to a business document or contract; the export/import of goods; the carriage of goods by land, sea, or air; insurance; banking and financial services; and business agency. The remit of the court therefore also represents a succinct statement of the type of disputes which might be regarded as commercial. The scope and extent of what commercial lawyers do is vast.

(3) HISTORICAL ORIGINS OF COMMERCIAL LAW

Another approach to defining contemporary commercial law is by examining its .
historical origins.[6] The existence of a body of law controlling mercantile life has been
recognised since medieval times when special courts existed for the purpose of dealing
with trade disputes. It was developed out of medieval law merchant (*lex mercatoria*),
which governed practices and disputes between merchants and traders before
incorporation by the common law, a process which began in the seventeeth century
and culminated in a series of codifications (for example the Sale of Goods Act 1893, the
Factors Act 1889).

One conclusion to be drawn from this is that modern commercial law is, and always has
been, a body of rules relating to trading and business relationships. This would explain
topics such as negotiable instruments and contracts of carriage. Of course, modern
business transactions are different from those in the nineteenth century. Modern
commercial law has added new topics. But even taking recent additions into account, the
overall picture remains unchanged: commercial law is driven by, and is responsive to, the
needs of commerce.

CONCLUSION

Yes, commercial law exists, but how do we go about defining commercial law?[7] As the
above different approaches show, different issues are buried in the question. If we take
the textbook approach, then commercial law is predominantly doctrinal (or 'black-letter')
in its methodology and orientation. If we take the commercial practice approach, then
commercial law is essentially pragmatic – it is the law of 'getting things done'. If we take
the historical approach, then modern commercial law is beginning to resemble medieval
law merchant. The answer is less important than what can be learnt by engaging in
debate. All that can be said is the commercial law is characterised by those principals,
rules and statutory provisions concerned to uphold and protect acceptable customs and
practices of merchants.

---

6   With this type of question, placing the topic into its historic context helps to show the development of
     the law and demonstrates your knowledge and understanding.
7   It is always good to finish your answer with a conclusion which summarises your findings. Be sure not to
     introduce new points.

QUESTION 2

'The strength of English commercial law has been its concern to provide solutions to practical problems facing commercial parties.'

▶ Discuss.

How to Answer This Question

This question is not an opportunity to discuss commercial law in a general way. A good answer requires you to identify what the needs of the commercial community are and then identify how the courts and legislature have responded to those needs. You need to illustrate these points by drawing from a range of areas of commercial law.

Answer Structure

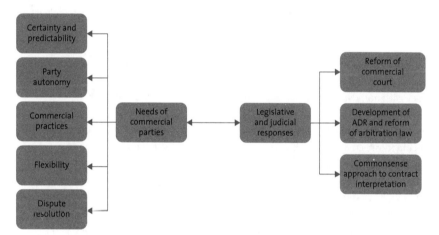

This diagram illustrates the main factors to consider for both commercial parties and possible legal responses.

ANSWER

In order to answer the question, it is necessary to identify what problems commercial parties face and how English commercial law helps them by providing solutions. If commercial law is about commercial activity, then the fundamental purpose of commercial law is the facilitation of commercial activity.[8]

---

8   As with every essay question, the provision of a brief outline of the issues to be discussed is the first step to ensure that your essay has a structure.

(1) CERTAINTY AND PREDICTABILITY

The commercial community values legal certainty above all.[9] Business people want to know that courts will be reliable and will consistently interpret transactions in a particular way. This allows for planning and anticipation of liability. Many transactions (many of high value) are undertaken on the basis that courts will continue to follow rules laid down in preceding cases. Business people do not want the law to be based on a random application of local custom and idiosyncrasies of individuals. Of course, this is not guaranteed because judges' thinking will change over time but, on the whole, courts have consistently promoted certainty of outcome over those of fairness and justice. This is what business people want.

As Lord Mansfield said, it is more important that a rule is certain than what the rule is.[e] An example is the postal rule (Adams v Lindsell (1818)). It does not matter if acceptance is deemed to take place at the time of posting or receipt. Parties to a contract merely need to know.

If the law is clear and certain, the outcome of a dispute may be predicted and parties may resolve it without having to litigate. If litigation is necessary, at least disputes can be dealt with quickly. This is especially important in a price fluctuation market.

The use of documentary credits is an example of courts' approach to ensure certainty.[10] Documentary credit is a bank's assurance of payment against presentation of specified documents. It is the most common method of payment in international sales. Although the Uniform Customs and Practice for Documentary Credits[f] only applies if it is expressly incorporated into a contract, because of its wide acceptance amongst international bankers, courts are likely to view the UCP as impliedly incorporated as established usage. There are two general principles involved with documentary credits. First, the doctrine of strict compliance dictates that a banker must comply exactly with its client's (the buyer) instructions as to payment. Even if the value of some documents required by the buyer is questionable, 'it is not for the bank to reason why'.[g] Even a minor discrepancy will disentitle the banker to reimbursement from its client. A clear example is the case of *Equitable Trust v Dawson* (1927)[11] where the buyer's instructions was payment against a certificate signed by experts, whereas the banker paid against documents signed by one expert. The House of Lords held that the banker had acted against his instructions and was thus not entitled to reimbursement.[h]

---

9   Where the question is about practical problems / implications, emphasise the practical aspects of a question. This shows that you are focused on the relevant issues.

10 The provision of a concrete example is a good way to illustrate the issues raised by the question and demonstrates understanding.

11 As the question refers to the provision of solutions to practical problems, it Is important to consider how the law has responded.

Secondly, the principle of autonomy of credit dictates that a bank is not concerned with any dispute that the buyer might have with the seller. As Lord Denning said[12] in *Power Curber v National Bank of Kuwait* (1981), a letter of credit ranks as cash and must be honoured. Courts have consistently defended the autonomy principle on grounds that an irrevocable letter of credit is the 'life-blood of international commerce'. It thus must be honoured and be free from interference by the courts, otherwise trust in international commerce would be damaged. The commercial value of the documentary credit system lies in the fact that payment under a letter of credit is virtually guaranteed (subject to the strict compliance principle). Certainty of payment is of paramount importance to the business community, thus irrevocable credits are treated like cash by courts.

(2) PARTY AUTONOMY

Business people should be free to make their contracts and they are entitled to receive what they bargained for. The aim of commercial law is to enforce the intention of the parties, not frustrate that intention by a rigid set of rules.[i]

Courts take a non-interventionist approach, justified on the basis that it promotes certainty. Courts should only intervene if the contract terms are so restrictive or oppressive that it offends public interest. Whenever there is a contest between contract law and equity in a commercial dispute, contract law wins hands down. This is one reason why so many foreigners select English law to govern their contracts and English courts to decide the case. Business people know where they stand with English law and English judges.[j]

(3) RECOGNITION OF COMMERCIAL PRACTICES

Courts have always recognised and given legal effect to customs and practices of the business community. The most common way is by implying a term into the contract, for example where the parties are in the same trade and there is a particular custom of that trade. By judicial recognition, commercial practice has become part of the common law.[k] An example is the agency doctrine of the undisclosed principal. In this situation, the existence of an agency is not disclosed to the third party, who therefore thinks he is contracting only with the agent in his own right and is unaware that the agent is acting for another. Nevertheless, the general rule is that the principal can intervene and enforce contract with the third party. This is an exception to doctrine of privity under the common law.[13][l] It is important to bear in mind that the initial contract is between the agent and the third party. The undisclosed principal intervenes in an existing contract.

---

12   Stating by whom a legal principle was stated in a case demonstrates a deeper knowledge and is likely to attract additional marks.

13   Showing an awareness of the exceptions to the rule is a good way to attract additional marks as it demonstrates knowledge.

The justification for the doctrine of the undisclosed principal has been the subject of much discussion by academic writers. It is generally accepted that although it runs against the fundamental principles of privity of contract (that is, there must be agreement between the parties), the doctrine is justified on grounds of commercial convenience. Generally, in commercial law, courts assume that buyers and sellers are willing to buy/sell to anyone.[14] Contracts are not personal and business people are not concerned about the identity of the other contracting party.[m] There is no reason for the undisclosed principal rule other than that courts recognise that this is what business people do. It is purely a matter of recognising commercial practice.

(4) FLEXIBILITY

Commercial people keep finding new ways of doing business. The internet is a good example.[15] The internet environment is constantly changing and the law must respond. Business people need the law to adapt to accommodate these changes. The English courts have been flexible. Legislation has also been flexible; whenever reform is proposed, extensive consultation takes place with the business community before a Law Commission report is produced. For example, amendments to the **Sale of Goods Act 1979** include s 20A.[16,n] Business buyers had complained that they had paid for goods but where the seller became insolvent before delivery, their claim against the receiver failed on grounds that the buyer has no property in unascertained goods. Commercial people wanted this change. **Section 20A** essentially gives a buyer who has paid for goods before delivery some measure of protection if the seller becomes insolvent. The buyer acquires property in an undivided share and he becomes an owner in common of the bulk pro rata.

However, flexibility is often at the expense of certainty. For example, s 15A says that if a buyer is not dealing as a consumer and the breach of description or quality of the goods is so slight that it would be unreasonable for the buyer to reject the goods, such a breach may be treated as a breach of warranty unless it is reasonable for the business buyer to reject. Although this allows for some flexibility, its application is uncertain.

(5) RESOLUTION

No matter how certain and predictable the law is, there will always be disputes. What commercial people need is a quick, inexpensive and efficient way to deal with problems. This need has been met in several ways. For example, commercial courts are special courts. These are separate courts of the Queen's Bench Division. They do nothing but hear

....

14   The provision of a practical example demonstrates understanding of the law and will attract a good mark.

15   Placing the essay question into its practical, wider context is another way to demonstrate knowledge and understanding.

16   Showing an awareness of the exceptions to the rule is a good way to attract additional marks as it demonstrates knowledge.

commercial disputes. The procedure is flexible with relatively little formality. Courts themselves have been willing to develop new remedies, for example, the development of the *search and seize order*, allowing seizure of evidence which might otherwise be destroyed.[o]

(6) FAIRNESS AND GOOD FAITH

A contemporary argument is that the law should promote fairness and good faith (especially if commercial law is to include consumer transactions). But English law has developed without a general duty of good faith. Examples include *The Mihalis Angelos* (1971), where a party can exercise the right to terminate a contract for breach even though the breach causes him no loss. This is so even if the sole motive for termination is market price fluctuation.[p]

Many countries have a general duty of good faith. In England, the idea of good faith is the subjective standard of honesty, rather than an objective one of fair dealing. Partly because of harmonisation of commercial law in the European Union, there is a growing reference to an objective standard of good faith. For example, under the **Unfair Terms in Consumer Contracts Regulations 1999**, the test is no longer *you* are being unfair, merely *it* looks unfair (*Director General of fair Trading v First National Bank* (2001)).

SUMMARY

The main challenge for commercial law is to strike the right balance between these competing principles to provide solutions to problems faced by commercial parties.[17] Where the balance should lie depends on the circumstances of the case. For example, if the parties involved are multinational corporations in the shipping trade, certainty might take precedence, whereas if there is a significant imbalance between the parties (especially if one party is a consumer), some certainty may be sacrificed in favour of fairness or flexibility.

Tensions are unavoidable. Business people want the law to be predictable in its application. But this is not always possible. More predictability means more detailed rules. At the same time, business people want flexibility, to allow them to develop new ways of doing business. This is very well, but how does commercial law deal with these competing principles? Essentially, it is a balancing act. Commercial law rules need to be sufficiently predictable to generate confidence so business people can depend on it. At same time, the law must be responsive and flexible enough to allow the development of new markets. On the whole, English commercial law does provide solutions to practical problems facing commercial parties.

---

17 Ending your answer with a conclusion, i.e. a summary of the results of your discussion/analysis, ensures that you present a complete picture to the examiner.

QUESTION 3

'Despite developments in recent times, the law of sale of goods is still permeated with the following key concepts: freedom of contract, privity of contract and *caveat emptor.*'

▶ Discuss the extent to which this is true.

How to Answer this Question

This question is a generalised one of a type often treated by students as one to tackle as a desperate last resort. Being generalised, it requires a good overall knowledge of the subject. In this particular question, three different concepts are expressly referred to and therefore it is required that each be addressed. There is every reason to take a straightforward approach and deal with one concept at a time.

Applying the Law

This diagram illustrates the factors to consider around sale of goods law in this scenario.

ANSWER

FREEDOM OF CONTRACT[18]

The law of sale of goods was originally developed by judges in deciding cases.[19] In the first **Sale of Goods Act** of **1893**, Parliament set out to incorporate this common law into statute form and the **1893 Act**, in its **Preamble**, described itself as an Act to codify the law. Most of the provisions of the **1893 Act** are now contained, often word for word, in the current **1979 Act**. There is no doubt that the freedom of contract philosophy underpinned much of the common law development, this philosophy being that the parties were free to decide for themselves what contract to make and what terms to incorporate into it. The law set out to provide for what would be the position if the parties had not themselves determined what it should be. Thus, throughout the **1893 Act**, one finds provisions such as 'unless otherwise agreed' and also a general provision (now to be found in an amended form in s 55 of the **1979 Act**) that where any right or liability would arise by implication of law, it can be negatived (excluded or varied) by express agreement between the parties. This was the embodiment of the freedom of contract principle. The amendment now found in s 55 relates to the rules on exclusion clauses. Since the original **Act** of **1893**, it had become clear that the freedom of contract principle could be abused by a party who was in a very strong bargaining position and who could insist on (often quite harsh) terms being in the contract. This was particularly true of standard form contracts made between a business and an ordinary private consumer and was not confined to contracts of sale of goods.[20] It occurred in hire purchase contracts and contracts such as those to buy railway tickets or to park one's car in a car park. The abuse often took the form of an insistence on the incorporation of clauses excluding liability towards the consumer. After initial legislative attempts to control these exclusion clauses in particular contracts (for example, hire purchase agreements), Parliament enacted general legislation on exclusion clauses in the **Unfair Contract Terms Act 1977**. This Act has introduced a very clear restriction on the freedom of contract principle in the following ways. First, it deals with the terms as to title, description, quality and sample implied by **ss 12–15** of the **Sale of Goods Act** (and by other Acts in relation to other contracts involving the passing of property or the hire of goods). It distinguishes between consumer deals and non-consumer deals and, broadly speaking, it makes it impossible for a seller to exclude or restrict liability for breach of the implied terms as to title and, where the buyer is a consumer, makes it impossible for a seller to exclude or restrict the other implied terms just referred to. Where the buyer is not a consumer, a clause purporting to exclude or restrict liability for these latter terms is subject to a test of reasonableness, which is also the position with any other exclusion clause using standard terms.

18 Dissecting the question into its constituent parts and considering these parts on a point-by-point basis ensures that your answer is structured logically.

19 Given that the question asks about developments, it is important that you refer to the development/ history of the area in question.

20 Supporting your discussion with concrete and relevant examples demonstrates understanding. Understanding is an important assessment criterion.

The Unfair Contract Terms Act 1977 deals only with exclusion clauses. With that important exception, the freedom of contract principle remains largely intact. Thus, for example, whether an express term is a condition or a warranty is a matter the parties are free to determine. A term as to the time of delivery will normally be construed by the courts as a condition, but it is still open to the parties expressly to state otherwise. Similarly, the rules in ss 17–20 of the Sale of Goods Act on the passing of property and risk apply only where the parties have not expressed a contrary intention.

A further significant inroad into the principle has derived from the 1993 European Directive on Unfair Contract Terms. This was implemented in Britain by the Unfair Terms in Consumer Contracts Regulations 1994, which have since been replaced by the 1999 Regulations of the same name. These apply with certain exceptions to any term (in a consumer contract) which, contrary to a requirement of good faith, causes a significant imbalance in the parties' rights and obligations to the detriment of the consumer. It is not just exclusion clauses which can be declared 'unfair' and thus of no effect; provided it is not a core term (for example, in a sale of goods contract, a term which states the price (*Office of Fair Trading v Abbey National plc and Others* (2009)), almost any term is subject to this possibility. An important feature of this piece of legislation is that it gives the Office of Fair Trading and other approved enforcers such as Local Trading Standards Authorities (Pt 8 of the Enterprise Act 2002) the duty to consider complaints about unfair terms and the power to bring court proceedings seeking an order or injunction to prevent a trader from using unfair terms (see, for example, *Director General of Fair Trading v First National Bank* (2001)). These Regulations apply, of course, only to contracts between a business and a consumer – the typical example where there is a substantial imbalance of bargaining power between the parties.

In 2002, the Law Commission published a Consultation Paper[21] in which it proposed that the two pieces of legislation referred to above (the Unfair Contract Terms Act 1977 and the Unfair Terms in Consumer Contracts Regulations 1999) be: (a) combined; and (b) rewritten to make the language more accessible and user-friendly. In February 2005, the Law Commission submitted its final recommendations together with a draft Bill.[9] The Bill proposes that the 1999 Regulations be extended to apply not only to business-to-consumer contracts but also to business-to-business contracts. That would mean that in a business-to-business contract, it would not only be exclusion or limitation of liability clauses which would be challengeable under the legislation. Any standard term (other than a core term) in a business-to-business contract would be open to challenge as being unfair/unreasonable. Arguably, this is necessary since, even in business-to-business contracts, there is no guarantee that there is a level playing field. There can, in such a contract, be a great disparity between the bargaining power of the two parties. The proposal would involve a further inroad into the freedom of contract principle, but this may be necessary in order to redress an imbalance in bargaining power.

....

21 The inclusion and consideration of material such as consultation papers demonstrates knowledge which goes beyond the normal textbooks and will attract additional marks.

To sum up:[22] the freedom of contract principle is, and is likely to remain, largely intact except for those instances where legislation proves necessary in order to protect a weaker party (often a private consumer) from the abuse of power that that principle would otherwise allow to the stronger party.

PRIVITY OF CONTRACT

This is still a central element of sale of goods law. Thus, the implied terms which create strict liability generally apply only as between seller and buyer. This has two effects. First, a buyer (let us call him Harold)[23] who has bought, say, a defective car which is not of satisfactory quality can in general sue only his seller for breach of the implied term as to satisfactory quality. Although his seller can then sue the person from whom he bought the car, Harold cannot take the shortcut of himself suing someone further up the distribution chain. This could leave Harold without a remedy in the situation where his seller has become bankrupt. There is, however, one important inroad into this principle of privity of contract which could assist Harold if he has used credit to purchase the car. This can be found in **s 75** or **s 75A** of the **Consumer Credit Act 1974** which would allow a buyer to bring the claim for the seller's breach of contract (or misrepresentation) against the creditor – though important to note this is a derivative action you can only sue the credit card company if you have a 'like claim' against the seller. This is a section which can apply where the creditor is someone different from the seller, where the credit agreement was a regulated debtor–creditor–supplier agreement within the meaning of the **Consumer Credit Act** and where the cash price of the item exceeded £100 and did not exceed £30,000. In this age of e-commerce, it is worth noting that if Harold bought his car on the Internet with his credit card, he could still rely on **s 75** even though the contract of sale was with a non-UK supplier (*Office of Fair Trading v Lloyds TSB plc* (2005)).[28,r]

Section 75A is an alternative route in cases where the cash price of the item exceeds £30,000 and under £60,260. However in this situation, unlike that in **s 75** Harold would have in the first place to seek recovery from the supplier of the car only if that failed could he pursue the credit card company – it is a form of secondary liability.

The second effect of the doctrine of privity is that only a party to the contract can sue on it. So, if Harold and his wife are both injured because the car is not of satisfactory quality, his wife will not (unless she was a joint purchaser) be able to seek a remedy by relying upon the implied (or express) terms in Harold's contract. There is now an important

---

22 Drawing an interim conclusion is a good way of signposting the relevant issues and also helps you to structure your answer logically.

23 The provision of a practical example demonstrates understanding of the law and will attract a good mark.

24 It is often not necessary to provide details of the cases you cite as you are merely using them as authorities (i.e. references) for the legal principles you have just explained/referred to.

exception to this second effect of the doctrine. Thus, a third party can now enforce a contract where the third party is able to rely on the **Contracts (Rights of Third Parties) Act 1999**. This enables a third party to enforce a term of a contract if either: (a) the contract expressly provides that he may; or (b) the term purports to confer a benefit upon the third party. To be able to enjoy this right, the third party must be expressly identified in the contract by name or as a member of a class or as answering a particular description. The effect of the statute is clearly very limited and does not extend to anyone who is neither expressly given a right in the contract nor purported to be given a benefit by the contract.[5] Harold's wife is unlikely to be able to rely upon it unless, perhaps, the contract expressly referred to the fact that Harold was buying it as a present for his wife. Even that may not be sufficient, for it is arguable that even then the contract does not purport itself to confer a benefit on Harold's wife, but rather to put Harold in a position where he can confer a benefit upon her by making a gift to her.

There is now, however, a different way – that is, outside the law of contract – where a buyer (or indeed a consumer who, like Harold's wife, was not a buyer) may have a remedy against someone for damage caused by defective goods. This is by relying on **Pt I of the Consumer Protection Act 1987**. This introduces a regime of strict liability into the law of tort to enable a claim to be brought against the manufacturer (or importer into the European Union). This is not so much an inroad into the doctrine of privity of contract as the provision of a way round it. The consumer brings the claim outside contract altogether. This is not, however, a complete solution to the problems presented to consumers by the doctrine, because although the **1987 Act** allows an action for damage caused by the defective product, it does not allow a claim to be brought in respect of damage to that product or in respect of the fact that the product is worth less than it should be; to put it another way, the **1987 Act** does not provide for a claim in respect of loss of bargain. A buyer of a defective product which has caused no damage is left with only the possibility of a claim against the seller or (if the purchase was financed by the relevant kind of consumer credit agreement) against the creditor under **s 75** of the **Consumer Credit Act** (*Office of Fair Trading v Lloyds TSB plc* (2005)). The only way round that restriction at present is if someone else, for example the manufacturer, has given a guarantee which could then be relied upon. Any doubts about the enforceability of such guarantees (for example, on grounds of lack of privity of contract) have now been removed since the **Sale and Supply of Goods to Consumers Regulations 2002** came into force on 31 March 2003. These regulations implement the **1999 European Directive on Consumer Guarantees**.[25] They also, in **reg 15**, make the seller liable to the consumer in respect of a guarantee given by the manufacturer (or any other third party, such as an importer or distributor).

---

25 Showing that you are aware of the development of the relevant legal rules will set your answer apart from an average answer.

CAVEAT EMPTOR

The notion 'buyer beware' is to some extent tied up with the two concepts already discussed. The freedom of contract principle means that the buyer can, if he can make the seller agree, have all sorts of protections and guarantees built in as express terms of the contract.[26] Of course, the reality is that this seldom happens and that therefore the buyer receives only such legal protection as is automatically built into the contract. This amounts to the following: the ability to rely upon any misrepresentation which was one of the causes that induced him to make the contract; the ability to rely upon any express term of the contract (for example, as to the date of delivery); the ability to rely upon the terms implied into the contract by ss 12–15. The latter include the terms as to satisfactory quality and fitness for purpose, which constitute the buyer's principal legal protection as to the quality of the goods he is buying, and which are implied only where the seller is selling in the course of a business. Thus, the notion 'buyer beware' is particularly strong where the buyer buys from his neighbour, or at the church fete, or as a result of replying to a small advertisement in the newspaper, or in some other way from someone who is not selling in the course of a business.

The buyer's ability to rely upon any misrepresentation, express term or implied term of the contract is backed up by the provisions in the **Unfair Contract Terms Act** and the **Unfair Terms in Consumer Contracts Regulations**, discussed above.[27] As we saw, the consumer as buyer is guaranteed the benefit of the implied terms and, so far as liability for misrepresentation or breach of an express term is concerned, any exclusion clause will need to satisfy the requirement of reasonableness. Thus, so far as the consumer buyer is concerned, there is quite a degree of protection. It is fair, however, to say that the buyer does need to 'beware' in some sense. He really needs to ask questions and also to let the seller know for what purpose(s) he wants the goods. This is because the seller is liable for any misrepresentation, but this does not extend to making him liable for not making a statement and, turning to s 14(3) of the **Sale of Goods Act**, there can be no liability for the goods not being reasonably fit for a particular purpose if the buyer has not made known to the seller what that purpose was.[t]

It also should be pointed out that the consumer's legal protection is no longer confined to the contractual liability of the seller. As we have seen, there can be strict liability under the **Consumer Protection Act 1987** for damage caused by defective goods – although, as observed, there is no liability under that provision for loss of bargain.

....

26 You need to provide an explanation of the relevant legal rules; without such explanation, it is more difficult for you to properly apply the law to the requirements of the question and thus also more difficult to demonstrate your knowledge and understanding.

27 Build upon points you have raised previously; this gives your answer structure and saves valuable time.

In conclusion, the notion *caveat emptor* still applies so that the wise buyer still asks questions, makes tests and makes known why he wants the goods. The notion is less strong in the case of a consumer as buyer. The privity of contract doctrine has been relaxed for consumers (or made circumventable) in certain circumstances (see s 75 of the **Consumer Credit Act** and the provisions of the **Consumer Protection Act**). Also, the **Contracts (Rights of Third Parties) Act 1999** has created an exception for the third party upon whom the contract purports to confer a benefit. The principle of freedom of contract is still intact, but is subject to some exceptions (see the **Unfair Contract Terms Act 1977** and the **Unfair Terms in Consumer Contracts Regulations 1999**). The common theme is that these three notions, each derived from a body of commercial law developed largely to regulate the position between merchants, have had to be qualified to some extent in order to achieve justice for consumers. It is worth noting that both domestic and EU consumer protection measures can be enforced on behalf of the collective interest of consumers, reluctant to pursue individual litigation by the Office of Fair Trading and other UK and EU-qualified enforcers under **Pt 8** of the **Enterprise Act 2002** – this injunctive procedure, though not providing compensation for individuals but only restricting future conduct, further strengthens the position of modern consumers.

QUESTION 4

Is the **Vienna Convention on Contracts for the International Sale of Goods (CISG)** better suited to international contracts than existing English sales law?

▶ Critically evaluate this question.

How to Answer this Question

This question gives you an opportunity to compare the main provisions in the **CISG** against existing English contract law, with particular emphasis on matters relating to commercial contracts. The amount of detail required will be restricted to the time available, so do not get carried away!

Adoption of the **CISG** would provide important benefits to UK exporters and importers of goods. Parties negotiating international sales contracts often find the 'choice of law' issue to be among the most contentious. Each party is familiar with its own domestic sales law, and prefers that its local rules apply to the transaction. A widely acceptable and accepted uniform and generally understood set of rules avoids all of those problems. The **CISG** attempts to eliminate obstacles to cross-border contracts by putting into place internationally accepted substantive rules on which contracting parties, courts and arbitrators may rely.

Answer Structure

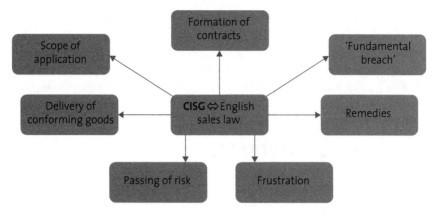

This mind map illustrates the main factors around CISG and English Sales law that will be considered in this answer.

ANSWER

The **Vienna Convention on Contracts for the International Sale of Goods (CISG)** now accounts for two-thirds of all world trade international sales law[u] and, in practice, supersedes the sales law of many of the countries with which the UK trades.[28] Adopting the CISG gives parties the advantage of a widely accepted and increasingly understood text. The CISG does not seek to deprive parties of the freedom of contract; its provisions merely act as a gap filler governing the parties' rights and obligations where their contract is silent on these issues. There are considerable differences between the contract laws of individual countries, and a common core has to be found. An attempt is made by CISG to eliminate obstacles to cross-border contracts.

The CISG recognises the basic principle of contractual freedom in the international sale of goods. **Article 6** enables parties to exclude the application of the CISG and parties have the right to pick and choose those parts of the CISG by which they agree to be bound. The CISG depends in important ways on standards such as reasonableness and good faith, which are familiar ideas and concepts to English lawyers. Another important feature of the CISG is its very limited use of technical legal terms and concepts. It has the characteristics of simplicity, practicality and clarity. It is free of legal shorthand, free of complicated legal theory and easy for business people to understand.

---

28 You need to evaluate the law, especially when dealing with a question that asks you to 'critically analyse'. This means that you need to be prepared to challenge the assumptions made by the question.

APPLICATION

The CISG only applies to international commercial sale of goods. Each of the following elements constitutes an important limitation on the scope of the CISG's applicability.[29] First, the sale must be international in character, that is, it involves parties whose places of business are in different States. Secondly, the CISG covers the sale of goods and does not automatically apply to service contracts. Finally, the CISG only applies to commercial transactions, that is, sales between merchants of goods. Amongst other limitations, it does not cover consumer sales, auction sales, sales of negotiable instruments or securities, nor does it cover sales of ships or aircraft.

FORMATION OF CONTRACTS

The CISG does not subject the contract of sale to any requirement as to form.[30] There are, however, aspects of the CISG relating to irrevocable offers and counter-offers which are novel – novel, that is, to English lawyers.

Under English law, the offeror's right to withdraw an offer is not restricted where the offeree has not given consideration, even if the offer is expressed to be irrevocable (*Payne v Cave* (1789)). Under **Art 16** of the CISG, an offer can be made expressly irrevocable because a time for acceptance is fixed; this is contrary to *Routledge v Grant* (1828). An offer is also irrevocable if it was reasonable for the offeree to rely on the offer as irrevocable and the offeree has acted in reliance on it.

The rationale behind **Art 16** is that commercial interests are enhanced by the greater certainty of dealing that arises from irrevocability. It is interesting to note that the law of major trading countries, including the USA and much of Europe, is consistent in this respect with the CISG.

Under English law, an acceptance which is not the mirror image of an offer does not give rise to a contract – it is regarded as a counter-offer, not an acceptance (*Hyde v Wrench* (1840)).[31] Under **Art 19** of the CISG, a reply to an offer which purports to be an acceptance but contains additional or different terms which do not materially alter the terms of the offer constitutes an acceptance rather than a counter-offer. This is subject to the absence of a timely objection by the offeror. **Article 19** is designed to maintain the contract if the differences between the offer and 'acceptance' are immaterial. Such a provision would do away with the problem in English law of 'battle of the forms'.

---

29 The consideration and explanation of limitations as to the CISG's applicability narrow your analysis down to what is relevant and demonstrates understanding.

30 As the question requires a comparison of the CISG with existing English sales law, it is important to outline the different sets of law.

31 It is important to refer to relevant authorities to substantiate your argument – this might be case law or a statutory provision. Remember, it is the application of law upon which you are assessed.

Furthermore, under the **CISG**, an acceptance of an offer becomes effective at the moment the indication of assent reaches the offeror; to that extent, the English postal acceptance rule would be abolished.

The **CISG** thus facilitates serious dealing, removes the differences arising from different forms of communication and takes account of new technology. Although none of the changes should present any difficulty, care should be taken in respect of irrevocable offers.

The **CISG** is concerned with neither the validity of the contract nor the rights of third parties.[32] Possible issues left to be determined by national legal systems are thus many: contractual capacity, mistake, penalty and liquidated damages clauses, illegal and unconscionable contracts, for instance, which may make a contract or a contract term void or voidable.

CONCEPT OF FUNDAMENTAL BREACH

The **CISG** imposes a much stricter standard for rejection and cancellation (referred to as 'avoidance'). Under the **CISG**, a buyer cannot reject defective goods unless there has been a fundamental breach. 'Fundamental breach' under the **CISG**[v] is quite distinct from the concept under English law.[33] English law permits a buyer to reject the goods or the tender of documents if they fail to comply with conditions of the contract (subject to qualifications, such as s 15A of the **Sale of Goods Act 1979**). By contrast, the **CISG** restricts a buyer's right to avoid the contract in circumstances where the buyer would be substantially deprived of what he is entitled to expect under the contract.

(a) *Partial/excessive delivery*[34] **Articles 51–52** of the **CISG** regulate partial and excessive performance and these differ in detail from existing English law. For example, under the **CISG**, a shortfall in the quantity delivered justifies the buyer's avoidance of the contract only if the failure amounts to a fundamental breach and, in the case of excess performance, only the excess can be rejected. By contrast, **s 30** of the **Sale of Goods Act 1979** allows the buyer to reject the whole delivery, unless the shortfall (or excess) in the quantity of goods delivered to the non-consumer buyer is so slight that it would be unreasonable for him to do so.

(b) *Anticipatory breach* Under the English doctrine of anticipatory breach, the innocent party is entitled to avoid the contract by reason of the other party's repudiatory breach. Under **Art 72** of the **CISG**, the right to avoid for anticipatory breach arises only if 'it is clear that one of the parties will commit a fundamental breach' (**Art 72**).

....

32 Pointing out areas of law still left to national law demonstrates understanding and ensures completeness of your answer.

33 Simplicity and clarity of expression are more likely to attract a good mark than highly complex statements – be accurate in what you are saying however.

34 Signposting (e.g. by use of bullet points) enhances clarity of expression.

DELIVERY OF CONFORMING GOODS

Under the CISG, the seller must deliver the goods, hand over any documents relating to them and transfer the property in the goods as required by the contract. These duties are unlikely to cause difficulty for English lawyers.

The basic obligation of conformity of the goods is that the seller must deliver goods which are of the quantity, quality and description required by the contract (including packaging). Conformity is spelled out in terms of fitness for ordinary purpose and for any particular purpose known to the seller, unless the buyer did not reasonably rely on the seller's skill and judgement. Again, these duties are unlikely to cause difficulty for English lawyers, but the wording of the obligations differs from the **Sale of Goods Act 1979** – for instance, there is no reference to conditions and warranties – but the substance appears not to differ in any significant way.

The rules relating to the consequence of non-conformity are, however, new. The CISG buyer loses the right to rely on a lack of conformity of the goods unless notice is given within a reasonable time after discovery of the defect or within two years of the actual delivery of the goods (whichever is the earlier).

REMEDIES

Remedies are critical in the effective operation of law in an area such as this.[35] It is not surprising that the CISG gives them a great deal of emphasis, introducing a range of remedies not to be found in English law.

(a) *Seller's right to cure* The CISG emphasises saving the contract by enabling the seller to cure the breach. The CISG permits a seller to remedy a tender of defective documents (**Art 34**) and non-conforming goods (**Art 37**) up to the time fixed for delivery, as long as the exercise of these rights does not cause the buyer unreasonable inconvenience or unreasonable expense. **Article 48** gives a seller the right to remedy 'any failure to perform' if he can do so without unreasonable delay and without causing the buyer unreasonable inconvenience. This right to remedy applies to a breach by failure to deliver on time. The procedure to be followed is that the seller must give notice to the buyer suggesting a new deadline for delivery. If the buyer does not answer within a reasonable time, the seller has the right to perform and the buyer has the obligation to accept performance within the new deadline. Since the seller's notice to the buyer is assumed under the CISG to include a request that the buyer consent or refuse his consent, this means that a buyer who does not respond to a notice that the seller will deliver late will be in breach if the buyer refuses to accept delivery.

---

35 Given the importance of remedies, it is essential to consider this point – otherwise your answer isn't complete.

(b)   *Price reduction* Under **Art 50**, if the seller delivers goods which do not conform to the contract, whether or not the price has already been paid, in addition to recovering damages, the buyer may unilaterally reduce the price in the same proportion as the value that the goods actually delivered bears to the value that conforming goods would have had at that time. If the goods are delivered late, but they do conform to the contract, **Art 50** does not apply. The right to reduce the price is a substantial right and there are situations in which **Art 50** can provide better relief than a damages claim (for example, in the case of a falling market). This is good news for the buyer but bad for the seller (the seller may, of course, revise the limitation of liability clause in the contract to reduce the effect of **Art 50**).

(c)   *Damages* The basic right to damages under **Art 74** of the **CISG**^W is stated in terms of foreseeability and appears to conform with the basic rule of damages in *Hadley v Baxendale* (1854). There is under the **CISG** an obligation on a party relying on breach to mitigate the loss.

(d)   *Specific performance* **Articles 46** and **62** of the **CISG** permit both the buyer and seller to require performance of the other party's obligations under the contract. However, this is subject to the qualification that a court need not grant an order for specific performance unless it would do so under its own law in non-**CISG** cases involving similar contracts of sale. English courts have invariably been reluctant to grant specific performance where damages are an adequate remedy (*Harnett v Yielding* (1805)).

PASSING OF RISK

Although the **CISG** deals with passage of risk of loss or damage, it does not contain provisions governing what we call transfer of 'title' or 'property'. Of course, the **Sale of Goods Act 1979** contains detailed provisions specifying when title passes.[36] Although the **CISG** does not regulate the transfer of property, it does provide a clear basis on which relevant arrangements, including insurance, can be made. Under the **CISG**, risk in general passes on the handing over of the goods to the carrier (**Art 67**) or to the buyer if he is taking direct delivery (**Art 69**).

FRUSTRATION

The **CISG**^X deals with the issue of the excusing of a non-performing party because of impossibility in a similar way to the doctrine of frustration in English law. However, **Art 79** operates only to prevent an action in damages. It does not bring the contract to an end, which is unlike the English law position (*Hirji Mulji v Cheong Yue Steamship Co* (1926)). However, if a failure to perform is a fundamental breach, the other party may declare the contract rescinded for breach.

---

36   Focus on the issues raised by the question; don't simply write down everything you know about a particular area of law.

CONCLUSION

Because the CISG is still so new, the ramifications of its provisions are uncertain.[37] However, with so many nations having become parties to it, and with so many alternative sources and markets available to purchasers of manufactured goods or producers of raw materials, British exporters and importers are no longer in a position to have their way with respect to choice of law and forum selection. The attitudes and lack of a widely accepted alternative that made the 'laws of England' the common contractual choice of law in international commercial transactions are gone, or are changing. A seller or buyer who refuses to deal on the CISG terms may find himself losing business opportunities to competitors who will.

> **Aim Higher** ★
>
> One crucial issue is, of course, the failure of the UK to adopt the Vienna Convention. A good answer would express a view whether the UK is justified in its refusal to adopt the Convention.

Notes

a   Eg agency law. There is no justification for the undisclosed principal rule. It is generally accepted that although it runs against the fundamental principals of privity of contract (i.e. there must be agreement between contracting parties), the rule is justified on grounds of commercial convenience. See Question 39.

b   See Question 48.

c   Eg retention of title clauses. These are often used in commercial contracts, but they are not created by statute. Retention of title clauses evolved through commercial practice and courts give recognition to the practice. See Question 12.

d   Eg the exceptions to the nemo dat quod non habet rule. The exceptions are sometimes difficult to justify, but commercial law needs to take a pragmatic approach. See Chapter 4.

e   *Vallejo v Wheeler* (1774): 'In all mercantile transactions the great object should be certainty; and therefore, it is of more consequence that a rule should be certain, than whether the rule is established one way or the other. Because speculators in trade then know what ground to go upon.'

f   The current, seventh, edition, is often known as UCP 600.

g   Devlin J in *Midland Bank v Seymour* (1955).

h   *Lord Sumner*: 'There is no room for documents which are almost the same, or which will do just as well.'

i   Lord Goff of Chieveley in an article analysing the objectives of judges when interpreting commercial contracts in *Commercial Contracts and the Commercial Court* (1984) LMCL Q 382: 'We are there to help businessmen, not to hinder them; we are there to give effect to their transactions, not to frustrate them; we are there to oil the wheels of commerce, not to put a spanner in the works, or even grit in the oil.'

j   Around 65% of disputes heard before the Commercial Court involve only foreign parties, that is, parties have expressly chosen England as the jurisdiction for dispute resolution.

k   For example, the bill of lading is recognised as a document of title to goods at common law.

l   This is not an exception under the **Contracts (Rights of Third Parties) Act 1999**, because the undisclosed principal is not identified nor identifiable at the time of the contract, so the Act does not apply.

37   Make sure that your conclusion follows on logically from your discussion / analysis in the main body of your answer; don't introduce new arguments.

m Lord Lindley in *Keighley, Maxsted v Durant* (1901): '. . . in the great mass of contracts it is a matter of indifference to either party whether there is an undisclosed P or not.'

n Inserted as an amendment by the 1995 Act.

o Other ways developed to deal with disputes include arbitration and alternative dispute resolution (such as mediation).

p Another example is *White & Carter v Macgregor* (1962) where a party can perform his obligations against the other party's wishes and remains entitled to claim the full value of the contract price.

q No implementation date has yet been set. Indeed, the Law Commission has recently reviewed its recommendations and consider they remain appropriate. Consultations on this issue run until 25 October 2012, followed by an Advice to the Department for Business Innovation and skills in spring 2013. The full text of the Bill can be found at: www.lawcom. gov.uk/docs/lc292bill.pdf.

r See Question 27.

s *Avraamides v Colwill* (2006). Successful third party claims under the 1999 Act were however made in *Laemthong v Artis (No 2)* (2005) and *Prudential v Ayres* (2007).

t Unless of course the description of the goods points to one purpose only, eg a hot water bottle: *Priest v Last* (1903).

u As at 1 September 2012, the following 78 countries subscribe to the CISG:

> Albania, Argentina, Armenia, Australia, Austria, Belarus, Belgium, Benin, Bosnia and Herzegovina, Bulgaria, Burundi, Canada, Chile, China, Colombia, Croatia, Cuba, Cyprus, Czech Republic, Denmark, Dominican Republic, Ecuador, Egypt, El Salvador, Estonia, Finland, France, Gabon, Georgia, Germany, Ghana, Greece, Guinea, Honduras, Hungary, Iceland, Iraq, Israel, Italy, Japan, Kyrgyzstan, Latvia, Lebanon, Lesotho, Liberia, Lithuania, Luxembourg, Mauritania, Mexico, Mongolia, Montenegro, Netherlands, New Zealand, Norway, Paraguay, Peru, Poland, Republic of Korea, Republic of Moldova, Romania, Russian Federation, Saint Vincent and the Grenadines, San Marino, Serbia, Singapore, Slovakia, Slovenia, Spain, Sweden, Switzerland, Syrian Arab Republic, The former Yugoslav Republic of Macedonia, Turkey, Uganda, Ukraine, United States of America, Uruguay, Uzbekistan, Venezuela (Bolivarian Republic of) and Zambia.

v A breach is fundamental, according to Art 25 of the CISG:

> '. . . if it results in such detriment to the other party as substantially to deprive him of what he is entitled to under the contract, unless the party in breach did not foresee and a reasonable person of the same kind in the same circumstances would not have foreseen such a result.'

w Article 74:

> 'Damages for breach of contract by one party consist of a sum equal to the loss, including the loss of profit, suffered by the other party as a consequence of the breach. Such damages may not exceed the loss which the party in breach foresaw or ought to have foreseen at the time of the conclusion of the contract, in the light of the facts and matters which he then knew or ought to have known, as a possible consequence of the breach of contract.'

x Article 79 states the basic rule:

> 'A party is not liable for a failure to perform any of his obligations if he proves that the failure was due to an impediment beyond his control and that he could not reasonably be expected to have taken the impediment into account at the time of the conclusion of the contract or to have avoided or overcome it or its consequences.'

Description and Quality

2

INTRODUCTION

The questions in this chapter relate to the statutory implied terms as to description, quality and fitness for purpose, to exclusion clauses and also to product liability. In some courses, the law of trade descriptions is dealt with in questions which also raise contractual issues (for example, under s 13 of the **Sale of Goods Act 1979**). This has not been done in this book because a number of sale of goods courses do not include trade descriptions in their syllabuses.

QUESTION 5

Sarah is a physiotherapist who works from home. She sees a poster in the window of Cutprice Ltd, a furniture shop: 'Massage tables £300. Suitable as an occasional bed or table for the discerning masseuse. Self assembly.' On the notice is a photograph of a pink table. The table is much cheaper than equivalent tables sold in nearby shops. Sarah points to the poster and tells Shelly, the sales assistant, 'I will buy a massage table.' She then adds, 'I will also need a side chair.' This is selected from a photograph of a range of chairs sold by Cutprice. It is agreed that the items will be delivered to Sarah's home on 1 February.

On 1 February, the table and chair are delivered in sealed cardboard boxes, but Sarah had to leave that day to visit her mother who had fallen ill. She returns on 15 February, but she is too upset to assemble the furniture until 1 March. It is only then that she discovers the table is green. She had particularly wanted pink because that is the colour of the decoration in the room she uses for her clients. In addition, one of the table's safety screws is missing, the table is not long enough to take anyone taller than five foot lying down, and the table is too high for the chair she bought from Cutprice.

▶ Discuss Sarah's possible remedies.

How to Answer this Question

This question involves a lot of points being included. It is testing your ability to spot each of the issues raised, as well as your ability to deal with them. So, a good answer must acknowledge each of the points raised, and must not concentrate on some of the issues to the exclusion of others. The main points that need to be discussed are as follows:

* description: s 13 of the Sale of Goods Act 1979;
* satisfactory quality: s 14(2);
* fitness for purpose: s 14(3);
* misrepresentation;
* when a buyer loses the right to reject goods;
* remedies.

Applying the Law

s 14(3) Sale of Goods Act 1979

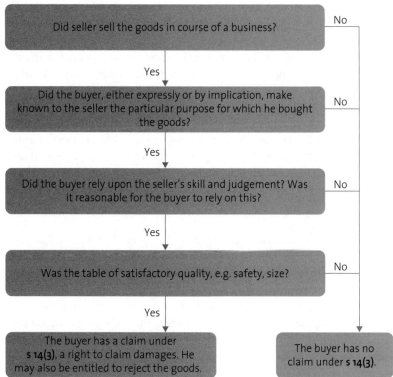

This diagram illustrates the factors to consider in relation to a right to claim under s 14(3) of the SGA 1979 when putting together this answer. You will also need to consider in this question the implied terms in s 13 (sale by description) and s 14(2) (satisfactory quality), as well as issues of inspection, rejection (s 34 and 35 of the SGA 1979) and remedies.

ANSWER

Sarah wants to know what remedies she might have against Cutprice Ltd.[1] She agreed to buy a table and chair from the shop and has found that the table is defective because (i) it is the wrong colour, (ii) one of the safety screws is missing, (iii) it is not long enough, and (iv) it is too high for the chair she bought.

WRONG COLOUR[2]

The shop poster included a photograph of a pink table. This was the colour Sarah had assumed her table would be when delivered. In fact, the table she received was green in colour. If Sarah had specifically agreed with Cutprice that she was buying a pink table, it seems clear that if a green one was supplied, then Cutprice would be in breach of an express term of the contract, as well as being in breach of s 13 of the Sale of Goods Act 1979. What appears to have happened here is that nothing was said in relation to colour, but that Cutprice's poster included a photograph of a pink table. The question is whether this was sufficient to imply into the contract that the table was to be pink.

If it does amount to an express term of the contract, the fact that the table as delivered was green would amount to a breach, and Sarah's remedy depends on whether this breach substantially deprives Sarah of what she might have expected under the contract. It is likely that the court will consider this breach a slight one, not entitling Sarah to terminate the contract, but that Sarah may be entitled to damages if she suffers any loss (*Hong Kong Fir Shipping v Kawasaki Kisen Kaisha* (1962)).

Whether a photograph of a pink table forms part of 'description' for s 13 of the Sale of Goods Act 1979 purposes is debatable.[3] If Sarah has specifically agreed the colour, the delivery of a green table would certainly amount to a breach of s 13. If 'pink' forms part of the description of the goods for s 13 purposes, it is immaterial that Sarah suffers no loss (*Re Moore and Landauer* (1921)). This is because s 13 is a condition implied into her sales contract. Although Sarah is a physiotherapist and she buys the table and chair in order for her to work from home, she does not buy the goods for the purposes of reprocessing and resale in the course of her business. Thus, following *R and B Customs Brokers v United Dominion Trust* (1988) and the more recent *Feldaroll Foundry v Hermes Leasing* (2004), Sarah is a consumer for the Sale of Goods Act purposes, and the court's discretion under

---

1   In your introduction, you should clearly identify the legal issues raised by the question. This is a good way to convince the examiner that you have understood what is relevant and will make him to be positively inclined towards your answer.

2   In the main body of your answer, you should develop the issues outlined in the introduction each at a time, i.e. analyse the points which are relevant to the question on a point by point basis; this adds structure to your answer.

3   The consideration of, or reference to, possible alternative arguments makes your answer stand out from the rest and demonstrates both deeper knowledge and understanding.

s 15A of that Act does not apply. As long as Sarah relied on Cutprice Ltd's description of 'pink' table, Sarah will be able to claim breach of s 13, entitling her to reject the table.

However, in the circumstances, it is a little unlikely that the courts will view 'pink' table as forming part of the description of the goods. We are told, however, that a further problem with the table is that one of the screws is missing. This is very serious indeed.

SAFETY SCREW MISSING

Cutprice Ltd sells in the course of business (*Stevenson v Rogers* (1999)), thus further conditions under the **Sale of Goods Act** are implied into the sales contract, namely **s 14(2)** and **s 14(3)**. As discussed earlier, Sarah will be treated as a consumer under the Act. Even if the court holds that the contract with Cutprice Ltd is not a consumer transaction, the fact that a safety screw is missing is a serious breach and the court is unlikely to exercise its **s 15A** discretion to disallow a business buyer from rejecting defective goods.

Under **s 14(2)**, the table is required to be of satisfactory quality. The test is what a reasonable person would regard as satisfactory, bearing in mind the price, description and other relevant circumstances.[4] Although we are told that the table is much cheaper than equivalent tables sold in nearby shops, this is not sufficient to imply that the defect in the table, the missing safety screw, was brought to Sarah's attention. Furthermore, although Sarah paid a fairly low price and therefore cannot expect too high a standard in goods (*Brown v Craiks* (1970)), the fact that one safety screw is missing cannot be regarded as anything but unsatisfactory (*Rogers v Parish* (1987)). Aspects of the quality of goods include the purposes for which goods of that kind are commonly bought, freedom from minor defects and safety. A reasonable person would not regard a table with one safety screw missing as anything but defective. Thus, it appears that Cutprice is in breach of the implied condition as to satisfactory quality.

Since the description 'massage table' points to its use (*Priest v Last* (1903)), s 14(3) implies a condition that the goods supplied by Cutprice must be fit for that purpose. It is reasonable in the circumstances for Sarah to rely on Cutprice's skill and judgement to supply a table fit for use as a massage table (*Teheran Europe v Belton (ST)* (1968)). Since one safety screw is missing, this amounts to a breach of s 14(3).

Sarah's remedies for breach of s 14(2) and 14(3) will be discussed later under Remedies.

....

4   You need to explain the relevant legal rules and how they relate to the question at hand. Don't assume that what you are saying is self-explanatory in its relationship to the question; it is necessary to relate the law properly to the question and to explicitly spell out the link.

TABLE NOT LONG ENOUGH TO TAKE ANYONE TALLER THAN FIVE FOOT LYING DOWN

Cutprice's poster advertised the table as 'suitable as an occasional bed or table for the discerning masseuse'. Not every statement about the quality or fitness of the goods can be treated as part of description. For s 13 to apply, words must constitute an essential part of the description of the goods. The key to s 13 is identification, that is, the words must constitute a substantial ingredient of the identity of the goods sold. Cutprice's statement is unlikely to constitute words forming part of the description of the goods. In *Ashington Piggeries v Christopher Hill* (1972), herring meal, which had been contaminated with a substance rendering it not suitable for feeding to mink, was sold to the buyer for use as mink food. The House of Lords held that there was no breach of s 13, because the goods had been properly described as herring meal. This is because not all descriptive words form part of the terms of the contract. So, the fact that the table was not suitable for use as a massage table because it was not long enough to take anyone taller than five foot lying down is unlikely to amount to a s 13 breach.

However, the advertisement might amount to a misrepresentation of material fact (*Smith v Land and House Properties* (1884)) which Cutprice intended buyers to rely on and which Sarah did rely on. Cutprice cannot argue that no reasonable buyer would have relied on their notice. If Sarah did rely on it, this will be sufficient (*Museprime Properties v Adhill* (1990)). As long as one of the reasons Sarah bought the table was because of Cutprice's statement that it was suitable for use as a massage table, this will found an action for misrepresentation (*Edgington v Fitzmaurice* (1885)). Sarah's action against Cutprice would be for negligent misrepresentation and, by virtue of s 2(1) of the **Misrepresentation Act 1967**, Sarah is entitled to claim damages as if the misrepresentation was made fraudulently, unless Cutprice can prove that they had reasonable grounds to believe and continued to believe up to the time of the sales contract with Sarah that the statement was true. It does not seem likely that Cutprice will be able to discharge this heavy burden of proof (*Howard Marine v Ogden* (1978)), thus entitling Sarah to damages in the tort of deceit (*Royscot Trust v Rogerson* (1991)). Whether or not Sarah may rescind her contract with Cutprice will be discussed later under Remedies.

TABLE TOO HIGH FOR THE CHAIR SHE BOUGHT

Whether Sarah has a remedy against Cutprice because the table was too high for the chair she bought from them depends on whether Sarah's statement to the sales assistant Shelly ('I will also need a chair') amounts to impliedly making it known to Cutprice the purpose for which Sarah needed the chair, that is, to be used with the table which she is buying from Cutprice. If Sarah has impliedly made it known, then it would be reasonable to rely on Cutprice to supply her with a chair suitable for that purpose. Since the chair is not suitable for the table, Cutprice may be in breach of s 14(3).

REMEDIES

As discussed above, Cutprice may be in breach of ss 14(2) and 14(3). Since these are conditions of the contract, this means that Sarah is entitled to reject the goods and claim damages. However, the right to reject goods is lost if Sarah keeps the goods beyond a reasonable time in which to examine them (s 35).[5] We are told that the goods were delivered to Sarah on 1 February in sealed boxes. By virtue of s 34, a buyer must be given a reasonable opportunity to examine the goods to ensure they conform with the contract. Sarah does not examine the goods because she left almost immediately to visit her mother until 15 February. The approach taken by the Sale of Goods Act is that as long as the buyer has a reasonable opportunity to examine, then s 34 is satisfied. Sarah is not under an obligation to inspect the goods. Section 34 merely requires that a buyer is given an opportunity to do so if she wishes. It is unlikely the courts will interpret s 34 subjectively to extend the period of time Sarah has to examine the goods due to her absence to visit her mother. By s 35, if the buyer retains the goods and does not complain about them beyond a reasonable length of time, she is deemed to have accepted the goods. We are told that Sarah only discovers the defects in the goods on 1 March. This is some four weeks after delivery. Whether or not this is beyond a reasonable time in which to examine is a question of fact. Although *Bernstein v Pamson Motors* (1987) has been criticised, the court indicated that three weeks may be beyond a reasonable time to examine a car. The goods here are a table and chair, not such complex goods, and Sarah has had them for four weeks. It is likely that Sarah will be deemed to have accepted the goods.

Thus, if Sarah has lost her right to reject the table and chair because she is deemed to have accepted them under s 35, she will nevertheless be entitled to damages as long as her loss satisfies the remoteness rule (*Hadley v Baxendale* (1854)).[6] It is unlikely Sarah will be entitled to non-pecuniary loss to cover for her disappointment (*Addis v Gramophone* (1909)), although the court may award damages if Sarah suffers loss of reputation and goodwill if she was unable to provide her physiotherapy service to her clients due to incomplete equipment (*Gibbons v Westminster Bank* (1939); *Anglo-Continental Holidays v Typaldos* (1967)). This will depend on whether Cutprice knew at the time the contract was made with Sarah that Sarah required the table and chair for her work at home (*Victoria Laundry v Newman* (1949)).

Furthermore,[7] since Sarah is a consumer, she has additional remedies under s 48A. She may demand that Cutprice repair the table at their cost; failing that, Cutprice could replace the table, or agree to reduce the purchase price, or if none of these is possible,

---

5 Pointing out any potential limitations of the application of a particular legal principle is a good way to demonstrate that you have understood the complexities of the rule in question.
6 Considering different possibilities ensures that your advice is complete.
7 Pointing out an alternative course of action is a good way to attract marks as it demonstrates knowledge and understanding.

Sarah will retain her right to rescind the contract. **Section 48A(3)** raises a presumption that if the goods are defective within six months of delivery, the goods were defective at the time of delivery, although the presumption depends on the nature of the goods. The table and chair are not complex goods, as discussed, and they were delivered some four weeks ago. It may be that Sarah can no longer claim her **s 48A** rights.

As far as Sarah's claim in misrepresentation is concerned, her primary remedy is rescission. This equitable remedy is lost if the misrepresentee has affirmed the contract (*Long v Lloyd* (1958)), or due to a lapse of time (*Leaf v International Galleries* (1950)).[8] What is clear is that the innocent party loses her right to reject goods for breach of contract more quickly than she loses her right to rescind the contract for misrepresentation. So, although Sarah may have accepted the goods for **Sale of Goods Act** purposes, Sarah may nevertheless retain her right to rescind the contract for misrepresentation.

> **Common Pitfalls**
>
> Students need to discuss the application of the law. Clearly, s 13 of the Sale of Goods Act applies, but often students just point out that there was a breach of s 13 without explaining what the section means, how it is applied and why it might have been breached. It is never sufficient to avoid these issues by saying that 'it is up to the court to decide'.

QUESTION 6

Shakespeare Ltd is a British manufacturer of Shakespeare electrical switches. It supplies them to, among others, Isis Cie, an Egyptian company which makes Isis microwaves in Cairo. These microwaves are imported into Britain by Watson plc and supplied to the retail market through a distribution system. A year ago, Beth bought an Isis microwave for £250 from Duncan's electrical shop in London. Yesterday, the Shakespeare switch in the microwave smouldered and set fire to the microwave. Beth was badly burnt in putting out the fire, but managed to limit the damage so that, apart from her burns, the only damage done was that the microwave was a write-off and Beth's kitchen carpet (worth £250) was burnt and has had to be replaced.

Advise Beth, bearing in mind that Duncan's shop has stopped trading since Duncan became bankrupt last week.

How, if at all, would it affect your advice if the Shakespeare switch which caused the fire was a replacement one supplied and fitted three months ago by Duncan's electrical shop

---

8   The consideration of potential limitations on the availability of remedies demonstrates understanding and will attract a higher mark.

after Beth had complained about the microwave not switching on at a sufficiently low temperature?

How to Answer this Question

This question demands a discussion of product liability. A claim by Beth under the Sale of Goods Act 1979 is clearly ruled out by the statement that Duncan has become bankrupt, but this must be stated in your answer. That leaves the answer to deal with two possible grounds of liability, at common law for negligence and for product liability under the Consumer Protection Act 1987. Some, maybe many, commercial law (or consumer law) courses are taken by students after they have taken basic subjects such as tort. It is therefore not always easy to know how much basic tort law, such as negligence, to include in an answer. In a question such as this, as a priority, make sure that you deal fully with the issues raised under the statute and that you do cover in some way the negligence issues. It is a matter to some extent of your own judgement as to how much space you can afford to give the negligence issues.

Most commercial law courses will not specifically include coverage of conflict of laws issues; thus, in this answer, those problems in relation to Isis Cie are no more than hinted at.

Applying the Law

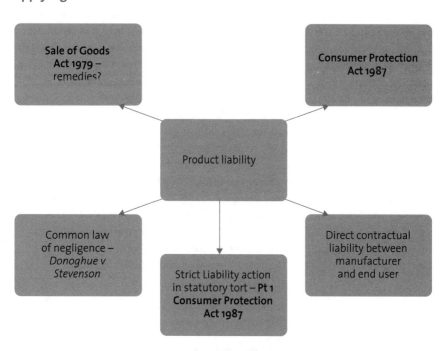

This diagram shows the main factors to consider in relation to product liability in this scenario.

ANSWER

The claim which Beth may very well have for breach of express or implied terms in her sale of goods contract with Duncan is clearly not going to yield much, if anything, for her, since Duncan is bankrupt.[9] Nor can Beth bring that claim against the manufacturer or importer or anyone else earlier in the distribution chain, as there is no privity of contract between her and any of them. Thus, any claim against one of the other parties will have to be a claim in negligence under the principle in *Donoghue v Stevenson* (1932) or a product liability claim under Pt I of the **Consumer Protection Act 1987**.

NEGLIGENCE

Beth has a claim in negligence against anyone in respect of whom she can establish three things:[10] (1) that that person owed her a duty of care; (2) that that person (or one of his employees in the course of his employment) failed to take reasonable care; and (3) that that failure to take care caused her damage which was of a foreseeable type occurring in a generally foreseeable sort of way. Given that the source of the damage was an apparently defective electrical switch, it is unlikely that those three elements could be shown except in relation to Shakespeare Ltd which manufactured it, or possibly Isis Cie which incorporated it into one of its machines. The principal difficulty in the case of Shakespeare Ltd would be proving a failure to take reasonable care, since clearly Shakespeare Ltd owed a duty to the ultimate consumer to take care in the design (or in its adoption) and manufacture of the switch. Whether reliance on the doctrine of *res ipsa loquitur* would help Beth prove negligence would depend very much on what evidence of care and systems is put forward by Shakespeare Ltd. So far as Isis Cie is concerned, there is no doubt in English law that a duty of care in the manufacture of machines was owed to the ultimate consumer, and little doubt that this extends to taking reasonable care to ensure that only safe components are used. The difficulties with a claim in negligence against Isis Cie are: (1) getting an English court to take jurisdiction; (2) proving that the duty just outlined was broken, that is, that Isis Cie failed to take reasonable care; and (3) the fact that, even if the claim were successful, damages would be recoverable only for Beth's burns and the damage to the carpet. Damages would not be recoverable in respect of the loss of the microwave itself, just as damages would not have been recoverable by Mrs Donoghue for the value of the ginger beer, this loss being an unrecoverable economic loss (*Murphy v Brentwood* (1990)). Thus, so far as negligence is concerned, Beth's best bet is a claim against Shakespeare Ltd, in which case, Beth will face the difficulty of proving a failure to take reasonable care. In the event of such a claim succeeding against Shakespeare Ltd, it is debatable whether the damages would include compensation for the loss of the microwave. On the one hand, that is damage caused 'by' and not 'to' the item (the switch) manufactured and put into

---

9   Providing a brief introduction which not only sets out the issues you are going to address but which also refers to the question set is a good way to demonstrate that you have understand what is relevant; relevancy is an important assessment factor.

10 The explanation of a legal principle is an important factor for its successful application to the requirements of the question.

circulation by Shakespeare Ltd. On the other, the switch was clearly designed to be incorporated into and subsequently supplied as a component of another item.

PRODUCT LIABILITY

Beth's best claim may well be one in respect of a defective product under Pt I of the Consumer Protection Act 1987.[11] She has, it seems, been the victim of two defective products, a switch and a microwave. They almost certainly were defective, that is, not as safe as persons generally are entitled to expect (s 3). Liability is strict and therefore negligence does not need to be proved. Nothing given in the problem suggests that any of the defences in s 4 will apply, unless perhaps the damage was entirely attributable to something in the microwave design, as opposed to something in the switch. In that case, there would be no liability under Pt I in respect of the switch, but only in respect of the microwave (s 4(1)(f)).

In the problem, there is no one who is an 'own brander'. So, the persons potentially liable (see s 2) are the manufacturers, that is, Shakespeare Ltd and Isis Cie, and the importer into the European Community, Watson plc. The problem does not precisely state that Watson plc imported the microwaves direct into Britain from Egypt. If, in fact, someone else imported them from Egypt into another country of the European Community, for example France, and Watson plc only imported the goods from France into Britain, then Watson plc would not be liable. Instead, liability could be fixed on whoever imported them into France. It will now, however, be assumed that Watson plc did import them from Egypt directly into Britain.

Shakespeare Ltd as producer can be held liable in respect of the defective switch, and Isis Cie as producer can be held liable in respect of the defective microwave. Watson plc as the importer can be held liable in respect of both. Given the possible difficulties of proceeding against a foreign company, with maybe no presence in Britain or even in the European Community, it may make sense therefore for Beth to contemplate claims only against Shakespeare Ltd and Watson plc. These claims would certainly include a claim in respect of Beth's personal injuries, that is, her burns. So far as property damage is concerned, no claim can succeed unless the property damage claimable amounts to more than £275 (s 5(4)). This means that Beth's claim can succeed only if she is able to claim for both the loss of the microwave (£250) and the damage to the carpet (£250). If she is able to claim both, then she is entitled to recover the whole of the £500, that is, including the first £275. There is nothing (apart from the need to exceed £275 in total property claims) to rule out her claiming for the carpet, which is clearly property for private, as opposed to business, use. However, Beth cannot claim for the damage to the microwave. So far as the claim (against Watson plc) in respect of the defective microwave is concerned, the damage to the microwave is unrecoverable (s 5(2)). It can be observed that, although Pt I of the Consumer Protection Act talks about liability for defective products, it defines 'defective' in terms of safety and thus, in truth, creates liability for

---

11   Evaluating the chances by giving reason is a good way to demonstrate knowledge.

dangerous products.[12] It creates a liability for damage caused by them, but not for damage caused to themselves. The position is exactly the same when one considers the claim against Shakespeare Ltd (and also Watson plc) in respect of the defective switch. Any argument that the damage caused by the defective product (here, the switch) to other things includes the damage to the microwave is ruled out completely by s 5(2). This subsection prevents recovery of damage for loss or damage to any product (here, the microwave) which has been supplied with the defective product (here, the switch) comprised within it. Thus, the damage to the microwave is not recoverable and thus it follows that the damage to the carpet is also ruled out because it does not exceed £275 in value.

In conclusion, therefore, it appears that in respect of her burns, Beth has a good claim under Pt I of the Consumer Protection Act 1987 against Shakespeare Ltd and Watson plc. The claim against Watson plc may be a little more secure in that, even if Shakespeare Ltd were able to show (under s 4(1)(f)) that the defect was not in the switch but in the unsuitability of the microwave for the particular switch, Watson plc would be still be liable as the importer into the European Community of the defective microwave. It seems, however, that any claim in respect of the carpet would have to be brought in negligence.

CONTRIBUTORY NEGLIGENCE

It is possible, if unlikely, that in trying to put out the fire, Beth was herself negligent.[13] It is unlikely since instinctive reactions in the heat (literally perhaps) of the moment are not normally regarded as amounting to contributory negligence (*Jones v Boyce* (1816)). If she were contributorily negligent, then her damages for her burns, whether under the common law of negligence or under the Consumer Protection Act (see s 6(4)) would be reduced proportionately. It does not follow, however, that any damages (that is, assuming they are recoverable) for the damage to the carpet or microwave would also be reduced, since although it is very likely that any negligence of Beth in choosing to fight the fire may have been one of the causes of her being burnt, it is unlikely that that negligence caused the damage to the microwave and the carpet. Indeed, her fighting the fire, far from being a cause of property damage, almost certainly prevented more occurring.

THE RIDER

There are two possibilities.[14] The first is that the switch was defective. The second is that the microwave was defective, a defect wholly attributable to its design, making it unsuitable for a switch which presumably was listed as one of its replacement parts. If the second possibility is the reality, then Shakespeare Ltd will not be liable, but the advice

---

12 The proper application of the relevant law to the requirements of the question is what the examiner is looking for.

13 The explanation of why a particular legal principle may not be applicable in relation to a question is as important as the explanation of why a particular legal rule may be applicable in relation to a question: on the one hand, this is because it narrows your answer down to the discussion of what is relevant; on the other hand, this is because it demonstrates your understanding.

14 Do not lose out on valuable marks by not discussing the 'alternative' question.

given above as to the liability of Watson plc for product liability will remain unaltered. It seems more likely that the first possibility is the reality. In that case, Shakespeare Ltd will remain liable for product liability, but Watson plc will not be liable at all, since presumably Watson plc did not import into the European Community the replacement switch which Beth fitted and which caused the damage. Furthermore, Shakespeare Ltd's liability can now include liability for the loss of the microwave, since Beth's microwave was not supplied to her with that switch comprised within it. This means that Shakespeare Ltd's liability under the 1987 Act will include liability for the microwave and the carpet, the two together amounting to property damage exceeding £275.

QUESTION 7

Merton plc recently bought two used cars, each six months old, for its executives to drive. Anthony, managing director of Merton plc, first saw the two cars at Sloppy's Garage a month ago, when he noticed that one, a Dolomite, had an engine oil leak and the other, a Winson, had a water leak in the boot. He did not, however, look in the boot of the Dolomite. Sloppy assured him: 'They are good little buses; you can rely upon them.' After test-driving both cars, Anthony, on behalf of Merton plc, signed two contracts of purchase, one for each car. Anthony left the Dolomite with Sloppy to have the oil leak repaired and drove away in the Winson. Two weeks later, he returned the Winson for its boot leak to be repaired and collected the Dolomite. The next day, he discovered firstly, that the Dolomite had a water leak in its boot; secondly, that the engine oil leak had not been repaired and was irreparable (meaning that a new engine was necessary); and, thirdly, that soon after delivery to its first buyer, the Winson had been in an accident and subsequently treated by its owner's insurance company as a 'write-off'. Upon learning these facts, Anthony informed Sloppy's Garage that he was rejecting the cars and demanded the return of the purchase price to Merton plc.

▶ Advise Merton plc.

How to Answer this Question

This question follows a certain style of setting questions, which involves a lot of points being included. The question is testing your ability to spot each of the issues raised as well as your ability to deal with them. Thus, a good answer must acknowledge each of the points raised and must not concentrate on some of the issues to the exclusion of the others.

The issues raised in this question are:

❖ liability for breach of the conditions as to satisfactory quality and fitness for purpose;

❖ liability (for an express term and/or misrepresentation) arising out of the statement about the cars being 'good little buses', etc;

❖ the remedies available to the buyer and, in particular, whether there has been acceptance of the goods so as to preclude rejection.

A sensible order of treatment is:

❖   implied conditions in s 14;
❖   express term/misrepresentation;
❖   remedies.

Applying the Law

s 14(2) Sale of Goods Act 1979

This diagram illustrates how to consider the application of the SGA s 14(2) in this scenario. You will also have to touch on liability for misrepresentation and/or breach of an express term and s 14(3) (fitness for purpose). In addition rights of rejection and remedies for breach of the contract will have to be considered.

ANSWER

This question raises issues of liability for express and implied terms of the contract, for misrepresentation, and the extent of any remedies available to Merton plc.[15] There may be liability in respect of the implied conditions as to satisfactory quality and fitness for purpose, liability for breach of an express term that the cars were 'good little buses', and liability for misrepresentation arising out of the same assertion by Sloppy. These possible liabilities will be considered, as will the remedies that may be available to Merton plc. It is to be observed that a separate contract was signed in relation to each car and, therefore, presumably the parties intended two distinct contracts. This answer will proceed upon that assumption.[16]

SATISFACTORY QUALITY

Because Sloppy clearly sells in the course of business, terms regarding satisfactory quality and fitness for purpose are implied as conditions into the contracts of sale negotiated with Merton plc. However, one condition, in s 14(2) of the **Sale of Goods Act 1979**, is not implied as regards any defect specifically drawn to the buyer's attention before the contract was made or, given that Anthony made a pre-purchase examination of the cars, as regards any defect which 'that' examination ought to have revealed. The engine oil leak in the Dolomite and water leak in the boot of the Winson both appear to be defects falling into one or both of these categories, most clearly the latter category, since we are told that Anthony noticed them. Assuming the water leak in the Winson can be repaired, it seems clear that in respect of that leak, no reliance can be placed by Merton plc upon s 14(2).

The engine oil leak of the Dolomite has turned out, however, to be irreparable without a complete engine replacement. This suggests that the true nature and/or extent of the defect was not something which was either drawn to Anthony's attention or which ought to have been revealed by his pre-contract examination of the car. Neil LJ in *R and B Customs Brokers v United Dominions Trust* (1988) indicated, *obiter*,[17] that a defect of which the buyer is aware but which he reasonably (and mistakenly) believes will be rectified at no cost to himself is not excluded from the effect of s 14(2). It seems therefore that Merton plc can rely upon the condition in s 14(2) as regards the engine oil leak in the Dolomite. The condition as to satisfactory quality might also apply to the water leak in the boot of the Dolomite and to the fact that the Winson had been an insurance 'write-off'. The first of these *might* be a defect which Anthony's

15 In your introduction, you should clearly identify the legal issues raised by the question. This is a good way to convince the examiner that you have understood what is relevant and will make him to be positively inclined towards your answer.
16 Considering ambiguities demonstrates understanding and will attract a higher mark.
17 Stating by whom or how (obiter or ratio) a particular legal principle was stated in a case demonstrates a deeper knowledge and will attract additional marks.

pre-purchase inspection *ought* to have revealed. It seems clear that that inspection did not in fact reveal it because Anthony did not in the course of that inspection look into the boot of the Dolomite. In *Thornett and Fehr v Beers* (1919), it was held that a buyer who had, before the purchase, inspected the outside of some barrels but not the inside was precluded from relying on the condition as to satisfactory quality as regards defects which would have been revealed if he had inspected the inside. It is submitted, however, that a minor change to the wording of s 14(2) effected in 1973 (to the then Sale of Goods Act 1893), namely, the change from 'such examination' to 'that examination' has reversed the effect of the 1919 case. Thus, Merton plc is precluded from relying on those defects that ought to have been revealed by the examination which Anthony actually made, but is not prejudiced by him having made a less extensive examination than he might have made. Put another way, the leak in the Dolomite's boot was not a defect which ought to have been revealed by the examination which Anthony actually made.

So, do the engine oil leak and boot leak in the Dolomite make the car of unsatisfactory quality, and does the fact that the Winson was an insurance 'write-off' make the Winson of unsatisfactory quality? Section 14(2A) requires us to ask in each case whether the car reached a standard that the reasonable person would regard as satisfactory, taking account of any description given to the goods, the price and any other relevant circumstances.[18] Undoubtedly, one of the relevant circumstances is the fact that, in each case, the car was not new but was six months old. Section 14(2B) lists a number of aspects of the quality of the goods, including their 'fitness for all the purposes for which goods of the kind in question are commonly supplied'. Thus, the purposes for which a car is bought include not merely the purpose of driving it from place to place, but of doing so with the appropriate degree of comfort, ease of handling and pride in its outward and interior appearance (*Rogers v Parish* (1987)). This general approach applies also to second-hand cars and the question is whether, in this case, the defects were sufficiently serious to render even these second-hand cars of less than satisfactory quality. A second-hand car which, unknown to the buyer at the time of the contract, had been an insurance 'write-off' has been held for that reason not to have reached the necessary standard (*Shine v General Guarantee Corp* (1988)). The two leaks in the Dolomite are less easy to decide upon. On the one hand, one is to expect minor defects in a second-hand car (*Bartlett v Sydney Marcus* (1965)). On the other hand, it could be said that the oil leak which requires a new engine for it to be remedied is actually a major defect. As regards the newly discovered water leak in the Dolomite, much will depend upon its extent and the ease with which it can be repaired. Therefore, it is submitted that in the case of both cars, Merton plc has a valid claim under s 14(2), but whether that

----

18 In order to attract a good mark you need to ensure that you don't merely describe the law; you need to explain and apply it to the requirements of the question.

extends to the boot leak in the case of the Dolomite will depend upon the seriousness of the latter.

FITNESS FOR PURPOSE

Merton plc's claim in respect of the defects discussed above might equally be made under s 14(3). Anthony told Sloppy of a particular purpose for which Merton plc wanted the cars, namely, the purpose of being driven by the company's executives. The defects already being relied upon under s 14(2) render the cars not reasonably fit for that purpose. Merton plc may have no claim under s 14(3) in respect of defects of which it was aware (for example, the Winson's leaky boot) if Merton plc placed no reliance upon Sloppy's skill and judgement in respect of them. It will still have a claim in relation to the other defect (*Cammell Laird v Manganese Bronze and Brass* (1934)).

'GOOD LITTLE BUSES'

Sloppy's assertion that the cars were 'good little buses' arguably implied that the cars were in good condition (*Andrews v Hopkinson* (1957)). This may have amounted to:

(1)   an express term, either a condition or a warranty, of the contract; and
(2)   a misrepresentation.[19]

Assuming it was an express term of the contract, it is submitted that that express term was broken in the case of the Dolomite by virtue of its engine oil leak necessitating a new engine. Whether the same can be said of water leaks in the boot is more problematic. Much will depend upon the seriousness of those leaks and the ease with which they can be repaired.

A claim for misrepresentation can succeed only if Anthony relied upon Sloppy's statement. Did his pre-purchase examination of the cars indicate a lack of such reliance? Presumably not, because the statement appears to have been made *after* those examinations. Did Anthony's subsequently going for test drives indicate that he was not relying on Sloppy's statement? It seems not, since Sloppy's statement referred to the cars' reliability (that is, presumably, over a period of time) and one or two test drives could not disclose the truth or otherwise of that. It is not necessary for Merton plc to have relied exclusively upon Sloppy's statement.

An untrue statement of fact by Sloppy which was one of the reasons Merton plc was induced into buying will give Merton plc a right to rescind the contract. If, however, Merton plc wishes to claim damages for a misrepresentation, it may do so, either as an alternative to rescission (when the issue of whether to award damages is at the discretion of the judge – s 2(2) of the **Misrepresentation Act 1967**) or as an independent

---

19   The consideration of different possibilities ensures completeness of your analysis and attracts additional marks.

claim for damages under s 2(1). In the latter case, Sloppy will have a defence if he can show, on a balance of probabilities, that at the time of the contract he had reasonable grounds to believe, and did believe, the statement to be true (s 2(1) of the Misrepresentation Act 1967).[a]

REMEDIES

Remedies for misrepresentation have just been discussed. For any breach of contract, there is a right to claim damages. Merton plc has also purported to reject the cars and required the return of the price for each. Assuming that there was breach of the implied term in either s 14(2) or s 14(3), Merton plc undoubtedly had a right of rejection, since both of those terms are implied *conditions*. The same is not necessarily true of the express term encompassed by the words 'They are good little buses; you can rely upon them'. Assuming that this amounted to an express term of the contract, it would have to be decided whether the parties intended it to be a condition, that is, a term any breach of which would give Merton plc the right to reject the goods and regard the contract as repudiated. The tendency of the courts is not to regard as a condition any express term (other than one as to the time of delivery), unless the parties have very clearly indicated it (*Cehave v Bremer, The Hansa Nord* (1976)).[20] Thus, the test of whether Merton plc had any right of rejection/repudiation for breach of the express term depends upon whether the breach was sufficient to deprive Merton plc of substantially the whole of the benefit of the contract (*Hong Kong Fir v Kawasaki Kisen* (1962)). It is submitted that neither the boot leak in the case of one car nor the boot leak and the engine oil leak in the case of the other was sufficiently serious.

Assuming that Merton plc was, because of the breach of the conditions in s 14, within its rights in rejecting the cars and demanding the return of the price, it will nevertheless have lost that right if, by the time it rejected the cars, it had already 'accepted' them within the meaning of s 35. Merton plc rejected the Winson just over two weeks after taking delivery. After a similar period of time, the buyer in *Bernstein v Pamson Motors* (1987) was held to have accepted the car. Even under the law as it then stood, that decision was controversial.[21] Since then, however, s 35 has been amended so that, in determining what is a reasonable length of time, it is relevant to ask whether the buyer has had a reasonable opportunity to examine the goods for the purpose of ascertaining whether they comply with the contract. It is thus arguable that Merton plc had not, in just over two weeks, had the Winson long enough to have examined it for that purpose. If it had not, then it was entitled to act as it did in rejecting it. Similarly, Merton plc arguably had not had the car long enough that it could be said to have affirmed the contract – and thus was entitled to rescind the contract (and reject the car) for misrepresentation.[b]

----

20 Stating exceptions to a particular principle is a good way to show greater knowledge of the area in question.

21 Showing that you are aware of controversies surrounding a particular legal principle will set your answer apart from an average answer.

Whatever may be a reasonable period of time for the buyer to examine the goods to see if they conform to the contract, there may be added to that period of time a further reasonable period. This may, for example, be a period during which the buyer investigates any apparent non-compliance (*Clegg v Andersson* (2003)) or a period during which the seller repairs the goods under an arrangement with the buyer (s 35(5)). So, Merton plc clearly had not lost its right to reject the Dolomite. Indeed, Merton had taken delivery of the Dolomite only one day before rejecting it.

Consequently, Merton plc is entitled to the return of the Dolomite's purchase price.[22] It might also claim damages, although these are unlikely to be substantial in the case of the Dolomite. In the case of the Winson, if Merton plc is held to have lost its right to reject the car, the damages would be more substantial. Assuming that the breach in relation to the Winson was due to the fact that it had been an insurance 'write-off', the amount of damages would be the difference between the market value the car would have had it not got that particular history and the lower value it currently has.

QUESTION 8

Trevor is a well-known dealer in antique vases. On 1 March, he went into China Emporium and asked the shop assistant if they had anything special. He was shown a vase described by the shop assistant as a 'Shiming' vase and, after examining it behind a glass case, Trevor agreed to buy it for £3,500 and took the vase with him. Trevor was very pleased with the purchase because he had a customer who would pay handsomely for such a vase.

On 12 March, Trevor left the vase with his customer to see if he would be interested in buying it for £4,000. The vase was returned two days later because it emerged that it was not genuine and that it was worth less than £250. A week later, during a dinner party, Trevor discovered that water leaked from the vase which he was using to display a bunch of flowers.

Trevor contacted China Emporium immediately, demanding his money back, and was told that it was not the shop's policy to make refunds in any circumstances.

▶ Advise Trevor.

How to Answer this Question

The central issue in advising Trevor is whether he is better off arguing that the pre-contractual statement that the vase was a 'Shiming' vase had become part of the

---

22   The provision of a conclusion by means of a few sentences which summarise your findings ensures that you present a complete answer and leaves a good impression on the examiner.

contract or suing for misrepresentation. The main points that need to be considered are as follows:

- ❖ China Emporium's policy about not refunding money (was this part of the contract anyway?);
- ❖ description: s 13 of the Sale of Goods Act 1979;
- ❖ satisfactory quality: s 14(2);
- ❖ fitness for purpose: s 14(3);
- ❖ misrepresentation, common law and the Misrepresentation Act 1967;
- ❖ when a buyer loses the right to reject goods (acceptance/affirmation);
- ❖ remedies.

Applying the Law

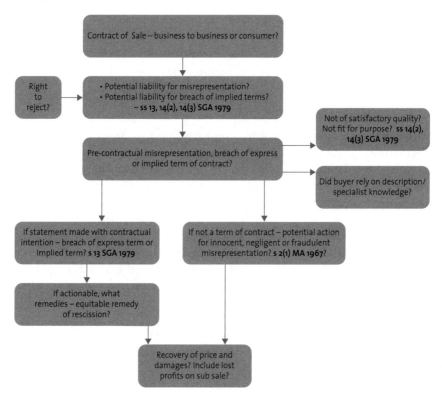

This diagram shows how to consider the contract of sale in relation to this scenario.

ANSWER

Trevor has bought a vase which he now wishes to return and has been told that he is not entitled to a refund of the purchase price.[23] It is clear that any attempt to restrict or limit liability is subject to the strict requirements of incorporation. China Emporium's policy of refusing refunds in any circumstances cannot be effective to prevent Trevor from pursuing the matter against them if a term to that effect has not been incorporated into their contract. We are not told what the express terms and conditions were under the contract, or whether reasonable notice of the policy had been given before or at the time of the contract.[24] Indeed, if there was such a notice displayed, perhaps in the shop, then such a term will be incorporated within their contract even if Trevor did not read it. Assuming that there was no such notice, China Emporium is not entitled to rely on a policy which has not been disclosed to Trevor, and the question of whether or not the policy is reasonable is not in issue. If there were such a notice, it would probably be ineffective by virtue of the **Unfair Contract Terms Act 1977**.

It is clear that Trevor was not dealing as a consumer. Thus, the amendments to the law made by the **Sale and Supply of Goods to Consumers Regulations 2002** do not apply.[25] Whether Trevor has the right to return the vase will depend on finding a breach of a term of the contract or an actionable misrepresentation. There are four possible grounds here:

❖ description;
❖ satisfactory quality;
❖ fitness for purpose;
❖ misrepresentation.

DESCRIPTION

The relevant description in this case is that it was a 'Shiming' vase. **Section 13 of the Sale of Goods Act 1979** states that where goods are sold by reference to a description, it is an implied term that the goods should correspond with the description. In considering whether the sale is one by description, the court will have regard to *Harlingdon and Leinster v Christopher Hull Fine Art Ltd* (1990), that is, whether the seller in making the description has held himself out as having special knowledge and whether the buyer has relied on that description. In that case, a painting was sold described by art dealers, who were not experts in German art, as one by the German painter Gabriele Münter. The buyer, who did not make further inquiries but was an expert in German art, bought the

---

23 Your introduction should clearly set out the relevant issues raised by the question, this demonstrates to the examiner that you have understood what the question requires. Remember that relevancy is an important assessment criterion.

24 Considering ambiguities demonstrates understanding and will attract a higher mark.

25 The explanation of why a particular legal principle is not applicable in relation to a question is as important as the explanation of why a particular legal rule is applicable in relation to a question. This is a good example of how to do this in a succinct manner.

painting for £6,000. It later transpired that the painting was a fake, worth less than £100, and the buyer rejected the painting on the ground that it did not comply with its description. The Court of Appeal held that the sale was not one by description since the description was not influential in the sale.[26]

Applying the *Harlingdon* case to the question, although we are told that Trevor is a well-known dealer in antique vases, we are not told whether China Emporium, with its name, was a known expert in this type of vase. Only if it was within the reasonable contemplation of the parties that Trevor would rely upon the description 'Shiming' could there be a sale by description. If China Emporium was, unlike the art dealers in *Harlingdon*, knowledgeable in 'Shiming' vases, or held itself out to be, Trevor would be entitled to reject the vase and claim damages.

We are told that Trevor examined the vase before agreeing to buy it. A sale of goods is not, however, prevented from being a sale by description solely because the buyer himself selects the goods (**s 13(3)** and *Beale v Taylor* (1967)).

SATISFACTORY QUALITY

China Emporium clearly sells in the course of business so the implied term in **s 14(2)** applies. The goods will not be of satisfactory quality if they do not meet the standard a reasonable person would regard as satisfactory, taking account of the price, any description and all other relevant circumstances (**s 14(2A)**). One relevant aspect of their quality is their fitness for all the purposes for which goods of the kind in question are commonly supplied. The issue which needs to be looked at here is whether the vase was fit for the purposes for which it might commonly be supplied. Trevor paid £3,500 for the vase. It is reasonable to assume that most people paying this high price for a vase will be buying it as an investment or for its resale value. Thus, the vase should be of satisfactory quality as an investment, but what of the fact that the vase is only worth £250? The Court of Appeal considered this point in the *Harlingdon* case, and Nourse LJ's view was that the purpose or purposes for which goods of this kind are commonly bought are the 'aesthetic appreciation of the owner or anyone else he permits to enjoy the experience'.[27] Thus, even if there was a defect in the quality of the vase, it was not one which made it 'unsaleable'. The question of whether goods are reasonably fit for resale cannot depend on whether they can or cannot be resold without making a loss. The test is an objective one, not dependent on the purpose for which Trevor himself required the vase. It seems, therefore, that since most people would have bought the vase for its aesthetic appreciation, the fact that it was not a 'Shiming' vase did not make the vase unfit for aesthetic appreciation

---

26 Outlining the facts of a particular case is a good way to illustrate the relevant legal rules and thus strengthens your argument.

27 The critical consideration of a statement given either in a case or by a noted expert is a good way to attract additional marks.

which, despite its value being so much lower than the price, did not mean that the goods were of unsatisfactory quality.

We are told that Trevor subsequently discovers that the vase leaks when he uses it to display a bunch of flowers. Can Trevor claim that this rendered the vase of unsatisfactory quality? Before the 1994 amendments to s 14, there was authority that the term as to merchantable quality did not require that the goods were reasonably fit for all the purposes for which goods of that description were commonly supplied, and that it was sufficient if they were fit for one of those purposes (*Aswan v Lupdine* (1987)).[28] Now, however, s 14(2B) provides that one aspect of the quality of the goods is their fitness for all the purposes for which goods of that kind are commonly supplied. Certainly, vases are commonly supplied for use as display containers holding fresh flowers and water. It is difficult to know whether that is one of the purposes for which 'Shiming' vases are commonly supplied. If it is, then the fact that the vase leaks suggests that it is not of satisfactory quality. If such vases are, however, commonly supplied for only one purpose, aesthetic appreciation (without containing fresh flowers), then the fact that it leaks will not make it of unsatisfactory quality.

FITNESS FOR PURPOSE

Section 14(3) provides that where goods are required for a particular purpose which has been made known to the seller, there is an implied term that the goods should be reasonably fit for that purpose. This will not apply if Trevor did not rely or it was unreasonable for Trevor to rely on China Emporium's skill and judgement in supplying the goods. In relation to the problem, two questions therefore need to be asked. First, did Trevor make known to China Emporium the exact purpose for which the vase would be required? Second, if so, was it reasonable for him to rely on China Emporium's skill and judgement? The answer to the first question seems likely to be 'yes', as Trevor is a well-known dealer and it is therefore reasonable to assume that if China Emporium is aware of this, it would also know that Trevor would have bought the vase for resale as an antique item. The answer to the second question, however, is likely to be 'no', because, as was discussed in relation to 'description' (above), as between the parties Trevor was the expert in 'Shiming' vases and it would be unreasonable for him to rely on China Emporium's skill and judgement. It seems, therefore, that China Emporium is not liable under s 14(3).

MISREPRESENTATION

The false statement that the vase was a 'Shiming' vase may amount to an actionable misrepresentation, entitling Trevor to rescind the contract and claim damages. The requirements of an actionable misrepresentation are that there was a false statement of an existing fact by one party which induced the other party to enter the contract. It must be a statement of fact and not opinion, although an opinion which is not honestly held at

28 Showing an awareness of the historical development demonstrates your knowledge.

the time or is based on facts which the maker of the statement ought to have known may be actionable.[29]

It is clear from this question that the shop assistant did describe the vase as a 'Shiming' vase. Trevor's reliance on this description does not have to be reasonable (*Museprime Properties v Adhill* (1990)). The court held in the *Museprime Properties* case that the reasonableness of the reliance was relevant to determining whether there was actual reliance, but that the test of reliance is subjective (the more unreasonable the reliance, the less likely the court is to believe that it did actually affect the buyer's decision to enter into the contract). It is also clear that the statement does not have to be the sole reason for entering into the contract: it is sufficient that it was one reason (*Edgington v Fitzmaurice* (1885)). It may be, therefore, that Trevor has a stronger claim in misrepresentation than under the implied conditions under the **Sale of Goods Act**.

Once it has been established that an actionable misrepresentation has been made, the remedies will depend on whether the misrepresentation was made innocently, negligently or fraudulently.[c] It is unlikely that the shop assistant will have made the statement that it was a 'Shiming' vase fraudulently. Either he made it innocently (that is, in genuine ignorance of the fact that it was untrue) or negligently (that is, he had no reasonable grounds for believing that the statement was true) under **s 2(1)** of the **Misrepresentation Act 1967**.[30,d] If the misrepresentation was made innocently, Trevor will be entitled to rescission of the contract. If the misrepresentation was made negligently, Trevor will be entitled not only to rescission, but may recover for all losses caused by the misrepresentation, unrestricted by the rules of remoteness (*Royscot Trust Ltd v Rogerson* (1991)). Moreover, following *Parabola Investments v Browallia* (2009), he will be entitled to lost profits.

One final point which needs to be made is that whether Trevor decides to pursue the matter for breach of contract or for misrepresentation may depend on the fact that it was some three weeks after he bought the vase that he tried to reject the goods against China Emporium.[31] Any action for breach of contract is subject to the rules of acceptance under **s 35** of the **Sale of Goods Act** which, *inter alia*, deems the buyer to have accepted the goods if, after a lapse of reasonable time, he retains the goods without intimating to the seller that he rejects them. In *Bernstein v Pamson Motors* (1987), a period of three weeks was regarded as beyond a reasonable time in which to examine a motor car. Since then, **s 35** has been amended and a reasonable period now will normally include a

---

29 You need to explain the relevant legal rules and how they relate to the question at hand. Don't assume that what you are saying is self-explanatory in its relationship to the question; it is necessary to relate the law properly to the question and to explicitly spell out the link.

30 The consideration of different options ensures completeness of your analysis and attracts additional marks.

31 The consideration of possible limitations on the availability of a particular claim will result in the award of a higher mark as this demonstrates a deeper understanding of how the law works.

reasonable opportunity for the buyer to examine the goods for the purpose of ascertaining whether they conform to the contract. This may well mean that the reasonable period of time before the buyer is taken to have accepted the goods will be longer than previously (*Clegg v Andersson* (2003)). Trevor had in fact had the vase for over three weeks before giving notice of rejection. Furthermore, he discovered after two weeks that it was not a 'Shiming' vase. Assuming that that is a breach of condition, it is arguable that keeping it a further week afterwards before rejecting it amounts to acceptance. If, however, he was using that week in order to have experts examine it to confirm whether or not it was a 'Shiming' vase (although we are told nothing to suggest that he was), that would have the effect of lengthening the reasonable period of time (*Truk v Tokmakidis* (2000)). If he has accepted the goods, then his only remedy for breach of contract would be a claim for damages, the amount of which would depend greatly on whether, on the one hand, he could establish a breach of contract arising out of the description 'Shiming' vase or, on the other, was able only to rely on the fact that the vase leaked.

An action in misrepresentation is not subject to the acceptance rules and a buyer is only deemed to have lost his right to rescind if he has affirmed the contract which, after three weeks, it may be held that he has done. If it were established that the misrepresentation were fraudulent, then time would begin to run only from when Trevor discovered the truth. It seems that Trevor knew of the lack of authenticity of the vase around 14 March and it was only a week later that he contacted China Emporium. Thus, if it was a fraudulent misrepresentation, Trevor would be able to rescind the contract. He would in any case be entitled to damages for misrepresentation, unless China Emporium could show that it had reasonable grounds to believe it was a 'Shiming' vase.

QUESTION 9

Agatha wants to buy a washing machine. She walks into a branch of Machines-R-Us Ltd and asks Paolo, the sales assistant, for his advice. She tells him that she needs a machine that has a quick wash cycle. Paolo recommended the Helper because, on average, it requires just 30 minutes for a wash cycle at 50 degrees Celsius. The machine is delivered later that day.

It turns out that for a wash cycle at 50 degrees Celsius the machine in fact requires 60 minutes. Two weeks later, the machine is beginning to make funny noises and starts belching smoke. The load it is washing at the time is completely destroyed. When Agatha phones Paolo to ask for her money back, Paolo tells her that the contract Agatha signed included a clause stating: 'All conditions relating to the quality or condition of any machine are hereby excluded. The seller accepts no liability in respect of any statements made prior to the contract unless such statements have been put in writing.'

▶ Advise Agatha.

How to Answer this Question

The issues raised in this question are:

- ❖ liability for breach of the conditions as to satisfactory quality and fitness for purpose;
- ❖ liability (for an express term and/or misrepresentation) arising out of the statement about the washing machine needing only 30 minutes for a wash cycle;
- ❖ the remedies available to the buyer and, in particular, whether there has been acceptance of the goods so as to preclude rejection;
- ❖ the exclusion clause. The method of dealing with it is, after quickly acknowledging that it was incorporated into the contract, to deal with the interpretation of the clause and then the effect of the **Unfair Contract Terms Act 1977** and the **Unfair Terms in Consumer Contracts Regulations 1999**.

Applying the Law

The diagram illustrates how the exemption clause can be considered in this question once the status of the contract has been determined.

In addition to the issue of the exemption clause you will have to consider the status of the statements by the employee and whether the item was of satisfactory quality (**s 14(2)**). Also whether the machine can be rejected and the remedies including new consumer remedies for breach of contract.

ANSWER

This question raises issues of liability for express and implied terms of the contract and the extent of any remedies available to Agatha, bearing in mind the seller has purported to exclude liability.

EXPRESS TERM

When Agatha told Paolo she needed a washing machine capable of a quick wash cycle, he recommended the Helper because, he said, it needed just 30 minutes for a wash cycle. This may have amounted to an express term. Assuming it was an express term of the contract, it is clear that that express term was broken in Agatha's case because the wash cycle, in fact, took 60 minutes.[32]

SATISFACTORY QUALITY

Because Machines-R-Us sells in the course of business, terms regarding satisfactory quality and fitness for purpose are implied as conditions into the sale contract with Agatha. Under **s 14(2)** of the **Sale of Goods Act 1979** there is an implied condition that goods sold should be of satisfactory quality. No reasonable person would regard the washing machine as satisfactory if after such a short period of time (two weeks) it makes funny noises and starts belching smoke.[33] It is unlikely that Paolo specifically drew this defect to Agatha's attention before the contract was made. We are not told whether Agatha made a pre-purchase examination of the washing machine, as regards any defect which 'that' examination ought to have revealed. Even if she did examine the machine, it is unlikely this would have revealed the defect. It seems therefore that Agatha can rely upon the condition in **s 14(2)**. The machine belched smoke, ruining the load it was washing at the time. A reasonable person would not regard the machine as satisfactory, taking account of any description given to the goods, the price and any other relevant circumstances (**s 14(2A)**). We are not told what price Agatha paid for the machine nor whether it was bought as new or second-hand goods. The general approach is that the higher the price paid, particularly for new goods, the higher the standard the buyer can expect. However, in Agatha's case, the defects are sufficiently serious to render even second-hand goods of less than satisfactory quality (*Crowther v Shannon Motors* (1975)). Therefore, it is submitted that Agatha has a valid claim under **s 14(2)**.

FITNESS FOR PURPOSE

Agatha's claim in respect of the defects discussed above might equally be made under **s 14(3)**. Since the description of the goods ('washing machine') points to one

---

32 Don't state all you know about the area of law in question, remember to focus on the relevant issues – it is as much your ability to apply the relevant legal rules to the question as your knowledge that is assessed.

33 You need to go beyond mere description of the law; it is the proper application of the relevant legal rules that demonstrates your knowledge and understanding. Remember that it is this upon which you are assessed. This is a good example of how to achieve this aim.

purpose only, the washing machine must be fit for that particular purpose (*Priest v Last* (1903)) and it is clear that the defects already being relied upon under s 14(2) render the washing machine not reasonably fit for that purpose and this a breach of the implied condition in s 14(3). In addition, Agatha told Paolo that she needs a machine that has a quick wash cycle. The machine recommended to her was not capable of this. Since it is reasonable for Agatha to place reliance upon Paolo's skill and judgement in respect of his recommendation, Agatha will have a claim under s 14(3).

EXCLUSION CLAUSE

Like any exclusion clause, the clause in this case will not have any effect unless it satisfies each of the following requirements:[34]

- ❖ it was incorporated into the contract;
- ❖ as a matter of interpretation, the wording of the clause is effective to exclude liability which otherwise the seller would incur;
- ❖ the clause is not rendered invalid by either the **Unfair Contract Terms Act 1977** or the **Unfair Terms in Consumer Contracts Regulations 1999**.

Clearly, in the present case, the first of these requirements is satisfied as we are told that Agatha had signed the contract (*L'Estrange v Graucob* (1934)).

INTERPRETATION OF THE CLAUSE

As regards the second requirement, the first half of the clause would clearly exclude liability for breach of the implied condition as to satisfactory quality in s 14 of the **Sale of Goods Act 1979**. The words of the clause are clear and there is no longer any presumption (at common law) that the clear words of a clause are not to be given effect, and that is so even if they clearly purport to exclude what used to be referred to as a fundamental breach of contract (*Photo Productions v Securicor Transport* (1980)). Does it also exclude liability for the condition of fitness of purpose? The *contra proferentem* rule of construction which the courts use in construing exclusion clauses requires that, where a clause is truly ambiguous, the meaning which gives the clause the lesser effect is adopted.[35] This is the rule as applied over the years in such cases as *Wallis and Wells v Pratt and Haynes* (1911) and *Andrews v Singer* (1934). Nothing in the *Photo Productions* case does away with the *contra proferentem* rule in cases of true ambiguity. Referring to the wording of the clause, the condition as to fitness is excluded if it relates to the 'quality or condition'

---

34 The identification of the constituent parts of a legal rule is a good way to attract marks as it not only demonstrates knowledge but also helps to provide a logical structure to your answer.

35 You need to explain the relevant legal rules and how they relate to the question at hand. Don't assume that what you are saying is self-explanatory in its relationship to the question; it is necessary to relate the law properly to the question and to explicitly spell out the link.

of a machine. Clearly, on the facts of the problem given, it is the quality that is in issue and, undoubtedly, the quality of a washing machine can affect its fitness for a particular purpose. However, the fitness for purpose condition implied by s 14(3) is not confined to matters of quality or condition. A machine can be of excellent quality and in excellent condition and still not be fit for a particular purpose for which the buyer has indicated she wants it. Here, Agatha told Paolo that she wants a machine capable of quick wash cycles. If the clause in issue here were held to exclude the condition as to fitness for purpose, it would rule it out in the latter situation, as well as where the unfitness is caused by defects in quality or condition. Applying the *contra proferentem* rule, therefore, it seems likely that a court would hold that the fitness for purpose condition was not excluded.

It appears then that the first sentence of the clause, as a matter of interpretation, does exclude liability for breach of the condition as to satisfactory quality, but may well not do so as regards the condition of fitness for purpose.[36]

Let us turn to the matter of Machines-R-Us's possible liability in respect of the pre-contract statement about the washing machine being capable of a 30-minute wash cycle. The latter part of the clause would appear to exclude that liability, since there is no indication that Paolo's statement was put into writing. There is, however, an argument which might prevent such a conclusion.[37] It is possible that Paolo's words might give rise to liability for breach of an express term of the contract (*Andrews v Hopkinson* (1957)). The clause refers to statements made 'prior to the contract'. It does not refer to statements which are part of the contract itself, which an express term – even one not reduced to writing – would undoubtedly be. So it might be argued that the clause was not intended to exclude express terms. The point is clearly an arguable one, since it could alternatively be said that the intention of the clause is to exclude all liability in respect of pre-contract statements, including terms of the contract itself, unless those terms are in writing.

UNFAIR CONTRACT TERMS ACT 1977

Assuming that the clause is effective at common law to exclude at least some possible liabilities, is it robbed of that effect by the **Unfair Contract Terms Act (UCTA) 1977**?[38] This Act applies differently to different heads of liability. **Section 6** deals with the clause[39]

....

36 Drawing an interim-conclusion is a good way of signposting the relevant issues and also helps you to structure your answer logically.

37 The provision, and consideration, of more than one possible legal argument or opposing views demonstrates wider knowledge and deeper understanding.

38 Pointing out any potential limitations of the application of a particular legal principle is a good way to demonstrate that you have understood the area of law in question.

39 Clear signposting of the issues discussed enhances the readability of your answer and helps to achieve clarity of expression.

insofar as it purports to exclude liability for breach of the implied conditions in **s 14** of the **Sale of Goods Act 1979**. Since Agatha dealt as a consumer in buying the washing machine, neither of those implied terms can be excluded.

Let us turn to the effect of the **UCTA** on the clause insofar as it purports to exclude liability for breach of unwritten express terms of the contract. The clause is subject to the requirement of reasonableness. This is provided for by **s 3** of the **UCTA**. **Section 3** will apply since it appears that the clause in question is one of Machines-R-Us's standard terms. Technically, **s 3** does not refer to **Sched 2** which offers guidelines as to whether or not a clause is reasonable. However, there is little doubt that similar considerations will be applied. The court is very likely to consider the clause as a whole in deciding whether it satisfies the requirement of reasonableness.

In any case where that requirement is under consideration, account needs to be taken of the factor, highlighted in the cases, that a clause which does not merely limit liability but purports totally to exclude it is much less likely to satisfy the requirement of reasonableness[40] (compare *Mitchell v Finney Lock Seeds* (1983) and *Ailsa Craig Fishing v Malvern Fishing* (1983)). It has already been said that perhaps the clause in Agatha's case will, on its wording, be held not to exclude liability for the condition as to fitness for purpose or for breach of an express term of the contract. Even so, in relation to those liabilities which it does purport to exclude, its exclusion of liability is complete. This fact strengthens the argument that the clause fails to satisfy the requirement of reasonableness.

UNFAIR TERMS IN CONSUMER CONTRACTS REGULATIONS 1999

Because Agatha has contracted as a consumer, the **1999 Regulations** will apply to her contract with Machines-R-Us (**reg 4**). The effect of these Regulations will render the exclusion clause of no effect since, contrary to a requirement of good faith, the clause causes a significant imbalance in the parties' rights and obligations to the detriment of the consumer. The exclusion clause in question is likely to be declared 'unfair'.

REMEDIES

For any breach of contract, there is a right to claim damages. Because the **Sale and Supply of Goods to Consumers Regulations 2002** are in force, Agatha has additional rights if an item purchased is not of satisfactory quality or not reasonably fit for its purpose. She is in principle entitled to claim a remedy of repair or of replacement

----

40 Showing an understanding of any subtleties/intricacies of a particular rule demonstrates a deeper knowledge and understanding and will attract a higher mark.

of the item, unless such a claim would be disproportionate. If such a claim would be disproportionate or, alternatively, if such a claim is made and not complied with within a reasonable time, then Agatha is entitled to a reduction in the price or to rescind the contract. It appears that these additional rights are not what Agatha wishes to claim for. We are told that she wants to reject the machine. Assuming that there was breach of the implied term in either s 14(2) or s 14(3), Agatha undoubtedly has a right of rejection, since both of those terms are implied *conditions*. The same is not necessarily true of the express term (that the wash cycle is complete in 30 minutes), since it would have to be decided whether the parties intended it to be a condition, that is, a term any breach of which would give Agatha the right to reject the goods and regard the contract as repudiated. The tendency of the courts is not to regard as a condition any express term (other than one as to the time of delivery), unless the parties have very clearly indicated it (*Cehave v Bremer, The Hansa Nord* (1976)). Thus, the test of whether Agatha had any right of rejection/repudiation for breach of the express term depends upon whether the breach was sufficient to deprive Agatha of substantially the whole of the benefit of the contract (*Hong Kong Fir v Kawasaki Kisen* (1962)). It is possible that the fact that the machine needs more than 30 minutes to complete the wash cycle was not sufficiently serious.

Assuming that Agatha was, because of the breach of the conditions in s 14, within her rights in rejecting the machine and demanding the return of the price, she will nevertheless have lost that right if, by the time she phones Paolo, she had already 'accepted' the machine within the meaning of s 35. Agatha rejected the machine about two weeks after taking delivery. After a similar period of time, the buyer in *Bernstein v Pamson Motors* (1987) was held to have accepted a car. Even under the law as it then stood, that decision was controversial. Since then, however, s 35 has been amended so that, in determining what is a reasonable length of time, it is relevant to ask whether the buyer has had a reasonable opportunity to examine the goods for the purpose of ascertaining whether they comply with the contract. It is thus arguable that Agatha had not, in just two weeks, had the washing machine long enough to have examined it for that purpose.

CONCLUSION

In conclusion, whatever interpretation is held to be the correct construction of the clause, it seems very likely that the clause will not satisfy the requirement of reasonableness in the **Unfair Contract Terms Act** nor 'fair' under the **Unfair Terms in Consumer Contracts Regulations**. It will therefore be of no effect. Consequently, Agatha is entitled to the return of the machine's purchase price. She may also claim damages, in particular for the load the machine was washing but which was completely destroyed. Such damages would not be too remote under the rule in *Hadley v Baxendale* (1854).[41]

....

41 Your conclusion should summarise the findings made in the main part of your answer in a succinct and clear way. This will ensure that the examiner finishes reading your answer in a positive frame of mind.

QUESTION 10

Agnes, in the course of her business, agreed to buy from Rodney '2,000 Christmas trees, Scots Pine, five feet to six feet high, fair average quality for the season, packed 50 to a pallet, delivery to Agnes's premises on 10–12 December'. The contract contained an exclusion clause which satisfied the requirement of reasonableness in the **Unfair Contract Terms Act 1977** and which excluded liability for any breach of the statutory implied conditions as to satisfactory quality and fitness for purpose. On 12 December, Rodney tenders delivery to Agnes.

Consider the legal position on 12 December in each of the following alternative situations:

(a)   90% of the trees are between five feet and six feet high but 5% of them are slightly less than five feet and 5% are slightly over six feet high;

(b)   a number of the trees are unevenly tapered in shape and are thus not 'fair average quality for the season';

(c)   the trees are packed 75 to a pallet;

(d)   the delivery tendered is of 2,020 trees.

How to Answer this Question

This question, with its exclusion clause, plainly effective to exclude the implied conditions as to satisfactory quality and fitness for purpose, is clearly concentrated on the implied condition as to description and to the (often) related issues that arise in relation to delivery of the wrong contract quantity or of contract goods mixed with non-contract goods. A simple approach here is to deal with each numbered part of the question in turn, taking care to refer back where necessary to an answer already given rather than to repeat issues that are the same in relation to the different parts of the question.

Applying the Law

s 13 Sale of Goods Act 1979

How the law relating to the right to reject can be understood in this answer can be seen above. In addition to the issue above you will have to consider the impact of the express term re fair average quality, the effect of the exclusion clause and delivery of the wrong amount. The remedies available to the buyer will need to be looked at.

ANSWER

(A)

The fact that 10% of the trees are outside the definition of 'five feet to six feet high' could cause the seller to be in breach of the condition, implied by s 13 of the **Sale of Goods Act 1979**, that the goods must correspond with their description. So far as we are informed, the shortness or extra length does not render the trees of any less quality or likely to be less fit for any purpose for which Agnes had indicated to Rodney that she wanted them. It seems clear that the description 'five feet to six feet high' was part of the contract description and thus any failure to comply would be a breach of the condition in s 13. We are not told how short of five feet or how much in excess of six feet the non-conforming trees measured, except that we are told that the deviation was 'slight'.[42] Rodney might seek to invoke the maxim *de minimis non curat lex* and thus argue that any deviation was so small that it ought to be ignored. However, the measurements of five feet to six feet, given in the contract description, are precise measurements and it has been held by the House of Lords that a contract requirement on the seller to supply staves 'half an inch thick' was exactly that and that supplying staves up to nine-sixteenths of an inch thick was a breach of the implied condition implied by s 13 (*Arcos v Ronaasen* (1933)).[43] If the seller had wished for a margin, he should have stipulated for it in his contract. In the present case, that reasoning can be taken further by the observation that there *was* a margin stipulated for in the contract, that is, anything from five to six feet high. Thus, it seems that Rodney is in breach of the condition in s 13.

Normally, a breach of condition entitles the buyer to reject the goods. In the case of a breach of the conditions in ss 13–15 of the **Sale of Goods Act**, however, this is subject to an exception which applies where (like Agnes) the buyer is not dealing as a consumer. This exception means that Agnes will not be entitled to reject the goods if the breach was so slight that it would be unreasonable for her to reject them (s 15A). Although we are told that some of the trees were 'slightly' over or under the contract height, we are not given enough facts to know if s 15A does apply – and it is for Rodney, the seller, to show that it does. If it does not apply, then Agnes has a whole range of options open to her. Firstly,[44] she could waive her right to reject the goods (which would leave her in exactly the same position as if s 15A does apply) and simply claim damages for her loss, if any, arising from the fact that some of the trees were too short and some too long. If she suffered no damage or loss because of that, then she would be entitled only to nominal damages. Secondly, she could reject the whole consignment and, assuming that Rodney is unable

---

42 Noting the lack of information provided by the question and pointing out the likely implications of any such lack show an understanding of the area of law in question.

43 The reference to examples supports and strengthens your analysis; it also demonstrates your knowledge.

44 The consideration of alternative courses of action is a good way to attract marks as it demonstrates knowledge and understanding.

to supply a complete consignment of complying trees by the end of the contractual delivery deadline (12 December), she could claim damages which would be assessed on the difference between what she was contracted to pay Rodney and the market price (if higher) on 12 December of 1,000 trees matching the contract description (**s 51**). Thirdly, Agnes could accept those trees which did conform to the contract description and reject some or all of the 10% which did not (**s 35A**). In this scenario, she must pay for those she accepts *pro rata* at the contract rate. She will also be able to claim damages in relation to the 10% she rejects, the damages being the difference between the contract price for the number of rejected trees and, if higher, the market price on 12 December for that number of trees conforming to the contract description.

(B)

Given the facts that (i) Agnes was not dealing as a consumer, and (ii) the exclusion clause satisfies the requirement of reasonableness, the implied conditions as to satisfactory quality and fitness for purpose cannot be relied upon by Agnes.[45] Unless there is some special statutory provision relating to Christmas trees or to trees, there are no other implied conditions as to quality (**s 14(1)**). That leaves two possible causes of action available to Agnes. The first is that Rodney is in breach of the condition as to description, in that the trees do not conform to the contract requirement that they be of 'fair average quality for the season'. However, it seems unlikely that the court would regard those words as part of the contract 'description' (*Ashington Piggeries v Hill* (1972)). This is because the contract description does not normally include quality requirements but is confined to those elements in the contractual requirements which help to 'identify' the goods. The result of this, combined with the exclusion clause, is that reliance on the implied conditions as to description and quality is ruled out. This means that Agnes is thrown back on her other possible cause of action, namely, a claim for breach of an *express* term of the contract, that is, a term that the trees be of fair average quality for the season. This term is unlikely, however, to be regarded by the court as a condition of the contract since the parties have not, it appears, indicated that it was their intention that any breach of the term would entitle Agnes to regard the contract as repudiated. That being so, the term is only a warranty (or intermediate term) of the contract and Agnes could not regard the contract as repudiated by a breach of that term unless the breach deprived Agnes of 'substantially the whole benefit' of the contract (*Hong Kong Fir v Kawasaki Kisen* (1962); *Cehave v Bremer* (1976)). We are told of neither the severity of the poor shape of the trees nor of the number affected. If more than half are affected and they are severely misshapen and if, as a result, Agnes cannot sell them without damaging her own commercial reputation, then the court would very likely be prepared to regard the breach as a repudiatory one. If the breach is sufficiently severe to

---

45 The explanation of why a particular legal principle is not applicable in relation to a question is as important as the explanation of why a particular legal rule is applicable in relation to a question: on the one hand, this is because it narrows your analysis down to what is relevant; on the other hand, this is because it demonstrates understanding.

amount to a repudiatory breach, then Agnes is entitled to accept those which conform to the contract and to reject some or all of those which do not. Whether Agnes refuses to accept all or just some of the goods, the risk for her is that the court may subsequently hold that the breach did not deprive her of substantially the whole benefit of the contract. In that case, then, Agnes would herself be in breach of contract for refusing to take delivery and would be liable to Rodney for non-acceptance of the goods. The measure of damages would be the difference between the contract price for the number of trees rejected and the market price, if lower, on 12 December. Agnes should therefore be advised to consider accepting the trees and reselling them for whatever she can get.[46] She would in those circumstances be able to claim damages for breach of the express term that the trees be of fair average quality for the season. Her measure of damages would, *prima facie*, be the difference in the value to her of the trees actually delivered and the higher value they would have had if they had been of fair average quality for the season (s 53(3)).

(C)

Even if the fact that the trees are packed 75 instead of 50 to a pallet renders them of unsatisfactory quality or unfit for their purpose, Agnes will be unable to rely upon the implied conditions in s 14 of the Sale of Goods Act, for the reasons just given in relation to the contract requirement that the trees be of fair average quality for the season.[47] Again, therefore, Agnes has two possible causes of action. The first is for breach of an express term of the contract and the second is for breach of the implied condition as to description. As regards the former, again, it seems unlikely that the court would construe the express term as a condition of the contract and therefore, again, any right of Agnes to regard the contract as repudiated (and, hence, to reject the goods) must depend upon whether the breach (the trees being packed 75 instead of 50 to a pallet) deprives Agnes of substantially the whole benefit of the contract. Unless there are some unusual facts which are not disclosed by the words of the problem as set, it seems unlikely that Agnes has suffered such a breach. Thus, Agnes's only right is to claim damages for breach of the express term, on the same basis as just explained in relation to the requirement that the trees be of fair average quality for the season. That is so, unless she can claim that Rodney is in breach of the condition as to description in s 13. Such a claim depends upon the requirement 'packed 50 to a pallet' being accepted by the court as being part of the contract 'description'. In *Re Moore and Landauer* (1921), a somewhat similar requirement was accepted by the Court of Appeal as being part of the contract description. This has the result that any deviation (even if quite a small one) from the requirement is a breach of condition and entitles the buyer to reject the goods.[48] In *Re Moore and Landauer*, the

....

46 Concluding your analysis with tailored advice to the advisee will ensure completeness of your answer.

47 Referring back to a previously drawn conclusion or an explanation made earlier not only demonstrates that you understand what is relevant, it also saves valuable time as you don't have to repeat yourself.

48 Providing an outline of a case which resembles the facts of the problem strengthens your argument/conclusion.

buyer was held entitled to reject a consignment of tinned fruit because although the correct contract quantity had been delivered, some of them were packed in cases of 24 tins instead of (as the contract required) in cases of 30 tins. That decision has, however, since been doubted in the House of Lords (*Reardon Smith Line v Hansen Tangen* (1976)). It is clear now that the courts are unlikely to find that an express term of the contract comprises part of the contract description unless it helps to 'identify' the goods. This means that the court is highly unlikely to regard the requirement that the trees be packed 50 to a pallet as anything other than a warranty (or intermediate term) of the contract. Furthermore, **s 15A** has been added to the **Sale of Goods Act 1979** by the **Sale and Supply of Goods Act 1994** with the result that, even if there has been a breach of condition, Agnes has no right to reject the goods if the breach was so slight that it would be unreasonable for her to reject them. Agnes therefore should be advised not to reject the trees but to accept them and to claim damages for any loss as a result of the trees being packed 75 to a pallet.

(D)

This question seems no more than a straightforward example of the seller tendering more than the contract quantity. However, it must also inevitably be that the trees are not all 'packed 50 to a pallet', since 2,020 is not divisible by 50! For a discussion of that aspect of the matter, see the answer to (c) above.[49] Leaving that issue aside, there remains the matter of the extra quantity. The normal rules on over-supply are as follows. Firstly, Agnes can reject all the goods for breach of the condition to supply 2,000 trees (**s 30(2)**). Secondly, she can accept the contract quantity and reject the surplus 20 (**s 30(2)**). Thirdly, she could accept the lot and pay for the extra *pro rata* at the contract rate (**s 30(3)**). However, the operation of s 30 is subject to any custom and practice between the parties and to any usage of the trade (**s 30(5)**). Even if there is no such relevant custom, practice or usage, the court may well regard the over-supply of 20 trees (that is, a mere 1% of the contract quantity) as *de minimis*. In that case, Agnes has suffered no breach and will be required to pay nothing for the extra 20 trees.

Common Pitfalls ✗

This question includes a lot of points. A good answer must acknowledge each of the points raised and must not concentrate on some of the issues to the exclusion of the others.

---

49 Don't assume that the issues raised by the question are self-explanatory. They might not!

QUESTION 11

Selborne agreed to sell to Marley 900 pine desks. The contract required delivery to be made in three equal instalments on 20 January, 25 January and 30 January. It also contained the clause 'This entire contract is governed by English law'. On 20 January, Selborne delivered 280 desks (260 pine desks and 20 teak desks). Today is 25 January and Selborne has delivered 295 pine desks. Marley has now found a cheaper supplier and wishes to return all the desks delivered so far and to cancel delivery of the third consignment.

▶   Advise Marley.

What difference, if any, would it have made to your advice if today is 3 February and Selborne has only just delivered the second consignment?

How to Answer this Question

There are two particular issues in the question which, on the facts given, it is impossible to determine for sure. These are 'has Marley accepted the first consignment within the meaning of s 35 of the **Sale of Goods Act 1979**?' and 'is the contract severable or entire?'. Because of this, it is important not just to point these things out, but also to identify the position in the different possible eventualities. Thus, it is essential to use that wonderful word 'if', which is so often useful to examinees in law examinations.

As the question gives a story of two defective deliveries, the structure adopted for the answer here is to deal with them each in turn and then, at the end, to deal with the rider to the question.

Answer Structure

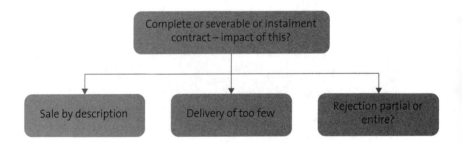

ANSWER

It is proposed to deal initially with the effect of the defective first delivery five days ago and then with the effect of today's defective delivery.

THE FIRST DELIVERY[50]

When Selborne delivered the first consignment, he was in breach of contract in one or both of two respects. First, 20 of the desks were not pine and therefore did not comply with what must have been part of the contract description. That put Selborne in breach of the condition implied by s 13 of the **Sale of Goods Act 1979**.[51] Secondly, one can say that Selborne delivered too small a quantity of the contract goods (that is, pine desks). Either way, there has been a breach of condition, giving the buyer the right to reject the goods (see **s 30(1)** of the 1979 Act)[52] and this, we are told, is what Marley wishes to do. There are, however, two problems with that. Firstly, it is not clear whether the contract is a severable one. If it is, the defective first delivery may not give Marley the right to reject the later two consignments. Secondly, it is possible that Marley may have lost his right to reject the goods because he may be held to have 'accepted' the first defective delivery.

To take the second of these issues first, a buyer who accepts the goods or part of them is precluded from rejecting the goods (**s 11(4)** of the **Sale of Goods Act 1979**). **Section 35** of the **1979 Act** states three things which will amount to acceptance. The problem simply gives us no information on the first two; we are therefore unable to state whether Marley has either intimated to Selborne his acceptance of the goods or else done any act inconsistent with rejecting them. As to the third thing (**s 35(4)**) listed in **s 35**, it is debatable whether a lapse of a reasonable length of time has occurred. Marley has had the desks for five days. It is true that a reasonable period of time will not have elapsed if Marley has not had the goods long enough to have been able to examine them to see if they conform with the contract. However, it must have been fairly obvious almost immediately upon delivery that: (a) 20 of the desks were missing; and (b) 20 of those which were delivered were teak and not pine.[53] It is arguable in those circumstances that five days is more than a reasonable period of time in which to reject. Certainly, three weeks was held to be more than a reasonable period of time in the first instance decision (on the very different facts of a defective motor car) in *Bernstein v Pamson Motors* (1987). We are not told what were the provisions of the contract regarding the time of payment. If a period of, say, one month was allowed for Marley to pay, then it may be that a reasonable period of time would be held to last at least until the deadline for payment (*Truk v Tokmakidis* (2000)).

Since **s 35** was amended, there is now a right of partial rejection which would allow Marley to reject the desks which do not conform to the contract and to accept the rest

....

50 Clear signposting of the issues discussed (e.g. by means of headings) enhances the readability of your answer and helps to achieve clarity of expression.

51 Restrict yourself to what is relevant, don't write down everything you know. Remember that relevancy is an important part of the assessment criteria.

52 It is important to refer to relevant authorities to substantiate your argument – this might be case law or a statutory provision. Remember: it is the application of law upon which you are assessed.

53 Don't assume that the issues raised by the question are self-explanatory. They might not!

(the other 260). However, it is clear from the facts that Marley would prefer to reject the lot. Thus, assuming that Marley has not 'accepted' the first consignment, he will have the right to reject that consignment (the whole of it). Whether that gives him the right to reject the later consignments also depends upon whether the contract is an entire contract or is a severable one.[54] If it is not severable, then the breach of condition entitles Marley to reject all consignments. The test of whether a contract is severable is one of construction (interpretation) of the contract, that is, one is trying to discover from the words of the contract what was the intention of the parties. Was it their intention that a breach in relation to one consignment should entitle the purchaser to reject all? If not, then the contract is severable – see generally *Jackson v Rotax Motor and Cycle Co* (1910). The fact that the desks were to be delivered in instalments is some evidence that the contract was severable. We are not told, however, whether under the contract, the consignments were each to be paid for separately. If they were, then that would be strong evidence that the contract was severable. It may be argued that the parties had themselves clearly labelled the contract as not being severable but as being entire, because of the clause in the contract which read that the 'entire' contract was governed by English law. It is submitted, however, that this clause is nothing more than a choice of law clause and that the word 'entire', in the particular context of that clause, does not bear upon whether the contract was severable, but merely means that all of the contract, as opposed to part of it, was to be governed by English law.

If Marley has not 'accepted' the first consignment and if the contract is not severable, then he is entitled to reject all the goods, including the later two consignments. If he has not 'accepted' the first consignment and the contract is severable, then he may still be able to regard the whole contract as repudiated and thus be able to reject the two later consignments.[55] Whether the whole contract is repudiated depends upon the following two factors: (a) the ratio that the breach bore quantitatively to the whole contract; and (b) the likelihood of the breach being repeated in later instalments (*Maple Flock Co v Universal Furniture Products* (1934)). This is not so easy to determine. At the time that the breach occurs, one cannot tell anything about the second of these factors. As to the first, it could be said that the breach is fairly small in relation to the whole contract. First, it relates to only one consignment out of the three and, within that consignment, it affects only a small proportion of the total quantity of the desks.

Thus, based on the first defective delivery, one's advice to Marley would be cautious since: (a) he may have 'accepted' the goods; (b) the contract may be severable; and if it is, the *Maple Flock* test may not be satisfied so as to allow him to regard the whole contract as repudiated.

....

54 Discussing different possibilities is a good way to attract marks as it shows that you have understood the potential implications of a particular legal rule.

55 Remember to aim for completeness in your answer. This means that you have to analyse the problems raised by a question in their entirety, whether you 'like' the potential outcome or not.

THE SECOND DELIVERY

The breach in relation to the second delivery is simply a delivery of too small a quantity.[56] The missing five desks would appear too many for the courts to be prepared to ignore the breach on the *de minimis non curat lex* principle. Thus, it is a breach of condition.

If the contract was not severable and Marley has not 'accepted' the first consignment, then he is entitled to reject all three consignments because of the breaches of condition in relation to the first two consignments. If the contract was not severable and Marley has 'accepted' the first consignment, then the position is clouded by the fact that the effect of s 11(4) and the new s 35A is not entirely clear.[57] Section 35A introduced the concept of partial rejection, allowing the buyer to reject some or all of the non-conforming goods, provided he accepted all of the conforming goods. One thing which does seem clear is that ss 11(4) and 35A do not allow the buyer to reject any goods (whether conforming or not) which he has actually accepted. Thus, if the contract is not severable and Marley has 'accepted' the first consignment, he cannot now reject any of the first consignment (though he may claim damages in respect of the breaches relating to the first consignment). As regards the second consignment, he is entitled to reject any non-conforming goods, but not conforming goods. However, there are no non-conforming goods, since the only breach relating to the second consignment is a shortfall in the number of desks. Section 30(1) entitles the buyer to reject all the goods if a quantity smaller than the contract quantity is tendered. The buyer appears, however, to be precluded from exercising this right by his acceptance of the first consignment. This is the effect of s 11(4) in the case of a non-severable agreement. Although s 11(4) is subject to s 35A, the latter is of no help to the buyer in this instance. Section 35A(1) applies only where it is non-conforming goods which are being rejected. Section 35A(2) also appears to be of no help, since it applies only where the buyer has a right to reject an instalment, and that is the very issue which we have to determine (that is, does the buyer have a right to reject the second instalment?). If this seems an odd result, it is explicable on the basis that the agreement is not severable. In the case of a non-severable agreement, acceptance by the buyer of any conforming goods precludes rejection of any goods. Perhaps this makes it more likely that the courts will regard contracts for delivery in instalments as severable contracts.

If the contract was severable, then Marley would certainly be entitled to reject the second consignment because of the breach of condition in relation to that consignment, and that is so even if he had 'accepted' the first consignment; s 11(4) does not apply to severable

---

56 Simplicity and clarity of expression are more likely to attract a good mark than highly complex statements – be accurate in what you are saying, however.

57 Pointing out uncertainties in either the problem or the law ensures completeness of your answer and demonstrates your understanding.

contracts.[58] In the event that the contract was severable, then the *Maple Flock* test again needs to be applied to determine whether Marley is entitled to reject the third instalment as well. This time, however, it seems much more likely that the test is satisfied. This is because, on two out of the three instalments, Selborne has made a non-conforming delivery. Thus, the ratio that the breach(es) bear quantitatively to the whole contract is much higher and would also seem to suggest a higher probability that he will repeat this with the third and last delivery. On that interpretation, Marley is entitled, even if the contract is severable, to regard the whole contract as repudiated and thus to reject the third consignment as well as the second. Whether that entitles him also to reject the first consignment is debatable. Although on its wording s 11(4) does not apply to severable contracts, it would seem unlikely that the law is such as to allow rejection of any goods which have actually been accepted.[59] Of course, if Marley has not 'accepted' the first instalment, then the breaches relating to the first two instalments entitle him, for the reasons just given, to regard the whole contract as repudiated, to reject all the goods delivered under the first two instalments and to refuse to accept the third.

THE RIDER

Would it have made any difference if the second delivery had been made only on 3 February?[60] This would affect the consideration of two issues discussed above. Firstly, the time lapse between the first delivery and today would be longer (that is, from 20 January to 3 February) and that would increase the likelihood that Marley would be held to have accepted the first consignment and thus be precluded from rejecting that consignment or, if the contract was not severable, any of the consignments. Secondly, it would increase the seriousness of the breach in relation to the second consignment, which would suggest that there is a greater degree of breach compared to the contract as a whole, for there would be no doubt that the breach in relation to the second consignment did indeed affect the whole of that consignment. Thus, if the contract is severable, it would be much more likely that by the time the second delivery has come, several days late and with five desks short, Selborne has committed a breach entitling Marley to regard the contract as repudiated and therefore to reject the third consignment immediately.

Notes

a   This burden is a very heavy one to discharge (*Howard Marine v Ogden* (1978)) and it is unlikely that Sloppy will manage to prove such a defence.

b   In *Feldarol Foundry v Hermes Leasing* (2004), the Court of Appeal held that a period of five to six weeks in relation to a defective car was not beyond a reasonable time in which to examine it, and thus the contract had not yet been affirmed.

....

58   The consideration of different options ensures completeness of your analysis and attracts additional marks.

59   Showing an understanding of any subtleties of a particular rule demonstrates a deeper knowledge and understanding and will attract a higher mark.

60   A logical structure is the first step towards gaining a good mark. You need to present your arguments in an organised manner, don't jump. This is a good example of how to achieve this aim.

c   A detailed knowledge of misrepresentation is not usually required on commercial law courses, but bear in mind that the examiner is entitled to test you on the general principles of contract law.

d   It is possible, of course, to bring the action under the common law, that is, under the rule in *Hedley Byrne v Heller* (1964). Since the **Misrepresentation Act 1967**, however, s 2(1) is the preferable cause of action because then the burden of proof is on the defendant to show that there were reasonable grounds for believing that the statement was true.

Passing of Property and Risk

INTRODUCTION

This chapter covers the passing of property and risk. It incorporates the topic of retention of title clauses, and also deals with perishing goods.

QUESTION 12

Neon Textiles plc sells silk to various garment makers on terms that require payment 30 days after delivery. About 50% of its sales are to regular customers and the rest are to 'one-off' customers. Some of its customers resell the silk, whereas other customers use it in the manufacture of dresses and other garments which are then stored or sold.

▶ Advise Neon Textiles plc on why it ought to consider incorporating a retention of title clause into its standard terms of sale and what protection such a clause might provide.

How to Answer this Question

The question invites an explanation of the purpose of retention of title clauses and a discussion of the effects and effectiveness of them. You should approach the question as follows:

❖ explain the purpose of retention of title clauses;
❖ deal with the passing of risk;
❖ state the requirements for an effective clause;
❖ explore the limits on effectiveness without being registered where:
  (a) the buyer sub-sells the goods (and can the seller take an interest in the proceeds of the sub-sales?);
  (b) the buyer pays for the goods (and what if he only makes part-payment or if the buyer owes other money to Neon Textiles plc?);
  (c) the goods lose their identity.

Applying the Law

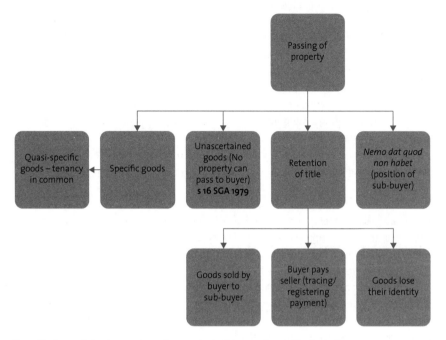

How the law relates to passing of property in this question is illustrated here.

ANSWER

The reason why Neon Textiles plc ought to consider incorporating a retention of title clause into its standard terms of sale is to protect itself against the risk of one of its customers becoming insolvent and hence going into liquidation before the customer has paid Neon Textiles plc for the silk supplied.[1] Without a retention of title clause or some other form of security, Neon Textiles plc would in that event be a mere unsecured creditor of the insolvent buying company and would be lucky to get more than a small proportion of the debt owed to it. The purpose of a retention of title clause would be to put Neon Textiles plc in a stronger position in the event of the buyer going into liquidation – that is, if the goods had not been paid for, to enable Neon Textiles plc to retake possession of the goods (Neon Textiles plc's goods) and to do so irrespective of how many other creditors the insolvent buyer might have.

---

1   Your introduction should clearly set out the relevant issues raised by the question; this demonstrates to the examiner that you have understood what the question requires. Remember that relevancy is an important assessment criterion.

PASSING OF RISK

Before dealing with the effectiveness of a retention of title clause to protect Neon Textiles plc, a warning should be given about the passing of risk. A retention of title clause, when it works, will result in title (that is, ownership, or what the **Sale of Goods Act 1979** terms 'property') being retained by Neon Textiles plc (that is, not passing to Neon Textiles plc's buyer) for some considerable time after delivery. However, by s 20(1) of the **Sale of Goods Act**, the goods will, unless the contrary is agreed, remain at the seller's risk until the property in them passes to the buyer.[2] Thus, Neon Textiles plc would be well advised, when including a retention of title clause in its conditions of sale, either to include also a clause stating that the goods will be at the buyer's risk from the moment of delivery, or else to see that Neon Textiles plc is covered by its own insurance for loss or damage caused after delivery by accident, act of God or act of a third party.

EFFECTIVENESS WITHOUT BEING REGISTERED

By a properly drafted retention of title clause, Neon Textiles plc can ensure that it retains property in the goods supplied until one of three events occurs. As soon as one of these events occurs, property will pass (that is, Neon Textiles plc will lose title to the goods). Those three events are: firstly, that the goods are sold by the buyer and property passes under that contract to the buyer's sub-buyer; secondly, that the buyer pays Neon Textiles plc; thirdly, that the goods, although still unsold by the buyer, lose their identity on becoming incorporated in something else.[3] The point is that, until one of these events occurs, Neon Textiles plc will have *retained* title to the goods and will be able, on the buyer going into liquidation, to retake the goods, thereby enforcing its rights of ownership. Such a right does not have to be registered as a charge, because the requirement (in s 860 of the **Companies Act 2006**) to register applies only to charges *created* by the buying company. Thus, both the Court of Appeal (in *Clough Mill v Martin* (1985)) and the House of Lords (in *Armour v Thyssen* (1990)) have held that retention of title clauses are enforceable without being registered.[4] Attention will now be paid in turn to each of the three possibilities that will cause Neon Textiles plc to lose ownership in the goods even where there is a retention of title clause.

BUYER SELLS THE GOODS

Neon Textiles plc may think that it would be wise to retain title until the goods have been paid for and to ensure that if they have not been paid for, Neon Textiles plc still retains title even if the buyer sells the goods. This, however, would be unrealistic. It is very likely that Neon Textiles plc's buyer needs to be able to sell the goods in order to maintain its

---

2   You need to provide an explanation of the relevant legal rules; without such explanation, it is more difficult for you to properly apply the law to the requirements of the question and thus also more difficult to demonstrate your knowledge and understanding.

3   Don't be reluctant to 'repeat' the wording of the question in the course your analysis, this demonstrates that your answer is focused on the relevant issues and also helps you to structure your answer logically.

4   Referring to examples supports and strengthens your analysis; it also demonstrates your knowledge.

own cash flow and thereby to be able to settle its debts, including those owed to Neon Textiles plc. On the other hand,[5] if that buyer were unable to pass on good title to a sub-buyer to whom it sold the goods, it would be very unlikely to be able to find willing sub-buyers. In any case, even if the retention of title clause were to purport to retain title for unpaid goods even after they had been sold on to a sub-buyer, there is always the risk that the sub-buyer, if unaware of the retention of title clause, would claim nevertheless to obtain title by virtue of one of the exceptions to the principle *nemo dat quod non habet* – in particular, the one in s 25(1) of the **Sale of Goods Act 1979**. Therefore, a sensibly drafted retention of title clause will authorise the buyer to sub-sell the goods (see the *Romalpa* case) so that the buyer in sub-selling the goods will, *vis-à-vis* the sub-buyer, be selling as a principal and, *vis-à-vis* Neon Textiles plc, be selling as an agent of Neon Textiles plc.[6] Technically, of course, Neon Textiles plc would not lose ownership and the sub-buyer would not acquire ownership until, according to the terms of the sub-sale, property passes from the buyer to the sub-buyer.

If then, as seems inevitable, Neon Textiles plc is not to retain ownership after the time when property is to pass to the sub-buyer, is there any way that Neon Textiles plc can continue to protect itself against the subsequent insolvency of the buyer?[7] The answer, confirmed by the decision in the *Romalpa* case, is that an appropriately worded clause *may* give Neon Textiles plc an interest in the proceeds of sale received by the buyer from the sub-buyer. For such a result to be achieved, the clause will need to make it clear that in having possession of and sub-selling the goods, the buyer is agent of, bailee of, fiduciary of, and selling for the account of the seller. Then, if the buyer has kept any such proceeds of sale in a separate account, Neon Textiles plc will, in priority over the buyer's other creditors, be able to take those proceeds of sale to satisfy the outstanding debt due to Neon Textiles plc. If the proceeds have been mixed by the buyer with other monies, then Neon Textiles plc would be able to trace according to the equitable principles of tracing (*Re Hallett's Estate* (1880)). It is important that the clause complies with the requirements set out above. Even then, there is uncertainty surrounding clauses aimed at securing to the seller (here, Neon Textiles plc) an interest in the proceeds of sub-sales by the buyer. Some of this uncertainty was exposed in *Pfeiffer GmbH v Arbuthnot Factors* (1988), where the clause authorised the buyer to sub-sell and required the buyer to pass on to the seller all the buyer's rights under those sub-sales contracts, requiring this to be done up to the amount of the buyer's indebtedness to the seller. It was held in the High Court that this was a charge created by the buyer and was void because it was not registered under the **Companies Act**. There were two significant distinctions between the clause here and that in *Romalpa*. Firstly, the clause providing that the buyer in sub-selling

5 The consideration of possible alternative arguments makes your answer stand out from the rest and demonstrates both deeper knowledge and understanding.
6 Drawing an interim-conclusion is good way of signposting the relevant issues and also helps you to structure your answer logically.
7 Proceeding from the conclusions previously drawn gives your answer a logical structure.

was doing so for the account of the seller was expressly limited to the amount of the outstanding debts owed by the buyer to the seller. Secondly, it failed expressly to state that the buyer was, in selling the goods, a fiduciary of the seller. One possibly significant uncertainty in all of this is that in *Romalpa*, the one case where a seller has successfully claimed an interest in the proceeds of sub-sales, the decision rested on a concession made by counsel for the buyer's receiver, namely, a concession that the relationship of seller and buyer was that of bailor and bailee. Advice to Neon Textiles plc is therefore to include in the contractual retention of title provisions a clause which deals with the proceeds of sub-sales and satisfies the requirements indicated above, but to recognise the uncertainty over its legal effect, if not registered as a charge created by the buyer.

BUYER PAYS NEON TEXTILES PLC

For those customers of Neon Textiles plc that are 'one-off' customers, the clause need retain title only until the purchase price has been fully paid. The effects of such a clause were set out in *Clough Mill v Martin* (1985) (partly *ratio* and partly *obiter*).[8] If the buyer goes into liquidation before paying for the goods, then Neon Textiles plc can retake the goods. Neon Textiles plc can then resell the goods itself, since they are its property. If Neon Textiles plc sells them for more than the original price that the buyer had agreed to pay, then Neon Textiles plc will make a profit which it would not have made if the buyer had paid for the goods before going into liquidation; Neon Textiles plc will be entitled to retain that profit. If Neon Textiles plc is able to resell the goods only for a lower figure than the buyer had agreed to pay, then Neon Textiles plc will have a claim for damages against the buyer for the consequent loss; however, Neon Textiles plc will be unlikely to recover much of that loss, in respect of which it will be merely an unsecured creditor of the insolvent buyer. If, at the time when the buyer had gone into liquidation, the buyer had paid *part* of the purchase price to Neon Textiles plc, and if Neon Textiles plc, having repossessed the goods, is able to sell them for the same price that the buyer had agreed to pay, Neon Textiles plc will be under a duty to refund the buyer's part-payment. If, however, Neon Textiles plc has been able to resell the goods only at a lower figure than the buyer had agreed to pay, then Neon Textiles plc will be able to deduct that loss from the amount of any refund.

For Neon Textiles plc's regular customers,[9] the clause should, in the interests of Neon Textiles plc, be an 'all liabilities' clause; it should retain title until the buyer has satisfied all his liabilities to Neon Textiles plc, whether arising under this or any other contract. That such a clause can be effective was confirmed by the House of Lords in the Scottish

....

8   Stating how a particular legal principle was stated (*ratio* or *obiter*) or by whom demonstrates a deeper knowledge and is likely to attract additional marks.

9   A logical structure is the first step towards gaining a good mark. You need to present your arguments in an organised manner, don't jump. This is a good example of how to achieve this: the discussion of issues involving 'one-off' customers is followed by the discussion relating to the regular customers.

case of *Armour v Thyssen* (1990), and it is not thought that the law is any different in this respect in England. Indeed, the reasoning in that case would seem also to legitimise a clause which retains title to Neon Textiles plc until all debts owed to Neon Textiles plc by the buyer *or by any subsidiary or associated company of the buyer* have been paid.

GOODS LOSE THEIR IDENTITY

It has been established in various cases that a retention of title clause will cease to be effective once the goods have lost their identity by becoming incorporated in something else. This usually occurs in the buyer's manufacturing process, for example, resin becoming incorporated in chipboard (*Borden v Scottish Timber Products Ltd* (1981)), or pieces of leather becoming incorporated into handbags made by the buyer (*Re Peachdart Ltd* (1984)).[10] It seems that Neon Textiles plc cannot retain title to the silk once that silk has been used in the manufacture of other products, such as suits, jackets, bedspreads, etc. It seems unlikely that the silk (unlike the engines in *Hendy Lennox v Grahame Puttick Ltd* (1984)) could be incorporated in something else without losing its identity. Thus, Neon Textiles plc cannot protect itself where the silk has been incorporated in something else in the buyer's manufacturing process, without registering a charge created by the buyer over the manufactured product.

CONCLUSION

Neon Textiles plc would be well advised to include retention of title provisions in its contracts, which, if carefully drafted, should serve to give some security against the risk of the buyer becoming insolvent. Without being registered as a charge, those provisions should be effective in the case of unmixed goods and, possibly, the proceeds of sale of unmixed goods.

> **Common Pitfalls**
> Students need to categorise the goods in order to ascertain where property in the goods is vested so that risk can be considered.

QUESTION 13

Belmont Wines Ltd is a wine merchant. Its stock in its warehouse a month ago was:

❖ 100 bottles of 1960 Château Rockport;
❖ 200 bottles of 1970 Château Nafite which, unknown to Belmont Wines Ltd, were the last bottles of that vintage remaining unconsumed anywhere in the world;

---

10 The inclusion of concrete examples demonstrates your knowledge and understanding of the relevant legal rules and also substantiates your analysis.

❖   350 bottles of 1980 Château Saint-Lam;
❖   assorted other wines.

In the last month, Belmont Wines has made and received no deliveries of wine, but has made the following agreements to sell wine:

❖   '100 bottles of 1960 Château Rockport' to Vladimir;
❖   '200 bottles of 1970 Château Nafite' to Mikhail;
❖   '300 bottles of 1980 Château Saint-Lam, currently in Belmont Wines' warehouse' to Fedor;
❖   '50 bottles of 1980 Château Saint-Lam' to Tolstoy.

As regards payment: Vladimir paid Belmont Wines when he made the contract; Mikhail agreed to pay upon collecting the goods from Belmont Wines' warehouse; Fedor and Tolstoy each agreed to pay upon delivery by Belmont Wines to their respective premises.

Yesterday, Belmont Wines despatched to Tolstoy 50 bottles of 1980 Château Saint-Lam. Unfortunately, the lorry (Belmont Wines' own) crashed en route and all the wine on board was lost. Last night, a fire destroyed Belmont Wines' warehouse and its contents.

▶   Advise Vladimir, Mikhail, Fedor and Tolstoy.

How to Answer this Question

This question is plainly concerned with the issue of whether risk had passed from the seller to the buyer. However, the answer must not be confined to that, because it is important to know whether the contracts are still binding and, if not, what the position is.

Applying the Law

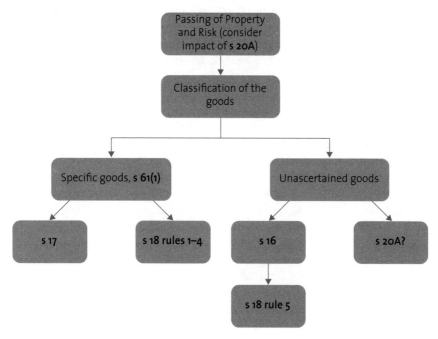

This diagram illustrates how passing of property is discussed in the answer.

ANSWER

Each of the buyers will be advised as to whether the risk in the goods had passed to him and, if not, whether the contract is still binding.[11]

We are not told whether the contracts contained any provision stating when risk was to pass to the buyer or when property was to pass. It will be assumed that there was no such provision.[12] In any case, even if there were a provision that property was to pass to the buyer at a particular stage, that provision could not, in the case of a contract for the sale of unascertained goods, come into effect until those goods were ascertained (s 16 of the **Sale of Goods Act 1979**).

....

11 A good introduction clearly identifies those legal rules which are raised by the question; this ensures
    that a logical structure to your answer right from the start and puts your examiner in a positive frame of
    mind.
12 Pointing out omissions in the information provided by the question and considering the impact these
    omissions might have on the outcome of your analysis will attract a higher mark as it demonstrates your
    understanding.

In the absence of contrary agreement, and subject to a couple of provisos, risk passes with property (s 20). Subject to the rule in s 16 just mentioned, property passes when the parties intend it to (s 17) and, unless a different intention appears, property passes according to the rules in s 18. The application of these rules depends upon whether the contract in question was for specific goods or unascertained goods.[13]

SPECIFIC OR UNASCERTAINED GOODS?

The time for determining whether goods are specific or unascertained goods is that at which the contract is made. If the contract is for goods which are 'identified and agreed upon' at the time the contract is made, then it is one for the sale of specific goods (s 61(1)). The agreement which Vladimir has is not one for specific goods, since, even if the parties had expected that Vladimir's contract would be fulfilled from Belmont Wines' stock, there was apparently no contractual agreement to that effect, but simply an obligation on Belmont Wines to deliver '100 bottles of 1960 Château Rockport'.[14] Thus, if Belmont Wines chose to keep for itself the 100 bottles in its stock at the time of the contract or if it chose to supply them to another customer, it could still comply with its contractual commitments to Vladimir by getting hold of 100 other bottles of 1960 Château Rockport and supplying those to Vladimir. That makes it a contract for the sale of unascertained goods, since the contract did not identify the 100 bottles in Belmont Wines' stock as the contractual bottles (*Re London Wine Shippers* (1986)).

Similarly, the contract with Mikhail did not identify the 200 bottles of 1970 Château Nafite in Belmont Wines' stock as being the contractual bottles. Had it been possible to do so, Belmont Wines could have bought a further 200 bottles and used those to fulfil its contract with Mikhail. It is submitted that it is irrelevant that it would in fact have been impossible to buy more such bottles. It may be argued that a contract to buy 'a painting of the *Mona Lisa* by Leonardo da Vinci' is no different from a contract to buy 'the painting of the *Mona Lisa* by Leonardo da Vinci', since there is only one such painting. However, in the present case, Belmont Wines was unaware that the bottles in its warehouse were the only ones in existence and, in those circumstances, it cannot be said that the 1970 Château Nafite bottles were 'identified and agreed upon at the time the contract was made' as being the contractual goods, since, so far as the parties were concerned, the contract allowed other goods to be supplied which corresponded with the contract description. Thus, Mikhail's contract also was for the sale of unascertained goods.

The contract with Fedor did identify Belmont Wines' stock as the source from which Fedor's bottles must come. However, it did not identify which of the 350 bottles in its

---

13   Be clear and precise in what you are saying. Don't use convoluted sentences as it distracts from your analysis; clarity of expression is another important assessment criteria.

14   The proper application of the relevant legal principle to the requirements of the questions is what the examiner is looking for. This is a good example of how to achieve this aim.

stock were to be supplied to Fedor. Thus, Fedor's contract was also a contract for the sale of unascertained goods (*Re Wait* (1927)).

Tolstoy's contract, apparently, did not even require his bottles to be supplied from Belmont Wines' current stock. So, for the same reasons as applied to Vladimir's contract, Tolstoy's was a contract for the sale of unascertained goods.

SECTION 20A

Section 20A provides for the buyer to obtain an undivided share of goods in unascertained goods from an identified bulk. There is, however, no question of s 20A applying to any of the goods in this problem.[15] There is only one lot of goods which are to come from a bulk which is identified by the parties, either in the contract or subsequently. Those are the 300 bottles that Fedor has agreed to buy. Section 20A does not apply to these goods, because it comes into operation only when the buyer pays for the goods and Fedor is not due to pay until delivery occurs. It follows that the passing of ownership and risk will be determined by reference to what the parties may have agreed and, failing that, by reference to ss 16–19.

PASSING OF PROPERTY

It may be that, in the case of Vladimir, the parties intended property to pass at an early stage, since Vladimir paid for the goods at the time of making the contract. However, nothing was done to ascertain which bottles were to be supplied to Vladimir. Therefore, no property ever passed to Vladimir, since no property can pass in goods until they are ascertained (s 16).

Where, after the making of the contract, goods become ascertained, property will not pass (unless a contrary intention appears) until goods are unconditionally appropriated to the contract by one party with the assent of the other (s 18 r 5). In the case of Mikhail, so far as we are told, nothing was done to appropriate the goods to the contract. Therefore, there being nothing to indicate a contrary intention on the part of the parties, property never passed to Mikhail.

If, contrary to the opinion advanced above,[16] the sale to Mikhail was in fact a sale of specific goods, then, assuming that the contract was an 'unconditional' one[a] and that the wine was in a deliverable state, property will have passed to Mikhail at the time the contract was made. At least, that is so according to s 18 r 1, which states that it is

....

15 The explanation of why a particular legal principle is not applicable in relation to a question is as important as the explanation of why a particular legal rule is applicable in relation to a question: on the one hand, this is because it narrows your analysis down to what is relevant; on the other hand, this is because it demonstrates understanding.

16 Considering different possibilities/solutions is a good way to attract marks as it shows that you have understood the potential implications of a particular legal rule.

immaterial that payment or delivery or both are postponed. However, the application of that rule coupled with the rule in s 20 would mean that risk had passed to Mikhail even though the goods were still in Belmont Wines' warehouse. That would be an unsatisfactory result to achieve unless the parties had very clearly indicated it to be their intention, as it would be quite likely that Belmont Wines was covered by insurance for the loss of or damage to its goods on its premises, and quite unlikely that a buyer would expect to have to take out insurance cover for goods of which he had yet to take delivery and for which he had yet to make payment. Maybe it was for that sort of consideration that Diplock LJ said in *Ward v Bignall* (1967) that in the case of specific goods, very little is needed to give rise to the inference that the parties intended property only to pass upon payment or delivery. If the court found the parties' intention by that means, then s 18 r 1 would not apply, since the s 18 rules apply only where the intention of the parties is not apparent. Therefore, it is submitted that even if the sale to Mikhail were of specific goods, the property was intended to pass only upon delivery and payment and that therefore no property in the wine passed to Mikhail.[17]

It could be that, in the case of Fedor, his 300 bottles became ascertained by exhaustion (see *Karlshamns Olje Fabriker v Eastport Navigation Corp, The Elafi* (1982)). This is because the contract requires his bottles to be supplied from the 350 in stock and as soon as the 50 are despatched to Tolstoy, Fedor's have become ascertained as being the remaining 300. However, although no property can pass before the goods become ascertained, it does not follow that the parties intended that property should pass as soon as the goods became ascertained. Unless the intention of the parties appears otherwise, the property has not passed unless there is unconditional appropriation of the goods to the contract. It might be argued that Belmont Wines made the unconditional appropriation by despatching the 50 bottles to Tolstoy, since Belmont Wines was thereby effectively committing itself to delivering the remaining 300 to Fedor. In that case, however, it would seem that Belmont Wines was unconditionally appropriating the 50 bottles to Tolstoy. But was it really? Certainly, it would have been had it consigned the 50 bottles to an independent carrier to deliver to Tolstoy (see s 18 r 5(2)). Is this still the case when it sends its own lorry? If this was an unconditional appropriation of the 50 bottles to Tolstoy, then it is submitted that there was an unconditional appropriation of the remaining 300 to Fedor. In that case, it seems likely that we can infer that Fedor impliedly assented in advance to that appropriation (as is possible; see *Aldridge v Johnson* (1857)), since he must have assumed that Belmont Wines was free to dispose of all but 300 of its stock of 1980 Château Saint-Lam. It is arguable, however, that consigning the goods to Tolstoy on Belmont Wines' own lorry did not amount to an unconditional appropriation and that such an appropriation would occur only upon delivery by Belmont Wines' lorry to Tolstoy. If the lorry had been recalled, for example by Belmont Wines calling the driver via a mobile telephone in the lorry's cab, then

---

17 The reasoned critical evaluation of a possible result demonstrates knowledge and understanding and will attract additional marks.

Belmont Wines would still have 350 bottles from which to select Fedor's. Thus, the despatch of 50 bottles in Belmont Wines' own lorry did not, it is argued, demonstrate an intention to attach those 50 irrevocably to Tolstoy's contract, or the remaining 300 irrevocably to Fedor's. It is submitted that, therefore, property did not pass to either Fedor or to Tolstoy. Even if the despatch to Tolstoy did amount to an unconditional appropriation, it would still be the case that no property would have passed to Tolstoy (as opposed to Fedor), since there is nothing from which to infer Tolstoy's assent given in advance to such an appropriation and thus his assent would only be given upon delivery to him, which never occurred because of the lorry crash.

PASSING OF RISK

It has been argued that no property passed to any of the buyers in the problem. It follows that no risk passed to them either (**s 20**) unless delivery was delayed for any of their faults (**s 20(2)**).[18] It is possible that delivery to Mikhail was delayed through his fault, depending upon whether he has taken more than the agreed (or else a reasonable) time in coming to collect his wine. If he did, then the 200 bottles of Château Nafite were at Mikhail's risk, since their loss in the fire is certainly something that might not have happened if he had collected them earlier (**s 20(2)**). This assumes that Mikhail was a business buyer because under **s 20(4)** where the buyer is a consumer, goods remain at the seller's risk until actual delivery to the buyer.

Risk not having passed (except possibly to Mikhail if he was a business buyer), Belmont Wines is not excused from having to deliver to Vladimir and to Tolstoy wine which corresponds to the descriptions in their respective contracts. Nothing has rendered their contracts impossible to perform, because they were contracts for the sale of purely generic goods. If Belmont Wines does not carry out those contracts, it will be liable to the buyers for non-delivery.

On the other hand, both Mikhail's and Fedor's contracts have become impossible for Belmont Wines to carry out: Mikhail's because there is no more of that wine left in the world and Fedor's because the contract provided for the goods to come from a particular source and that source is now void (*Howell v Coupland* (1876)). The contracts being for unascertained goods, **s 7** will not apply, but the contracts are frustrated at common law, assuming the frustration was not self-induced, that is, that the fire was not Belmont Wines' fault. That being so, Belmont Wines is not liable for non-delivery and nor are Fedor and Mikhail liable to pay the price. Even if (that is, in Mikhail's case) the contract had been for the sale of specific goods, the result would have been the same (that is, provided that risk had not passed) by virtue of **s 7**.

If risk had passed to Mikhail, that is, if delivery was delayed because he was contractually late in collecting, then Mikhail's contract will not be terminated or void for frustration, but instead he will be liable for the price.

18 Proceeding from the conclusions previously drawn gives your answer a logical structure.

QUESTION 14

(a) 'The rules in the **Sale of Goods Act 1979** relating to the passing of risk do not always place the risk upon the party who should sensibly bear it.'

▶ **Discuss this statement.**

(b) Jonas enters into a contract for the sale to Luka of 600 bags of horsebeans out of the 800 bags of Jonas' horsebeans currently stored in Peter's warehouse. On receiving a cheque for the purchase price, Jonas gives Luka the invoice and written delivery authority. A month later, when Luka goes to collect the horsebeans, it is discovered that, since the contract was made, 400 of Jonas' bags have been stolen. Luka is offered delivery of the remaining 400 bags and seeks your advice.

▶ **Advise Luka.**

How to Answer this Question

Many law examiners do not indicate how many marks are allocated to each half of the question. The only safe guide to adopt in such a case is that either the (a) and (b) parts carry equal marks, or else there will not be a very great disparity between the marks allocated to each part. It is certainly unreasonable to assume that, because the question in (a) is shorter, the answer should be.

The answer to (a) is to some extent a matter of taste. There is certainly no right answer. One could mount a good case for the rules being sensible. The approach taken in this model answer is to attack the rules on the basis that if you can come up with some plausible criticisms of the area of law under scrutiny, it is usually easier to attack the state of the law than it is to defend it.

Part (b) is a typical problem on the passing of risk. The most common cause of students throwing away marks on problems on this topic is a failure to do any more than consider who bears the risk, that is, a failure to spell out the consequences, such as a possible frustration of the contract and whether the buyer still has to pay the price. The plan adopted in (b) is to consider on whom the loss of the theft falls, and then to consider the possible consequences of it falling on Jonas or Luka.

Answer Structure

This mind map illustrates the key aspects of the SGA to consider in relation to passing of risk and property in this answer.

Passing of risk ⇕ Passing of property

- Passing of risk – link to physical control?
- ss 18 rules 1 – 5 – to use if parties express no intention
- s 20A SGA 1979
- s 20B SGA 1979
- s 19 SGA 1979
- s 18 SGA 1979
- s 17 SGA 1979 – Specific goods, passing of risk and property
- s 16 SGA 1979 – No property can pass in unascertained goods
- s 20 SGA 1979

ANSWER

(A)

Apart from the addition of **ss 20A** and **20B** in 1995, the rules referred to in the question have remained virtually unchanged since the first **Sale of Goods Act** was passed in 1893. That Act was itself a codifying Act which simply sought to put into statutory form rules that had been arrived at by judges deciding individual cases.[19] Thus, they do not result from a considered comprehensive approach to the whole range of issues that ought to bear upon a piece of legislation. They do, however, reflect the basic 'freedom of contract' philosophy which imbued the decisions in commercial cases by nineteenth-century judges. This accounts for the opening words of **s 20** ('unless otherwise agreed') which allow the parties to determine the rules within their own contract. To that extent, the comment in the question is certainly unjustified, since it is surely sensible to have risk borne by the party who it has been agreed in the contract should bear it.

Where the matter is more debatable is in those cases where the contract is silent as to who bears the risk. In this situation, apart from two exceptions specifically catered for in **sub-ss (2)** and **(3)**, the basic approach adopted is to tie the passing of risk to the passing of property.[20] This approach is flawed because the passing of property is significant for other purposes as well as for determining the passing of risk – those other purposes include the seller's right to maintain an action for the price (see **s 49**) and the right of the relevant trustee in bankruptcy to take the goods in the event of one or other of them becoming bankrupt. The rules on the passing of property are themselves subject to the freedom of contract principle which allows the parties to agree when they intend property to pass. In that case, the rules on the passing of risk and the passing of property are not lacking in sense, since the parties can presumably remember to cater for the one when making a specific provision for the other. It would certainly be quite absurd of the parties to include a retention of title clause whereby the seller retains title (that is, property) long after delivery to the seller without also including a clause stating that the risk passes with delivery.[b]

It is where the parties do not remember or think to include express provisions on these matters that the rules in **s 20** (on the passing of risk) and the related rules in **ss 16–19** (on the passing of property) appear particularly flawed. The plain fact is that it would be logical (apart from the clear justice of the exceptions in **s 20(2)** and **(3)**) to link the passing of risk with physical delivery of the goods, unless the parties have expressly agreed otherwise. There are two very sound reasons for this. First, it is obvious that in the vast

19 Showing an awareness of the development of the area of law in question demonstrates both knowledge and understanding.

20 Be prepared to challenge the assumptions made by the question, don't merely agree with the statement made because it is easy. You are assessed on the ability to think critically, i.e. your ability to consider opposing arguments.

majority of cases, it is the person in possession who has the greatest ability to take care of the goods to see that they are not stolen, burnt, damaged, etc. If he has to bear the risk of any loss, then he has the consequent incentive to exercise that care. The second reason is that it is likely to be much easier to secure insurance cover for goods on your own premises or otherwise within your own possession.[21] Of course, it is possible to secure insurance cover when they are elsewhere. One does wonder, however, how many businesses fail to insure goods of which they are not in possession but for which they are bearing the risk. The notion of insuring goods where, although the risk of loss or damage is borne by the insured, the property in the goods is with someone else may raise problems of whether the insured had in law an insurable interest. If that is a problem, then the law on insurable interest needs changing. Not only do the rules in **ss 16–20** not tie the passing of risk and of property to the transfer of possession of the goods, they expressly recognise that the passing of property and/or risk can occur independently of whether delivery has occurred – see the wording of **s 18 r 1** and **s 20**. There is undoubtedly something inconsistent about saying, as **s 20** does in its principal rule in **sub-s (1)**, that it is immaterial whether delivery has been made or not and then saying in an exception to that rule that where delivery is delayed due to the fault of one of the parties, any loss which might not have occurred but for the delay is to be borne by the party at fault.

There is, however, a further difficulty which would more commonly arise if the rule tying the passing of risk to the passing of property in the absence of contrary agreement were abolished.[22] This is the absurdity where, while the risk is with one party and the property is with the other, the goods are destroyed or damaged by the negligence of a third party; the party who suffers the loss is unable to maintain an action for damages against the culprit (*Leigh and Sillivan v Aliakmon Shipping Co* (1984)).

Finally, it must be acknowledged that the somewhat complicated rules relating to the sale of a specified quantity of unascertained goods out of an identified bulk were a sensible amendment to the law. They were introduced in 1995 and are stated in **ss 20A and 20B**. They were designed to deal with the situation where the buyer has paid for the goods and where they are still unseparated from the identified bulk at the time when the bulk is damaged or lost in whole or in part. Now, unless the parties have agreed something to the contrary, the buyer will no longer be a mere unsecured creditor in the event of the seller's insolvency. So far as risk is concerned, the seller's proportion of the bulk will be assumed to have perished or been damaged first, but if the loss or damage goes beyond that, each buyer will have to bear the risk of loss or damage to his share of the bulk.

....

21 Where the question relates to practical problems, emphasise the practical aspects of a question in your answer. This shows that you are focused on the relevant issues.
22 Showing an appreciation of the wider implications of a particular principle is a good way to attract marks. However, remember to focus on the relevant issues; don't simply write down all you know.

(B)

The question requires us to establish, if possible, at whose risk the goods were when 400 bags were stolen.[23] Much depends upon whether they were stolen before or after Luka paid for the goods (that is, gave over his cheque to Jonas). If they were stolen after that point, then ss 20A and 20B are relevant. These sections apply where there is a sale of a specified quantity (here, 600 bags) out of a bulk which is identified in the contract (here, Jonas' horsebeans stored in Peter's warehouse). Their effect is that, upon payment of the price, the buyer (Luka) acquires property in an undivided share of the bulk. From that point onwards, there is a possibility that loss of or damage to the bulk will to some extent fall upon Luka. Where only some of the bulk is lost or damaged, then that loss is taken first of all to have fallen on that share of the bulk retained by the seller, Jonas. The problem does not state that there is any other buyer to whom Jonas has agreed to sell any of the bulk. It appears therefore that after Luka paid the price of his 600 bags, the bulk of 800 bags comprised 600 for Luka and 200 retained by Jonas. The loss occasioned by the theft of 400 thus falls first on Jonas' 200 and thereafter on Luka's 600. Thus, after the theft, there are none of Jonas' left and only 400 bags of Luka's left. These remaining bags will then have become Luka's by a process of exhaustion. He is entitled to the remaining 400 bags, but is not entitled to recover any of the purchase price he paid.

The result whereby the loss is taken to have fallen first on Jonas' share of the bulk is challengeable by Jonas if he can rely on s 20(2) or if it can be said that the arrangement over giving the delivery authority to Luka indicated that the parties intended risk to pass on the handing over to Luka of the delivery authority. In either of those two eventualities, Luka and Jonas would bear the loss in the proportions of their respective interests in the bulk: 75% and 25%. As regards s 20(2), we are told that Luka went to collect the horsebeans 'a month later', that is, presumably a month after being given the written delivery authority. It is quite possible that a month was an unreasonable delay and that therefore one could describe delivery as having been delayed through Luka's 'fault'. If so, Luka has to bear the consequences of the theft if that loss might not have occurred if he had collected the goods within a reasonable period of time (say, within a week). We are not told when the theft occurred. If it is established that it occurred before the lapse of what would have been a reasonable length of time for Luka to turn up to collect the goods, then Jonas cannot rely on s 20(2). If it occurred after a lapse of that length of time, or if it might have done, then it is a loss which 'might' not have occurred if Luka had collected on time and s 20(2) applies.[24] Alternatively, the arrangement over the giving of the delivery authority, and Luka thus taking on the task of collecting the goods, could well

---

23 Your introduction should clearly set out the relevant issues raised by the question, this demonstrates to the examiner that you have understood what the question requires. Remember that relevancy is an important assessment criterion.

24 Considering different options is a good way to attract marks as it shows that you have understood the potential implications of a particular legal rule.

be something which a court would take as indicating the intention of the parties that risk should pass to Luka upon the handing over to him of the delivery authority (*Sterns v Vickers* (1923)). In the situation where either **s 20(2)** applies or else the theft occurred after the parties intended risk to pass (for example, on the handing over of the delivery note), the result is as in *Sterns v Vickers*, namely, that all 800 bags were *pro rata* (that is, 75%) at Luka's risk. This is because he had agreed to buy 75% of the 800 bags. In that case, he has to bear 75% of the loss of 400 bags, that is, the loss of 300 bags. In that case, he is entitled to take delivery of a further 300 bags, but must pay the full contract price. In this scenario, there is no possibility that the contract has become frustrated by virtue of the theft, since the only way to make sense of the rule that Luka has to bear the risk is to make him pay for the goods, despite the fact that some of them have been stolen.

We now consider the situation if Jonas had agreed to sell the remaining 200 bags to another buyer (B2) who had also paid for them before the theft from Peter's warehouse.[25] In that situation, both Luka and B2 would have an undivided share in the bulk in the proportions 75% and 25% respectively, and they would bear the loss in those proportions. This would mean that they would suffer the loss as follows: Luka would lose 300 bags and B2 would lose 100. This would mean that they would each be entitled to take from the remaining bulk 300 and 100 bags respectively. In that scenario, Luka would be entitled to 300, not 400, of the remaining bags. He would not, however, be entitled to any repayment of the price he has paid.

We now turn to the situation where the theft occurred before Luka paid Jonas. In that situation, Luka had not at that time acquired any property or any undivided share in the goods. Thus, the risk will have at that time been with Jonas. In that case, frustration becomes a possibility. **Section 7** of the **Sale of Goods Act 1979** will not apply because it refers only to contracts for the sale of specific goods. It is possible, however, for the contract to be frustrated at common law if it is a contract for the sale of unascertained goods out of a specific bulk (*Howell v Coupland* (1876)). This would certainly be the case where the whole of the bulk was lost or stolen.[26] In that case, Jonas would not be liable for non-delivery and Luka would not be liable to pay the price. However, the court may infer an intention on the part of the parties that, where only part of the bulk has been lost, the contract should not be regarded as frustrated, but that there was an implied term that: (a) the seller was excused from his obligation to deliver the whole contract quantity of 600 bags; and (b) the buyer was to have the option of buying what was left at a *pro rata* proportion of the contract price (*Sainsbury v Street* (1972)).[27] The solution

---

25 Dealing with the points raised in an essay question on a one-by-one basis ensures adds structure and clarity to your analysis.

26 The provision of a practical example demonstrates your understanding.

27 The consideration of alternative possibilities makes your answer stand out from the rest and demonstrates both deeper knowledge and understanding.

adopted in this latter case would leave Luka with a choice as to whether to take the remaining 400 bags at two-thirds of the contract price or to decline to take any at all. The solution adopted in *Sainsbury v Street* might not be quite so simple for a court to adopt in Jonas' and Luka's case if Jonas had in fact also made a contract to sell the other 200 bags to someone else. In that case, the option allowed to the two buyers, Luka and the other one, would presumably be an option to take a proportion (in Luka's case, 75%) of the remaining 400 bags and pay for them *pro rata* at the contract rate. Or could it be that, in the event of the other purchaser not wanting to take his proportion of the 400 bags, Luka would be given the option of taking all 400? These are some of the possible difficulties in the court adopting a *Sainsbury v Street* approach and could lead the court instead simply to decide that the contract is frustrated. In the latter case, Luka would have no right to take any of the remaining 400 bags, but might be able to negotiate a new contract with Jonas about them.

Notes

a   Ie, the contract does not contain a condition preventing s 18 r 1 from applying. In *Varley v Whipp* (1900), since the seller did not own the goods which were the subject of the contract, it was held that this was a conditional contract, ie a contract with the condition that the seller needed to acquire the goods first before property could pass to the buyer.

b   See Question 12 on retention of title clauses.

Nemo Dat Quod Non Habet

INTRODUCTION

This chapter covers the *nemo dat* principle and the exceptions to it, in particular:

- ❖ estoppel;
- ❖ mercantile agents (**s 2(1)** of the **Factors Act 1889**);
- ❖ voidable contracts;
- ❖ seller in possession (**s 8** of the **Factors Act** and **s 24** of the **Sale of Goods Act 1979**);
- ❖ buyer in possession (**s 9** of the **Factors Act** and **s 25** of the **Sale of Goods Act**);
- ❖ **Pt III** of the **Hire Purchase Act 1964**;
- ❖ the law enabling an owner to sue in conversion;
- ❖ the implied condition as to title in **s 12** of the **Sale of Goods Act**.

QUESTION 15

Sydney left his car for repair at Bromley Garage, carelessly leaving the car's registration document in the glove compartment which was unlocked. While the car was at Bromley Garage, Bromley telephoned Sydney and informed him that another customer had seen the car and wished to buy it for £3,000. Sydney said that he had not intended to sell the car, but that if Bromley were to receive an offer in excess of £4,000, he would be interested. Without again contacting Sydney, Bromley sold the car for £3,500 to Elizabeth, handing over the registration document and the ignition key.

❭ **Consider the legal position.**

How to Answer this Question

This question requires an understanding of the *nemo dat quod non habet* rule and the exceptions to it, in particular, the estoppel exception and the case law on **s 2(1)** of the **Factors Act 1889**. Sometimes, examiners allow you in the examination to refer to the statutory provisions. Without a knowledge of the case law, those provisions will take you only so far. Indeed, the question requires consideration of some possible distinctions between the facts of the problem set and those of a couple of the cases.

The sensible layout of an answer is very straightforward indeed. It is to consider first who now owns the car (no definite answer, however, can be given to that). That involves considering the two relevant exceptions to the *nemo dat* principle. Many candidates answering this type of question are content to leave it there. The question does, however, ask you to consider the legal position and that must also involve setting out the rights of the parties *vis-à-vis* each other in the light of the conclusion (or different possible conclusions) you come to as to who now owns the car. It is often important in questions such as this to consider possible claims in conversion and claims under **s 12** of the **Sale of Goods Act 1979**.

Answer Structure

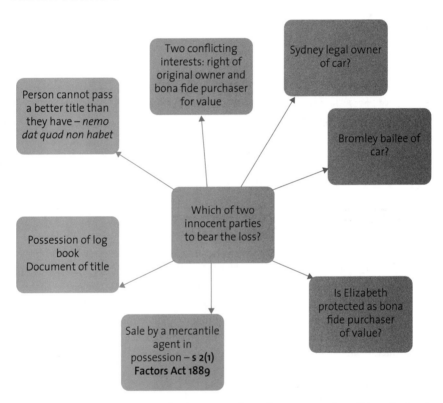

This mind map illustrates the key factors to consider in determining who will bear the loss in this scenario.

ANSWER

It is necessary first to establish who now owns the car, and then to advise the parties as to the legal position flowing from that.[1]

TITLE

The first issue is who owns the car now? Sydney, we are told, owned it to start with and since he has never agreed to sell it, he is still the owner unless one of the exceptions to the *nemo dat* principle applies. The *nemo dat quod non habet* principle states that someone who lacks title to goods (for example, Bromley) cannot transfer that title. Only if one of the exceptions to that principle applies will Bromley have conferred good title upon Elizabeth. Two such possible exceptions present themselves for discussion: estoppel and the mercantile agent exception. The first of these can be quickly dismissed, since it is now clearly established that the mere act of the owner of letting someone have possession of his goods is insufficient to enable an estoppel to be raised against him. The position is still the same even if the owner (here, Sydney) has parted not only with possession of the goods (here, a car), but also the ignition key and the registration book; the registration book is not a document of title (*Central Newbury Car Auctions v Unity Finance* (1957)).

Does the mercantile agent exception apply? There are a number of requirements, each of which must be complied with before this exception, in s 2(1) of the Factors Act 1889, will apply.[2] Firstly, Bromley must have been a mercantile agent, that is, someone having, in the customary course of his business as an agent, authority to sell. On the given facts, it seems likely that Bromley as a car dealer had such customary authority, including the customary authority to sell the goods in his own name (*Rolls Razor v Cox* (1967)). Secondly, Bromley must have been in possession of the goods (or documents of title) with the consent of the owner (Sydney) at the time of the sale to Elizabeth, which he clearly did, since he had possession of the car. Bromley must have also been at that time in possession of the car in his (Bromley's) capacity as mercantile agent. There is some ambiguity about this in the question, since originally Sydney left his car with Bromley for repair and therefore not with a view to Bromley selling it, or seeking offers for it. However, after Bromley's telephone call, Sydney could be said to have left the car with Bromley in two different capacities, one as a repairer and one as a factor (that is, authorised to seek and/or consider offers). This is because Sydney in that telephone call clearly contemplated the possibility of Bromley receiving further offers. Section 2(1) does not require that Bromley 'obtained' possession with the

---

1 Providing a brief introduction which not only sets out the issues you are going to address but which also refers to the question set is a good way to demonstrate that you have understand what is relevant; relevancy is an important assessment factor.
2 Applying the elements of a test/legal rule one by one to the requirements of the question ensures that your analysis is thorough and proceeds in a logical and structured manner.

consent of the owner, merely that he was (that is, at the time of the disposition to Elizabeth) in possession with that consent. The same presumably applies to the judicial gloss on the section which requires him to have been in possession in his capacity as a mercantile agent. Furthermore, there does not seem to be any logical reason why Bromley should not have been in possession in two capacities at the same time.

There is, however, a problem over the registration document. It is not a document of title but, for the mercantile agent exception to operate, the seller (here, Bromley) must be in possession of the goods, not just in his capacity as a mercantile agent, but also in such a way as to clothe the seller with apparent authority to sell; in the case of a motor vehicle, that really requires the seller to be in possession not just of the vehicle, but also of its registration document (*Pearson v Rose and Young* (1951)). This also ties in with the further requirement for the exception to apply, namely, that the seller in selling acts in the normal course of business of a mercantile agent. It was said in *Stadium Finance v Robbins* (1962) that selling a car without its registration document would not be a sale in the ordinary course of business. On the given facts, Bromley was in possession of the registration document which, together with the ignition key, he handed over to Elizabeth. However, it was held in *Pearson v Rose and Young* that not only must the seller be in possession of the registration book as well as the car, but also he must be in possession of the registration book (as well as of the car) *with the consent of the owner*.[3] In *Pearson v Rose and Young*, the seller was in possession of the registration book, but did not have the consent of the owner to that possession, since the seller had obtained possession of it by a trick he played upon the owner. This was taken one stage further in *Stadium Finance v Robbins*, where it was held that the owner accidentally leaving the document locked in the glove compartment did not amount to the seller having possession of it with the consent of the owner. The only possible distinctions between that case and the present problem are: firstly, that in Sydney's case, the document was in an *unlocked* glove compartment; secondly, that very possibly the key to the glove compartment in Sydney's car was the same as the ignition key which Sydney presumably left with the car; thirdly, that possibly (although we do not know) something was said in the telephone conversation between Bromley and Sydney which alluded to the registration document and indicated Sydney's 'consent' to Bromley's possession of it.

Subject to what has just been said about the registration book, it seems that all the requirements of the exception have been satisfied, including the requirement that

---

3   Showing an awareness of the development of the area of law in question demonstrates both knowledge and understanding.

Elizabeth took the car in good faith without notice of Bromley's lack of authority to make the sale.[4] There is nothing in the stated facts of the problem to indicate that Elizabeth should have been 'put on notice'; at least, that is so provided the sale price of £3,500 was not so low as itself to be a cause of suspicion. If there is a substantial doubt about Elizabeth's good faith, that could cause her a problem, since the burden of proof to show that she took in good faith is upon Elizabeth (*Heap v Motorists Advisory Agency* (1923)).

CONSEQUENCES

Assuming that all the requirements of **s 2(1)** of the **Factors Act** are satisfied, then Elizabeth now has good title to the car.[5] That means of course that Sydney, in any action for conversion, would fail against Elizabeth. Sydney would, however, have a good claim for conversion against Bromley. This is a tort of strict liability and, since Bromley has effectively disposed of the car to Elizabeth, could not result in an order for the goods to be returned to Sydney, but only in an award of damages. The *prima facie* measure of damages to which Sydney is entitled would be the value of the car at the time of the sale to Elizabeth. This would be a matter of evidence, but presumably Sydney will try to insist that it was worth at least £4,000, since that was a figure he would have been interested in. The value, however, is not necessarily the car's value to Elizabeth, but its market value. It is of course possible that, before selling the car, Bromley had carried out the repairs. In that case, the cost of the repairs will need to be taken into account in one way or another, either by a set-off of their cost or by deduction of an improvement allowance by virtue of the provisions of the **Torts (Interference with Goods) Act 1977**. That allowance might well be less than the cost of the repairs, since it is the proportion of the value of the car (that is, at the time of the sale to Elizabeth) which is attributable to the improvement effected by the repairs.

If Elizabeth did not satisfy the requirements of **s 2(1)** of the **Factors Act**, she will not have acquired good title.[6] In that case, Sydney would be entitled to succeed against Elizabeth in an action in conversion. It is assumed that the car was not unique. Therefore, the result of such an action would not be to compel Elizabeth to return the car, but would be an award of damages (with Elizabeth perhaps being given the option of returning the car). The damages would be calculated as in the case of the claim against Bromley just discussed. Thus, the improvement allowance (due to the repairs by Bromley – assuming Bromley had effected those repairs) would be deducted. If Elizabeth chose to

---

4   Drawing an interim conclusion is a good way of signposting the relevant issues and also helps you to structure your answer logically.

5   A good conclusion summarises the findings made in the main body of your answer and relates these findings to the question set.

6   Pointing out different solutions is a good way to attract marks as it shows that you have understood the potential implications of a particular legal rule.

return the car to Sydney, Sydney would be liable to pay the improvement allowance to Elizabeth.

If Elizabeth were to be held liable to Sydney in the way just outlined, Elizabeth would have a claim against Bromley for breach of the condition as to title in s 12 of the **Sale of Goods Act 1979**. She would be entitled to the return of her purchase price, but would have to give credit for any improvement allowance received by her from Sydney. The entitlement to the return of the purchase price is based upon the notion that, since Elizabeth never got title, she has suffered a total failure of consideration. Thus, according to the controversial decision in *Rowland v Divall* (1923), Elizabeth is entitled to the return of the full purchase price (minus, if applicable, the improvement allowance) even if she has had some months' use of the car before having to surrender it to Sydney, for example if it was some considerable time before the truth was discovered and the car's whereabouts traced to Elizabeth.

QUESTION 16

Blake had a car on hire purchase terms from Fortress Finance. He still owed three monthly instalments on the car when four months ago he sold it to Holbrook, a car dealer, who bought it for his wife to use as a runabout to do the shopping and collect the children from school. Before buying the car, Holbrook had a check done by HPI, of which he was a member. HPI responded that the vehicle in question was not registered with HPI as being the subject of a credit agreement. Two months later, Holbrook sold the car to another car dealer, Kingston, who has since sold it to Humphrey.

▶ Advise the parties as to who owns the car now and what claims and liabilities each might have.

How to Answer this Question

This is a problem dealing with the *nemo dat* principle and the exceptions to it. In this case, the problem is located in hire purchase and involves a consideration of the following: estoppel; Pt III of the **Hire Purchase Act 1964**; s 9 of the **Factors Act 1889** (and s 25 of the **Sale of Goods Act 1979**); and the doctrine of feeding the title. The punchline at the end of the question is unusually helpful because it alerts you to the need to deal not only with who now owns the car, but also with any claims which the parties may have between themselves. Always in this type of question, these latter matters involve a consideration of who can maintain an action for conversion against whom and similarly who can make a claim against his seller under s 12 of the **Sale of Goods Act**.

Applying the Law

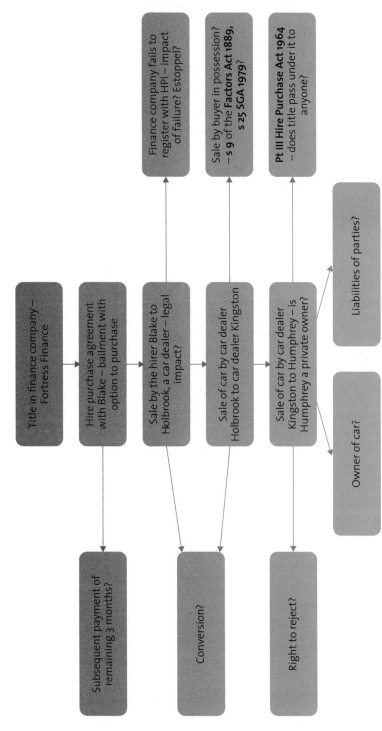

The flowchart illustrates the progress of the car from hirer to purchaser in this scenario and how this can be considered in relation to the nemo dat rule and possible exceptions.

Title in finance company – Fortress Finance

Hire purchase agreement with Blake – bailment with option to purchase

Subsequent payment of remaining 3 months?

Sale by the hirer Blake to Holbrook, a car dealer – legal impact?

Finance company fails to register with HPI – impact of failure? Estoppel?

Conversion?

Sale of car by car dealer Holbrook to car dealer Kingston

Sale by buyer in possession? – s 9 of the **Factors Act 1889,** s 25 SGA 1979?

Sale of car by car dealer Kingston to Humphrey – is Humphrey a private owner?

Pt III Hire Purchase Act 1964 – does title pass under it to anyone?

Right to reject?

Owner of car?

Liabilities of parties?

ANSWER

It is assumed that Fortress Finance had good title to the car, since there is nothing in the question to suggest otherwise. First, we must try to ascertain who now has ownership. We will do so by dealing with the transactions in the problem in chronological order. Blake did not have good title to the car. So, the *nemo dat quod non habet* principle means that he did not confer good title upon Holbrook unless it can be shown that the sale to Holbrook came within one of the exceptions to the *nemo dat* principle.[7] Certainly, someone who has possession of goods under a hire purchase agreement is not a *buyer* in possession of the goods and, therefore, when he sells the goods, the buyer in possession exception (in s 9 of the **Factors Act 1889** and s 25 of the **Sale of Goods Act 1979**) cannot operate to defeat the title of the owner (*Helby v Matthews* (1895)).

Also, when Blake sold the car to Holbrook, there is no question of **Pt III** of the **Hire Purchase Act 1964** applying, since Holbrook was a car dealer. That is so despite the fact that he bought the car for his own (or rather for his wife's) private use (*Stevenson v Beverley Bentinck* (1976)). Another means by which it might be argued that Holbrook obtained good title is by virtue of the doctrine of estoppel. That argument was used in a case involving very similar facts to this in *Moorgate Mercantile v Twitchings* (1976).[8] It failed because an estoppel has to rest upon a representation by the person to be estopped (here, Fortress Finance), and failing to register an agreement with HPI is not the same thing as making a representation. Rather, it is the opposite; it is an absence of doing something. Nor could it be said that the finance company was in breach of any duty of care in failing to register the agreement, since it was not under any duty to join HPI in the first place. We are not told anything about the current terms of membership of HPI. If, as at the time of the *Twitchings* case, the terms of membership do not impose a duty on members to register their credit contracts, then the result has to be the same, that is, Fortress Finance cannot be liable to Holbrook for failing to register and Holbrook cannot raise an estoppel against Fortress Finance.

In fact, the problem does not tell us that Fortress Finance failed to register with HPI the credit agreement it had with Blake.[9] It is possible that the reason that Holbrook was given the response he was given by HPI was that this was due to negligence by HPI. We are not told the terms of the agreement between Holbrook and HPI. Depending upon what those terms are, HPI may well be liable to Holbrook in negligence or for breach of the implied

---

7   Considering any potential exception after describing the general legal rule to the requirements of the question ensures that your analysis proceeds in a logical way.

8   When a problem scenario resembles what happened in a decided case, don't automatically assume that you have found the answer to the problem; this assumption might lose you valuable marks as the finer points of the question set might make an important difference to the analysis.

9   Pointing out omissions in the information provided by the question and considering the impact these omissions might have on the outcome of your analysis will attract a higher mark as it demonstrates your understanding.

term to carry out its service with reasonable care and skill (s 13 of the Supply of Goods and Services Act 1982). Any exclusion clause in its contract purporting to exclude such liability will be subject to the requirement of reasonableness in the Unfair Contract Terms Act 1977. Of course, even if the fault did lie with HPI, and even if HPI is liable in the way just canvassed, that will not alter the question of who owns the car. It will serve only to give Holbrook a claim in damages.

It seems unlikely then that any of the exceptions to the *nemo dat* principle will have served to give Holbrook good title. When Holbrook sold the car on to Kingston, it seems very likely that Blake had still not completed the payments to Fortress Finance under his hire purchase agreement, since when he bought the car, Blake still had three monthly instalments to pay and Holbrook sold the car after having it for only two months. If Holbrook did not have good title, then he could not confer title upon Kingston, unless some exception to the *nemo dat* principle applied. Again, Pt III of the Hire Purchase Act 1964 will not apply because Kingston also was not a private purchaser. However, does the 'buyer in possession' exception apply, that is, the exception stated in s 9 of the Factors Act 1889 and in s 25 of the Sale of Goods Act 1979? Undoubtedly, Holbrook was a buyer (someone who had bought or agreed to buy) who obtained possession of the goods with the consent of the seller (Blake). Undoubtedly, Holbrook delivered the car to Kingston and, presumably, Kingston took it in good faith unaware of the defect in title. Despite the fact that there was a compliance with the wording of the two sections, nevertheless, they do not apply. The House of Lords has held that the two sections can defeat the title only of an owner who has entrusted the possession of his goods to a buyer (*National Employers' Mutual General Insurance Association v Jones* (1988)). Thus, a disposition by Holbrook to Kingston cannot by virtue of those two sections defeat the title of anyone except the owner who entrusted them to Holbrook. The two sections cannot defeat the title of Fortress Finance.

Kingston sold the car to Humphrey. We are not told of Humphrey's status. If he was a private purchaser, he may be able to take advantage of Pt III of the Hire Purchase Act 1964. This is because although Humphrey did not buy the car from the hire purchase customer (Blake), the Act gives its protection to the first private purchaser provided that that private purchaser bought the car *bona fide* and unaware of the hire purchase agreement (s 27 of the Hire Purchase Act 1964, *Kulkarni v Manor Credit (Davenham) Ltd* (2010)). It is immaterial how expensive the vehicle was and it is immaterial whether Blake's hire purchase agreement was a regulated agreement within the Consumer Credit Act 2006. There are no financial limits to the operation of Pt III of the Hire Purchase Act 1964.

There is a further way in which either Kingston or Humphrey may have acquired good title to the car.[10] We are told that, four months before Kingston sold the car to Humphrey,

---

10 The consideration of possible alternative solutions makes your answer stand out from the rest and demonstrates both deeper knowledge and understanding.

Blake owed three monthly instalments on his hire purchase agreement. We are not told if Blake subsequently paid those off. If he did, then he will have done what is necessary for title to pass from Fortress Finance to Blake. If and when that happened, then title will have been fed automatically down the chain of buyers to Humphrey (*Butterworth v Kingsway Motors* (1954)). For this to happen, there is no need for the buyers to have been in good faith and, equally, it is immaterial if any or all of them were car dealers. If it did not, then we are left wondering whether Humphrey was a private purchaser or not.

CONSEQUENCES

If Humphrey was not a private purchaser, he will not have obtained good title unless Blake has paid off his hire purchase instalments. If Humphrey did not get good title, Fortress Finance is entitled to succeed against Humphrey in an action in conversion.[11] The measure of damages, however, would not be the value of the goods at the date of conversion (which is the usual measure of damages for conversion), but would be the lower of two amounts which are:

(a)   the value of the car at the date of conversion (that is, when Humphrey bought it or refused to hand it over to Fortress Finance);

(b)   the outstanding balance of the hire purchase price owed by Blake to Fortress Finance.

This is the rule in *Wickham Holdings v Brooke House Motors* (1967), confirmed in *Chubb Cash Ltd v John Crilley & Son* (1983).

If Humphrey is liable to Fortress Finance in the way just described, then he will have a claim for his losses against Kingston under s 12 of the **Sale of Goods Act** and Kingston will, in turn, have such a claim against Holbrook and Holbrook will have such a claim against Blake, although one guesses that the latter claim may not be worth much if Blake has no means of paying.[12]

If Humphrey was a private purchaser who obtained good title by virtue of the **1964 Act**, then Fortress Finance would have no valid claim against Humphrey, but would be entitled to succeed in conversion against either Kingston or Holbrook. Indeed, even in the scenario just considered, that is, that Humphrey was not protected by the **1964 Act**, Fortress Finance would not be required to bring proceedings against Humphrey; the finance company could choose instead to sue Holbrook and/or Kingston. They have each committed conversion by selling Fortress Finance's car. Conversion is a tort of strict liability and it is no defence to either of those dealers that, in selling Fortress Finance's car, they were unaware of Fortress Finance's interest in it. The measure of damages would again be calculated according to the rule in *Wickham Holdings v Brook House Motors*.

....

11   Build upon your previous discussion; this gives your answer structure.

12   Pointing out the implications of a particular conclusion for the parties concerned shows an in-depth understanding and will attract additional marks.

There is one further matter which is relevant if Humphrey does not have good title.[13] It is that he is then entitled to reject the car and demand the whole of his purchase price back from Kingston, who is entitled to do the same to Holbrook, who is entitled to do the same to Blake (although, again, Blake may not have the means to make the refund). The ability to reject the car depends upon the ruling in *Rowland v Divall* (1923) which, in the case of a breach of the condition as to title in s 12, regards the buyer as having suffered a total failure of consideration.

QUESTION 17

Abigail owns a jewellery shop in Islington. Nathan came into the shop, selected a ruby bracelet and paid for it. Nathan explained to her that he had an appointment to play football that afternoon and asked if it would be all right to leave the bracelet with Abigail until after his football game. A little later that same afternoon, Enrique, who looked the very image of Rafael Nadal, the famous tennis player, and had a strong Spanish accent, came into the shop and selected the very same bracelet (which by an oversight Abigail had failed to remove to be kept for Nathan). Abigail let Enrique pay the £1,000 price by cheque, which Enrique did – signing himself Rafael Nadal. Subsequently, the cheque was dishonoured and Abigail informed the police, who traced the bracelet to Paul's shop in Croydon. It has turned out that Enrique has a stall at Bermondsey market in South London and that he sold the bracelet (for £200) early one morning to Paul, a jewellery dealer, who considered at the time that he had a real bargain.

▶ Advise Abigail.

How to Answer this Question

The question deals with certain 'exceptions' to the *nemo dat* rule, namely:

❖ the position where a seller sells goods which the seller has already sold to an earlier buyer;

❖ when a buyer misrepresents (or a seller is mistaken as to) the buyer's identity;

❖ the rule (in s 25 of the Sale of Goods Act 1979) dealing with a buyer in posses-sion who sells the goods.

Also expected is the knowledge that the exception relating to market overt has been abolished. It is logical to deal with the transactions in chronological order. In that way, the passing of title can be traced through those transactions. As always in this sort of examination question, certain key facts are not given, with the result that the examinee cannot always be sure if an exception does or does not apply. This requires, as the answer progresses, copious use of the expressions 'if' or 'assuming that'.

---

13 Pointing to possible solutions demonstrates both understanding and knowledge of the legal area in question.

Answer Structure

This diagram illustrates the main factors to consider in the sale of the bracelet.

ANSWER

As there is nothing in the question to suggest otherwise, it will be assumed that Abigail was at the outset the owner of the bracelet. Therefore, each of the transactions (the sales to Nathan and to Enrique and the sale by Enrique to Paul) must be examined to see whether it operated to pass title.

ABIGAIL'S SALE TO ENRIQUE

The sale by Abigail to Enrique appears to have been affected by fraud on the part of Enrique, who passed himself off as being Rafael Nadal. Whether or not he said anything to that effect, he certainly made a representation of it by signing himself as Rafael Nadal. The effect of this was either to render the contract between himself and Abigail void for unilateral mistake or to render it voidable for fraud. In one case on somewhat similar facts (*Ingram v Little* (1961)), it was held that the contract was void for unilateral mistake. That case, however, is now generally regarded as having been decided on its own special facts. The law presumes that, as the parties were dealing face to face, Abigail intended to deal with the person there in the shop, albeit that she was mistaken as to that person's identity (*Lewis v Averay* (1972)). This is not a situation, like that in *Shogun v Hudson* (2001), where the parties were not face to face but contracted via an intermediary.[14] Thus, there was an agreement between Abigail and Enrique which, however, was a voidable contract, that is the agreement was valid unless and until Abigail avoided the contract for fraud. This was the result achieved in a case on remarkably similar facts, involving a sale of a ring by a jeweller (*Phillips v Brooks* (1919)). Thus, assuming for the moment that Abigail had title, good title passed to Enrique, unless and until such time as Abigail rescinded the contract. In circumstances like those in the present case, it is impractical to suppose that the seller (Abigail) can contact the buyer (Enrique) in order to rescind (set aside) the contract, since Abigail does not actually know who Enrique was. If, however, the seller, when she realises the fraud, does her best to rescind the contract, for example, by informing the police, that will be regarded as rescinding the contract (*Car and Universal Finance v Caldwell* (1965)).[15] This is what Abigail did. Giving such notice to a third party with an intention to rescind operates to rescind it and thus to cause the title to revert to the seller (Abigail). However, it will not have that effect if, as in *Phillips v Brooks*, the rogue buyer (Enrique) has already sold the goods to a purchaser who was ignorant of the fraud and who bought in good faith. We are not told whether Enrique sold the bracelet to Paul before or after Abigail informed the police of the fraud upon herself.[16] If it was afterwards, then Abigail's informing of the police will have operated to rescind her contract with Enrique and to cause title to the bracelet to revert to Abigail. If Enrique sold the bracelet to Paul before Abigail informed the police, then, since Enrique had title at that time, Paul will have received title and, assuming that he was ignorant of the fraud and a purchaser in good faith, his title will be unassailable by Abigail. The fact that the price which Paul paid was low would not seem to prevent him having been a purchaser in good faith. Indeed, one would expect prices in a street market to be significantly less than in, say, a Central London jewellers.

ABIGAIL AS SELLER IN POSSESSION

The position relating to the sale by Abigail to Enrique is complicated by the fact that the bracelet in fact belongs to Nathan. If the transaction between Abigail and Enrique was not avoided for fraud before Enrique sold the bracelet on to Paul, the question arises as to whether that transaction operated to transfer title from Abigail who did not have title so as to defeat the title of Nathan.[17] Abigail was a seller (she had sold to Nathan) and she continued being in possession of the goods with the consent of the buyer (Nathan). In those circumstances, if she sold and delivered the goods to another person who received them in good faith and without notice of the previous sale to Nathan, that transaction has the same effect as if Abigail had been expressly authorised by Nathan to make it (s 24 of

---

14 It is important to refer to relevant authorities to substantiate your argument – this might be case law or a statutory provision. Remember: it is the application of law upon which you are assessed.
15 Considering different possibilities ensures that your analysis is complete.
16 Pointing out omissions in the information provided by the question and considering the impact these omissions might have on the outcome of your analysis will attract a higher mark as it demonstrates your understanding.
17 Proceed in a logical manner; this attracts a higher mark.

the Sale of Goods Act and s 8 of the Factors Act 1889). Thus, it would operate to transfer Nathan's title to the innocent buyer. The question then arises as to whether Enrique was 'in good faith'. In one sense, he very clearly was not acting in good faith because he was himself fraudulent. Section 24 is clearly intended not to allow someone who takes in bad faith to benefit from the section. The difficulty is that if the absence of good faith prevents the sale from Abigail to Enrique transferring title to Enrique, it is not Enrique who suffers but the person (Paul) to whom Enrique sold.[18] The requirement of good faith may possibly simply relate to the matter of the previous sale (in this case, to Nathan). It may mean that the buyer is not acting in good faith – and s 24 does not operate – if the buyer (even though he may not have 'notice' of the previous sale) has reason to suspect that there is a previous sale. If that is what it means, then Enrique was (in that limited sense) presumably acting in good faith (that is, without the slightest suspicion of any earlier sale of the bracelet by Abigail). In that case, if the sale by Enrique to Paul took place before Abigail informed the police, Enrique (and, through Enrique, Paul) will have secured good title by virtue of s 24. In that case, Nathan will have lost title.

ENRIQUE'S SALE TO PAUL

It is necessary now to consider the position if the sale by Enrique to Paul occurred after Abigail informed the police. In those circumstances, Enrique was selling something to which he did not have title and, according to the *nemo dat quod non habet* principle, he will not have conferred title upon Paul. However, there is one exception to that principle which might have relevance.[19] This is the possibility of Paul relying upon s 25 of the Sale of Goods Act. First, however, it must be pointed out that the exception which used to exist in relation to any sale in market overt no longer exists, since s 22 of the Sale of Goods Act was repealed in 1995. Thus, the fact that it was in Bermondsey market that Enrique sold the bracelet is of no significance.

SECTION 25

It is possible that Paul can claim good title by virtue of s 25, which is virtually identical in its wording to s 9 of the Factors Act 1889. Assuming, as has been argued above, that the sale by Abigail to Enrique was a voidable (and not a void) contract, then Enrique was someone who had 'bought or agreed to buy'. He was in possession of the bracelet with the consent of the seller (Abigail) and he delivered the bracelet under a sale to Paul. That all being so, the conditions of s 25 were all satisfied, apart from the requirement that Paul received the bracelet in good faith. It would seem that Paul's belief that he had a good bargain would not cast doubt on his *bona fides* unless the price of £200 was so low that it ought to have put him on notice. Once the conditions of the section are satisfied, the sale and delivery of the bracelet by Enrique to Paul has the same effect as if Enrique were a

---

18   Point to existing difficulties. This demonstrates your awareness and will attract a higher mark.

19   Credit is given for pointing out and considering exceptions as this demonstrates knowledge and understanding.

mercantile agent in possession of the goods with the consent of Abigail. This wording of s 25 taken literally means that even if all the conditions of s 25 were satisfied, Paul will have obtained good title only if the conditions for the passing of title by a mercantile agent (that is, under s 2(1) of the **Factors Act 1889**) were also satisfied. This means that s 25 will operate to pass good title only if the buyer in possession (here, Enrique) sells the goods in the normal course of business of a mercantile agent – that is, even if he was not in fact a mercantile agent. This seems to have been the approach adopted by the Court of Appeal in *Newtons of Wembley v Williams* (1965), where the buyer in possession sold the goods (a car) in a street market where mercantile agents commonly sold cars.[20] It was held in that case that s 25 did operate to pass good title in circumstances (such as those in the present problem) where the buyer in possession had acquired the goods under a contract which was voidable for his own fraud, and which had in fact been avoided before the sale by the buyer.

However, s 25 is probably of no use to Paul unless he can use it to defeat the title of Nathan as well as that of Abigail, since we have seen that Nathan appears to have obtained good title prior to Abigail's agreeing to sell the bracelet to Enrique. We are here dealing with the situation where it is after Abigail contacted the police that Enrique sold the bracelet to Paul. In that situation, s 25 is of no use to Paul, because s 25 can be relied on to defeat the title only of the original owner (Abigail) who entrusted the goods to the buyer (Enrique) who has then sold them on to the innocent purchaser (Paul) (*National Employers' Mutual General Insurance Association v Jones* (1988)).

Thus, Abigail is advised that Nathan obtained title by virtue of having bought the bracelet from her.[21] If Abigail informed the police and thus avoided her contract for fraud with Enrique before he sold the bracelet to Paul, then Nathan still has that title. The sale to Paul will not operate to transfer title to Paul because: (a) the market overt exception to the *nemo dat* rule had been abolished; and (b) s 25 cannot operate to transfer to the buyer (Paul) any title other than that of the person (Abigail) who entrusted goods to the seller (Enrique). It will not operate to defeat Nathan's title. In those circumstances, Nathan could then demand return of the bracelet from Paul and, failing its return, would be entitled to succeed in an action against Paul in conversion. If Abigail did not inform the police before Enrique sold the bracelet to Paul, then (subject to the correct interpretation of the expression 'in good faith' in s 24) Paul will have obtained good title by virtue of having bought from someone (Enrique) who obtained good title by virtue of s 24 of the **Sale of Goods Act**. In those circumstances, Abigail will be liable in conversion to Nathan for having sold his bracelet.

....

20 Considering a case which resembles the facts of the problem strengthens your argument/conclusion.

21 Concluding your analysis with tailored advice to the advisee will ensure completeness of your answer.

Making and Cancelling a Credit Agreement

INTRODUCTION

This chapter deals with the common law and statutory provisions, both under the domestic law contained in the **Consumer Credit Acts 1974–2006**, and where relevant the **EU Consumer Credit Directive 2008/48/EC** relating to the advertising and marketing of credit, the position of credit-brokers if they do not hold a valid licence from the OFT, the making of a credit agreement, pre-contract disclosure and formalities, including coverage of the triangular scenario involving a customer, a garage and a finance company and cancellation of credit agreements.

Checklist ✔

The following topics should be prepared in advance of tackling the questions:

- definition of 'credit';
- definition of a 'regulated agreement' – **ss 8** and **9** of the **Consumer Credit Act 1974** (as amended by **ss 1–4** of the **Consumer Credit Act 2006**);
- definition of a regulated consumer hire agreement **s 15** of the **Consumer Credit Act 1974**;
- Office of Fair Trading's powers to impose requirements on licensees and civil penalties (**ss 38–43** and **ss 52–54** of the **CCA 2006**);
- effects of unlicensed trading – **s 40** of the **Consumer Credit Act 1974** as amended by **s 26** of the **Consumer Credit Act 2006**;
- criminal controls on false and misleading credit advertising – **s 44** of the **Consumer Credit Act 1974** and the **Consumer Protection from Unfair Trading Regulations 2008**;
- pre-contract disclosure requirements – **s 55** and **ss 55A-C 1974**;

- **ss 60–65** of the **Consumer Credit Act 1974** on the documentation formalities;

- **ss 66A–74** of the **Consumer Credit Act** on cancellation;

- **Cancellation of Contracts made in the Consumer's Home or Place of Work etc Regulations 2008/1816**;

- **s 56** of the **Consumer Credit Act 1974** on the agency of the dealer and the position at common law;

- the responsibilities of credit intermediaries **s 160A** of the **CCA 1974**.

QUESTION 18

The combined impact of the enactment of recent reforms to domestic UK consumer credit law and the implementation of the EU **Consumer Credit Directive, 2008/48/EU** means that creditors must pay more attention to whether the debtor can actually afford the credit and is aware of the implications of the transaction they are entering into and should provide more protection for vulnerable borrowers in the subprime section of the market.

How to Answer this Question

- ❖ Need to mention that the problem of exploiting vulnerable debtors still remains a topical and important issue – particularly in light of current economic situation flowing from credit crunch financial crisis.
- ❖ Look at OFT's enhanced licensing powers and new powers to issue requirement notices.
- ❖ Look at requirement to more accurately assess the debtor's creditworthiness and to try to avoid problems arising from overindebtedness.
- ❖ Pre-contract disclosure requirements.
- ❖ Moves toward more of a know your customer regime where creditors required to make more pre-contract disclosures and permit more scope for questions about a transaction and ability to ready the contract before signing.
- ❖ Introduction of an extended general cancellation right giving more opportunity to withdraw from ill-considered credit transactions.

Answer Structure

This flowchart illustrates the key points to cover in your answer, highlighting how the relevant legislation will be discussed.

INTRODUCTION[1]

Despite the fact that the **Consumer Credit Act 1974** created one of the most sophisticated and wide-ranging legislative regimes in Europe nearly forty years ago the problem of effectively protecting vulnerable debtors who do not have access to main stream forms of credit such as overdrafts, bank loans and credit cards has remained a persistent problem with authorities at times seemingly helpless to get to the roots of the problems. In recent years reform of the domestic law and the implementation of the **EU Consumer Credit Directive 2008/48/EU** it is hoped will at last provide effective weapons to deal with this area.[2]

---

1   It is always sensible to start with general overview introduction showing the examiner you are aware of issues raised by the question and general context.

2   Always try to have some context referring to current issues, reports or events to illustrate your answer.

LICENSING AND IRRESPONSIBLE LENDING

With new strengthened licensing powers granted by the **Consumer Credit Act 2006**, in particular the power to impose 'requirements notices' (**ss 38-42** of the **CCA 2006** inserting **ss 33A-D** of the **CCA 1974**) backed up with the power to impose civil penalties of up to £50,000 per breach (**s 52** of the **CCA 2006**) the OFT is focusing much more on undesirable lending practices including lending to borrowers who reasonably cannot safely take on any more debt despite the optimism of the debtor that they can cope.

For a list of formal requirement notices issued or proposed see:

http://www.oft.gov.uk/shared_oft/consumer-credit/enforcement-activity/CEA-activity-requirements.pdf

An example of a requirements notice particularly relevant to this area was issued to Swift Advances plc. The sub-prime lender Swift, trading as Swift Advances plc and Swift Securities Limited, had to improve its lending and collections practices or risk losing its credit licences.[3]

An OFT investigation found Swift was giving secured loans to customers with poor credit histories or limited access to credit without:

checking whether they could afford the loan
verifying their income
taking account of their other financial commitments and personal circumstances
fully checking the information provided in the application.

See OFT Press Notice 73/11 23 June 2011:

http://www.oft.gov.uk/news-and-updates/press/2011/73-11.

Under s 25(2)(2A) and (2B) the OFT can take into account the business practices of an applicant which can be considered both at the initial application stage and at any point when the revocation, variation or suspension of a licence is under consideration. A requirements notice could be issued under s 33A prescribing what the OFT considered to be irresponsible lending. To assist creditors to comply with best practice the OFT has issued guidance – *Irresponsible Lending*, OFT (Feburary 2011):[4]

http://www.oft.gov.uk/shared_oft/business_leaflets/general/oft1107.pdf.

---

3   Always try to avoid being simply descriptive and refer to cases and decisions of regulatory bodies to explain and illustrate what you are saying.
4   In answers concerning consumer credit consider reports and guidance issued by regulators such as the Office of Fair Trading.

In general terms, creditors should:

❖ not use misleading or oppressive behaviour when advertising, selling, or seeking to enforce a credit agreement

❖ make a reasonable assessment of whether a borrower can afford to meet repayments in a sustainable manner

❖ explain the key features of the credit agreement to enable the borrower to make an informed choice

❖ monitor the borrower's repayment record during the course of the agreement, offering assistance where borrowers appear to be experiencing difficulty and

❖ treat borrowers fairly and with forbearance if they experience difficulties.

As can be seen in the guidance, it covers the various aspects of the creditors' involvement with debtors or prospective debtors

1   Introduction of prospective debtor and creditor
2   Observing general principles of fair business practice
3   Explanations of credit agreements
4   Assessment of affordability
5   Pre-contractual issues
6   Contractual and post-contractual issues
7   Handling of default and arrears
8   Regulatory compliance
9   Creditor's responsibility for conduct of agents and third parties and
10   Dealing with vulnerable adults.

A holistic approach and failure to meet these standards may well lead to the imposition of a requirements notice or even revocation of a licence.

For example, the use of aggressive sales tactics contrary to **reg 7** of the **Consumer Protection Unfair Trading Regulations 2008** led to the revocation of a consumer credit licence in the case of *SAS Fire and Security Systems Ltd* and associated companies in relation to the use of aggressive sales techniques to persuade, often elderly consumers, to buy costly burglar alarm and fire alarm systems funded by the use of expensive credit see OFT Press Release 84/11, 22 July 2011 – http://www.oft.gov.uk/news-and-updates/press/2011/84-11.

In February 2012 the Office of Fair Trading launched an extensive[5] review of the payday lending sector, an area notorious for short-term high interest loans to vulnerable

---

5   An example of recent investigations or inquiries will always yield extra marks.

consumers often desperate for short-term credit. This was in part prompted by concerns that some payday lenders may be taking advantage of people in financial difficulty. The review will investigate compliance with the **Consumer Credit Act** and the OFT's guidance on irresponsible lending. Evidence gained during the review will be used to boost standards across the sector and to drive out companies that are not fit to hold consumer credit licences.

There were a number of issues of concern that the OFT will focus on during the review, including:

> Giving loans without first checking adequately that the borrower can afford to repay them.
> Inappropriately targeting particular groups of people with clearly unsuitable or unaffordable credit.
> Rolling over loans so that charges escalate and the loans become unaffordable.
> Not treating borrowers that get into financial difficulties fairly.

The review will involve on-site inspections of 50 major payday lenders and surveys of industry and consumer organisations. Leading up to the review the OFT had conducted a sweep of over 50 payday lending websites and written to the main trade bodies outlining areas where it considered advertising standards need to be improved.

See OFT Press Notice 11/12 February 24 2012 and weblink:

> http://www.oft.gov.uk/news-and-updates/press/2012/11-12.

FORMAL ASSESSMENT OF CREDITWORTHINESS

The Act now formally requires the creditor to carry out an assessment of the prospective debtor's creditworthiness – as set out in **s 55B** which states:[6]

(1)   Before making a regulated consumer credit agreement, other than an excluded agreement, the creditor must undertake an assessment of the creditworthiness of the debtor.

(2)   Before significantly increasing—

    (a)   the amount of credit to be provided under a regulated consumer credit agreement, other than an excluded agreement, or

    (b)   a credit limit for running-account credit under a regulated consumer credit agreement, other than an excluded agreement,

    the creditor must undertake an assessment of the debtor's creditworthiness.

(3)   A creditworthiness assessment must be based on sufficient information obtained from—

....

6   It is important to be up to date in relation to legislation. Remember, your text book may be a year to 18 months out of date – where possible make use of companion websites of books to keep up with recent developments.

(a) the debtor, where appropriate, and

(b) a credit reference agency, where necessary.

PRE-CONTRACT DISCLOSURE

The degree of ignorance about financial matters is quite high in the UK, some struggle to understand even basic concepts such as percentages and the differences between compound and simple interest. People will spend hours selecting the appropriate goods or services but rarely pay similar attention to buying money which of course credit is. Section 55A now requires the creditor to provide 'adequate explanations' of key issues relating to the agreement to enable the debtor to assess whether the agreement is adapted to his needs and financial situation and to consider the information provided in the written pre-contract disclosures provided for in s 55(1). The debtor must be allowed to take away the information and given the opportunity to ask questions and how further information may be obtained from the creditor. Key issues include features of the agreement which may make it unsuitable for particular uses; how much the debtor will have to pay periodically; any features of the agreement which may have adverse effects on the debtor and which the debtor is unlikely to forsee and the consequences of failure to make payments at the agreed times. The prospective debtor must also be advised of any right to withdraw.

This advice can be given orally or in writing – unfortunately the section does not stipulate a minimum period of reflection before proceeding to sign the credit agreement. The danger is that this may become an empty formality or tick box exercise.

However it is a breach of statutory duty not to give, if requested by the debtor, a copy of the prospective agreement or at least such of its terms that have been reduced to writing before a regulated agreement is made (s 55C).

Under the **Consumer Credit (Disclosure of Information) Regulations 2010** certain pre-contract information must be disclosed to the prospective debtor in 'good time before the agreement is made' in effect setting out the key obligations the debtor is undertaking, the APR and the nature of any goods or services being provided under the agreement. It will also include warnings about missing payments and information about any compulsory ancillary contract required to be entered into such as payment protection insurance. Special provision is made to adapt the provisions for telephone and distance contracts. Disclosure must be in that required by the Standard European Consumer Credit Information form set out in **Sched 1** to the regulations. A modified form of disclosure is created for authorized overdrafts and the information provided in the European Consumer Credit Information form set out in **Sched 2** to the Regulations.

GENERAL CANCELLATION RIGHT

Even if a consumer does enter into a pressurised or misunderstood credit transaction, particularly a straight money loan, the new general unilateral 14 day right of withdrawal in s 66A can be invoked by the consumer. Any credit advanced will have to be returned but there are not charges or compensation payable to the creditor to exercise the right. The application of the provision to hire-purchase and conditional sale agreements in relation to goods is not entirely clear but presumably the goods can simply be taken back by the creditor? Any ancillary contract such as a payment protection policy is cancelled as well s 66(A)(13).

CONCLUSION

A combination of more focused and tighter licensing controls;[7] responsible lending policies and more accurate assessment of the prospective debtor's credit worthiness and information access and disclosure policies will it is hoped lead to less abuse of vulnerable debtors and deal with the difficulties of overindebtedness. However, experience with the operation of the consumer credit regime has shown that it is extremely difficult to effectively monitor and regulate the area of sub-prime lending and to change the habits of debtors. In the end if a person is desperate for credit they will often ignore protections provided for them and be vulnerable to the overtunes of unscrupulous fringe or unlicensed moneylenders.

QUESTION 19

Bert, in partnership with his two brothers, runs a sub-post office and is worried about the continued viability of their postal business. The brothers agree that to try and stimulate business beyond core postal services, they need added value services to entice customers in. Bert is approached by Reg, a self-employed salesman, who acts for a variety of firms, including Stingray Photography, who specialise in placing photography booths in shops and other public areas. Reg is very experienced and has been dealing with Stingray Photography for over 10 years. The booth is equipped with computerised printing facilities, which allow customers to produce prints of various sizes and to carry out touching up of their photographs. Reg informs Bert that the hire is £300 per month and that the minimum duration of a hire agreement is 36 months, and he must give three months' notice of termination. Reg assures Bert that based on his considerable experience, and taking into account the location of the sub-post office, annual takings are likely to be of the order of £10,000. The partnership enters into a hire contract and the booth is installed. After six months Bert is extremely unhappy because takings from the machine are barely covering half the monthly hire fee; the computerised printing facilities are very temperamental and are continually jamming, and so he wants to terminate the hire contract, which Stingray Photography the owners of the booth are refusing to do.

---

7   Always useful to end answer with a conclusion bringing strands together showing your awareness of all issues raised by the question.

1   Advise the partnership; and
2   Would your advice differ if instead of hiring the machine, the partnership had licensed Stingray Photography to place the booth in their shop, agreeing to account for the takings on a monthly basis to Stingray Photography minus a 10% commission for doing this, dealing with customer queries and minor maintenance such as removing jams in the print facility?

How to Answer this Question

The question requires you to consider the scope of the CCA 1974 in relation to hire agreements (and in the second scenario, site licence agreements); the status of Reg and whether he is a principal in his own right or an agent, and if the latter, whether s 56 of the CCA applies; whether there is any liability for his misleading opinion about potential takings; whether there is a right to reject if the equipment is not working satisfactorily; and the position in relation to breach and termination if the equipment is not found to be unsatisfactory.

Applying the Law

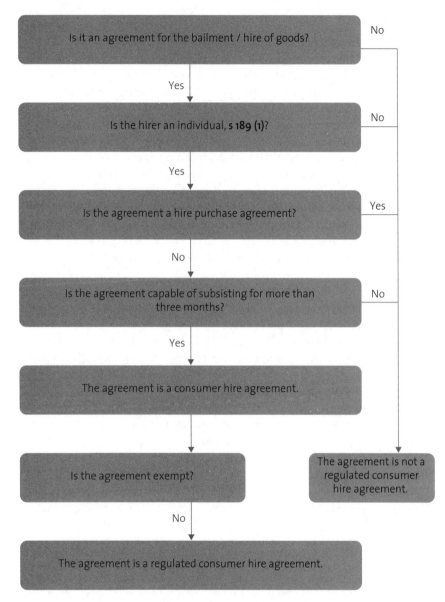

This diagram focuses on the status of the agreement in this scenario and how to determine whether it is a regulated consumer agreement. In addition to the issue you will also have to consider the application of s 56 CCA and whether any 'antecedent negotiations' is creating a statutory agency or liability for misrepresentation as well as the second scenario where there is an unregulated licensing arrangement.

ANSWER

Scope[8]

This is a hire agreement with a business partnership requiring minimum payments of £10,800 over 36 months. The title of the **Consumer Credit Act 1974** was misleading, in that it protected all debtors other than corporate debtors (and even those might be partially protected if there was a joint credit agreement with individual debtors – s185 of the CCA 1974). As part of an exercise in deregulation, the **CCA 2006** redefines 'individual' to include 'a partnership consisting of TWO or THREE persons not all of whom are bodies corporate and an unincorporated body of persons which does not consist entirely of bodies corporate and is not a partnership'.[9] The effect is that generally only small partnerships and not large-scale partnerships will benefit from the protections of the Act. The financial limit in s15(1)(c) excluding hire agreements where the required hire payments would exceed £25,000 has been repealed (ss1 and 2 of the **CCA 2006**). However, consumer hire agreements for wholly or predominantly business purposes where the required hire payments will exceed £25,000 are treated as exempt agreements under s16 of the **CCA 1974** (s4 of the **CCA 2006**). The agreement here is therefore a regulated consumer hire agreement.[10]

Agency

The partnership may be able to take advantage of the statutory agency in relation to Reg's statements under s56 of the **CCA 1974**.[11] The statutory agency' is very precisely defined and it is necessary to check whether the facts of a consumer credit or hire transaction fall within one of the three 'sub-categories of agency' in s56(1)(a)–(c) – see *Black Horse Ltd v Langford* (2007). The statutory agency does not apply to consumer hire agreements unless the statements are made by the creditor or owner himself (which can include his employees and agent) and not by third party credit-brokers or suppliers (*Moorgate Mercantile Leasing Ltd v Gell & Ugolini Dispensers* (1985) and *Lloyds Bowmaker Leasing Ltd v MacDonald* (1993)). It would be a question of fact whether at common law Reg is the agent of Stingray Photography, though the courts have been reluctant to create an agency in relation to intermediaries in credit transactions (*Branwhite v Worcester Works Finance* (1969)). If he were an agent, then as principal, Stingray Photography would be held liable for the statements of Reg if they gave rise to any legal liability as either misrepresentations or terms of the contract. The statements by Reg would probably be regarded as 'antecedent negotiations' made in relation to a regulated

---

8 Be careful here to remember when dealing with a pure hire agreement not a hire purchase insurance agreement or a regulated consumer credit agreement – you are dealing with a regulated consumer hire agreement. Always read questions carefully.

9 Showing an awareness of the development of the area of law in question demonstrates both knowledge and understanding.

10 Remember to draw conclusions from your analysis; this evidences your understanding of how to apply the law.

11 Section 56 is a good illustration of the need to read sections of this Act carefully, it is very precisely drafted and there is need to be within exact scope of the section for it to apply.

agreement, even though not directly concerned with the hire payments element, and such liability would be non-excludable (s 56(1)(a), (3) and (4) – see *Forthright Finance Ltd v Ingate & Carlyle Finance* (1997)). If Reg were deemed to be not an agent but a freestanding principal, then s 56 of the CCA 1974 would not apply.[12] The joint liability provisions in s 75 of the CCA 1974 do not apply to consumer hire agreements.

Misrepresentation[13]

On the face of it, Reg's remarks as to likely revenue from the booth look to be a mere opinion, but given his status and experience, the courts would probably imply a statement of fact that he had a reasonable basis for his opinion and if this did not exist, then potential liability might arise for misrepresentation. If he is an agent of Stingray Photography, an action for statutory negligent misrepresentation would be available under s 2(1) of the **Misrepresentation Act 1967**, with the added advantage that the onus of proving a reasonable factual basis for Reg's opinion would lie on Stingray Photography (*Howard Marine & Dredging Co Ltd v A Ogden & Sons (Excavations) Ltd* (1978)).[14] If Reg is a free-standing principal s 2(1) would not apply, as the consumer hire contract would not be with him but Stingray Photography, but here a common law tort action for negligent misstatement might lie, based on the principle in *Hedley Byrne v Heller & Partners* (1964), on the basis that Reg is aware that Bert is relying on his skill and judgement in relation to potential revenues and it is fair and just to impose liability on him.

IMPLIED TERM

If the computerised printing facilities keep breaking down and this is attributable to a defect in the equipment, there is the potential for the termination of the contract for breach of the implied term of satisfactory quality under s 4 of the **Supply of Goods and Services Act 1982** even though Bert has had the booth for three months (see *UCB Leasing v Holtom* (1987) and *Farnworth Finance Facilities v Attryde* (1970)).

TERMINATION

Unfortunately for Bert, the statutory right of termination of consumer hire agreements provided in s 101 of the CCA 1974 will not apply as the annual payments exceed £1500 and the agreement is for business purposes (s 101(7) of the CCA 1974). In the absence of any contractual right of early termination, the partnership would be bound by the minimum hire period of 36 months.[15]

....

12 Outlining different possible conclusions demonstrates both understanding and knowledge of the legal area in question.

13 Always remember consumer and commercial law is built on foundations of contract law; do not forget basic law on likes of terms and representations.

14 Explaining why a course of action might be preferable will attract additional marks.

15 The explanation of why a particular legal principle is not applicable in relation to a question is as important as the explanation of why a particular legal rule is applicable in relation to a question: on the one hand, this is because it narrows your analysis down to what is relevant; on the other hand, this is because it demonstrates understanding.

BREACH AND DAMAGES

In the absence of any contractual right to reject for breach of the condition of satisfactory quality, or contractual right of early termination, then the partnership would be in breach of contract if they sought to terminate the hire before the 36-month minimum period had elapsed and could, assuming proper default procedures had been followed (ss 87–89 of the CCA 1974), face an action for damages for breach of contract or face a demand for immediate payment of the hire charges under a valid acceleration clause (*Wadham Stringer Ltd v Meaney* (1981)), as well of course as the return of the photography booth to Stingray Photography.[16] It is quite probable that as this is a business contract there will be a liquidated damages clause in the hire contract, and provided this is a reasonable pre-estimate of the owner's loss, will be upheld by the courts even if the amount payable under the clause exceeds the actual loss on this occasion (*Robophone Facilities Ltd v Blank* (1966)). The statutory rebate provision in s 94 of the CCA 1974 does not apply to consumer hire agreements. It is unlikely on the facts that the hirer could claim relief under s 132 of the CCA 1974 on grounds that it is just that he be relieved from some or all of his future hire payments and recover any part of instalments already made.

LICENSING AGREEMENT[17]

In the second scenario, the partnership merely license Stingray Photography to place the machine in their shop and to account for any proceeds received for use of the machine, minus a commission. It follows from this that if no one used the machine, they would not be required to pay any money to Stingray Photography. The question then arises whether it is still a regulated consumer hire agreement within s 15 of the CCA 1974. The answer to that question appears to be no, as a result of the decision in *TRM Copy Centres (UK) v Lanwall* (2008), where it was held that for a bailment to fall within the scope of the Act, there must be an element of payment involved, and where in that case, involving a photocopier, in a post office the owner of the shop only had to account for the proceeds of use of the copier minus a commission, it was held that as there were no mandatory hire charges, it was not a regulated consumer hire agreement.[18] The outcome here is then that in the second scenario it would be an unregulated credit agreement governed by the common law and it would depend on the terms of the licence whether and under what conditions the partnership could terminate the licence – presumably if the machine did not work they might, in absence of any express provision, rely on an implied term to give business efficacy to the contract that the licensed equipment actually work satisfactorily (*Liverpool City Council v Irwin* (1977)).

....

16   The proper application of the relevant legal principle to the requirements of the questions is what the examiner is looking for in an answer.

17   This part illustrates importance in CCA area of being on top of basic category definitions.

18   It is important to refer to relevant authorities to substantiate your argument – this might be case law or a statutory provision. Remember: It is the application of law upon which you are assessed.

Aim Higher ★

A candidate looking to secure a first class mark will have picked up the more limited impact of the **Consumer Credit Act** regime on regulated hire agreements as opposed to regulated consumer credit agreements – in particular in relation to operation of **ss 56** and **101 CCA 1974**. Another key element in this and a number of other questions on consumer credit is to be able to apply the known **CCA 1974** dimensions – in this question in particular the scope and operation of the **Misrepresentation Act 1967** and the relevant common law provisions on breach and liquidated damages clauses in relation to hire agreements, to use a modern phrase, to 'think outside the box'. In other words, not all the aspects of a question will be dealt with by the **Consumer Credit Act 1974** regime – examiners will give extra credit for this broadness of vision.

Common Pitfalls 8 ✗

Often marks may be lost by simple errors such as confusing pure hire agreements with hire-purchase agreements and for example incorrectly applying the agency provisions in **s 56 CCA 1974** and the termination provisions in **ss 99** and **100 CCA** instead of the correct provision in **s 101 CCA 1974**. Another error is to fail to realise that the **CCA 1974** can apply to some business credit contracts in particular with small partnerships – the weak candidate will not have taken on board the narrowed definition of an '*individual*' in the amended **s 189(1) CCA 1974**. Another common oversight is failure to consider whether – which will commonly be the case – there is a valid liquidated damages clause in a business hire agreement. In relation to the second fact scenario, a weak student may not appreciate the parameters of the definition of a regulated hire agreement in **s 15 CCA 1974** and the impact of the House of Lords decision in *TRM Copy Centres (UK) v Lanwall* (2008).

QUESTION 20[19]

Pedro who has no regular employment, but who has inherited subject to mortgage with a building society his late mother's house, earns small sums of money from part-time decorating. As a result of his small and intermittent earnings Pedro owes a variety of

---

19 Read problem questions carefully candidates advised to do proper structure plan of answer before writing – as many marks lost by bad technique as by lack of knowledge – do not waste time with repetition you do not get double the marks by saying the same thing twice.

creditors some £30,000 unsecured debts. He sees an advertisement on the internet by Access Finance which states 'we can provide you with peace and security from pressing creditors, easy to arrange and cheap consolidation loans, contact us straightaway, no delays. Main stream lenders such as banks or credit card companies refusing you visit us.' The site goes on to give various examples of loans made to allegedly satisfied customers. It also states a £1500 arrangement fee will be charged upfront or deducted from the amount of the loan.

The advertisement fails to state that Access Finance are credit brokers and do not provide the loans themselves and that any loans they arrange will have to be secured by a first or subsequent charge on the debtors property, if the debtor owns any property. The advertisement does not specify the name of any lenders with whom Access Finance deal or has it been approved by any of those lenders.

Pedro contacts Access Finance to try and arrange a loan for £35,000, which will pay off his existing creditors and leave him with some money left over to meet urgent house renovation expenses. Access Finance arrange a secured loan with sub-prime lenders Severn Finance at an APR of 40% per annum and secured by a second charge on Pedro's house. This is in fact a different credit contract to the one Access Finance initially sent him with Cymru Finance for a loan at 30% APR and which would be unsecured but Pedro was later informed that this contract was not apparently available for 'reasons connected with the credit crunch'.

Pedro only gets £33,500 as Access Finance deduct a £1500 arrangement fee and Pedro is further informed that his future repayments will include a brokerage fee of £2,500 payable to them – this is set out in the consolidation agreement but no mention was made in Access Finance's internet advertisement.

Pedro has received no copy of either the unexecuted or executed consolidation loan agreement. Pedro is concerned about the transaction and in particular the way it was advertised and carried out.

(a) Advise Pedro and
(b) Would your advice differ if Pedro discovered that while Severn Finance are fully licensed under the **Consumer Credit Act** Access Finance hold no licence under the Act at all.[20]

How to Answer this Question

❖   Need to be aware of extent to which CCA applies to ancillary credit businesses such as credit-brokers.

....

20 Always read questions carefully to check whether more than one part to answer and in terms of timing etc got balance right because of allocation of marks between parts.

❖   Need to be aware of general controls on false and misleading advertising in
      Consumer Protection Unfair Trading Regulations 2008.
❖   Need to be aware of advertising regime laid down by **Consumer Credit
      Act 1974.**
❖   Need to be aware of licensing regime in relation to ancillary credit businesses
      and also impact of introduction by unlicensed credit-broker to licensed creditor.
❖   Need to be aware of structure of agreement and copies of agreements
      regulations under CCA.

Applying the Law

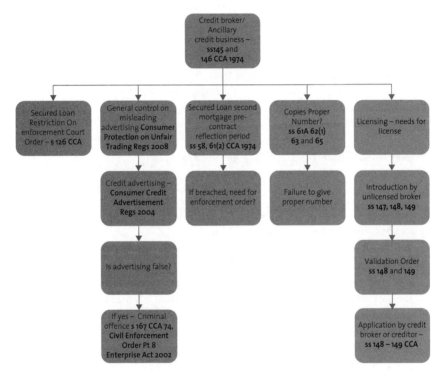

*This flowchart shows the main factors to consider in this scenario in relation to the law
around credit brokers.*

(A) ADVERTISING[21]

An initial point that might be made to Pedro is as the agreement is secured by a land
mortgage regulated by the consumer credit regime it cannot be enforce by a court order

21   In respect of advertising bear in mind consumer credit regime now less self-contained with the repeal of
      s 46 and need to bear in mind the very expansive and all embracing **Consumer Protection from Unfair
      Trading Regulations 2008**.

and at any such hearing concerns about the procedure for entering into the loan and mortgage might be raised (s 126).[22]

Serious questions must be raised about the content of the advertising by Access Finance – they have failed to omit they are brokers and also appear to be offering to arrange loans which they cannot in practice provide – is this an example of so-called 'bait and switch' advertising. There is a strong possibility that they may be in breach of the[23] It is questionable whether the cheaper credit deal was ever on offer.

It is suggested that the advertising would influence an average consumer in the vulnerable section of sub-prime borrowers into making or potential making a transactional decision to pursue a loan via the brokers (CPUTR 2008 reg 2(2), (3) and (5).

While Access Finance may face criminal prosecution (CPUTR 2008 regs 9, 10 and 12) or the possibility of a civil enforcement order by the OFT or other authorized enforcer under Pt 8 of the Enterprise Act 2002 to prevent the continuance of such conduct if adversely affecting the collective interest of consumers at the moment Pedro has no direct civil right of action for breach of the CPUTR 2008.

However, it also appears that the brokers are guilty of breach of the relevant advertising regulations made under s 44 and 151 . As the advertisement relates to agreements which may well be secured on land the Consumer Credit (Advertisement) Regulations 2004 (as amended) apply. Key breaches of these regulations appear to be

(a) Reg 7 failure to state that security will be required;
(b) Reg 8 does not seem to contain a 'typical APR' required in advertisements aimed at persons whose access to credit is restricted which Pedro's appears to be – a typical APR is defined as: 'an APR at or below which the advertiser reasonably expects, at the date on which the advertisement is published, that credit would be provided under at least 66% of the agreements which will be entered into as a result of the advertisement.' The impression from the facts appears to be that vulnerable borrowers may be being lured on to the site with falsely optimistic APRs;
(c) Reg 4 and Sched 2 para 6 – Failure to make clear the circumstances about the additional brokerage fee – in addition they appear to have omitted other matters specified in Sched 2.

An offence by the credit-broker is punishable as a criminal offence (s 167(2)) and subject to a due diligence defence (s 168 and *Coventry CC v Lazarus* (1996)). However breach of the

---

22 Extra marks may be made by putting incidental points which are relevant in wider sense to answer but be careful to stay within bounds of relevance as no marks for irrelevant material.
23 Consumer Protection Unfair Trading Regulations 2008 SI 1277: Regulation 5 (misleading advertising), Regulation 6 (misleading omission) and reg 3(4)(d) Sched I (automatically unfair practices) paras 5 and 18.

advertising regulations does not render any agreement entered into void, voidable or unenforceable.

The deemed agency provisions in **s 56** do not appear to apply to these facts and as the broker appears to act in relation to a range of lenders it appears difficult to argue an agency relationship, rather the broker is a free standing stakeholder in the arrangements (*Branwhite v Worcester Works Finance* (1969)).

AGREEMENT

There appears to be nothing to suggest that the principal credit agreement has not been properly executed in compliance with **s 61**. We are not told the exact procedures relating to the entry of the agreement by Pedro. It is also worth noting we are not told whether the lender has complied with the pre-contract reflection period provided for in **ss 58** and **61(2) & (3)** where certain land mortgage transactions are secured – this would be covered by these provisions and in effect if any approach had been made directly or indirectly by the creditor or the creditor broker in the seven day reflection period the subsequent credit agreement would be improperly executed and a court order or the free, informed and voluntary consent of the debtor would be required to the subsequent civil enforcement of the agreement.

COPIES[24]

However there appears to have been a breach of the statutory copy requirements. This is an excluded agreement as secured on land (**s 61A**) and if the document was unexecuted at the time he signed it – he should have been given a copy of the executed agreement (**s 62(1)**) and any other document referred to in the agreement which would presumably include the mortgage agreement and further a copy of the executed agreement should have been sent to him within the prescribed period along with a copy of any document referred to in the credit agreement (**s 63(2)**).

The impact of this is to make the agreement 'improperly executed' under **s 65** and thus enforceable only with a court order or the free and fully informed consent of the debtor given at the time enforcement is required (**s 65**). If Pedro refuses to pay then Severn Finance will have to apply for an enforcement order under **s 127** which the court can grant on a conditional or unconditional basis and subject to agreement to variation (**ss 135** and **136**). It might be in this case because the subsequent brokerage fee is buried away in the agreement and his attention was not drawn to it previously then an order might be enforcing the loan arrangements but subject to a reduction or removal of the subsequent brokerage fee.

---

24 This typifies what is in some ways a boring area but failure to comply can have major impact on enforceability of the agreement so need to know in broad terms number of copies of executed and unexecuted agreement debtor should normally have.

(B) LICENSING

Access Finance[25] are carrying on the business of credit brokerage which constitutes an ancillary credit business by virtue of s 21 and s 145(1), (2), (3) – they are affecting introductions of individuals desiring to obtain credit to persons carrying on a consumer credit business. It is a criminal offence to carry on a licensable activity without a licence (s 39). The credit brokerage agreement is not civilly enforceable unless the Office of Fair Trading grants a validation order covering the period when the relevant brokerage agreement was concluded (s 148). The OFT will consider, in deciding whether to make such an order, how far consumers (not only Pedro) were prejudiced by the traders conduct; whether the OFT would have been likely to grant a licence covering the relevant period and the degree of culpability for the failure to obtain a licence (s 148(4)). Such an order may be subject to conditions. Here there is a strong possibility that an order may not be made given the false impression in the advertising of the firm and also the failure to offer the provide the product initially offered but a different apparently more expensive one (see revocation of licence of Yes Loans by OFT – OFT Press Notice 15/12, 8 March 2012 – weblink:

http://www.oft.gov.uk/news-and-updates/press/2012/15-12.

Though Severn Finance are fully licensed the introduction of Pedro by an unlicensed credit broker means that the resulting principal credit agreement is civilly unenforceable (s 149). Severn Finance could apply for the agreement to be enforced as if the credit broker had been licensed at the time (s 149(2)). Again the OFT will take into account the prejudice to the debtor of the credit broker's conduct and the degree of culpability of the applicant in facilitating the carrying on by the credit-broker of his business when unlicensed (s 149(4)). The OFT can be made subject to conditions to ameliorate any prejudice to the debtor (s 149(5)).

---

25 Careful reading of question is important as it is here all too easy to assume a creditor-broker is licensed irrelevant that the credit broker was not

Default and Termination of Credit Agreements

INTRODUCTION

This chapter covers the termination of hire purchase agreements as well as other regulated agreements; challenges by the debtor to an allegedly unfair credit agreement; and the use of the Financial Ombudsman Service instead of the courts in the event of a dispute with the creditor.

Checklist ✔

The following topics should be prepared in advance of tackling the questions:

- need to issue arrears and default notices and arrears and default information sheets under **ss 8–12** of the **Consumer Credit Act 2006**;
- need for and effect of a default notice under **s 87** of the **Consumer Credit Act 1974**;
- non-default notice under **ss 76** and **98**;
- time orders under **s 129** of the **Consumer Credit Act**;
- liability of surety in relation to regulated agreements;
- protected goods provision in **s 90** of the **Consumer Credit Act**;
- accelerated payments clauses;
- hire purchase customers' right of termination under **s 99** of the **Consumer Credit Act**;
- claim by owner against a third party to whom a hire purchase customer has sold or bailed the goods;
- the consumer credit jurisdiction of the Financial Services Ombudsman under **ss 59–61** of the **Consumer Credit Act 2006**;
- the jurisdiction to intervene in an 'unfair relationship' between the creditor and the debtor **ss 19–22** of the **Consumer Credit Act 2006** replacing extortionate credit bargain provisions in **ss 137–40** of the **Consumer Credit Act 1974**;

- guidance on irresponsible lending set out in 'Irresponsible Lending' OFT Guidance for Creditors (OFT 1107, March 2010) and **Arts 8 and 9 EU Consumer Credit Directive 2008/48/EC**;

- the provisions of the **EU Consumer Credit Directive 2008/48/EC, 23 April 2008** and their implementation in the **Consumer Credit Act 1974**.

QUESTION 21

Just over five months ago, Fred traded in his old car in part-exchange for a new car which he acquired from XYZ Finance under a regulated hire purchase agreement. The hire purchase agreement showed the following details:

- ❖ a cash price of £21,000;
- ❖ a total hire purchase price of £24,000;
- ❖ a part-exchange allowance of £4,000.

Under the agreement, Fred agreed to make an initial cash payment of £2,000 and 36 monthly instalment payments of £500.[1]

Upon trading in his old car and taking delivery of the new one, Fred paid the initial payment of £2,000 and has since paid the first three of the £500 monthly instalments. However, he is now two months in arrears with his instalments and a week ago wrote to XYZ Finance, informing it that he was temporarily out of work and unable to keep up his payments.

Advise Fred as to his legal position now that he has received a default notice which complies with the requirements of the **Consumer Credit Act 1974** and states that unless he pays off his outstanding arrears within seven days, XYZ Finance will regard the agreement as terminated.

How to Answer this Question

This question demands a consideration of the area of termination of a hire purchase agreement. The plan is to consider the following:

- ❖ have the procedures in relation to dealing with arrears been followed?
- ❖ has a terminating event occurred?
- ❖ what are the consequences of termination arising from Fred's breach?

---

1   Where figures and limits are involved make sure you work out correctly the amounts involved in relation to the limit and also key in consumer credit questions in many areas the law distinguishes 'credit' from 'total charge for credit'.

❖   can Fred avoid those consequences, for example by paying off the debt before expiry of the default notice, or applying for a time order (and how in all of that does the fact that the goods are 'protected goods', if indeed that is what they are, help Fred)?

❖   is it worthwhile for Fred to exercise his own right of termination?

❖   is there any other way out of the mess for Fred, for example selling the car or refinancing the debt?

Applying the Law

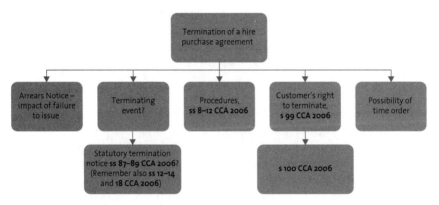

This diagram illustrates the factors to be considered in relation to a hire purchase agreement. When considering the agreement itself it is important to consider whether it is regulated or unregulated, and if they are protected goods.

ANSWER

The question states that the hire purchase agreement is a regulated one. No information is given about whether the formalities and documentation requirements of the **Consumer Credit Act 1974** have been satisfied, and it is assumed in this answer that they have been.

The problem requires a discussion of whether the agreement has been, or can be, terminated and the possible consequences of that for Fred.[2]

....

2   Providing a brief introduction which not only sets out the issues you are going to address but which also refers to the question set is a good way to demonstrate that you have understand what is relevant; relevancy is an important assessment factor.

ARREARS INFORMATION AND ARREARS NOTICE

The creditor would have to check whether it had to serve a notice of 'sums in arrears' under s 9 of the CCA 2006 which will be the case where the debtor is required to have made more than two payments under the agreement and the amount of the shortfall is no less than the sum of the last two payments which Fred is required to have made before the relevant time. This applies here, and within 14 days of these conditions being satisfied under a fixed-sum credit agreement, an arrears notice must be served and with this notice a copy of an OFT-issued 'arrears information sheet' must be given which is designed to inform debtors who receive an arrears notice of what steps they might take and the consequences of taking remedial action (s 8 of the CCA 2006 and see copy on OFT website: http://www.oft.gov.uk/shared_oft/consumer_leaflets/credit/OFT965a.pdf).[3] Failure to give such a notice will mean that while this default continues, the creditor may not enforce the agreement and the debtor will not be liable for interest or any default sum during the non-compliance period (s 11 of the CCA 2006).

TERMINATING EVENT – FRED'S BREACH

Has a terminating event occurred? There is no doubt that Fred is in breach of his agreement by becoming in arrears. There are three alternative ways in which this could be argued to be a terminating event.[4] The first is if it amounts to a repudiation by Fred. On the facts, that argument would be difficult to sustain, since there is no outright refusal by Fred to honour the agreement and his failure to pay two instalments, coupled with Fred's letter referring to him being *temporarily* out of work, hardly signifies a repudiation.

The second way that Fred's breach could be argued to be a terminating event is if the agreement expressly gives to XYZ Finance a right to terminate the agreement, for example if Fred falls into arrears exceeding seven days' delay in making any payment. The third way is if the agreement expressly stipulates that prompt making of payments by Fred is 'of the essence' of the contract (see *Lombard North Central v Butterworth* (1987)).[5]

Even if one of the last two possibilities proves to be the case, XYZ Finance would not be able to treat the agreement as terminated until the expiry of the default notice (s 87) The default notice issued under ss 87–89 of the CCA 1974 will also have to contain information required by a 'default notice' under s 12 of the CCA 2006 – the contents of which will be prescribed by statutory regulation; default interest will not be payable until the lapse of 28 days after the issue of the notice and interest on default sums can only be calculated on a simple interest and not a compound interest basis, e.g. no interest on interest, only

---

3   The inclusion and consideration of material such as consultation papers demonstrate knowledge which goes beyond the normal textbooks and will attract additional marks.
4   Considering different possibilities ensures that your analysis / advice is complete.
5   This question demonstrates that not all answers to consumer credit revolve around the statutory provisions. The common law on breach and assessment of damages in this area remain important.

on the outstanding principal (**ss 13** and **18** of the **CCA 2006**). It is also important to note that under **s 88(4A)**, to be valid notice a default information sheet must be included which will advise Fred on how he might deal with the default issue[6] (see copy on OFT website: http://www.oft.gov.uk/shared_oft/consumer_leaflets/credit/OFT966a.pdf).[7] If Fred makes good his default and pays off his arrears (together with any default interest) before the expiry of the default notice (and under **s 88** amended by **s 14** of the **CCA 2006** Fred must be given at least 14 days from the date of the service of the notice to rectify the breach – see *Brandon v American Express Services Ltd* (2011)), then Fred's breach will be treated as not having occurred (**s 89**) and therefore XYZ Finance will have no right to treat the contract as terminated.

Although there is no statutory sanction for a failure to serve a compliant default notice, a debtor can rely on non-compliance with **s 87** and/or **88** as a defence if the creditor seeks judicial enforcement of its claims.[8]

A non-compliant default notice might, therefore, have serious consequences for a creditor's claim. However, it might well be possible for a creditor to remedy a bad default notice by serving a "good" default notice. This was suggested in the case of *Harrison v Link Financial* (2011)[9] and it is also advocated by some practitioner texts.

CONSEQUENCES OF TERMINATION UPON FRED'S BREACH

If Fred's breach is a terminating event, what will be the consequences of termination (that is, assuming also that Fred does not pay off his arrears before expiry of the default notice)?[10]

If the termination arose because[11] the agreement gave XYZ Finance a right of termination upon the debtor falling into arrears, then the consequences of that termination would be those indicated in *Financings v Baldock* (1963). These would be that Fred would lose the right to keep the car and would be liable for the arrears due up to termination; assuming

----

6 In order to attract a good mark you need to ensure that you don't merely describe the law; you need to explain and apply it to the requirements of the question. This is a good example of how to achieve this aim.

7 Awareness of OFT guidance and advice very useful get marks for indicating regulator's position or guidance on areas – good student will know their way around OFT website in revising for the exam.

8 Always try and be aware of sanctions and penalties that flow from breach of provision and whether it will render agreement permanently or temporarily unenforceable.

9 Marks gained by mentioning relevant *obiter dicta* or suggestions by judges on what position might be even if not central to finding in the particular case as in *Harrison*.

10 Proceeding from the previously drawn conclusions gives your answer a logical structure.

11 The consideration of different options ensures completeness of your analysis and attracts additional marks.

that the agreement imposed upon him a requirement to take reasonable care of the vehicle, he would be liable also for any loss caused by any failure of his to take that care.

If the termination arose because the agreement made Fred's prompt payment of instalments 'of the essence', then XYZ Finance would be entitled to regard the termination as having come about as a result of a repudiation by Fred and would be able to claim not only the return of the car, but also damages assessed on a *Waragowski* (1961) basis, which would allow XYZ Finance to claim not only the arrears already fallen due, but also all the outstanding instalments minus the value of the vehicle recovered and minus a deduction to reflect the fact that XYZ Finance was getting early payment of some instalments. This deduction would be assessed on a rather rough-and-ready basis at common law (*Overstone v Shipway* (1962)) but, under the **Consumer Credit Act**, would be calculated according to the regulations (under **s 95**) governing the rebate for early payment.

It has been said that if termination on either basis just discussed occurred, then XYZ Finance would be entitled to recover the goods. That is in principle true, and at common law an owner is entitled simply to help himself to his own goods – at least if he can do so without trespassing (see *Bowmakers v Barnet Instruments* (1945)). However, XYZ Finance would not be able simply to help itself to the car, for example from the street, if the car was 'protected goods' within the meaning of **s 90**.[12] In this case, the goods will be protected goods if Fred has made or tendered payments totalling one-third (that is, £8,000) or more of the total price (of £24,000). Fred has actually paid a £2,000 initial cash payment, plus £4,000 trade-in allowance plus three instalments of £500, which totals only £7,500. If he were to tender payment of one more instalment, the goods would become protected goods. In that case, XYZ Finance would have to bring court proceedings for a return order (under **s 133**) in order to recover the car. If Fred does not offer that further payment, the goods will not be within the definition of protected goods. It would still be the case, however, that XYZ Finance would not be entitled to trespass to recover the car (for example, if it was in a garage on Fred's premises) (see **s 92**). Fred could, of course, waive the protection afforded by **ss 90** and **92** by giving permission to XYZ Finance to recover the goods – provided that that consent is given at the time of the repossession (**s 173(3)**). Even then, the consent would not be effective if Fred had not been informed of what his rights would be if he refused that consent (*Chartered Trust v Pitcher* (1987)), although it is thought that the default notice is likely to have given Fred that information.[13] Fred would be well advised not to give that consent. The ability or

---

12   Pointing out any potential limitations of the application of a particular legal principle is a good way to demonstrate that you have understood the complexities of the rule in question.

13   Showing an understanding of any subtleties / intricacies of a particular rule demonstrates a deeper knowledge and understanding and will attract a higher mark.

otherwise of XYZ Finance to recover possession of the goods without having to bring court proceedings could well be significant, since if it recovers possession of the goods – and especially if it then subsequently sold them, it would be very difficult in any later court proceedings for the court to keep Fred's hire purchase agreement alive. If, on the other hand, XYZ Finance has to bring court proceedings to recover the car, Fred will have a meaningful option to apply under s 129 for a time order. If evidence of his means is sufficiently convincing, the court could then allow Fred extra time to pay off his arrears (*Southern and District Finance v Barnes* (1995)). Furthermore, this being a hire purchase agreement, the court would have power in making a time order to reorganise the future payment pattern in relation to instalments which have not yet fallen due: s 130(2). In the event that the car is not within the definition of protected goods and is kept on the highway, then Fred might well consider applying immediately for a time order, so as to try to pre-empt any attempt by XYZ Finance to recover the goods. As a default notice has been served on him, Fred has the right to apply for a time order under s 129 without waiting for proceedings to be commenced against him. Under s 16(2) of the CCA 2006, after being served with an 'arrears information sheet' and an 'arrears notice' (ss 8 and 9 of the CCA 2006) Fred can apply for a time order but must give the creditor at least 14 days' notice of his proposed schedule of payments.

FRED'S RIGHT OF TERMINATION[14]

A different option open to Fred, rather than to await termination taking place upon his own breach of the agreement, is to exercise the right himself to terminate the agreement under s 99, which he could do simply by serving upon XYZ Finance a written notice to that effect. The effects of him doing that are laid down in s 100. He would have to return the car and would be liable to pay the arrears which have already fallen due: £1,000.

Also, he may be liable to pay such further sums as would be required to bring his payments up to one-half of the total price unless the loss suffered by the creditor is less than that amount. After payment of his arrears, his payments to date will be £8,500.[15] Thus, the final sum to be paid by Fred (in addition to the £1,000 arrears) could be up to £3,500, which would bring the £8,500 up to £12,000 (which is the total price of £24,000). This figure of £3,500 would be reduced to such sum, if any, stipulated in the agreement as payable upon termination. Normally, an agreement will state a formula which will produce exactly the same figure as, in this case, the £3,500; if the agreement fails to stipulate any sum as payable upon termination, the figure of £3,500 is reduced to zero. Assuming that the sum of £3,500 is stipulated in the agreement, the court still has discretion under s 100 to reduce the £3,500 to such lesser figure as it

---

14 Rarely one route to be followed in consumer credit problems always think of possible alternative routes extra marks for thinking around the issues.

15 Do not be frightened if figures are mentioned in vast majority of cases very simple calculations involved.

considers sufficient to compensate XYZ Finance. It might do this if, for example, the value of the car when recovered by XYZ Finance proved still to be very high (that is, over £12,000).

CONCLUDING ADVICE[16]

Which is the better (or least negative) option outlined above largely depends upon two things.[17] The first is the likelihood of Fred getting back into work which will enable him to resume full payments; this would certainly make an application for a time order look an attractive option if XYZ Finance can be prevented from helping itself to the car. Failing the first, the second is the value of the car at present. If it is still of a high value, exercising the s 99 right of termination might prove quite expensive and, even if Fred sat back and let XYZ Finance terminate the agreement, it might be galling to have to return a car when he has already paid £7,500 towards it and when he would still be liable for the £1,000 arrears. Of course, if he can summon up the financial resources, he could pay off the arrears before expiry of the default notice and thus put off the problem until he is next in arrears.

Otherwise, Fred might consider a different possibility. He could ask XYZ Finance for a settlement statement, thus discovering how much is required for him to pay off the whole of the outstanding debt (that is, getting the benefit of a rebate of charges under s 95), and then he could discover how much he could sell the car for. It may be that Fred would be better off selling the car and using the proceeds to pay off the debt to XYZ Finance than if he either simply let XYZ Finance terminate the agreement or he terminated it himself under s 99. If Fred could find a willing buyer at the right price, he has only either to get that buyer to pay direct to XYZ Finance the outstanding balance owed by Fred or else himself to pass that amount on to XYZ Finance. Either way, as soon as XYZ Finance is paid off, Fred will acquire title to the goods, which title would of course be 'fed' straight on to Fred's purchaser (*Butterworth v Kingsway Motors* (1954)). If Fred cannot sell the car for a figure which would help him out of his difficulties, he could possibly make a different use of his right (under ss 94 and 95) to pay off the debt early and earn the rebate of charges for doing so. That is, he might find that his bank is willing to make him a loan agreement at a significantly lower rate of interest than the hire purchase agreement is costing him. Because Fred is out of work, his credit rating may make the bank wary of any such agreement, but the possibility of refinancing the agreement could at least be investigated (note any firm advising him on how to 'clean up' his credit rating and remove anything likely to impede future granting of credit will need to be licensed as a provider of 'credit information services': s 25 of the CCA 2006).

....

16   Always try and tie up loose ends to question in good strong conclusion go out on good exit velocity!

17   Explaining why a course of action might be preferable / more successful will attract additional marks.

QUESTION 22

Harley had longed for a motorcycle which he had seen in the window of Cycles Sellers Ltd. On his 17th birthday, Harley acquired the motorcycle under the terms of a regulated hire purchase agreement which he made with Davison Finance. Davison Finance had refused to make the agreement until Harley's father, Gullible, had provided a guarantee of Harley's liabilities under the hire purchase agreement. Davison Finance also has a recourse agreement with the dealer, Cycles Sellers Ltd. The hire purchase agreement provided for an initial payment of £3,000 and 36 monthly payments of £200 each. After making the initial payment and paying one of the monthly instalments, Harley stopped making payments. Davison served a default notice upon him at a time when he was two instalments in arrears and, upon expiry of the default notice without Harley having paid off his arrears, Davison Finance terminated the agreement and repossessed the cycle, helping itself to it from outside Gullible's house where Harley had left it. That was yesterday. The motorcycle is now worth £3,000 and Harley has no assets.

▶ Advise Davison Finance.

What difference, if any, would it make if at the time when Harley fell into arrears, he had already paid three of the monthly instalments and if the agreement which Gullible signed was expressed as an indemnity?

How to Answer this Question

This question tells us that Harley has no assets and thus it requires us to consider any claims Davison Finance may have against Harley's father and the dealer. The fact that the agreement signed by Gullible is a guarantee means that we cannot avoid examining what claims in law Davison Finance may have against Harley. Since we are not told of the terms of the recourse agreement, it seems sensible first to consider the claim against Gullible. It is assumed that the correct procedures have been followed in relation to the issuing of any required arrears notice and default notice (s 9 of the CCA 2006 and s 87 of the CCA 1974).

Answer Structure

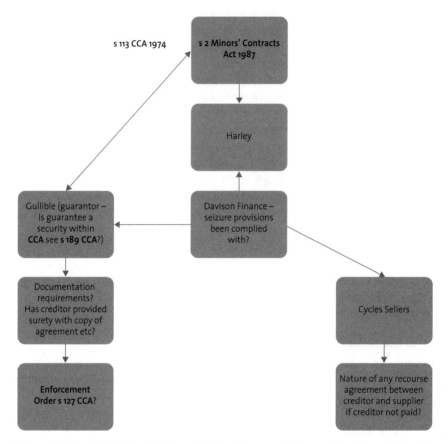

The application of the Minors' Contracts Act in this answer is shown above. You will need to be clear about the position of a guarantor/surety under the CCA 1974. In addition, the impact of any non-compliance with document and copy requirements will have to be considered under ss 65 and 127 of the CCA 1974.

ANSWER

GULLIBLE'S LIABILITY[18]

Since Harley has no assets, Davison Finance will not be advised to consider any proceedings against Harley. It is nevertheless necessary to ask what is the legal liability of Harley because the liability of Gullible, if not of the dealer, may well depend upon it. The

---

18 An easily overlooked area is the liability of sureties if the principal debtor does not pay. You need to know basic rules concerning giving of guarantees for debtor.

most obvious issue is that Harley was, at the time of the making of the contract, a minor. This might well make the contract unenforceable against Harley. Even if that is so, however, that particular defence will not be available to someone, here Gullible, who has guaranteed Harley's liability. If the only reason that the principal debtor is not liable is that he was a minor at the time of the contract, then that will not prevent someone who has guaranteed that liability from being liable on his guarantee (s 2 of the **Minors' Contracts Act 1987**).[19] Apart from that exception, Gullible, as Harley's guarantor, cannot be liable to any greater extent than Harley (s 113 of the **CCA 1974**).[20]

So, ignoring the fact that Harley was a minor, what is the extent of Harley's liability? The hire purchase agreement made by Harley was, we are told, a regulated consumer credit agreement. It provided for a total hire purchase price of £10,200. At the time of the termination, Harley had paid £3,200, which is less than one-third of the total price. In those circumstances, the motorcycle was not 'protected goods' within the definition in s 90 of the **Consumer Credit Act 1974**. That being so, once the contract had been validly terminated, Davison Finance had a right to possession of its own goods irrespective of whether the contract stated so in express terms (*Bowmakers v Barnet Instruments* (1945)). We are told that the cycle was repossessed from outside Gullible's house. We are not told if this means that it was in the street, that is, the public highway, or in Gullible's garden.[21] If the latter was the case, then despite the fact that Davison Finance was entitled to possession of the cycle, it was not entitled to trespass in Gullible's garden in order to retrieve it (s 92) and is liable to Gullible for breach of statutory duty (s 92(3)). There is no other sanction for the entry onto Gullible's premises (if that is what occurred) to recover possession of the cycle. It will thus have no bearing upon Gullible's liability under his guarantee, other than to afford him a counterclaim in any proceedings that Davison Finance may bring against him [22]

Harley's liability, and hence Gullible's, would certainly include a liability to pay off the £400 of arrears already due before the termination occurred. Beyond that, the liability depends upon the terms of the hire purchase agreement.[23] If it provided that prompt payment of all instalments under the agreement was 'of the essence' of the agreement, then that would result in a liability for the whole outstanding balance of the hire purchase price (*Lombard North Central v Butterworth* (1987)). From that would be

....

19 It is important to refer to relevant authorities to substantiate your argument – this might be case law or a statutory provision. Remember: it is the application of law upon which you are assessed.

20 Key point work out if debtor has any liability first because apart from case of infancy surety has no greater liability under CCA than principal debtor.

21 Pointing out omissions in the information provided by the question and considering the impact these omissions might have on the outcome of your analysis will attract a higher mark as it demonstrates your understanding.

22 Remember to draw conclusions from your analysis; this evidences your understanding of how to apply the law.

23 Proceeding from the general to the specific is a good way to structure your answer in a logical manner; it also demonstrates your knowledge and understanding.

deducted the value of the cycle when recovered (£3,000) and any rebate due for the consequent earlier payment of the outstanding instalments.

The mathematical process is thus as follows:[24]

1	Ascertain the total HP price	£10,200
2	Deduct from the total HP price all sums already paid	£3,200
3	That leaves the outstanding balance	£7,000
4	Divide the outstanding balance into:	
	(a) arrears owing at termination	£400
	(b) future payments owing	£6,600
5	Deduct from future payments owing, both:	
	(i) value of vehicle repossessed	£3,000
	(ii) amount of rebate for early settlement	£X
6	The total due is then:	
	(a) arrears owing at termination	£400
	(b) future payments owing minus the items at 5(i) and (ii) above	£3,600 *less £X*
7	The total due thus is	£4,000 *less £X*

£X is the statutory rebate for early payment of outstanding instalments.

If, however, the contract contained no provision making prompt payment 'of the essence' of the contract, then there will be no liability beyond an obligation to pay off arrears due before termination together with damages (if any) for any failure by Harley to take reasonable care of the cycle (*Financings v Baldock* (1963)). This is because, on the facts given, there is no evidence of Harley having committed a repudiation of the contract. In this situation, there is no question of Gullible being held liable to any greater extent than Harley would be, for example, for the outstanding instalments. This is because, apart from the exception which deals with the fact that Harley was a minor, a guarantor cannot be liable to any greater extent than the debtor whose debts or obligations he has guaranteed.

DOCUMENTATION

So, can Gullible be held liable to the extent indicated above? The answer is probably yes, but there are some documentation requirements which need first to be considered.[25] The guarantee given by Gullible is 'security' within the meaning of the **Consumer Credit Act** (see s 189(1)). Thus, it needs to be determined (the question does not tell us) whether the necessary documentation requirements were complied with, both in the making of the hire purchase agreement between Harley and Davison Finance, and also in the making of the guarantee agreement. So far as the first of these is concerned, any defence available to

---

24 Always sensible to set out clearly any calculations worth taking time on in pre-answer plan.

25 Clear signposting of the issues discussed (e.g. by means of headings) enhances the readability of your answer and helps to achieve clarity of expression.

Harley because of any failure to observe the documentation requirements is equally available to Gullible. This is a result of the nature of a guarantee and is reinforced by s 113 of the Consumer Credit Act. The court has a discretion whether to grant an enforcement order even when the documentation requirements have been infringed (see s 127, s 15 of the CCA 2006 has repealed s 127(3)–(5) so there are no longer any cases where the infringement of the documentation requirements automatically renders the credit and/or security agreements permanently unenforceable and also reverses the effect of the House of Lords decision in *Wilson v First County Trust (No 2)* (2003)).[26] There are documentation requirements which should have been observed in the making of the guarantee (see s 105), which include a requirement that Gullible receive a copy of Harley's hire purchase agreement. Again, however, the court has a discretion, under s 127, to grant an enforcement order against Gullible even if the requirements were not complied with (*Hurstanger Ltd v Wilson* (2007)).[27]

There is, however, one further documentation requirement to be mentioned. It is that Gullible should have been (we are not told whether he was) served with a copy of the default notice served on Harley (s 111). If he was not, then again the court has a discretion (under s 127) nevertheless to grant an enforcement order against Gullible. It is to be observed, however, that in exercising its discretion in all the above-mentioned cases, the court must take into account not only the culpability (that is, of Davison Finance) for the infringement, but also any prejudice caused by it. If there was a failure to serve Gullible with a copy of the default notice, then, unless Harley informed Gullible about Harley having received the default notice, the degree of prejudice to Gullible could have been very severe. Had he been served with the default notice, then he might well have paid off the arrears owing and thus prevented the termination of the hire purchase agreement.

LIABILITY OF CYCLES SELLERS[28]

We are informed that Davison Finance has a recourse agreement with Cycles Sellers. We are not told anything of its terms. It is usual, however, for these agreements to be expressed as indemnities and definitely not as guarantees. Thus, Cycles Sellers will have taken on a primary liability and, unlike Gullible, will not automatically have available to it any defence available to Harley. Also, the recourse agreement will not be within the definition of 'security' in s 189(1), since it is virtually certain that the recourse agreement was not entered by Cycles Sellers at the request (express or implied) of Gullible. Indeed, it is highly likely that Harley and Gullible will never have known anything of the existence of the recourse agreement. Thus, the agreement is not subject to the documentation provisions, nor to

---

26 Showing that you are aware of the development of the relevant legal rules will set your answer apart from an average answer.

27 You will not normally be asked questions which involve transitional provisions, you can normally assume current law fully in force but make clear if you are not assuming that or applying previous law and why.

28 As here clearly separate liability of different parties involved here clarity of answering important remember bad technique can lose you a lot of marks if examiner gets lost in a muddle maze of an answer.

s 113, discussed above in relation to Gullible.[29] Furthermore, since the recourse agreement is not (we can be reasonably sure it is not) a guarantee, it is possible for Cycles to be liable to a greater extent than Harley himself. Thus, for example, if Harley's hire purchase agreement did not make prompt payment of the instalments 'of the essence' and therefore Harley's liability was limited to *Financings v Baldock* damages, it is nevertheless possible for Cycles Sellers to be held liable for more than that if, by the terms of its recourse agreement, it had agreed to indemnify Davison Finance against any loss the latter might suffer as a result of Harley not paying the full hire purchase price (*Goulston Discount v Clark* (1967)).

THE RIDER[30]

If the agreement between Gullible and Davison Finance had been written as an indemnity instead of a guarantee that would make no difference at all to the answer above.[31] The agreement would still have been 'security' within the meaning of the Act (**s 189(1)**). That being so, it would have been subject to exactly the same documentation requirements as those already referred to. Furthermore, **s 113** would apply and that section has the effect of rendering an indemnity (which is security within the meaning of the Act) of exactly the same effect as a guarantee. Thus, Gullible cannot be liable to any greater extent than Harley (ignoring for this purpose that Harley was a minor).

The fact that Harley had made three instalment payments before falling into arrears would considerably alter the advice given. This is because in that case, Harley would, at the time the contract was terminated, already have paid over one-third of the hire purchase price, namely, £3,600 (the initial payment of £3,000 plus three instalments of £200 each). £3,600 is more than one-third of £10,200. Thus, the cycle was protected goods within **s 90**. It does not appear that Harley gave his permission to the repossession at the time the cycle was repossessed, and there is no suggestion in the facts that Harley had disposed of the cycle or had abandoned it. Thus, the repossession of the goods was an infringement of the protected goods provisions and Harley (and therefore also Gullible) are relieved of any further liability under the agreement (**s 91**). For the same reason, Davison Finance is liable to repay to Harley all payments he has made under the agreement.

QUESTION 23

'The **Consumer Credit Act 2006** has in three key respects strengthened the protection for vulnerable debtors borrowing in the sub-prime market: first, strengthened licensing controls, secondly introduced a wider regulation of unfair credit transactions, and thirdly a new alternative dispute resolution mechanism.'

---

29 By referring to a previously made explanation or discussion you link different stages of your analysis and thus present a more complete answer; it also saves valuable time.

30 Don't miss out on marks by not discussing more minor issues raised by the question.

31 Don't be reluctant to use the wording of the question in the course of your analysis; this demonstrates that your answer is focused on the relevant issues and also helps you to structure your answer logically.

▶ Critically discuss the above statement.

How to Answer this Question

The vulnerability of debtors who are offered unsuitable loans and forced to borrow, often on disadvantageous terms, from unscrupulous lenders in the so-called sub-prime market, has been an issue of concern to the Office of Fair Trading and other consumer groups for some years. The question requires candidates to consider three areas of reform introduced by the **Consumer Credit Act 2006**:

1. the enhanced licensing powers granted to the Office of Fair Trading in relation to applicants for, and current holders, of consumer credit licences by ss 38–54 of the **CCA 2006**;
2. new provisions to regulate unfair credit transactions in ss 19–22 of the **CCA 2006**;
3. the extension of the powers of the Office of the Financial Services Ombudsman, set up under the **Financial Services and Markets Act 2000**, to cover consumer credit disputes; and
4. the new focus on prevention of irresponsible lending.

The candidate should seek to assess whether these changes, taken together, will provide more effective protection for such vulnerable debtors, than those provided for in the Consumer Credit Act 1974.

Answer Structure

This diagram shows the main factors relating to the CCA *reforms that are relevant to the application of law in this answer.*

ANSWER

INTRODUCTION – CONTEXT OF REFORMS

At the time of its passage, the Consumer Credit Act 1974 was hailed as the most sophisticated and comprehensive consumer credit regime in the world. However, in the intervening period there have been massive changes in the amount of credit granted and the structure of the consumer credit market.[32] One area of concern, however, has proved stubbornly resistant to effective legal remedy, and that is the problem of poorer vulnerable debtors who borrow from sub-prime lenders, sometimes known as non-status lending (see *OFT Guidelines – Non-Status Lending: Guidance for Lenders and Brokers* (1997) OFT 192). A sub-prime loan is simply one made outside the prime market, which comprises mainstream lenders such as the major clearing banks and their subsidiaries. People who cannot borrow in the prime market are often forced to borrow in the sub-prime market on more expensive terms, in terms of both interest rates and expensive default charges, and often at the mercy of more unscrupulous lenders. In some cases these lenders will be unlicensed, and thus committing a criminal offence (s 39 of the CCA 1974). Illegal actions such as threats of violence, harassment and seizure of benefit books as security are not uncommon. Trading standards authorities have found it very difficult to assemble evidence in relation to such activities and to persuade frightened debtors to come forward and give evidence. One of the aims of the reforms introduced by the CCA 2006 is to address these issues.

SECTORAL REVIEWS[33]

Under their general oversight role in relation to consumer credit matters the OFT in February 2012 announced a review of the growing use of so-called 'payday loans', high interest short-term credit often to the most vulnerable consumers. Key issues to be focused on are:

❖ giving loans without first checking adequately that the borrower can afford to repay them;

❖ inappropriately targeting particular groups of people with clearly unsuitable or unaffordable credit;

❖ rolling over loans so that charges escalate and the loans become unaffordable; and

❖ not treating borrowers that get into difficulties fairly.

OFT Press Notice 11/12, 24 February 2012 'OFT Launches review into payday lending http://www.oft.gov.uk/news-and-updates/press/2012/11-12.

---

32 Be prepared to challenge the assumptions made by the question, don't merely agree with the statement made because it is easy. You are assessed on the ability to think critically, i.e. your ability to consider opposing arguments.

33 Credit always to be gained by referring to current reviews, inquiries and reports in overview questions shows you are in command of subject.

LICENSING

Part III of the CCA 1974 required those operating a consumer credit, consumer hire or ancillary credit business to hold either a standard licence or be subject to a group licence.[34] Unlicensed lending is a criminal offence (s 39 of the CCA 1974) and is civilly unenforceable without a validation order from the OFT (s 40 of the CCA 1974), but these deterrents often had little effect on fringe lenders.[35] These provisions remain in force but the objective now is for the Office of Fair Trading to aim for more focused, targeted and effective enforcement of the licensing provisions, with added enforcement powers. The majority of licences will now be granted for an indefinite period, and will not need to be renewed every five years so, releasing resources for more targeted enforcement against abuses (s 34 of the CCA 2006). The fitness criteria set out in s 25 of the CCA 1974 are expanded to allow the OFT to take into account the applicant's skills, knowledge and experience in relation to the relevant credit business and the practices and procedures the applicant proposes to implement in the conduct of the business (s 29 of the CCA 2006), thus allowing perhaps greater focus on the proposed business plan and compliance mechanisms of sub-prime lenders. Sections 44–51 of the CCA 2006 give the OFT greater enforcement powers, in particular in relation to acquiring information from the business and increased powers to enter premises to acquire information about breaches of the law. In addition to the rather cumbersome current procedure of revoking, varying or suspending a licence, the OFT is given more flexible powers under ss 38–43 of the CCA 2006 to impose *requirements* on licensees. The powers are very wide: the OFT can impose requirements if dissatisfied with the way a regulated business is, has been or is proposed to be carried on by a licensee or by an associate or former associate of the licensee. Dissatisfaction is not defined, although the OFT must publish guidance on when *they might be minded to impose requirements* (s 42 *of the* CCA 2006. The OFT can require the doing or ceasing from doing any act in relation to the licensee's business or proposed business (s 38 of the CCA 2006). Extensive supplementary powers are granted for the OFT to specify the time or period within which the required action is to be taken). An example is the *Requirements Notice imposed on Creation Consumer Finance Ltd* (OFT Press Release 65/10, 17 June 2010: http://www.oft.gov.uk/news-and-updates/press/2010/65-10); this notice required the firm to stop issuing proceedings against Scottish debtors in English courts. The OFT regarded this practice as unfair because of the unfamiliar law and procedure involved in a court claim in a different jurisdiction, and any associated travel costs might deter consumers from defending such action. This practice was in breach of the OFT's Debt Collection Guidance.[36]

---

34 Providing a clear and complete explanation not only helps you to properly apply the law to the requirements of the question, it also shows your knowledge. Remember that accuracy is an important assessment factor.

35 OFT website has a lot of good information about licensing. This is an area where regulatory rulings of more importance than rather meagre case law on the area.

36 Showing that you have read more widely than simply learning the basic principles is a good way to attract marks.

A licensee who is unhappy with the imposed requirements can appeal to the First Tier (Consumer Credit) Tribunal, which is part of the General Regulatory Chamber of the Tribunal Service – the appeal will be by way of a full rehearing on the merits, and there is a further right to appeal to the Administrative Appeals Chamber of the Upper Tier Tribunal on a point of law (replacing the Consumer Credit Appeals Tribunal created by **ss 55–58** of the **CCA 2006** under the unification of the Tribunal Service appeals structure created by the **Tribunal Courts and Enforcement Act 2007**). The OFT, again subject to a right of appeal to the First Tier (Consumer Credit) Tribunal, may impose a civil penalty of up to £50,000 for failure to comply with the requirement (**ss 52–55** of the **CCA 2006**). However, before imposing a penalty, the OFT must give the licensee the reasons for the imposition of the penalty, and give them a chance to respond. It is hoped these extended powers and the more flexible penalties should allow a more effective enforcement regime by the OFT. In *EEC Ltd v Office of Fair Trading* (Decision 01, 23 November 2009), the First Tier Tribunal ruled that the onus of proving that it was legitimate to revoke a licence once granted rested on the OFT: http://www.consumercreditappeals.tribunals.gov.uk/Documents/decisions/ecisiononpreliminaryissueson23November2009inEECLtdvOfficeofFair TradingwithdirectionsandNCN_dec09.pdf (see also *QSolvency Ltd* (Decision 07, June 2009[37] – rejection of an appeal against OFT's refusal to grant a licence in relation to an internet-based debt counselling service, based on acting before receiving a licence, lack of appropriate experience and misleading statements on the proposed website: http://www.consumercreditappeals.tribunals.gov.uk/Documents/decisions/0007_QSolvencyRowley.pdf).

The OFT has been using its new powers more aggressively in recent times. In March 2012, following the failure to follow requirements notices, the brokerage licence of Yes Loans, one of the UK's largest brokers of unsecured credit, was revoked under **s 32 CCA 1974**. Among the unfair business practices particularly targeted

❖   were using high pressure sales tactics to persuade consumers to provide their debit or credit card details on the false premise that they were required for an identity and/or security check;

❖   deducting brokerage fees without making it clear that a fee was payable and/or without the consumer's consent;

❖   failing to introduce some consumers to the product originally sought, frequently arranging short-term high interest loans instead;

and

❖   misleading consumers into believing it was a loan provider rather than a credit broker – see 'OFT acts to revoke Yes Loans' licence', OFT Press Notice 15/12, 8 March 2012. See weblink: http://www.oft.gov.uk/news-and-updates/press/2012/15-12.

---

37 The reference to more current cases shows that your knowledge goes beyond the basics; it also demonstrates that you have read more widely and will make your answer stand out from the rest.

UNFAIR CREDIT RELATIONSHIPS

Sections 137–140 of the CCA 1974 gave the courts a very wide discretion to reopen extortionate credit bargains,[38] which were agreements that required the debtor to make payments which were grossly extortionate or which otherwise grossly contravened the principles of fair dealing. The provisions, however, were not a great success, partly because they relied on the individual debtor taking legal action or raising the provisions by way of a defence, which few did, and the bar for court intervention was set at too high a level. The credit agreement did not merely have to be unfair or unreasonable but grossly exorbitant or grossly extortionate, which was a difficult hurdle to surmount. The CCA 2006 repeals these provisions, and by ss 19–22 of the CCA 2006 introduces new powers for the intervention if the agreement is unfair to the debtor. Unfairness is not defined but analogies may be drawn to the **Unfair Terms in Consumer Contract Regulations 1999** (see *Director General of Fair Trading v First National Bank* (2001)). In one key respect these provisions are wider, in that they cover both core and non-core terms, so can be used in relation to excessive interest rates.[39] The court can take account of the whole relationship between the debtor and creditor arising out of the principal credit agreement and any related agreement (such as a brokerage or payment protection plan) and is unfair because of any of the terms of the agreement or of any related agreement or by the way in which the creditor has exercised or enforced any of his rights under the agreement or related agreement. The powers are also wider than those in the CCA 1974 in that the courts can look not only at the position when the agreement is entered into but how the agreement is being enforced. The court can take account of any relevant factor relating to the debtor or creditor. Extensive powers are given to set aside the agreement, vary it, reduce or discharge any sum payable or set aside any security given. It is also important to note that if the collective interests of debtors are being affected by the use of unfair agreements the Office of Fair Trading (or other qualified body such as a local trading standards department) can seek a voluntary assurance that the creditor desist from using such agreements or if necessary apply for a court injunction restraining the creditor from continuing use the offending agreement or terms (**Pt 8** of the **Enterprise Act 2002**). It is important to note that these orders only apply to the creditor's future conduct and do not provide for payment of compensation to individual debtors for past breaches. The OFT has issued a guidance document, 'Unfair Relationships' OFT854, May 2008, on how they intend to use their powers under Part 8 to secure voluntary assurances and court orders in this area.[a]

Already a steady jurisprudence is building up on unfairness – see *Shaw v Nine Regions* [2009] EWHC 3514 (QB), 18/12/2009, *MBNA Europe Bank Ltd v Lynne Thorius* (Lawtel 4/1/2010),

---

38   When revising ensure you use up to date texts marks will be lost by discussing repealed provisions – companion websites good source where using edition which is a couple of years or more old.

39   Providing clear and complete descriptions and explanations not only helps you to properly apply the law to the requirements of the question, it also shows your knowledge. Remember that accuracy is an important assessment factor.

Upendra Rasiklal Patel v Vithalbhai Bikabhai Patel [2009] EWHC 3264 (QB) and *Tew v Bank of Scotland (Shared Appreciation Mortgages) No 1 Plc* [2010] EWHC 203 (Ch) 22/1/2010.[40]

The issue has been raised in a number of cases arising out of the PPI scandal – the mis-selling on an industrial scale of payment protection insurance polices by creditors. An important, if unsuccessful, invocation of the jurisdiction was the case of *Harrison v Black Horse Ltd* [2011] EWCA Civ 1128.[41] The court refused to set aside a credit agreement despite the fact that the bank received a wapping 87% commission on the PPI policy made with an associate company. Overall the policy was expensive and poor value relatively speaking. However the terms and conditions had been explained to the debtors and at this point the Insurance Conduct of Business Rules which applied under the **Financial Services and Markets Act 2000** did not require disclosure of commission. The Court of Appeal took the view that it would be wrong in effect to impose a higher duty under the **CCA 1974** on banks and insurers than that required by the Financial Services Authority under the FSMA 2000 regime. The case has been appealed to the Supreme Court.

NEW DISPUTE RESOLUTION REGIME[42]

Vulnerable debtors are extremely reluctant to use the courts even if they are aware of their rights, which in many cases they are not, and so many of the protections provided by the **CCA 1974** were theoretical rather than real. A key plank of the **CCA 2006** is to provide a less formal and cheaper method of dispute resolution. This is done by extending the jurisdiction of the Financial Ombudsman Service set up under the **Financial Services and Markets Act 2000**[b] (**ss 59–61** and **Sched 2** of the **CCA 2006**). The scheme is free for the individual debtor to use and is financed by fees and levies on the consumer credit industry. The FOS can award up to £150,000 in compensation (it can recommend higher payments but these recommendations are not binding), including damages for distress and inconvenience caused by the actions of the creditor. The awards are enforceable as court judgments. If a debtor is unhappy with how he has been dealt with by the creditor in relation to any matter connected with the credit agreement, the debtor, after first exhausting the creditor's internal complaints procedure, which he is required to have under the scheme, may take the matter to the FOS. Only if a complaint to the creditor fails to resolve matters can the complaint be taken to the FOS. If unhappy with the award of the FOS, the debtor can go the courts, but the creditor is bound by the ruling, subject to any judicial review challenge, for example that the FOS has exceeded its jurisdiction or acted unfairly. The defendant can contend that the complaint raises a novel point of law with significant consequences, and if

40 Showing an awareness of the development of the area of law in question demonstrates both knowledge and understanding.
41 Marks to be gained by reference to topical scandals and controversies such as mis-selling of Payment Protection Insurance – PPI.
42 Remember now consumers have access to a free dispute procedure lots of useful decisions and articles about this area are on the Financial Ombudsman Service Website. Marks are to be gained by reference to these on such things as unfairness disputes

the FOS agrees that it would be more suitably dealt with as a test case, it can be pursued in the courts, but the defendant creditor must agree to pay the costs of the complainant even if the complainant is unsuccessful. The courts accord the FOS a very wide discretion, and providing the decision is fair and reasonable in all the circumstances, the FOS is not bound to follow the strict letter of the law, subject only to their decision being set aside on the grounds that it was perverse or irrational (*R (on the application of Heather Moor & Edgecomb Ltd) v Financial Ombudsman Service* (2008)). Issues 68, 75 & 81 of the *Ombudsman News* feature a useful cross-section of decisions of the FOS: http://www.financial-ombudsman.org.uk/publications/ technical_notes/consumer_credit_resource.html.[43]

The FOS have received a number of complaints from consumers who believe their loan agreements may be "unenforceable at law". Because the ombudsman service is not a court, the FOS has no power to declare a loan agreement unenforceable – and so the ombudsman is not the best forum for this kind of complaint. However the FOS can consider issues relating to such an unenforceable agreement such as whether the loan was unaffordable from the outset or whether information provided by the lender was misleading about the cost (or other benefit) of taking out the loan. Huge numbers of complaints have made about the mis-selling of PPI policies.

A challenge to the largely documents based system and wide unfairness jurisdiction as being incompatible with **Art 6 European Convention on Human Rights 1950** was declared inadmissible in *Heather Moor & Edgecomb Ltd v UK* (2011) 53 E.H.R.R. SE18, 14/06/11.

IRRESPONSIBLE LENDING

One way of course of avoiding problems and disputes is to ensure that borrowers act prudently in the first instance and that creditors do not create debt problems building up by irresponsible lending. Among the reforms introduced by the **Consumer Credit Act 2006** was a new provision, s 25 (2B) of the Act, which made it explicit that among the business practices which the OFT may consider to be deceitful or oppressive or otherwise unfair or improper, for the purposes of considering fitness to hold a consumer credit licence, are practices that appear to the OFT to involve irresponsible lending. The OFT has now published guidance in *Irresponsible Lending – OFT Guidance for Creditors* (OFT 1107, March 2010); among the general criteria set out are:

❖ not use misleading or oppressive behaviour when advertising, selling, or seeking to enforce a credit agreement;
❖ make a reasonable assessment of whether a borrower can afford to meet repayments in a sustainable manner;
❖ explain the key features of the credit agreement to enable the borrower to make an informed choice;

....

43   The inclusion of other relevant sources rather than the 'mere' consideration of case law shows not only that you have researched and read more widely but also adds to the criticality of your analysis.

❖   monitor the borrower's repayment record during the course of the agreement, offering assistance where borrowers appear to be experiencing difficulty; and

❖   treat borrowers fairly and with forbearance if they experience difficulties (para 2:2).

Lenders engaging in irresponsible lending and encouraging debtors to take on unsuitable and unsustainable commitments may find they lose their licences. This is reinforced by Art 8.1 of the new EU Consumer Credit Directive, 2008/48/EC (CCD), which requires the creditor to assess the consumer's creditworthiness on the basis of 'sufficient information', which will include access on a non-discriminatory basis to databases across the European Union (Art 9 CCD).

It can also be noted that further reforms introduced by the EU Consumer Credit Directive 2008/48/EC require prospective creditors to assess the 'creditworthiness' of prospective debtors and to provide an 'adequate explanation of the nature of the credit agreement being entered into (implemented by s 55A and s 55B of the CCA 1974).[44]

QUESTION 24

Consider what have been, so far, the most significant impacts on the previous UK domestic consumer credit law brought about by the implementation of the EU Consumer Credit Directive 2008/48/EC of 23 April 2008?

How to Answer this Question

This is a question that requires the candidate to take an overview of the EU Consumer Credit Directive 2008/48/EC (CCD) and assess the main changes it will require in UK domestic law. The candidate will not be required to go into all the intricate detail of mplementation but to focus on significant changes required and the relationship of the new law to the pre-existing domestic regime. Among the main points to consider:

❖   the CCD is only a partial harmonisation of consumer credit law, e.g. it does not deal with provisions relating to unfair credit transactions or regulated hire agreements;

❖   however, where it does apply it follows the maximum harmonisation approach, not the traditional minimum harmonisation approach;

❖   the UK Government has retained much of the existing domestic law, particularly in areas where the CCD does not apply, e.g. to small business credit contracts and to hire agreements;

❖   outline the main areas of reform in relation to pre-contractual informational requirements;

❖   the information requirements in agreements, in particular the *Standard European Credit Information Sheet*;

---

44 Relating the essay question to its wider (here: European) context is another way to demonstrate knowledge and understanding.

❖   new unilateral right of withdrawal form credit agreements;
❖   new provisions in relation to credit intermediaries.

Applying the Law

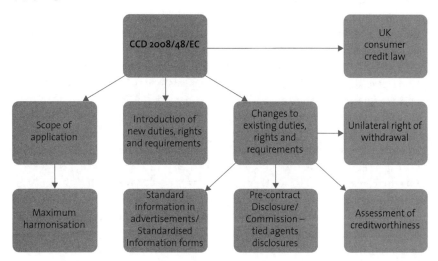

This diagram shows the main factors to consider in relation to the CCD in this answer and the relationship between these.

ANSWER

The **EU Consumer Credit Directive 2008/48/EC of 23 April 2008 (CCD)**[45] is a partial harmonisation of European consumer credit law in EU Member States,[46] e.g. it does not apply to provisions relating to unfair credit transactions, deal with damages for breach of consumer credit contracts or apply to certain categories of agreements, e.g. consumer hire agreements. However, where it does apply the approach adopted is that of maximum harmonisation, leaving Member States with no element of discretion, unlike the traditional minimum harmonisation approach where Member States could adopt stricter rules for their own nationals provided that credit agreements that complied with a directive provided by nationals of other EU Member states were acceptable (**Art 22 CCD**). As is common with most EU consumer law protection, the protections cannot be waived or excluded and cannot be avoided by a choice of law clause nominating the law of a non-EU country (**Art 22(2)–(4) CCD**). One major area that is untouched is the regulation of

---

45 Note complex way UK has incorporated Directive by amending existing law and a separate set of parallel provisions implementing Directive insofar as it goes beyond current UK law – see **s 75** and **s 75A** as illustration.
46 The provision of background information to a particular legal rule shows deeper understanding of the area of law in question and can also help to frame the issues raise in an appropriate manner.

creditors (**Art 20 CCD**) – so although creditors must be properly supervised, the UK can retain the current licensing system operated by the Office of Fair Trading.

The UK has largely adopted a 'bolt-on approach' with the regime being created by the **CCA 1974** and 2006[47] being largely retained and with the new rights being added on or interwoven into current provisions. This has complicated an already complex legal regime even more, and the UK Government has extended the time for compliance with the new hybrid regime to 1 February 2011, though the provisions should have been applicable from 12 May 2010 (**Art 27 CCD**).[48] The **CCD** does not apply to hire agreements (**Art 2(d) CCD**) but the UK will retain the provisions regulating hire agreements in the **CCA 1974**. The **CCD** only applies to agreements with '*a natural person, who in transactions covered by this Directive, is acting for purposes which are outside his trade, business or profession*' (**Art 3(a) CCD**); however, UK law will retain existing protections for small business debtors and in some cases extend the new protections to these debtors even though not required to do so by the **CCD**. A good example of the marrying of a UK provision with a provision required by the **CCD** is the connected lender liability provision in s 75 of the **CCA 1974**[49] – the UK managed to secure the right to retain such a connected-lender liability provision (**Art 15(3) CCD**) but to comply with linked liability provision in **Art 15(2) CCD** – adopting the approach commonly used in civil law in EU countries that you can only sue a creditor when an attempt to recover compensation from the supplier has failed. An additional alternative linked liability action is provided for in s 75A of the **CCA 1974** – which will apply where the main provision in s 75 of the **CCA 1974** does not apply but nevertheless the agreement falls within the scope of the **CCD**. So the linked liability provision will not apply where the cash price of the item is under £30,000 and so, within the scope of the main s 75 of the **CCA 1974**, and not where the amount of credit advanced exceeds £60,260 (75,000 euros), the upper limit in sterling of the application of the Directive. Small business debtors will be able to take advantage of this additional form of protection, though this is not required by the **CCD**. In some cases new definitional categories will exist alongside pre-existing similar domestic categories, e.g. '*credit intermediaries*' (**Art 3(f) CCD**), '*credit brokers*' (s 145(2) of the **CCA 1974**), '*linked credit agreements*' (**Art 3(n) CCD**) and '*linked transactions*' (s 19 of the **CCA 1974**). In some cases domestic rights will cease to apply where new EU rights are introduced, e.g. the new unilateral right of withdrawal (**Art 14 CCD** implemented in s 66A of the **CCA 1974**) will largely supplant the existing cancellation right in s 67 of the **CCA 1974**, but the cancellation regime will continue to apply to those cases not falling within s 66A of the **CCA 1974**.

Many of the changes will be of detail and the UK consumer will not see significant changes in the essence of protection.

----

47 In revising make sure you are looking at most up to date version of **Consumer Credit Act 1974** – amendments etc will be largely incorporated into parent Act.
48 Showing that you are aware of the development of the relevant legal rules will set your answer apart from an average answer.
49 Considering concrete examples demonstrates your knowledge and understanding of the relevant legal rules and also substantiates your analysis / argument.

The main changes will be[50,51]:

❖ standard information to be included in advertisements (**Art 4 CCD**);
❖ toughened pre-contractual information (**Arts 5** and **6 CDD**);
❖ an obligation to assess the creditworthiness of the consumer (**Art 8 CCD**);
❖ standardised information in relation to credit agreements and in particular the introduction of Standard European Credit Information (**Arts 10–12** and **Annex II CDD**);
❖ a unilateral right of withdrawal from a credit agreement (**Art 14 CCD**);
❖ a right to sue a creditor where action against a supplier has failed to produce compensation where the goods or services supplied are not in conformity or only partially in conformity with the contract (**Art 15(2) CCD**);
❖ standardised method for assessing early repayment rebate (**Art 16 CCD**);
❖ new standardised calculation of the annual percentage rate of charge (**Art 19** and **Annex I CCD**);
❖ new disclosure requirements in relation to receipts of commissions and whether tied to a particular creditor or independent imposed on credit intermediaries (**Art 21 CCD**);
❖ Member States to provide '*adequate and effective*' out-of-court dispute resolution procedures (UK already complies with the consumer credit jurisdiction of the Financial Ombudsman Service (FOS)) and encourage those bodies to cooperate in order to resolve cross-border disputes (**Art 24 CCD**).

Given that many consumers do not take advantage of or understand informational requirements in credit advertisements, agreements or copies of agreements, in many ways the chief advantage which will flow from the **CCD** is the ability of the creditors to take advantage of more cross-border opportunities for the provision of credit, e.g. aware that in advertisements the illustration of a '*representative example*' (e.g. that he can reasonably expect to supply at least 51% of debtors on those terms) will be the same throughout the EU, making pan-European advertising campaigns easier – see **regs 1, 4** and **5 Consumer Credit (Advertisement) Regulations 2010/1012**).

From a debtor perspective it should make entering credit agreements with creditors in other EU countries easier.[52] In practical terms the main improvements in relation to consumers will firstly be the stronger disclosure receipts of commissions and the nature of their relationship with the prospective creditor imposed on credit intermediaries –

....

50 Remember to draw conclusions from your analysis; this evidences your understanding of how to apply the law.
51 Good marks can be gained by constructive use of bullet points and even the odd diagram if it helps to show you are aware of area – particularly in essay questions which can degenerate into dense stream of consciousness answers with repetitions and contradictions even on same page.
52 You should avoid making unsubstantiated arguments or premature conclusions when you are asked to 'critically consider / analyse' a statement. Remember that it is the application of the law upon which you are assessed - simply saying that e.g. you don't think something is not fair is not good enough. This is a good example of how to achieve this aim.

particularly in the sub-prime market, where brokers are often used (see **s 160A** of the **CCA 1974** implementing **Art 21 CCD**). Secondly, the reforms increase the movement of consumer credit law towards a 'know-your-customer' approach that is common in such areas as the selling of investments and insurance. **Section 55A–C** implementing **Art 6 CCD** considerably tightens the pre-contractual requirements regime already in existence in **s 55** of the **CCA 1974** and **Consumer Credit (Disclosure of Information) Regulations 2004.**

New pre-contract disclosure requirements are also introduced by the **Consumer Credit (Disclosure of Information) Regulations 2010. Section 55A** of the **CCA 1974** introduces a requirement for an 'adequate explanation' of the prospective transaction (including some potential disadvantages – **s 55A(2)(c)** of the **CCA 1974**) – *'the features of the agreement which may operate in a manner which would have a significant adverse effect on the debtor in a way which the debtor is unlikely to foresee.'* **Section 55B** will require the creditor to undertake an assessment of the debtor's creditworthiness and this, linked to more joined-up access to databases as a whole throughout the EU, may mean fewer 'no questions asked' loans and recklessness in ignoring overextension by a prospective debtor.

Another major improvement is a movement to a unilateral 14-day withdrawal period (**Art 14 CCD** implemented by **s 66A** of the **CCA 1974**). This is a welcome move from the byzantinely complicated cancellation provisions in **ss 67–74** of the **CCA** – tied in to the often irrelevant fact that the agreement was signed off trade premises and the need for 'antecedent negotiations' to be conducted in the presence of the debtor, so ruling out telephonic communications. It will also bring consumer credit law more into line with other withdrawal rights.[53]

CONCLUSION[54]

Given that the UK had one of the most sophisticated consumer credit regimes in the EU, the changes being brought in by the **CCD** will not have a radical impact on the levels of protection. However, key changes in the pre-contract regime and the new right of withdrawal are welcome changes for consumers. For creditors, the third major set of legal reforms in six years means an unwelcome increase in compliance costs and the 'bolt-on approach' adopted by the UK increases the complexity of an already complex regime.[c]

QUESTION 25

Steve acquires a car which has a cash price of £4,000 under a conditional sale agreement with Fleece Your Finance (FYC) for a total price of £6,000 including interest and all other charges. He puts down a deposit of £1,500 and has made six further monthly payments of

---

53 Where possible try referring to any good academic literature on topic particularly where writer draws attention to key positives and negatives in relation to the provisions.

54 Do not forget your overall conclusion – good strong conclusion will yield extra marks.

£100 when he is declared redundant and makes no further subsequent monthly payments. He has missed three monthly payments so far. He then writes to FYF saying 'I am in trouble with this car contract, I want to pay but cannot pay. I will have to give it back.' Two days later FYF arrange for two mechanics from the garage which supplied the car to go to Steve's house where they go up his drive and proceed to drive away the car, using a duplicate set of keys, from Steve's open garage. FYF rely on a clause in the conditional sale agreement which states that the car can be re-possessed at any time if the debtor defaults on a monthly instalment repayment. Steve who is mowing his back garden lawn at the time is very angry and that night he goes to the supplier's garage, where the car is temporarily parked on their forecourt pending a decision as to its future, and using his set of keys takes the car back. Steve then decides to sell the car to his friend Mike who agrees over a pint in their local pub to pay him £2,000 cash for the car 'no questions asked'. Steve intends to use this money to help pay off his debt to FYF unfortunately he is so drunk leaving the pub he loses the envelope with the £2,000 cash Mike has given him. When FYF demand Mike return 'their' car immediately he refuses saying that he bought the car in good faith.

▶ Advise FYF

How to Answer this Question

❖ You will need to consider whether the agreement between Steve and Fleece Your Finance (FYF) has been validly terminated in particular whether the provisions of **ss 87–89** of the **CCA 1974** have been complied with?

❖ You will also need to look at whether the goods are 'protected goods' within **ss 90–92** of the **CCA**, and if they are, what is the impact of a wrongful seizure of them?

❖ You will also need to consider Steve's action In seizing his car back from the garage – who has title to the car at this point. Has Steven a right as bailee under an existing hire-purchase agreement to take back the car?

❖ If Steven has no title to the car what is the impact of his purported sale to Mike and in particular whether Mike can take advantage of ss 27–29 of the **Hire Purchase Act 1964** and claim he is a bona fide purchaser for value from a person holding under an existing hire-purchase or conditional sale agreement.

Answer Structure

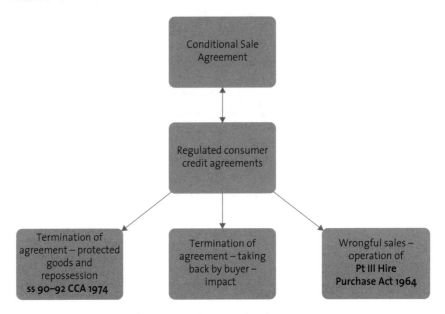

This diagram illustrates the key points to be covered in this answer.

DEFINITION

This agreement is a regulated fixed sum restricted-use debtor-creditor-supplier agreement (ss 8, 9, 11(1)(a) and s 12(a)). Under a conditional sale agreement title to the car remains in the finance company until the instalments are paid (ss 17 and 19 of the **Sale of Goods Act 1979**)[55] and it differs from a hire-purchase agreement only in that the buyer has irrevocably committed himself to the purchase at the outset of the contract. Steve will have permitted possession of the car under the contract and is in effect a bailee of it (see It can be assumed that all the necessary formalities have been completed the statutory copies of the credit agreement provided to Steve and FYF are properly licensed under the **CCA 1974**.

BREACH

Steve is clearly in default by the non-payment of three successive monthly instalments[56] and that in addition to his letter to FYF saying he cannot go on with the agreement and that they better take the car back would it is suggested amount to a repudiation of the contract. However before FYF accept that repudiation and terminate the contract for breach they must issue a statutory termination notice in the prescribed form under

---

55 Questions can involve more than one Act or piece of legislation.

56 Always read a problem questionc carefully and note material facts - fact that Steve has not paid three successive instalments why is three mentioned does it have any relevance to your answer.

ss 87–89.[57] Under s 88(1)) the notice must be in the prescribed form and set out the nature of the alleged breach; if the breach is capable of remedy what action needs to be taken to remedy it and the date before which such action is to be taken and if not remediable the amount of compensation which is payable (s 88(1)). Attached must also be a copy of the current default information sheet required under s 86A. Steve must be given at least 14 days from the date of the service of the notice – allowing two days for receipt if notice sent by first class post – to carry out these actions (s 88(2)) and if he can remedy the breaches within this period the breach is treated as never having taken place (s 89). No such notice appears to have been issued here – though no sanction appears to be provided for breach of the section it is suggested any legal action against Steve will be stayed until a proper default notice is issued (*Brandon v American Express Services* (2011)). A further problem which might exist for FYF is that Steve is more than two payments in arrears and there is no reference to them having issued a notice of arrears as required by s 86B and while this failure continues the creditor or owner shall not be entitled to enforce the agreement while this failure continues (s 86D). Further while this default continues Steve is not liable for any default interest or pay any default sum (s 86D(4)).

PROTECTED GOODS

Steve has paid a total of £2,100 out of a total price of £6,000 and as this amounts to more than one-third of the total price the car has become 'protected goods' under s 90. This means that the creditor is not entitled to recover possession of the goods without an order of court (*Bentinck Ltd v Cromwell Engineering Co Ltd* (1971)) or the free, informed and voluntary consent given at the time possession is sought (ss 90(1) and 173(3) *Mercantile Credit Co Ltd v Cross* (1965), *Chartered Trust plc v Pitcher* (1988)). Further, and even if the goods were not protected goods the creditor is not entitled to enter the land of the debtor to repossess the goods without the debtor's consent and thus here a statutory trespass has occurred as Steve has obviously not consented to the repossession (s 92). The consequences of this is the regulated agreement, if not previously terminated, shall terminate and the debtor shall be released from all liability under the agreement and shall be entitled to recover from the creditor all sums paid by the debtor under the agreement (s 91) and so on the face of it Steve is no longer required to make any future payments and can recover the £2,100 he has already paid. However the restriction on creditor repossession does not apply if it is the debtor who has terminated the agreement (s 90(5)) and here Steve seems to have terminated by saying he cannot carry on with the agreement and asking FYF to take the car back?[58] However under equivalent provisions in the **Hire-Purchase Act 1965** the courts have often interpreted such statements as a repudiation of the contract by the debtor which the creditor by retaking possession of

---

57 Consumer credit regime quite strong on formalities and following proper procedures in making and terminating agreements whilst not necessary to down all complex technical details it is necessary to be aware of broad requirements in these areas.

58 Important to consider carefully the legal impact of what is being done all too easy to assume Steve has forfeited his rights here because he is terminating but what does that mean in legal terms?

the car has accepted so in fact it is the creditor by accepting the debtor's repudiation who terminates the contract (*United Dominions Trust (Commercial) Ltd v Ennis* (1968), *F.C. Finance v Francis* (1970)). Thus Steve may still be in a strong position.

PART III HIRE PURCHASE ACT 1964[59]

Title in the car never passed to Steve so he has no right to sell it and arguable is committing conversion or wrongful interference with goods by retaking possession of the car if we regard the contract as terminated he no longer has any legal right to possession of the car. In any event even if he has a right to possession of the car he has no property in it as title has not passed to him and therefore on the face of it he cannot pass any title to *bona fide* purchaser for value who would be liable in the strict liability tort of conversion or wrongful interference with goods to FYF. However there is a possibility that Mike might be able to take advantage of one of the exceptions to the 'nemo dat non quod habet' rule (that you cannot pass better title than you have) contained in **ss 27–29** of the **Hire Purchase Act 1964**. Where a motor vehicle has been bailed under a hire-purchase agreement or sold under a conditional sale agreement and before property in the vehicle has become vested in the debtor, he disposes of the vehicle to a good faith private purchaser (though not to a trade purchaser – *Stevenson v Beverley Bentinck* (1976) and *GE Capital Bank Ltd v Rushton* (2005)) that private purchaser will obtain good title to the car as against the finance company. Good faith means having no actual notice of the prior agreement between the debtor and finance company (*Barker v Bell* (1971), **s 29(3)** of the **HPA 1964**) and onus of proving lack of good faith lays on the finance company – FYF (*Dodds v Yorkshire Bank Finance* (1992)). The major problem for Mike here is firstly at the time he acquired the car from Steve it appears that Steve is a trespasser and is no longer holding the car under a subsisting conditional sale agreement and thus **s 27(1)** is not satisfied (*Shogun Finance v Hudson* (2003)[60]) and secondly given that he appears to be buying the car in a public house at a considerable discount to the recent cash valuation of the car, even allowing for the dramatic levels of depreciation which occur to cars as soon as they leave the forecourt, questions may be raised about whether he has actual notice of the facts and the dispute over the prior agreement between Steve and FYF? If that is the case Mike must either return the car or at least pay its equivalent value in damages to FYF, though he might be able to recover his price and consequential damages for breach of **s 12** of the **Sale of Goods Act 1979** (breach of the implied term as to title in contracts for sale of goods) from Steve. However given Steve's current financial position that might be a forlorn hope!

------

59 Question illustrates the importance of remembering a question can involve multiple issues – need to understand core implications of common credit agreements such as hire-purchase agreements.
60 Always consider analogous cases. *Shogun* is not on this issue but shows the scope of **s 27** and the need for existence of a hire purchase or conditional sale agreement for section to operate.

CONCLUSION

The question highlights the need for finance companies to have proper systems in place to ensure the proper issue of notices of arrears under s 86 and default notices under ss 87–89 and to act precipitately in repossession and seizure of goods where the debtor is default and so falling foul of the draconian provision for breach of the protected goods provisions (ss 90–92). It is also worth noting that Steve could possibly have exercised his statutory right of termination by paying a maximum of an additional £900 to bring up his payments to a maximum of 50% of the total price under (ss 99–100) or sought a time order and presented a proposed re-scheduling of repayments of a lesser sum over a longer period of time (ss 129 and 130)

Notes

a   This can be seen on the OFT website: http://www.oft.gov.ac.uk.
b   See the website of the FOS for more detail: www.financial-ombudsman.org.uk.
c   Two useful websites providing information on consumer credit and the reform consumer credit law are the Department for Business, Innovation and Skills website (http://www.bis.gov.uk/policies/ consumer-issues/consumer-credit-and-debt/consumer-credit-regulation) and the Office of Fair Trading website (http://www.bis.gov.uk/policies/consumer-issues/consumer-credit-and-debt/consumer-credit-regulation).

Connected Lender Liability

INTRODUCTION

This chapter covers the liability of the creditor for breaches of contract or misrepresentation by the dealer/supplier. The **Consumer Credit Act 2006** does not amend either s56 or s75 dealing with connected lender liability and deemed agency. The EU Consumer Credit Directive 2008/48/EC (CCD) does not amend the deemed agency provision in s56, leaves intact the connected lender liability provision in s75 (**Art 15(3)** CCD), but has required the introduction of an additional liability against creditors in relation to 'linked credit transactions' ('linked liability') in **Art 15(2) CCD**.

Checklist ✔

The following topics should be prepared in advance of tackling the questions:

- definitions in the **Consumer Credit Act 1974** and, in particular, that of debtor–creditor–supplier agreements;
- **s56** of the **Consumer Credit Act**;
- **s75** of the **Consumer Credit Act**;
- **s75A** of the **Consumer Credit Act**;
- **Art 15** of the **EU Consumer Credit Directive 2008/48/EC (CCD)**.
- rules on modifying agreements **s82** of the **Consumer Credit Act 1974**
- rules on provision of copies during currency of running account agreements in **s78** of the **Consumer Credit Act 1974**

QUESTION 26

(a) Despite the connected lender liability provision of s75 of the **Consumer Credit Act** being regarded by the credit industry as a 'flawed provision', successive UK governments have refused to amend s75 and the new EU Consumer Credit Directive 2008/48/EC permits the UK to retain the provision.

▶ Discuss.

(b) Betty decided to have a new kitchen installed. At Kitch Kitchens Ltd, she contracted to have the work done according to an agreed specification. She needed to borrow money to finance the new kitchen and, at Kitch Kitchens Ltd, she also signed a proposal form for a loan from Flash Finance. This was a loan of £5,000 to be paid direct to Kitch Kitchens and to be repaid by Betty by monthly instalments spread over five years. All documentation and other formalities required under the provisions of the Consumer Credit Act were observed in the making of the loan agreement. It is now three months since the new kitchen was installed and Betty has found that the new waste disposal unit is defective, the new cupboards are falling off the walls and the turbo-charged oven will never work properly, since it needs an outlet to the outside. Therefore, it must be installed immediately in front of an outside wall, and Betty's kitchen has no outside wall.

It is going to cost £3,000 for Betty to get a substitute oven and to have the other matters put right. Kitch Kitchens Ltd is insolvent and has gone into liquidation.

(i)   Advise Betty;

AND

(ii)   Would your advice differ if the kitchen had a cash price of £50,000 and Betty had borrowed the money from Flash Finance?

How to Answer this Question

This is a typical two-part question, where (a) requires some critical discussion of an area of law and (b) requires an application of those same rules of law to two specific situations. As with all such questions, it is wise to spend a roughly similar amount of time on each part. When dealing with a question, such as in (b), which demands an application of the rules in s 75, it must be established that there is legal liability on the part of the supplier and that the basic requirements for s 75 and s 75A have been satisfied. Those two issues are dealt with in that order followed by the consequences for Betty. It is also important in answering not to overlook the second sub-part of question (b), which involved new law introduced by the EU Consumer Credit Directive 2008/48/EC and implemented in the UK by s 75A of the Consumer Credit Act 1974.

Applying the Law

Has the right of withdrawal under **s 66A CCA 1974** passed? — No

Yes ↓

Is it a 'non-commercial agreement'? — Yes

No ↓

Is it a debtor–creditor–supplier agreement? — No

Yes ↓

Are the creditor and the supplier one and the same person? — Yes

No ↓

Is the cash price of the item to which the claim relates £100 or less? — Yes

No ↓

Is the cash price of the item to which the claim relates more than £30,000? — Yes

No ↓

s 75 applies. The debtor can claim against the creditor or the supplier for misrepresentation or breach of contract by the supplier.

s 75 does not apply.

This diagram focuses on the debtors right to clam under the CCA in this scenario. In addition to connected lender liability under s 75 set out below you will also have to consider 'secondary liablity' under s 75A where s 75 does not apply.

ANSWER

(a)

The origin of **s 75** is to be found in the Crowther Report, which laid the policy foundations for the **Consumer Credit Act 1974**.[1] That report described the close business link sometimes to be found between a supplier (of goods or services) and a finance house.[2] Those links would arise from the fact that a supplier would need to be able to offer credit to his customers. Thus, a finance company would be quite keen to have a supplier hold a stock of that finance company's proposal forms and to have the supplier suggest that a customer wanting credit should fill out the form. The arrangement often to be found between the finance company and the supplier includes the understanding that the finance company will make finance available to such of the supplier's customers who apply for it and who satisfy the finance company's usual creditworthiness criteria. The Crowther Committee described such suppliers and finance houses as being in a 'joint venture for mutual profit'. The Committee pointed out that the existence of this link and the ready supply of credit to customers of the supplier meant that sometimes a supplier was kept in business for longer than would occur without such support. The Committee recommended that there should be 'connected lender' liability, that is, that the finance company should share liability towards the customer for breach of contract or misrepresentation by the supplier. It is important to note that **s 75** applies both to three-party arrangements, where there is a consumer–supplier–credit card company, and also to the increasingly prevalent four-party arrangements, where there is a consumer–supplier–merchant acquirer–credit card company. In this four-party situation the merchant acquirer, usually a bank, recruits suppliers to the network and processes vouchers from customers and deals with the credit card company, subject to commission and interchange fee arrangements, so there need be no direct link between the credit card company and the supplier for **s 75** joint liability to apply (*Office of Fair Trading v Lloyds TSB* (2007)).

In all of this, the credit industry argues that there is one clear flaw in the policy and there are several others, which are flaws either in the policy or else in its implementation in **s 75**. Consumer groups, on the other hand, have strenuously argued for the retention of **s 75** as one of the most effective consumer protection measures in the **1974 Act**.[3, 4]

---

1   Outlining the context of/rationale for a particular legal rule demonstrates deeper knowledge and will attract a higher mark.
2   It is always important to try and be aware of history and rationale for a provision and perhaps to question whether that rationale still holds good particularly when asked to critique the provision.
3   Don't merely agree with the statement made because it is easy. You are assessed on the ability to think critically, i.e. your ability to consider opposing arguments.
4   Always remember to put the pros and cons of any proposition even though you may favour one side of argument or the other try to be dispassionate and look at matter from attitude of both debtors and creditors.

The first and obvious flaw is that although it is no doubt beneficial for the credit customer to have the liability of his supplier towards him effectively guaranteed by the creditor, there is actually no reason why the credit customer should have this guarantee and the cash, charge card or debit card customer should not. Thus, the customer who has saved up for his purchase and then paid cash has no remedy for the defective goods or services once the supplier has become insolvent, but the credit customer is given such a remedy. Not only does this not encourage thrift and saving up prior to purchase, but it then positively favours the credit customer. When an unbonded travel agent becomes insolvent, it is the cash customer who is penalised and the credit customer who is saved. Yet, the latter is no more deserving than the former.

The second flaw is the fact that there is no limit on s 75 liability.[5] The creditor who supplies only a relatively small amount of credit under a regulated agreement can be held liable under s 75 for unlimited damages. Thus, an oven costing £500 might be paid for by use of a regulated credit card and, because it is defective, might burn down the house causing, say, £100,000 worth of damage. The creditor, who is not in the business of supplying ovens, has nevertheless to pick up the £100,000 bill. It is true that s 75 gives the creditor a right of indemnity against the supplier. However, where the supplier is insolvent, this is of little use, though the credit card company may have a claim against the insolvent supplier's insurers under any relevant third-party liability policy by virtue of the Third Parties (Rights Against Insurers) Act 1930[9] (see *First National Tricity Finance v Ellis* (2004)). Many creditors have the opinion that if it is right for there to be a s 75-type liability, it should be confined to the amount of credit advanced in relation to the transaction in question.[6]

A further flaw in s 75 is in relation to subs (3). This sub-section was intended to prevent creditors being made liable for relatively trivial claims. As drafted, however, it does not work to rule out claims according to their size, but rather according to the cash price attached to the item in question. Thus, there is in s 75(3) a lower figure of £100, the result of which is that if the cash price of the item in question is £100 or less, no s 75 claim can be made.[7] That is so even if the item in question causes a vast amount of damage.

Thus, the defective toaster which burns down the house will not attract s 75 liability, since its cash price will not have exceeded £100. Section 75(3) seems to be encouraging

---

5   Dealing with the points raised in an essay question on a one-by-one basis ensures adds structure and clarity to your analysis.

6   Always remember the role of insurance which often lies behind many disputes in commercial law who should bear the loss.

7   The explanation of why a particular legal principle is not applicable in relation to a question is as important as the explanation of why a particular legal rule is applicable in relation to a question: on the one hand, this is because it narrows your analysis down to what is relevant; on the other hand, this is because it demonstrates understanding.

creditors to give credit for a lot of small items, but not to give a lot of credit for any one item – unless the item costs more than £30,000. The sense of doing this is difficult to see. This is especially so where, in the case of a misrepresentation by the supplier, the debtor may be able to avoid this limitation in s 75 by the simple device of relying upon the deemed agency provision in s 56. Section 56 has no equivalent limitation.[8]

There is a further flaw in the implementation of the policy. It is that, quite apart from the limitation in s 75(3), s 75 does not always work to protect the debtor in circumstances where the supplier is effectively in a joint venture for mutual profit. This is because there are other ways in which the creditor can help to finance the supplier or the supplier's customers without incurring liability under s 75. One of these ways is simply to lend money direct to the supplier. This might, on the one hand, avoid s 75 and, on the other, still leave the creditor reasonably well protected against the risk of the supplier's insolvency by virtue of charges over the supplier's assets granted to the creditor. Another way of arranging the finance is for the finance company to enter into an arrangement with the supplier whereby it is the latter who himself makes the credit agreement with the debtor, but where subsequently the supplier assigns the benefit of the credit agreement to the finance company. Thus, the latter becomes entitled to the receivables (that is, the debtor's repayments) under the credit agreement, but avoids being liable to the debtor. This is because an assignee takes only the benefits of the contract and not the burdens. Of course, where a debtor has a claim under the credit agreement against the supplier, that claim could be used as a set-off against money owed by the debtor (to the assignee, that is, the finance company) and this would then, by a roundabout way, make the finance company 'liable' (that is, by way of set-off) for the supplier's default towards the debtor. That 'liability' would, however, be limited to the amount of credit (and interest) due under the credit agreement.

Thus, there are serious flaws in s 75. It should also be pointed out that there were other 'difficulties' in s 75, which are not least the cross-border implications (for example, those arising out of the use of regulated credit card agreements abroad) and the doubt over the position of the second credit cardholder *vis-à-vis* s 75.[9,b]

The cross-border issue has now been resolved by the House of Lords decision in *Office of Fair Trading v Lloyds TSB* (2007), ruling that s 75 liability does apply where a credit card covered by a regulated agreement is used outside the UK.

The **Consumer Credit Act 2006** which introduced significant reforms to the 1974 regime did not amend or change s 75, which suggests the Government at least is happy with its

----

8   Always draw attention to parallel or related provisions particularly if they do not have a draw back that the provision you are discussing has why the £100 limit in s 56 but not s 75?

9   Drawing an interim-conclusion is another way of signposting the relevant issues and also helps you to structure your answer logically.

operation. Some of the issues discussed here in relation to **s 75** were discussed at a European level as a result of the European Commission's proposal for a revised **Directive on Consumer Credit**. Draft proposals were published in 2002. These proposals suggested a type of connected lender liability (such as that which **s 75** imposes) which: (a) would not extend to credit cards other than store cards; (b) would, apparently, not include claims for consequential loss; and (c) would require the removal of the lower and upper price limits to the application of **s 75** liability.[10] However, a second modified version produced in 2005 dropped any reference to harmonising national rules on connected lender liability. Ultimately **Art 15(3)** of the **EU Consumer Credit Directive 2008/48/EC** permitted the UK to retain the 'joint and several' liability provision in **s 75**, which the UK has done. However in the complex way the UK has superimposed the new EU requirements on top of the existing UK regime even if a claim fails under **s 75** the creditor may face 'secondary liability' under **s 75A** of the **CCA 1974**. Here however the consumer must have attempted to recover damages from the supplier first, though not necessarily having used the courts, before they can pursue the creditor. However this secondary liability will only apply where the cash price of the goods exceeds £30,000 and the linked credit agreement is more than £60,260 and the goods or services acquired are not wholly or predominantly for business purposes. Thus despite strong lobbying by the credit industry, it seems that they will continue to face 'joint and several' liability under **s 75** for the foreseeable future.

(b)(i)

It seems reasonably clear that Betty has a good claim in law against Kitch Kitchens for breach of implied (or express) terms of the contract of supply. This appears to have been a contract for the provision of services or work and materials, with some goods being incidentally supplied. Even so, there are still implied terms as to satisfactory quality and fitness for purpose (**s 4** of the **Supply of Goods and Services Act 1982**).[11] In the case of the waste disposal unit, it appears that there is a breach of the term as to satisfactory quality and, in the case of the oven, a breach of the term as to fitness for purpose, since she must have indicated to Kitch Kitchens the particular purpose (installing it in her kitchen) for which she wanted the oven. So far as the cupboards are concerned, it appears that there has been a breach of the term in **s 13** of the same Act, that the work will be carried out with reasonable care and skill (see *Jones v Callagher t/a Gallery Kitchens and Bathrooms* (2004)).[12] The problem in this case is that it is of no use to Betty that she has a good claim in law against Kitch Kitchens Ltd, because the latter is insolvent.

---

10 Build upon points you have raised previously; this gives your answer structure.
11 Remember consumer credit questions involving goods will nearly always require some awareness of implied terms in **Sale of Goods Act 1979** or **Supply of Goods and Services Act 1982**.
12 Don't state all you know about the area of law in question, remember to focus on the relevant issues – it is as much your ability to apply the relevant legal rules to the question as your knowledge that is assessed.

The issue is what remedies Betty may have against Flash Finance by virtue of the Consumer Credit Act. Section 75 provides that in certain circumstances, the debtor (here, Betty) may bring a claim against the creditor (here, Flash Finance) for breach of contract or misrepresentation by the supplier (here, Kitch Kitchens Ltd). For s 75 to apply, the credit contract must be a regulated debtor–creditor–supplier agreement within s 12(b) or (c). It seems highly likely that the loan agreement satisfies this requirement and falls within s 12(b). It does not fall within s 12(c) since it appears to be an agreement for restricted-use credit, because the loan was to be paid not to Betty, but direct to Kitch Kitchens. The agreement will fall within s 12(b), however, only if it was made under 'arrangements' between Kitch Kitchens and Flash Finance. Since it appears that Kitch Kitchens had a stock of Flash Finance loan proposal forms, it would seem quite likely that there were such arrangements. If there were a commission paid by Flash Finance to Kitch Kitchens (or indeed vice versa), that would be conclusive. Assuming such arrangements exist, Betty has a like claim against Flash Finance as she has against Kitch Kitchens. According to a Scottish case (*United Dominions Trust v Taylor* (1980) but outcome in that case that both the supply contract and linked loan contract could be rescinded simultaneously not followed in *Durkin v DSG Retail Ltd* [2010] CSIH 49 (IH (1 Div) and discussed by Macqueen in 'Faulty goods, rejection and connected lender liablity' Edin LR 2011, 15(1) 111–115),[13] a like claim means that in circumstances where the debtor has a right to rescind the supply contract, the 'like' claim under s 75 is to rescind the loan contract. This case is controversial in the way it reached the result. That, however, is perhaps unimportant in the case of the problem here, since it appears that this being a contract for services (and not a sale of goods contract) the debtor, Betty, will not be seeking to recover all her money paid to Kitch Kitchens, but will wish to make simply a money claim, that is, for damages. There might be some problems if she wanted to reject the physical components of the kitchen in that she may be taken to have 'accepted' them, especially if they have been altered in the fitting, though the fact that three months had elapsed would not seem to amount to 'acceptance of the goods' (see *Jones v Callagher t/a Gallery Kitchens and Bathrooms* (2004)). That claim being a valid legal claim against Kitch Kitchens, Betty is entitled to succeed with it against Flash Finance.

In this sort of situation, it is quite common for the finance company still to expect the debtor to maintain monthly payments under the loan agreement while the other claim is still being contested and, if the debtor ceases to maintain those payments, the finance company will keep sending reminders; and of course there will be default interest, which the finance company will show on each successive statement, though the pressure is less with the bringing into force of s 13 of the CCA 2006 which stipulates that only simple interest can be charged on default sums under regulated consumer credit agreements and not compound interest, which of course involves charging interest on interest. This operates as a clear pressure upon the debtor, who may doubt the likelihood of success

---

13   The reference to academic literature rather than the 'mere' consideration of case law shows not only that you have researched and read more widely but also adds to the criticality of your analysis.

with her claim under s 75. Cautious advice to Betty is therefore to maintain her loan repayments while also pursuing her claim against Flash Finance.

(b)(ii)

Most European Union states did not have the equivalent connected lender liability provisions that the UK had but rather a substituted liability in relation to contracts financed by a credit company where the consumer had failed to get redress from the supplier. If action to get redress from the supplier had failed, action for redress could be taken against the creditor but the debtor always had to take reasonable steps against the supplier first. Article 15(2) of the EU Consumer Credit Directive 2008/48 (CCD) provides for this type of liability. The UK has provided for such an action in those cases falling outside the connected lender liability provision in s 75 of the CCA 1974 but within the scope of the CCD. This is done in s 75A of the CCA 1974.[14] This can be described as the 'linked liability' provision and would only kick in if Betty had failed to get redress from Kitch Kitchens. There are four situations where the section can apply:

❖   the supplier cannot be traced;
❖   the debtor has contacted the supplier but the supplier has not responded;
❖   the supplier is insolvent;
❖   the debtor has taken reasonable steps, which need not include litigation, to pursue the claim against the supplier but has not obtained satisfaction of his claim – satisfaction includes accepting a replacement product or service or other compensation from the supplier in settlement of the claim.[15]

However, this provision will only apply where the cash value of the goods or services is in excess of £30,000 and the linked credit agreement is for credit which does not exceed £60,260 (the upper limit of the Directive converted from euros to sterling at date of UK's adoption of the Directive).[16] Betty is covered here as the cash value of the kitchen is £50,000 and the linked credit agreement for less than £60,020. Neither has Betty seemingly acquired the kitchen 'wholly or predominantly' for business purposes carried on by her – if she had, the protection would not have applied (s 75A(6) of the CCA 1974).

The sole issue that might cause problems is whether the provision of a loan for the acquisition of the kitchen and its fitting is a 'linked credit agreement'. A 'linked credit agreement' means a regulated consumer credit agreement that serves 'exclusively' to finance an agreement for the supply of specific goods or the provision of a specific service and where:

....

14   It is all too easy to overlook recent reforms; many students would have assumed as s 75 not applying meant end of the story and lost marks by not discussing s 75A. You get extra merit for being up to date.
15   This shows where a statute book is useful in an exam. It is helpful for those detailed qualifications to a general liability proposition, in area like this if you can take statute into exam may be a good investment.
16   Considering any potential limitation after outlining and applying the general legal rule to the requirements of the question ensures that your analysis proceeds in a logical way.

(a) the creditor uses the service of the supplier in connection with the preparation or
     making of the credit agreement; OR
(b) the specific goods or provision of a specific service are explicitly specified in the credit
     agreement (s 75A(5) of the CCA 1974).

The question says she signed the Flash Finance loan form at Ktich Kitchen's premises,
which suggests that condition (a) is satisfied and probably condition (b) as well.[17] If this is
the case and she has failed to secure compensation from Kitch Kitchens, and on the facts
she seems to have taken reasonable steps to do so, she can then pursue her claim for
£3,000 against Flash Finance under s 75A of the CCA 1974.

QUESTION 27

Andrew works as a debt adviser in a debt advice centre and has been approached by
several clients in connection with disputes with their credit card company, the Excess
Credit Card Company ('Excess'):

(a) Iain has used his Excess credit card to buy a Persian carpet from a dealer in Morocco
     while on holiday there. He has discovered a number of moth holes in the carpet and
     wishes to reject it on the grounds that it is not of satisfactory quality and recover his
     price and consequential damages. Excess have rejected his claim on the grounds
     that he was abroad when he used the card and has not attempted to pursue his
     claim against the retailer in the first instance. Further as the Moroccan retailer has
     now gone out of business they will not be able to indemnify themselves if they have
     to compensate Iain.
(b) Mark is refusing to pay his outstanding balance of £12,000 on his Excess Credit card
     because Excess cannot supply him with a copy of the original agreement which Mark
     entered into in 1996. Mark has been sent by Excess copies of the standard terms and
     conditions in operation at the time instead.
(c) David has purchased a vintage car for a cash price of £100,000, paying part of the
     price, some £58,000 using his Excess Platinium Super Credit Card. The car has
     frequently broken down and David wishes to reject for breach of s 14 of the Sale of
     Goods Act 1979 and recover his price. The vintage car firm have gone into liquidation
     and were not insured and Excess say as the cash price of the card exceeds £30,000,
     s 75 of the CCA 1974 is inapplicable and they have no joint liability with the retailer
     under the section.
(d) Nan is refusing to pay her credit card balance of £5,000 on the grounds that in 2003
     her Greens Ltd store card, which was operated for Greens by Excess was 'upgraded'

---

17 Remember to relate your analysis to the issues raised/facts outlined by the question; it is the proper
     application of the relevant legal rules to the requirements of the question upon which you are assessed
     not the abstract discussion of the law.

to an Excess Card but she was not sent a copy of the new credit card agreement for her signature.

(e) Suzannah bought a kettle for £60 which was described on the box as 'super efficient and safe to use' with her Excess Credit Card. Due to faulty wiring the kettle causes a fire and Suzannah's kitchen is severly damaged and will cost an estimated £50,000 to restore. Suzannah has no property insurance and is claiming the money from Excess.

How to Answer this Question

❖ Need to consider the operation of connected lender liability provisions under s 75 of the CCA.

❖ Need to consider new 'secondary liability' under s 75A of the CCA.

❖ Need to consider the 'deemed agency' provisions in s 56 of the CCA.

❖ Need to consider the documentation requirements during currency of a credit card running account agreement in s 78.

❖ Need to consider whether upgrading a store card to a credit card amounts to a modifying agreement within s 82 of the CCA and implication of this.

Answer Structure

ANSWER

(a) Does the **Consumer Credit Act** apply to cards used abroad? It has been decided that the Act does apply to regulated agreements governed by English law,[18] as Iain

---

18 Always remember CCA only applies to credit agreements regulated by English law but can apply where sales or services contract is governed by foreign law.

appears to be, where the card is used to purchase goods abroad (*Office of Fair Trading v Lloyds TSB plc* (2007)). A credit card agreement contains what amounts to a standing offer, that is, an offer to supply credit on the terms of the credit card agreement. The offer is accepted *pro tanto* each time an authorized user uses the card to finance a transaction. Liability however is derivative Iain must have a claim either for misrepresentation or breach of contact against the retailer. That would appear to be the case here even if the contract were governed by Moroccan law. If there is such a claim Iain has a *'like claim'* against Excess. There is no requirement on Iain to seek to pursue his claim with the Moroccan retailer before seeking compensation from the Excess. The liability of the credit card company is primary and not secondary under s 75. The credit card company has a statutory right to be indemnified, subject to any agreement to the contrary, under s 75(2). The fact that this right cannot be effectively exercised here is irrelevant to Iain's claim Excess will either have to bear the loss or possibly claim against any insurance they have taken out to meet such a contingency. Excess cannot exclude this liability to Iain by virtue of s 173(1) of the CCA 1974.

(b) Mark's refusal to pay may at least be temporarily justified.[19]

The failure to provide him with, after payment of a small fee, of a copy of a regulated running-account agreement along with such details as are practicable to provide of the current state of the account means that while the default continues the creditor is not entitled to enforce the agreement (s 78(1) and (6)). In *Phoenix Recoveries (UK) v Kotechna* (2011) a creditor had failed to satisfy a debtor's request under s 78(1) for a copy of a credit agreement as it had not, on the evidence, included the original terms and conditions in respect of interest rates then in force. The creditor was accordingly not entitled to proceed to enforce the debt. Though enforcement does not prevent a notice indicating the debtor has defaulted to a credit reference agency (*McGuffick v Royal Bank of Scotland* (2009)). This has become a major problem for some companies with records of original agreements being discarded on lost on mergers of companies etc. There is also no dispensing provision allowing court to either wholly or partially disregard any breach of the provision unlike the case where the original agreement is improperly executed. A large number of claims often instigated by claims management companies have been launched though the courts have not always been sympathetic to debtors seeking to use 'technical defences' to avoid payments clearly due. In *HSBC Bank plc v Brophy* (2011) where the Court of Appeal rejected the argument that a signed and returned credit card application was not a contractual

---

19 Remember questions may well involve separate areas. You cannot always expect a question to focus on a single issue or section.

document and therefore there had been a failure of the credit card agreement regulations.

In *Carey v HSBC Bank plc* (2009) it was common ground that the s78 copy did not need to be a photocopy or other form of literal copy of the executed agreement. However, a creditor also did not need to prove execution of the agreement by reference to the document itself. It could instead satisfy its duty under s78 by providing a reconstituted version of the executed agreement which might be from sources other than the actual signed agreement. The debtor's name and address at the date of the executed agreement had to be provided in the copy but could be provided within the reconstituted copy from whatever source the creditor had of those details. It did not have to take them from the executed agreement itself. A reconstituted copy agreement had to include a heading, names and addresses of the debtor and creditor and any cancellation clause which was applicable to the executed agreement. That information could be provided on a sheet which was separate from the full statement of terms and conditions which also formed part of the reconstituted agreement. Its format should not be such as to mislead the debtor as to what he agreed to. Thus provided Excess can do this they should be able to enforce the credit card agreement.

(c) Excess are correct in asserting that s75 is inapplicable because the cash price of the vintage car exceeds £30,000 (s75(3)(b)).[20] However they have overlooked that as result of the implementation of the **EU Consumer Credit Directive 2008/48/EC** David may have an alternative claim under s75A. Assuming that the purchase was made with the card after 1 February 2011 when the s75A came into force David may be able to recover his price from Excess. The liability of Excess under s75A is secondary; that is in the first instance David must pursue his claim against the retailer but if one of four conditions in s75A(2) is satisfied David may make a claim against Excess:
   (a) that the supplier cannot be traced,
   (b) that the debtor has contacted the supplier but the supplier has not responded,
   (c) that the supplier is insolvent, or
   (d) that the debtor has taken reasonable steps to pursue his claim against the supplier but has not obtained satisfaction for his claim.

It should be noted that under s75A(3) 'reasonable steps' need not include litigation.

The vintage car must have been purchased under a 'linked agreement which is defined in s75A(5) as a regulated consumer credit agreement which serves exclusively to finance an agreement for the supply of specific goods or the provision of a specific service and where—

---

20 Here poor students would stop and move on but important to consider whether any other options open to claimant and would get credit for being up to date with alternative form of secondary liability.

(a)   the creditor uses the services of the supplier in connection with the preparation or making of the credit agreement, or

(b)   the specific goods or provision of a specific service are explicitly specified in the credit agreement.

Under s 75(A)(6) the cash price of the car exceeds £30,000 and the amount of credit advanced is under £60,260 and the vintage car appears not to being purchased wholly or predominantly for business purposes David will be able to make a claim against Excess providing only he has not been able to secure satisfaction of his claim from the retailer.

(d)   Whether Nan can refuse to pay the balance depends on whether the agreement and copy provisions of the **CCA 1974** have been satisfied in relation to the 'upgrading' of her store card to a credit card. In its original form (and assuming that the appropriate formalities were carried out at the initial stage) it was a restricted use debtor-creditor-supplier agreement to finance transactions with Green Stores under ss 11(1)(b) and 12(b)[21] it was then modified to permit the card to be used at any supplier accepting Excess Cards. This would be a 'modifying agreement' under s 82(2) which varies or supplements an earlier agreement – this modified agreement is treated as revoking the earlier agreement and containing provisions reproducing the combined effect of the two agreements. **Reg 7** of the **Consumer Credit (Agreements) Regulations 1983/1553** apply the rules on agreements and copies as to the original principal agreement. This would mean that the agreement is 'improperly executed' under s 61(1)(a) in that an agreement containing all the prescribed terms, in the prescribed form and signed by the debtor in the prescribed manner does not exist. This in turn given that the agreement was entered into before the 6 April 2007 means that the agreement is permanently unenforceable by the creditor by virtue of s 127(3) [*the repeal of s 127(3)–(5) removing the category of permanently unenforceable agreements by s 15 of the **Consumer Credit Act 2006** did not affect agreements entered into before the 6th April 2007*].

The only possibility is for Excess to argue[22] that they had a power of unilateral variation permitting the upgrade of the card from a store to a fully fledged credit card (*Lombard Tricity Finance Ltd v Paton* (1989) CA). There are two problems with this firstly such a wide ranging power might be considered to be 'sham' and also the Office of Fair Trading has argued that such a power is 'unfair' within the terms of the **Unfair Terms in Consumer Regulations 1999** which imposes control on unilateral variation clauses in **Sched 2 para**

---

21   Important in questions concerning consumer credit to get definition of relevant agreement clear – as different parts of the Act apply in different ways to different classifications of agreement.

22   Always consider potential defences but try to keep treatment of these clear and separate so answers are easy to follow.

1(j) and **Para 2(b)** – query the upgrade was for a 'valid reason' and was Nan given the opportunity to dissolve the pre-existing store card? This issue arose in 2003 when Marks and Spencer sought to unilaterally upgrade its customers from a Marks and Spencer store card to a credit card. The OFT has challenged the standard term in the MSFS store card agreement that purported to give Marks and Spencer Financial Services (MSFS) an unrestricted unilateral right to change the terms of the agreement. The OFT considered that this term was legally unfair. MSFS, without accepting the OFT's view, gave the OFT an undertaking that it wiould amend the challenged term to limit its applicability. In particular permitting customers to retain their cards as store cards or to reject the 'upgrade' and to take steps to positively activate their new card if they wanted the upgrade.

The OFT took no further enforcement action at that time. It recognised that there might be advantages to consumers in having the choice of replacing a store card by a credit card with a lower APR as in that case. The OFT also noted that MSFS, in line with principles of responsible lending, has taken care to make a proper credit assessment of individual cardholders being invited to change to the &More credit card and on deciding credit limits. (see OFT Press Notice 128/03, 8 October 2003 'M&S agrees to amend conversion of store cards to credit cards':

http://www.oft.gov.uk/news-and-updates/press/2003/pn_128-03).

(e)   As the cash price of the kettle purchased by Suzannah has a cash price of less that £100 s75 does not apply s75(3)(b). However she may have an alternative claim under the 'deemed agency' provision in s56.[23] The argument would be that the statement on the box constituted 'antecedent negotiations' within s56(1)(c). 'Antecedent negotiations' under s56(4) shall begin then the negotiator and the debtor or hirer first enter into communication (including communication by advertisement) and to include any representations made by the negotiator to the debtor and any other dealings between them. It is suggested the statement on the box although placed there by the manufacturer has been adopted by the retailer and can therefore be deemed to be a 'communication' in the wide sense used in s56. It is suggested the retailer is a 'negotiator' within s56(1)(c). In that he is a 'supplier' in relation to a transaction financed or proposed to be financed by a debtor-creditor-supplier agreement within s12(b) or (c). A credit card agreement is a debtor-creditor-supplier agreement under either of one of these sections given the wide concept of 'arrangements' adopted by the House of Lords in *OFT v Lloyds TSB plc* (2007). The supplier would therefore be deemed to be the agent of Excess and this statutory agency cannot be excluded (s56(3)). This would mean that as the kettle is unsafe this is an actionable misrepresentation under the section and Excess would be liable for

---

23   Common area in connected lender questions to forget related deemed agency provision which can assist claimant – examiners give credit for considering alternative options in making claims

reasonably foreseeable loss flowing from the breach which it is suggested would include damage to Suzannah's kitchen and damages to restore it to its original condition.

Notes

a   This will shortly be replaced by the **Third Parties (Rights Against Insurers) Act 2010** but the position would be the same under the new Act in this respect.

b   For general criticism of the policy behind **s 75**, see: 'Credit cards and section 75: time for a change in the law?', Andrew Campbell (1996) 11 JIBL 527–32 and Bisping, 'The case against **s 75** of the **Consumer Credit Act 1974** in credit card transactions' (2011) JBL [5] 457–474.

General Principles of Agency

INTRODUCTION

The doctrine of privity in contract law normally prevents a person acquiring rights under a contract unless he is a party to it. The long-established exception to that rule is the concept of agency. The most important feature of the relationship created by an agency agreement is that where a contract is concluded by an agent on behalf of a principal, the agent's acts are treated as if they were the acts of the principal and the principal becomes a party to the contract through the agreement. Examiners often set questions dealing with the general concept of agency contracts, either in the form of whole-essay questions or part-essay questions.

A contract of agency is governed by the general law of contract and is subject to the same rules as other contracts. However, unlike other types of contract, there are special terms which are implied into agency contracts, such as the fiduciary relationship between the principal and the agent as a result of which a number of duties are cast on the agent and, similarly, the agent has rights as against the principal. In addition, in relation to one type of agent – the 'commercial agent' – the relationship will be at least partially governed by the **Commercial Agents (Council Directive) Regulations 1993**. These Regulations, deriving from a European Directive, are particularly important in relation to the rights of the agent on termination of the agreement. They apply only to self-employed agents engaged to arrange contracts for the sale or purchase of goods.

The questions in this chapter concentrate on the general principles of agency contracts, and those in Chapter 9 deal with the scope of an agent's authority to bind the principal.

Students should be familiar with the following areas:

- ❖ general concept of agency and its relationship to the doctrine of privity;
- ❖ rights and duties of an agent *vis-à-vis* the principal;
- ❖ ratification – when can it be used and what are its effects;
- ❖ termination of an agency contract;
- ❖ the **Commercial Agents (Council Directive) Regulations 1993**.

QUESTION 28

The duties owed by agents to their principals may or may not be dictated by the express terms of the contracts between them.

▶ Explain the duties of an agent in the context of this statement.

How to Answer this Question

As with any other contract, the express terms of a contract of agency primarily determine the obligations of the parties to it. However, by the very nature of the relationship, the agent stands in a position of trust *vis-à-vis* the principal. A fiduciary relationship therefore exists between them and other important duties are implied into the contract, based on the notion of good faith, save insofar as these are not excluded or modified by the express terms of the contract.

In relation to commercial agents falling within the **Commercial Agents (Council Directive) Regulations 1993**, there is a duty to act 'dutifully and in good faith' which cannot be modified by the contract between principal and agent. Even where an agent acts gratuitously (and therefore there is no question of contractual obligations arising), the agent still owes fiduciary duties and the lack of consideration *per se* is no bar to these arising, and the possibility of a general liability in tort arises.

The following points need to be considered:

❖   express contractual duties determined by the terms of the contract;
❖   fiduciary duties which, if not expressly provided for in the contract, are either implied or enforceable *per se*;
❖   in the case of a gratuitous agent, a general duty of care in tort.

Answer Structure

This diagram shows the main points to consider in your answer, illustrating the way these relate to the commercial agent.

ANSWER

Any contract between a principal and an agent may expressly impose duties on the agent and, in the absence of any relevant express duties, the obligations of the agent are regulated by a number of duties as a matter of law. Even in the absence of a contract, an agent who acts gratuitously owes fiduciary duties to the principal in the law of tort.[1]

Where there is an agency contract, the terms of that contract will generally dictate the internal obligations between the principal and the agent. In relation to commercial agents falling within the **Commercial Agents (Council Directive) Regulations 1993**, however, there is a non-derogable duty on the agent to look after the principal's interests and to act dutifully and in good faith. Subject to this, an agent's duties will include the following.

OBEDIENCE[2]

An agent must obey the principal's lawful instructions and must not exceed his authority. This applies to both paid and gratuitous agents. Where the agent's instructions are ambiguous, however, he will not be liable if he acts on a reasonable interpretation of them (*Weigall v Runciman* (1916); *The Tzelepi* (1991)), although a duty will be imposed on the agent to seek clarification of the instructions.

A paid agent must act according to the terms of the contract and is liable for loss caused either by a failure to act or acts in excess of the authority. In *Turpin v Bilton* (1843), for example, an agent who was instructed to insure his principal's ship but failed to do so was liable in damages to his principal when the ship was lost.

A gratuitous agent is generally under no duty to act so that, albeit liable for exceeding his authority, he cannot be liable for a complete failure to act. There is generally no liability in tort for negligent omissions. However, some academic authorities maintain that liability could arise if the agent does not warn the principal that he has not or does not intend to perform the agency.[3,a] On this basis, a gratuitous agent acting in *Turpin* above would still have been liable to the principal.

CARE AND SKILL

All agents owe a duty of care to their principals to exercise reasonable care and skill in the execution of their authority. A paid agent is expected to exercise care and skill which is

---

1   Don't be reluctant to use the wording of the question in the course of your analysis; this demonstrates that your answer is focused on the relevant issues and also helps you to structure your answer logically.
2   Dealing with the points raised in an essay question on a one-by-one basis adds structure and clarity to your analysis.
3   Showing that you have read more widely than simply learning the basic principles is a good way to attract marks.

usual and proper in the type of business or work for which the agent is employed. An unpaid agent's duty of care arises in tort, and his actions are judged against the skill actually possessed. Whether or not an agent has fulfilled this duty is a question of fact in each case. Any attempt by an agent to exclude or limit liability for failure to exercise care and skill is subject to the **Unfair Contract Terms Act 1977**.

The standard of care required is whatever is reasonable in the circumstances of each case. Where the agent holds himself out as being a member of a profession, the standard of care and skill expected of him is that of a reasonably competent member of that profession, irrespective of the degree of skill he may personally possess. In deciding what care is reasonable, the court will take into account whether or not the agent is paid.

In *Chaudry v Prabhakar* (1988), P, who had recently passed her driving test, asked a friend, A, to buy a car on her behalf, stipulating that the car must not have been involved in an accident.[4] A, who was not a mechanic and acted gratuitously, bought a one-year-old car for P. When P discovered that the car had been badly damaged in an accident, P sued A. The Court of Appeal, taking into account that A acted gratuitously, held that, on the facts, A had failed to exercise reasonable skill and was liable to P.

PERSONAL PERFORMANCE

As a general rule, an agent must personally perform the task because, in every case, the principal places trust in the agent: 'confidence in the particular person employed is at the root of the contract of agency', *per* Thesiger LJ in *De Bussche v Alt* (1878). This is often expressed in the Latin maxim *delegatus non potest delegare*. There are exceptions to the rule, but If the agent delegates duties without authority to do so, the agent is liable to the principal for breach of duty. The principal is not bound by an unauthorised sub-agent's acts unless the agent had apparent authority to delegate and the principal is thereby estopped from denying the want of authority. There are some exceptions to this rule.[5]

Firstly, where the agent is expressly authorised to delegate. In *De Bussche v Alt*, for example, an agent employed to sell a ship at a specified price at one of a number of specified places was unable to do so and obtained the principal's authority to appoint a sub-agent who subsequently sold the ship according to the principal's instructions. This was held to be a permissible delegation by the agent of his authority. Secondly, where the agent has implied authority to do so in the circumstances because of a custom in a

---

4   Outlining the facts of a relevant case is a good way to illustrate the relevant legal rules and thus strengthens your argument / conclusion.
5   Stating exceptions to a particular principle is a good way to show greater knowledge of the area in question.

particular trade or profession. For example, a solicitor practising outside London generally has authority to appoint a London-based solicitor to conduct litigation on his behalf in London courts (*Solley v Wood* (1852)). Thirdly, where the principal is aware, at the time of making the contract of agency, that the agent intends to delegate part or all of his authority and the principal does not raise objections. Fourthly, where the circumstances necessitate delegation, for example, where a company is appointed as an agent, it must delegate performance to its employees since it must act through human agents. Finally, where the task delegated does not require the exercise of discretion, for example signing documents or sending notices. In *Allam v Europa Poster Services* (1968), for example, it was held that an agent who was instructed to revoke certain licences could delegate to his solicitor the task of actually sending the notices of revocation. Estate agents provide a common example where authority cannot normally be delegated. Selling the principal's property is not a purely ministerial act and, should they delegate their task to sub-agents without authority, they are not entitled to commission on a sale effected by the sub-agents.

NO CONFLICT OF INTEREST

This fiduciary duty of good faith is paramount and applies whether or not the agent receives payment. The duty is very strict and applies even where it can be proved that there was no actual conflict of interest. It is enough that there is the possibility of conflict. In *Boardman v Phipps* (1966), for example, where the duty was strictly applied, a solicitor, while acting as agent, acquired information relating to the value of certain shares.[6] Acting in good faith, he used this information for his own benefit after the principal had declined to use it for him. The House of Lords held that the agent was accountable to his principal for the profit made, because the information that he had acquired and used for his own benefit belonged to his principal.

More generally, this duty is reflected in the principles that an agent should not purchase the principal's property nor act for both parties in a transaction. Where, for instance, an agent is instructed to buy property on behalf of the principal and the agent sells his own property to the principal, the agreement reached will be a breach of the duty owed to his principal. This is true even if it is a custom of a particular market (for example, the London tallow market) that agents in that market could sell their own goods to the principal (*Robinson v Mollett* (1875)). In such a situation, the potential for conflict is clear, since a seller's interest is to get the best price, whereas the buyer's is to pay as little as possible. Even if the agent acts fairly and pays a reasonable price, he will be in breach of duty unless there is full disclosure to the principal and the principal consents to the transaction.[b]

---

6   Stating the facts of a particular case can be helpful in explaining a legal principle.

NOT TO MAKE A SECRET PROFIT

An agent must not make a secret profit over and above the agreed commission. Again, this rule is strictly applied and it is irrelevant that the agent acted in good faith or that the principal suffered no loss (see *Boardman v Phipps*). If a secret profit is made and discovered, it may be claimed by the principal (*Imageview v Kelvin Jack* (2009)). The duty applies equally to unpaid agents. In *Turnbull v Garden* (1869), for example, an agent was employed without payment to purchase clothes for his principal's son.[7] He was allowed a trade discount on the transaction by the seller, but sought to charge his principal the full price. The court held that the agent had to account to his principal for the discount that he had received.[c]

NOT TO TAKE A BRIBE

A bribe is a particular form of secret profit and arises where a payment between a third party and an agent is kept secret from the principal. If an agent takes a bribe, the principal is entitled to claim the amount of the bribe as money had and received (*Logicrose v Southend United Football Club* (1988)) or to damages against either the agent or the third party. The principal can also refuse to pay commission to the agent on that transaction (or recover any commission already paid) and summarily dismiss the agent, and can set aside the transaction with the third party.[8] The principal's remedies are cumulative save that, in *Mahesan v Malaysia Government Officers' Co-operative Housing Society Ltd* (1979), the Privy Council held that the principal must choose between recovering the bribe or an action for damages (to prevent the principal receiving a windfall profit). If, however, property constituting or representing the bribe has increased in value, the principal can claim the full value (*Attorney General of Hong Kong v Reid* (1994)).

Furthermore, both parties to the bribe may be liable to prosecution under the **Bribery Act 2010**.

TO ACCOUNT

An agent must keep his principal's property strictly separate from his own and is treated in equity as though he was a trustee of the property.[9] On the termination of the agency, an agent must account for all such property.[d] For example, in *Lupton v White* (1808), it was held that where an agent fails to keep the principal's property separate, the principal is entitled to a charge on the entire mixed property unless the agent is able to establish who owns what.

---

7   The provision of concrete examples is a good way to illustrate the issues raised by the question and demonstrates understanding.

8   Considering options is a good way to attract marks as it shows that you have understood the potential implications of a particular legal rule.

9   As accuracy and clarity of expression are important, the use of clear, precise, technical language will help to gain a good mark.

An agent is also required to keep proper accounts and present these to his principal.

Common Pitfalls

Students need to focus on the question asked. Those who use this question as an excuse to write all they know about the fiduciary duties of agents will not score well.

QUESTION 29

(a)   When is an agent entitled to claim commission?

(b)   Dylan engages Sonya to sell Dylan's 'Supaclean' industrial carpet-cleaning service. The terms of the contract specify that Sonya may only give 14 days' credit to purchasers, and provide for Sonya to be paid 2% commission on all sales arranged by her. Sonya negotiates contracts with Philip and Duncan, incurring considerable travelling and subsistence expenses in order to do so. In her negotiations, Sonya discloses her agency to Philip, but not to Duncan. In addition, Sonya agrees that Duncan can have 30 days' credit. Sonya communicates her dealings to Dylan and Dylan agrees to allow Duncan 30 days' credit. Contracts are entered into between Dylan and Philip, and Sonya and Duncan, Dylan subsequently confirming the latter contract directly with Duncan. Subsequently, a dispute arises between Sonya and Dylan, and Dylan refuses to supply the Supaclean service to Philip and Duncan. She also refuses to have any further dealings with Sonya. Discuss the legal position of the parties involved.

How to Answer this Question

The first part of the question concerns the right of an agent to claim commission. The conditions for such payment at common law are as follows:

- ❖   the agent is acting with the principal's authority;
- ❖   the contract expressly or impliedly provides for commission to be paid;
- ❖   the event has happened on which payment was made conditional;
- ❖   the acts of the agent were the effective cause of that event happening.

The provisions of the **Commercial Agents (Council Directive) Regulations 1993** in relation to the payment of commission to commercial agents will also need to be noted.

The second part of the question deals with an agent's right to claim remuneration and expenses necessarily incurred in the course of her agency. The question also involves a discussion of an agent's rights and liabilities under a contract which she makes on behalf of an undisclosed principal. Finally, we need to consider whether an undisclosed principal may ratify a contract.

Applying the Law

Undisclosed agency	Disclosed agency	Subsequently disclosed agency; agent has actual authority
A ⟷ TP	P ⟷ TP	P ⟷ TP

A can be used by TP

A

This diagram focuses on how to determine the nature of agency in this scenario. Issues of ratification and breach of warranty of authority will also have to be considered.

ANSWER

(A)

The general rule is that an agent is only entitled to commission if that has been agreed with the principal.[10] There are, however, instances where the court will imply a term giving the agent a right to be paid for his services even if there is no express agreement.

If the contract is silent as to *when* commission is payable, the normal intention of the parties is that the agent can claim commission when the contract of sale is concluded, particularly where the agent is acting in the course of a profession or business. As regards commercial agents falling within the **Commercial Agents (Council Directive) Regulations 1993**, the time for payment of commission is dealt with by **reg 10**. In the absence of any more favourable agreement, commission will be payable when either the principal or the third party has 'executed the transaction', and at the latest when the third party has executed his part of the transaction (or should have done if the principal had executed his part as he should have). At common law, it is only rarely, however, that a court will interfere where to do so varies or is contrary to the express terms of the agency contract. For example, in *Kofi Sunkersete Obu v Strauss & Co Ltd* (1951), the contract provided for the agent to receive £50 per month as expenses but that the scale of commission was solely at the company's discretion.[11] The Privy Council in that case was not prepared to intervene to determine the rate and basis of the commission that the agent claimed he had earned.

The principal's duty to pay commission only arises where the agent has earned it.[12] If the agent acts contrary to instructions, therefore, under common law, no right to commission

---

10 Proceeding from the general rule to specific points is a good way to structure your answer in a logical manner; it also demonstrates your knowledge and understanding.

11 Providing details of relevant cases demonstrates deeper knowledge and substantiates your argument.

12 Proceed in a logical manner; this attracts a higher mark.

will arise. For example, in *Marsh v Jelf* (1862), an auctioneer was employed to sell property by auction and was held not to be entitled to commission when he sold the property by private contract. If the agent is in breach of instructions under the contract of agency, but a contract of sale has been concluded between the principal and a third party, the agent may still be entitled to commission if her breach was done honestly and in good faith (but she does forfeit her commission if she acted in bad faith).[e] As regards a commercial agent payable by commission, the right will only be lost if a contract concluded between the principal and a third party is not executed for a reason for which the principal is not to blame (for example frustration, or where the third party withdraws) (**reg 11** of the **Commercial Agents (Council Directive) Regulations 1993**). The Regulations make no provision for the right to commission to be lost as a result of the agent acting contrary to instructions, even where this is in bad faith. The agent will of course be in breach of the duty of good faith, and if this has resulted in loss to the principal, compensation could be sought, but commission cannot be withheld on this basis.[13]

An agent will only earn her commission when she has been the direct or effective cause of the event upon which the principal has agreed to pay commission. The relevant phrase in the **Commercial Agents (Council Directive) Regulations** is where a contract 'has been concluded as a result of [the agent's] action' (**reg 7**). It is to be assumed that this will be interpreted in the same way as 'effective cause'. The question of causation is ultimately a question of fact in the absence of judicial definition of 'effective cause'. If some event breaks the chain of causation between the agent and the event on which payment of commission depends, then the agent will not be entitled to commission. Thus, in *Coles v Enoch* (1939), A was employed to find a tenant for P's property. T overheard a conversation between A and an interested party and, although A only gave T a general description of the location, T found the property himself and made an offer directly to P which was accepted. The court held that A was not entitled to commission since his actions had not been the direct cause of T's agreement with P.[14]

A commercial agent may also be able to claim commission in relation to contracts between the principal and a customer previously introduced by the agent, even though the agent has not taken any action in relation to the later contracts (**reg 7(1)(b)** of the **Commercial Agents (Council Directive) Regulations 1993**).

In some cases, an agent will be entitled to commission where the principal wilfully breaks his contract with a third party whom the agent has introduced and whom the

---

13 Providing clear and complete explanations not only helps you to properly apply the law to the requirements of the question, it also demonstrates your knowledge. Remember that accuracy is an important assessment factor.
14 The inclusion of a concrete example is a good way to substantiate your argument by showing the practical implications; as such, it demonstrates understanding.

principal has accepted. In *Alpha Trading Ltd v Dunnshaw-Patten Ltd* (1981), a principal was introduced to a buyer for a quantity of cement. The principal accepted the introduction and contracted with the buyer accordingly. In order to take advantage of a rising market, the principal decided not to perform the contract of sale (preferring instead to pay damages for breach of contract). The agent claimed damages for lost commission. The Court of Appeal held that the agent was entitled to commission because it was an implied term of the agency contract that the principal would not deprive the agent of his commission by breaking the contract with the third party. As noted above, this common law principle also operates under reg 11 of the Commercial Agents (Council Directive) Regulations 1993. If a contract is not performed for a reason for which the principal is to blame, the commercial agent is still entitled to commission.

Where a person is appointed 'sole agent', he is entitled to be paid even if the sale is not effected by him but by some other agent.^{f}

(B)

SONYA'S POSITION *VIS-À-VIS* DYLAN

Sonya's position here depends on applying the rules relating to an agent's rights against her principal. These are: the right to be remunerated; the right to be indemnified for expenses properly incurred; and the right to a lien over items of the principal's property in her possession.[15]

Because the contracts negotiated by Sonya are for the supply of a service rather than the sale of goods, the Commercial Agents (Council Directive) Regulations 1993 will not apply to this situation.[16] The precise conditions to the right of remuneration will therefore depend on the terms of the agency contract but, in essence, the agent must have acted within the scope of her authority and her acts must have been the effective cause of the event she was employed to bring about. Whether or not the agent's acts were the 'effective cause' will be a question of fact in each case.

In the case of the contract with Philip, Sonya has fulfilled the criteria for payment and is entitled to her commission.

---

15 Pointing out that you are going to discuss / analyse something at a later stage in your answer is a good idea for two reasons: first, it gives you more time to focus on the relevant issues rather than having to constantly repeat yourself and thus wasting valuable time; second, it might also enhance the readability of your argument and shows a certain degree of planning ahead on your part.

16 The explanation of why a particular legal principle is not applicable in relation to a question is as important as the explanation of why a particular legal rule is applicable in relation to a question: on the one hand, this is because it narrows your analysis down to what is relevant; on the other hand, it demonstrates understanding.

Unless excluded from doing so by her contract with Dylan (of which there is no evidence), Sonya can also claim her expenses from Dylan in relation to the contract with Philip, since these have been properly incurred in the performance of the agency. The right to indemnity covers all expenses and liabilities necessarily incurred by the agent while acting within her actual authority. Furthermore, should Sonya be in lawful possession of property or documents of title belonging to Dylan, she may protect her rights by exercising a lien[g] over them for unpaid commission and expenses.

The position in relation to the contract with Duncan is more problematic. Sonya exceeded her authority by giving Duncan 30 days' credit. Where an agent acts outside her authority, she is generally not entitled to commission, even though her principal may be bound by the transaction. Although Dylan purported to ratify the contract, at law, an undisclosed principal cannot do so (*Keighley Maxsted & Co v Durant* (1901)). In that case, the agent entered into a contract for the purchase of wheat at a price in excess of the limit on behalf of himself and his principal.[17] The agent did not disclose to the seller of the wheat his intention to contract on the principal's behalf as well as his own. Later, the principal purported to ratify the agent's act. The House of Lords unanimously held that an undisclosed principal cannot ratify. It seems therefore that whatever the position as between Duncan and Dylan or Duncan and Sonya, Sonya is not entitled to commission on the contract made with Duncan.[18]

As for Sonya's expenses, in order to render Dylan liable to indemnify her, she must have acted within the scope of Sonya's authority. For the same reasons as above, Sonya will not be entitled to claim for her expenses because she has acted in breach of her instructions.

SONYA'S POSITION *VIS-À-VIS* PHILIP AND DUNCAN

Where an agent acts with authority and names or sufficiently identifies the principal in such a way that it is clear to the third party that the agent is acting as such, the contract is made between the principal and the third party, and the agent drops out of the transaction entirely. This is Sonya's position with regard to Philip – she incurs neither rights nor liabilities on the contract made between Philip and Dylan.[19]

In relation to Duncan, Dylan's purported ratification of Sonya's actions is without legal effect, because a principal can only ratify if he was identified at the time the contract was

---

17   It is a good idea to provide details of the cases you cite as it supports your argument by illustrating the points you have just made.
18   Remember to draw conclusions from your analysis; this evidences your understanding of how to apply the law.
19   Remember to relate your analysis to the issues raised / facts outlined by the question; it is the proper application of the relevant legal rules to the requirements of the question upon which you are assessed not the abstract discussion of the law.

made (*Keighley Maxsted & Co v Durant* (1901)). Thus, the position is exactly the same as it was when the contract was made – Duncan thought the contract was made with Sonya and, therefore, Sonya is contractually liable to Duncan. No question of breach of warranty of authority arises here, because Sonya was, at law, the principal when the contract was entered into. It is clear that an agent is personally liable on a contract where it has been negotiated on behalf of an undisclosed principal. If the agent is unable to supply the Supaclean service under the contract made personally with Duncan, Sonya will be liable to pay damages for breach of that contract.

DYLAN'S POSITION *VIS-À-VIS* PHILIP AND DUNCAN
Once again, the position in relation to Philip is straightforward. Sonya acted within her authority and identified Dylan as her principal; the contract was therefore solely between Dylan and Philip. Thus, if Dylan refuses to supply the Supaclean service to Philip, he is in breach of this contract and Philip has a right of action against Dylan alone. In relation to Duncan, Dylan is able to rely on the rule in *Keighley Maxsted & Co v Durant* (1901) that an undisclosed principal cannot ratify.

QUESTION 30
To what extent is it true to say that, once an agent has brought his principal and a third party into a contractual relationship, the agent drops out, and has no rights or liabilities as against the third party?

How to Answer this Question
This question requires you to know, and to explain, the exceptions to the general rule that an agent is neither liable under, nor entitled to enforce, a contract he makes on behalf of his principal. It goes a little further than that, however, in that there are some actions which may be taken by the third party against the agent which are not strictly speaking based on the contract. Examples are liability on a collateral contract, or liability for breach of the implied warranty of authority. The issues to be discussed are:

- intention to contract personally;
- custom;
- undisclosed principal;
- principal non-existent;
- collateral contract;
- implied warranty of authority.

It may also be useful to say a little about the power of the third party to choose whom to sue in a situation where both principal and agent may be potentially liable.

Applying the Law

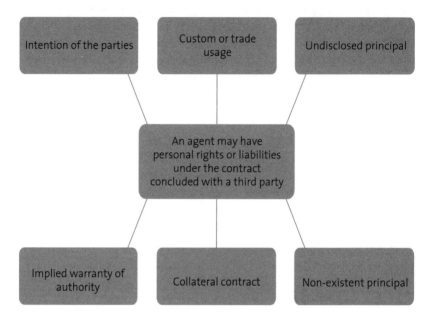

ANSWER

There is no doubt that it is true to say that, in the normal course of events, once the principal and the third party have made a binding contract, the agent has no further rights or liabilities against the third party.[20,h] The agent may, of course, have outstanding claims on, or obligations towards, the principal, but that is a separate issue, arising from their continuing relationship rather than the specific contract which has resulted from the agent's activities. It is also true, however, that, in certain situations, the agent will have rights and liabilities either alongside, or in place of the principal, and it is to those exceptions which we now turn. Some of them relate to rights and liabilities on the contract itself; some are independent of the contract.

The first exception which must be considered is where the parties themselves intend that the agent should have personal rights or liabilities. At one time, much stress seemed to be placed on the exact form in which the contract was signed, for example, to sign 'as

20 Don't be reluctant to use the wording of the question in the course your analysis, this demonstrates that your answer is focused on the relevant issues and also helps you to structure your answer logically.

solicitors' left the agent liable (*Burrell v Jones* (1819)), whereas to sign 'on behalf of' or '*per pro*' was taken to indicate an intention that the agent should not be liable. The more recent approach, set out by Brandon J in *The Swan* (1968), suggests that is a question of looking carefully at the contract and the surrounding circumstances to try to determine the intention of the parties.[21,i] *The Swan* involved a one man company, JD Rodger Ltd, which had hired a boat belonging to JD Rodger himself, who was a director of the company. The company gave instructions, through JD Rodger, for repairs to be carried out. It was held that, in all the circumstances, although the order for the work had been signed simply as 'Director' (which carried no implication of personal liability),[j] JD Rodger, the agent, was personally liable. It was natural for the ship repairers to assume that the ship owner would accept personal liability.

By way of contrast, in *The Santa Caterina* (1977), the defendants requested the claimants to supply bunkers to the ship, *Santa Caterina*.[22] The claimants forwarded the invoice to the defendants who denied liability on the basis that they had requested the bunkers as agents of the time charterers of the ship. The Court of Appeal held that, since on the facts the claimants *knew* the defendants were agents, the onus was on the claimants to introduce evidence to enable an inference to be drawn that the defendants were personally liable. In the absence of such evidence, the court held the agents not personally bound by the contract.

It is also clear that, if there is a custom or trade usage (for example, in the tallow trade: *Thornton v Fehr* (1935)) that agents are personally liable or entitled, the courts will give effect to it, provided that it is consistent with the express terms of the contract, and the surrounding circumstances.

The rights and liabilities of the principal and agent against third parties may differ according to whether the agency is disclosed or undisclosed. Agency is disclosed where the agent reveals that he is acting as an agent.[k] Agency is undisclosed where the agent does not reveal the fact of agency at all and appears to be acting on his own behalf. Where the principal is undisclosed, then it is only fair that the third party, who thinks that the agent is the other party, should be able to take action against the agent (*Sims v Bond* (1833)). Once this is established, it must also be fair to allow the reciprocal right to the agent (*Siu Yin Kwan v Eastern Insurance* (1994)).

There may also be rights and liabilities where there is, in fact, no principal standing behind the agent. This might occur in two ways. It may be that the agent is, in fact, the

....

21 Stating by whom or how (*obiter* or *ratio*) a particular legal principle was stated in a case demonstrates a deeper knowledge and is likely to attract additional marks.

22 The consideration of possible alternative arguments makes your answer stand out from the rest and demonstrates both deeper knowledge and understanding.

principal and is simply pretending to act as an agent. Secondly, the principal may not be in existence at the time the contract is made.

If the agent is simply pretending to be acting for a principal (real or imaginary), while really acting on his own behalf, then there is no doubt that he will be liable on the contract. He will also be able to enforce the contract provided that he gives due notice of the fact that he was acting on his own behalf, and the contract is not one where the personal characteristics the other party are important, as they would be, for example in an employment contract, or an underwriting contract (*Collins v Associated Greyhound Racecourses Ltd* (1930)).[l]

More difficulty can arise where the principal was not in existence at the time of the contract. This can happen in relation to contracts made on behalf of a company which has yet to be incorporated. The common law approach was demonstrated by *Kelner v Baxter* (1866) where it was held that the promoters were personally liable for the contract. This has now been given statutory force by **s 51** of the **Companies Act 2006**. The section deals with liability, rather than ability to enforce. At common law, the only authority in this area was *Newborne v Sensolid* (1954) where the decision against allowing the agent to enforce turned on a very pedantic argument about the precise form of the signature on the contract.[m] This kind of technical argument has been disapproved in later cases, and in particular by the Court of Appeal in *Phonogram v Lane* (1982). The balance of opinion seems to be that, following the statutory intervention noted above, the agent should be able to sue as well as being liable, where a contract is made on behalf of a company not yet incorporated.

The situations we have looked at so far have involved the agent being liable on the contract itself.[23] There are two situations, however, in which the agent may have a separate type of liability to the third party. The first is where there is a collateral contract between the agent and the third party. The kind of situation where this could arise is exemplified by the case of *Andrews v Hopkinson* (1957). The claimant wanted to acquire a car on hire purchase. The dealer said 'It's a good little bus. I would stake my life on it'. The claimant entered into a hire purchase contract with a finance company for the car, arranged through the dealer. When the car turned out to be defective, it was held that the claimant, although, at first sight, having no contractual remedy against the dealer, could in fact sue him on the basis of a collateral contract. At the time, the dealer was in fact held not to be the agent of the finance company, but that has now been changed by statute.[n] The case illustrates how a statement made by an agent which encouraged the third party to enter into the contract could make the agent liable for breach of a collateral contract.[24]

---

23 Proceeding from the general to the specific or to exceptions is a good way to structure your answer in a logical manner; it also demonstrates your knowledge and understanding.

24 Where the question relates to practical problems, emphasise the practical aspects of the question. This shows that you are focused on the relevant issues.

The final way in which the agent may be liable to the third party is for breach of the implied warranty of authority. This will occur where the agent has held himself out as having authority from the principal, when in fact he does not. Of course, in some circumstances, the principal may nevertheless be liable for the contract on the basis of usual or apparent authority. If the principal is not liable, however, the agent will be liable for breach of this implied warranty. The remedies that the third party will be able to recover, however, are limited to what could in practice have been recovered from the principal. Thus, if the principal is insolvent, it may not be worth suing the agent for breach of the implied warranty.

The existence of the warranty does not depend on the agent's awareness of the lack of authority. This was established in *Collen v Wright* (1857) and taken to its logical extreme in *Yonge v Toynbee* (1910).[25] In this case, the warranty was held to operate against a solicitor who had continued to act for a client who, unknown to the solicitor, had become mentally incapacitated (which had the automatic effect of terminating the solicitor's authority). The fact that the solicitor had acted in good faith throughout was regarded as irrelevant.

A final issue which may need consideration is the position where the third party has the possibility of suing either the agent or the principal. Judgment cannot, of course, be enforced against both, but supposing judgment has been obtained against the principal, who turns out to be unable to pay. Can the third party then sue the agent in respect of the same loss? Or does he have to make a choice at an earlier stage. The rules are not very clear. It used to be the case that once judgment has been obtained against either principal or agent, that precluded any action against the other. That was changed, however, by the **Civil Liability (Contribution) Act 1978**, so that there is no longer any automatic effect of this kind. In all situations now, the test is whether the third party has 'elected' to sue one party. If so, this will bar any action against the other. The problem is in deciding what amounts to an 'election'. In *Clarkson Booker Ltd v Andjel* (1964), it was held that what was required was a 'truly unequivocal act'. It might have been thought that the institution of proceedings was such an act, but the Court of Appeal thought that this was only *prima facie* so. The election to be binding must be made with knowledge of all relevant facts. In the case before them, the third party had issued a writ against the principal, but had subsequently discovered that the principal was insolvent. It was held that, because they were not in possession of the full facts, the issue of the writ against the principal was not a binding election. Proceedings could be started against the agent. The question of the precise requirements for an election remains unclear.

As we have seen, there is a variety of ways in which the agent may have rights against, and liabilities towards, a third party. Most of the rules seem to operate in a reasonably

---

25 Providing details of relevant cases demonstrates deeper knowledge and substantiates your argument.

satisfactory way. Some criticism might be made, however, of the rather strict approach to the implied warranty of authority. Moreover, as has just been pointed out, the rules relating to 'election' are in considerable need of clarification.[26]

QUESTION 31

'Agents are in a vulnerable position in relation to their principals and, accordingly, stand in need of protection. The Commercial Agents (Council Directive) Regulations 1993 has gone some way towards providing agents with an appropriate level of protection, but much more remains to be done.'

Critically evaluate this statement and, in particular, consider the contribution made by the Commercial Agents (Council Directive) Regulations to the protection of an agent.

How to Answer this Question

This is a straightforward question which simply requires you to demonstrate a good understanding of the 1993 regulations. Topics which will need to be covered are:

- ❖ definition of a 'commercial agent';
- ❖ duties of a commercial agent as regards the principal;
- ❖ duties of the principal as regards the agent, including the payment of commission;
- ❖ rights of termination, including the agent's right to compensation or indemnity.

There is some case law on the regulations, most of which deals with the issue of compensation. The case of *Lonsdale v Howard and Hallam* (2007) will need to be mentioned.

Answer Structure

---

26 Finishing your essay with a conclusion ensures completeness of your analysis; this should summarise your findings in a clear and succinct manner. Don't introduce new arguments here.

ANSWER

The **Commercial Agents (Council Directive) Regulations 1993** were introduced to give effect to a European directive intended to provide protection for a particular type of agent, and to ensure equivalent treatment across the European Union. In England, the regulations sit alongside the common law, supplementing it in some areas and replacing it in others. In general, an agent covered by the regulations is better protected as regards relations with the principal than under the common law. The regulations do not affect the relationships between principal or agent and third parties with whom the agent negotiates.

The regulations only apply to a particular type of agent, described in reg 2 as a 'self-employed intermediary who has continuing authority to negotiate the sale or purchase of goods' for a principal.[27] The regulations do not, therefore, apply to agents who are employed by the principal, or who act for a single transaction, or who do not act in relation to sale of goods contracts. In addition, the regulations specifically exclude company officers, partners and insolvency practitioners from their scope. They are therefore limited in scope, and there are many agents who in the broadest sense might be regarded as 'commercial' but who will fall outside the regulations. Their relationships with their principals continue to be governed solely by the common law.

The duties of the commercial agent as regards the principal are set out in reg 3. Overall, the duty is to 'look after the interests of his principal and to act dutifully and in good faith'. This seems to add little to the common law duties to follow instructions and to comply with an agent's fiduciary obligations (for example, to avoid conflicts of interest, not to make a secret profit).[28] There are two specific duties mentioned in reg 2, however, which seem to go a little further. The first is to 'make proper efforts' to negotiate and conclude transactions. This seems to amount to a duty of 'due diligence', expecting the agent to be rather more pro-active than the common law would require. The second obligation is to communicate 'all necessary information' to the principal. This has no equivalent under the common law. Again, it is requiring the agent to be pro-active in providing information, rather than the common law approach of prohibiting the concealment of relevant information (for example, as regards secret profits).

Turning to the duties of the principal in relation to the agent, reg 4 sets out some general duties which mirror those imposed on the agent under reg 3.[29] Thus, the principal is also required to act 'dutifully and in good faith' in his dealings with the agent. There is no parallel to this under the common law, where the principal's main general obligation is simply to act in accordance with the contract. More specific duties relating to information

---

27 You need to provide an explanation of the relevant legal rules; without such explanation, it is more difficult for you to properly apply the law to the requirements of the question and thus also more difficult to demonstrate your knowledge and understanding.

28 You need to evaluate the law, especially when dealing with a question that asks you to 'critically analyse'. This means that you need to be prepared to challenge the assumptions made by the question.

29 Addressing each of the issues raised by the question ensures that your analysis is thorough and proceeds in a logical and structured manner.

and documentation are, however, set out in the rest of **reg 4**. These require, first, that the principal should obtain for (and presumably communicate to) the agent, the information 'necessary for the performance of the agency contract'. This is very general, and the precise limits of the information are not clear, though it will obviously cover practical information such as the details of prospective buyers or sellers. There is also a specific obligation to notify the agent if the volume of transactions appears to be going to be significantly lower than the agent could have expected. Finally, the principal must inform the agent of any action taken in relation to a transaction arranged by the agent. Thus, the agent must be told whether the principal has accepted or refused the transaction, or not executed it. These actions have potential consequences for the agent's remuneration, and as regards the agent's relationship with the third party with whom the transaction has been negotiated, and, therefore, it is desirable that the agent should have this information. The common law does not impose any such obligations on a principal.[30]

Similarly, the final obligation contained in **reg 4** has no equivalent under the common law. This is that the principal must provide the agent with the relevant documentation relating to the goods concerned. This is an unexceptional and uncontroversial duty (which might indeed be implied by the common law on the basis of 'business efficacy'). If the agent is to deal with goods on behalf of the principal, relevant documentation necessary to the transaction (for example, documents of title, customs clearance) must be made available. Breach of any of these obligations (which cannot be changed by the contract between principal and agent) will amount to a breach of contract by the principal – but the regulations do not provide for any specific remedies.

The most important obligation is for the principal to remunerate the agent. The obligation to do so is at common law regulated by the contract between the principal and agent, and that largely remains the case in relation to commercial agents, except that where the contract is silent as to payment the regulations provide that the agent is to be paid 'reasonable remuneration', which is not necessarily the common law position (*Kofi Sunkersette Obu v Strauss & Co* (1951)).[31] Where the agent is paid wholly or partly on the basis of commission, however, the regulations contain some provisions (in **regs 7–12**) as to how this is to be calculated and paid (though the rate of commission is left to the parties).

The entitlement to commission will arise when a transaction has been concluded 'as a result of [the agent's] action'. Presumably, this will be approached in the same way as the question of whether the agent's actions were the 'effective cause' of the transaction under the common law. The regulations also give the agent the right to commission, however, in two situations where there has not been any direct involvement in negotiating a transaction (**reg 7**). Both apply for as long as the agency contract between

---

30 Simplicity and clarity of expression are more likely to attract a good mark than highly complex statements - be accurate in what you are saying however.

31 Showing an awareness of the exceptions to the general rule is a good way to attract additional marks as it demonstrates knowledge.

agent and principal subsists. The first is where the principal concludes a transaction with a third party previously 'acquired' by the agent as a customer for transactions of the same kind. So, once a customer has been found by the agent, all subsequent transactions with the principal raise the possibility of commission. Secondly, where the agent has exclusive rights in a particular geographical area, or with a specific group of customers, the agent will be entitled to commission on all transactions of the relevant type entered into by the principal with customers from that area or group. Neither of these rights would apply under the common law unless specifically provided for in the agency contract.

The regulations also contains provisions relating to transactions completed after the termination of the agency (**reg 8**). For example, where an order is received prior to termination, though the transaction is not concluded until after termination, the agent may be entitled to commission. In addition, commission may also be recovered where a transaction is mainly attributable to the agent's efforts, and is entered into within a 'reasonable period' of the termination of the agency. The language here is rather vague, and, as yet, there has been no case law on it. It clearly goes further than the common law, but the precise scope of the agent's rights is difficult to determine without some clarification of the terms used in the regulations.[32]

Regulation 10 contains detailed provisions as to when commission becomes due, and by when it should be paid. These override any common law rules, or anything in the agency contract which is less favourable to the agent. They mean that there should not be undue delay in paying an agent his or her commission.

The right to commission on a concluded transaction is lost in only one circumstance – when the transaction is not executed for a reason for which the principal is not to blame (for example, frustration, or withdrawal by the third party) (**reg 11**). The regulations make no provision for the right to commission to be lost as a result of the agent acting contrary to instructions, even where this is in bad faith. The agent will, of course, be in breach of the duty of good faith, and, if this has resulted in loss to the principal, compensation could be sought, but commission cannot be withheld on this basis.

Finally, in relation to commission, there are obligations imposed by **reg 12**, going beyond anything that would be implied under common law, for the principal to supply information to the agent in order to allow him or her to check what commission is due.

As has been seen, the provisions so far discussed supplement the common law in various ways and, to some extent, supersede it.[33] The most significant difference, however, is in relation to the payment of compensation on termination of the agency agreement. Under the common law, this is governed by general contractual principles, so that what the agent will recover, even if the agency has been terminated in breach of contract, will

....

32 Pointing out ambiguities in the law ensures completeness of your answer and demonstrates your understanding.

33 Build upon points you have raised previously; this gives your answer structure.

normally be based simply on the rules governing the assessment of contractual damages. The regulations take a very different approach, however.

First, as regards termination by notice, the regulations specify minimum periods for such notice, which will override anything less favourable contained in the agency contract (reg 15). The most important provisions, however, are contained in reg 17, which deals with the rights to compensation or indemnity where the contract is terminated (other than as a result of the fault of the agent (reg 18)). An agent wishing to make a claim under these provisions must give notice within one year of the termination of the agency. It was held in *Hackett v Advanced Medical Computer Systems Ltd* (1999) that no particular formality is required. A letter which gave a clear indication of an intention to seek compensation was sufficient, even if it did not specify the regulations which would be relied on.

Regulation 17 provides for the agent to seek recompense on an 'indemnity' basis, or 'compensation'. Unless the agency contract specifies otherwise, however, the compensation, rather than the indemnity, approach will be taken. The European origins of these remedies are shown in the fact that the indemnity approach is derived from the German system whereas the compensation approach follows the French system. Under reg 17, if the agency contract term specifies that the agent is entitled to an indemnity, then in money terms, this is calculated as one year's commission. If the agency contract does not specify whether an indemnity or compensation is payable, reg 17 provides that an agent has the right to compensation. However, the regulations do not give any guidance as to how much compensation is payable. For years, courts have been grappling with this.[34] Bearing in mind that the reasoning behind the Council Directive is to protect commercial agents, the European Commission published a report recommending the French approach, which is that two years' gross commission (based on the average earnings of preceding years) be paid. Scottish courts have followed this French approach and although the decisions are not binding on English courts, some English cases have awarded agents compensation under reg 17 of two years' gross commission. The House of Lords has now made the English position much clearer. In *Lonsdale v Howard & Hallam* (2007), Mr Lonsdale was a commercial agent selling ladies shoes for 13 years. The principal company's business declined, so it sold its brand name to a competitor. The new company employed most of the principal's agents but not Mr Lonsdale. Instead, Lonsdale was offered £7,500 compensation under reg 17. Lonsdale argued the two-year approach and said that he had earned approximately £12,000 per year. No expert valuation was given in court. The court awarded £5,000 in compensation (indeed, less than what Lonsdale had been offered). Lonsdale appealed. The House of Lords dismissed the appeal, because, on termination, an agent suffers loss of goodwill attaching to the agency business, which the court had valued at £5,000.

Goodwill can be traded (in same way as businesses are sold). In *Lonsdale*, the court said that compensation under reg 17 should be based on the value of agency business, that is,

....

34 Consider existing difficulties. This demonstrates your awareness and will attract a higher mark.

the value of goodwill at the date of termination. The value is whatever a notional buyer might pay for the agency business. In *Lonsdale*, since the principal's business was in financial difficulty and was thus terminating the agent's contract, the value of the agency business to a notional buyer was small because the commission-earning power was small. The result of *Lonsdale* is a more flexible approach to the calculation of compensation under **reg 17**. Of course, parties will need to seek accountants' advice as to the value of an agency business, but this would be less rigid than the French approach of two years' gross commission. The two-year rule is such an arbitrary approach. It is surely better for the court to take into account the facts of an individual case.

Potentially significant is the more recent High Court decision in *Michael McQuillan, Lorna McQuillan v Darren McCormick, Wizzeweb Limited, Pandora Jewelry Ltd*.[35] When the agency was terminated, the agents claimed for compensation under **reg 17**. Each party instructed its own expert and the experts ultimately agreed that the valuation of the business was some £342,895. The Judge declined to adopt this figure on the basis that the agency was terminable on one year's notice on either side. He held that it was unlikely that any potential purchaser would pay more than one year's income stream for it. The experts had determined that the annual income stream was £149,000, and so the Judge awarded **reg 17** compensation of £150,000. The judge clearly based his decision on the notice period on which the agency could be terminated. This is not a factor that was identified either in the *Lonsdale* case or in the regulations themselves.

Although *McQuillan* is a High Court decision and thus not binding authority, it will be of persuasive value. This decision is perhaps more in keeping with the general approach of the English courts to determine loss-based compensation. If followed, it could represent a shift in the balance of protection offered to agents on termination. It would mean that the compensation under **reg 17** could be capped by the termination notice period of the agency agreement. Where there is no express provision for notice periods, as mentioned above, the regulations specify a minimum period of notice. Depending on the duration of the agency contract, the notice period is somewhere between one and three months. Thus, an agent whose agency is terminated on, say, three months' notice might find his compensation under **reg 17** capped at a sum equivalent to only three months' net profit.[o]

As discussed above, under **reg 17**, if the agency contract term specifies that the agent is entitled to an indemnity, this is calculated as one year's commission. If the agency contract does not say whether an indemnity or compensation is payable, **reg 17** provides that an agent has the right to compensation. Previously, it was often thought that providing an indemnity on termination would produce a more certain outcome for the principal. The impact of *McQuillan* may be that principals will prefer the compensation option combined with the minimum notice period under **reg 15**. It will be interesting to see how the *McQuillan* principle is applied.

....

35 The reference to more current cases shows that your knowledge goes beyond the basics; it also demonstrates that you have read more widely and will make your answer stand out from the rest.

In conclusion, it is the case that the common law is still important in relation to many aspects of commercial agency agreements.[36] In certain areas, however, particularly in relation to the information to be provided to agents, the payment of commission, and the consequences of termination, the European approach set out in the 1993 regulations operates to provide rather more protection for the agent than would otherwise be the case.

Notes

a   *Hedley Byrne & Co Ltd v Heller & Partners Ltd* (1964) suggests that liability will be imposed for loss caused by a failure to warn the principal where the agent had voluntarily assumed such a responsibility, although the point remains undecided in English law.

b   Where an agent deals with the principal in breach of his duty, the principal may rescind the contract. His right to rescission subsists until the breach is actually discovered. (In *Oliver v Court* (1820), the principal was able to rescind 13 years after the transaction.)

c   See also *Hippisley v Knee Bros* (1905), where the court found that although the agent, acting in good faith, was in breach of duty, he was allowed to keep his commission on the transaction. Similarly, in *Boardman v Phipps* (1966), the agent was allowed some reimbursement for his expenses.

d   In recent years, sellers of goods have increasingly sought to rely on reservation of title clauses in their contracts of sale by making the buyer the seller's 'agent'. In practice, courts are reluctant to require such buyers to act as true agents in the sense of owing fiduciary duties, preferring that the agent should be a debtor to the principal.

e   See also *Hippisley v Knee Bros* (1905), where the court found that although the agent, acting in good faith, was in breach of duty, he was allowed to keep his commission on the transaction. Similarly, in *Boardman v Phipps* (1966), the agent was allowed some reimbursement for their expenses.

f   This takes the form of damages for breach of the term that he should be the 'sole' agent.

g   Agents normally exercise a particular lien, that is, the agent is entitled to retain the principal's property until debts relating to that property are discharged (cf a general lien exercised by certain types of agent, for example bankers and solicitors).

h   'The contract is that of the principal, not that of the agent, and *prima facie* at common law the only person who can sue is the principal and the only person who can be sued is the principal' (*per* Wright J in *Montgomerie v United Kingdom Mutual Steamship Association* (1891)).

i   The test is, as in most other areas of contract law, objective, that is, the question is not what the two individuals actually intended but what 'two reasonable businessmen making a contract of that nature, in those terms, and in those surrounding circumstances, must be taken to have intended' (*per* Brandon J in *The Swan* (1968)).

j   Though it did nothing to avoid liability either.

k   It is sufficient that the fact of agency is revealed without the need for the principal to be named.

l   In this case, the problem was that an undisclosed principal wanted to take over the contract, but there is no reason why it should not also apply where the agent is wanting to step into the shoes of the supposed principal. See, also, *Schmalz v Avery* (1851).

m   It was taken to have been signed in the name of the company, that is, 'Leopold Newborne (London) Ltd'.

n   That is, **s 56** of the **Consumer Credit Act 1974** – thought is important to note that this statutory agency is quite precisely defined and the general rule remains where **s 56** does not apply: see *Black Horse v Langford* [2007] RTR 38.

o   Had the notice period in *McQuillan* been three months, on this basis, the compensation would have been only £37,500.

---

36 Ending your answer with a conclusion, i.e. a summary of the results of your discussion, ensures that you present a complete picture to the examiner.

Relationship with Third Parties

INTRODUCTION

This chapter is concerned with the scope of an agent's authority and when a principal will be liable, or be able to sue, on a contract made by the agent without authority. The different types of authority must be understood, in particular, apparent authority (sometimes known as 'ostensible' authority) and usual authority. Furthermore, students must pay sufficient attention to the important concept of the doctrine of the undisclosed principal. The general rule is that an undisclosed principal can sue and be sued on the contract made by the agent on his behalf, if it was within the scope of the agent's actual authority. The justification for the doctrine of the undisclosed principal has been the subject of much discussion by academic writers. It is generally accepted that, although it runs against the fundamental principles of privity of contract (that is, there must be agreement between the parties), the doctrine is justified on grounds of commercial convenience.

QUESTION 32

Homes Ltd appoints Polly to act as its agent in the sale and purchase of furniture for sale through its shops in England. Polly is instructed to obtain the consent of the company's board of directors before making any purchase above £15,000. Polly has undertaken various actions.

(i) Beds-R-Us bed manufacturer contacts Polly offering to sell a consignment of beds. Beds-R-Us is in financial difficulties and, therefore, offers the beds for £20,000, which represents a substantial discount on the normal price, but Beds-R-Us requires an immediate decision. Polly says, 'I need to check with the company's board for such a large transaction, but they usually back my opinion on such matters, especially in an emergency like this.' Polly, therefore, agrees to buy on behalf of Homes Ltd. The next day, Beds-R-Us receives a better offer for the beds from another furniture retailer. Beds-R-Us telephones Polly and says it is withdrawing from the deal. That afternoon, the board of directors of Homes decides it wishes to go ahead with the purchase from Beds-R-Us.

(ii) Polly is offered by Chest Ltd wardrobes for £10,000, which is the normal price. During negotiations, the sales manager of Chest says to Polly, 'Once this deal goes through, you'll be on the top of the list for a Christmas hamper which contains a voucher for a one-week all expenses paid caravan holiday'. Polly agrees to buy the wardrobes, but manages to persuade Chest to agree to a price of £9,500. Later, she receives a Christmas hamper containing the holiday voucher from Chest. When asked about this by the board of directors, Polly strongly denies that she was influenced by the promise of a Christmas hamper. Polly points out that Chest wardrobes have always been popular with customers.

(iii)   Polly contracts to buy table lamps from a manufacturer in Latvia for £5,000. The lamps do not conform to safety standards and cannot be sold in England.

▶   Advise Homes.

How to Answer this Question

This question concerns the extent to which a principal can be bound by contracts which the agent has made without authority. Part (i) involves the principal's attempt to ratify its agent's act. The general requirements of ratification need to be stated. Beds-R-Us is aware that Polly has no authority to accept its offer. Since ratification requires an agent to purport to act for the principal, there is no agreement for the board of directors to ratify. In Part (ii), Polly may be in breach of her fiduciary duties not to make a secret profit nor take a bribe. An agent is required to perform with honesty and good faith for the benefit of the principal. The consequences of such a breach need to be discussed. Part (iii) requires a discussion of the Latvian manufacturer's possible breaches of the **Sale of Goods Act 1979**, namely, under s 14.

Answer Structure

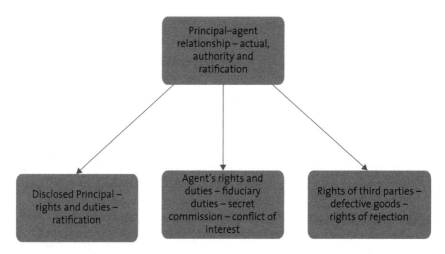

This diagram shows key points to be discussed in the answer.

ANSWER

Homes want to know whether they are bound by the transactions carried out by Polly. In order for Homes to be bound, Polly, as their agent, must have had some form of authority from Homes to enter into the transactions. If Polly had no authority, then Homes cannot be bound to the contracts made with the third parties. We will look at the individual situations to see if Homes are bound.[1]

(I) BEDS-R-US

An agent has actual authority when what is done has in fact been previously authorised either expressly or impliedly by the principal. Homes instructs Polly to obtain the consent of the company's board of directors before making any purchases above £15,000. There is nothing vague or ambiguous about these instructions (*Weigall v Runciman* (1916)). So Polly does not have actual authority to conclude the contract to purchase beds for £20,000. Although this was what Polly explained to Beds-R-Us, Polly agreed to buy the beds anyway, in the belief that the board would approve the transaction. Indeed, she is correct, because the board of directors in fact does wish to go ahead with the deal.

Although a principal may ratify an agent's unauthorised act, there are limitations to this rule.[2] The right to ratify depends on whether the agent purported to act on behalf of the principal at the time of agreeing to the transaction (*Keighley, Maxsted v Durant* (1901)). Beds-R-Us knew Polly did not have authority, because Polly specifically told Beds-R-Us this. Even though Polly believed that the Homes board would approve the transaction, when she agreed to purchase the beds from Beds-R-Us, Polly did not purport to act on behalf of Homes. Thus, there was no unauthorised transaction which Homes's board of directors could ratify. This is unlike the situation in *Bolton Partners v Lambert* (1889), where the managing director of a company accepted the offer to purchase a property on behalf of the company without its authority.[3] When the third party wanted to withdraw from the contract, the court held that it was too late, because when the company ratified the agent's unauthorised act, ratification related back to the time when the unauthorised act was concluded. It was thus too late for the third party to withdraw. Here, Polly did not conclude the unauthorised act on behalf of Homes. She specifically told Beds-R-Us that she did not have the company's authority. Thus, there is no concluded transaction which Homes's directors could ratify. The effect of ratification is that an unauthorised contract made by an agent becomes an authorised one from when it was made. Here, Homes

---

1   Providing a brief introduction which not only sets out the issues you are going to address but which also refers to the question set is a good way to demonstrate that you have understood what is relevant; relevancy is an important assessment factor.

2   Pointing out any potential limitations to the application of a particular legal principle is a good way to demonstrate that you have understood the complexities of the rule in question.

3   Outlining a relevant contrasting case shows your understanding and supports your argument.

cannot ratify because there was no unauthorised contract to which they were a party. Thus, there is no binding contract with Beds-R-Us and Beds-R-Us can withdraw their offer at any time up to the point of acceptance (*Payne v Cave* (1789); *Byrne v Van Tienhoven* (1880)).[4]

Homes have no action against Polly, since she had followed her instructions and had acted within the limits of her purchasing power on behalf of Homes. She has not acted in excess of her actual authority.

(II) CHEST LTD

Polly has express authority to purchase furniture. So, *prima facie*, Homes are bound by contract to purchase wardrobes with Chest. But as Homes's agent, Polly owes a fiduciary duty and is in a position of trust and confidence.[5] So equity will intervene and place fiduciary duties on an agent to protect the principal from an abuse of trust. A major consequence of this is that an agent must not put herself in a situation where there might be a conflict of interest and duty. The fiduciary duty of good faith has been applied very strictly (*Boardman v Phipps* (1966)) and it appears that Polly is in breach of this paramount duty. Furthermore, Polly must not make a secret profit nor take a bribe. She cannot accept commission from a third party.

It seems clear that Chest is aware that Polly is an agent. Nevertheless, they offer her a Christmas hamper containing a holiday voucher. This constitutes a bribe. It is conclusively presumed against Chest that their motive was corrupt and that Polly was affected and influenced by the offer of the hamper and holiday. It is irrelevant that Polly managed to persuade Chest to reduce the price to £9,500. In this situation, Polly may be summarily dismissed, even if appointed for a fixed period. We are not told what Polly's remuneration package was, but certainly Polly would lose her right to commission on this transaction.[6] If Polly has already consumed the contents of the hamper and used the holiday voucher, Homes could claim damages from Polly and Chest for any loss they suffer as a result of the bribe. Homes can, if they wish to do so, set aside the transaction with Chest (*Logicrose v Southend UFC* (1988)). Furthermore, Polly and Chest may incur criminal liability under the **Bribery Act 2010**.

---

4   Restrict yourself to what is relevant, don't write down everything you know about a particular case. Remember that relevancy is an important part of the assessment criteria.
5   Considering any potential limitation after outlining and applying the general legal rule to the requirements of the question ensures that your analysis proceeds in a logical way.
6   Pointing out omissions in the information provided by the question and considering the impact these omissions might have on the outcome of your analysis will attract a higher mark as it demonstrates your understanding.

It is not clear whether Polly is a commercial agent within the **Commercial Agents (Council Directive) Regulations 1993**.[7] The Regulations would apply if she is a self-employed intermediary with continuing authority to negotiate the sale and/or purchase of goods (**reg 2**). If Polly is a commercial agent, she is certainly in breach of her duties to look after the interests of Homes and to act 'dutifully and in good faith' (**reg 3**). Although the Regulations state that an agent is entitled to commission where a transaction is concluded as a result of an agent's action (**reg 7**), the Regulations are silent as to whether an agent loses the right to commission if the agent acts contrary to instructions – even if the agent acts in bad faith. Certainly, Polly is in breach of her duty of good faith under **reg 3** and, if this resulted in loss to Homes, compensation could be sought, but it seems that her commission on this transaction cannot be withheld. Although an agent has the right to an indemnity or compensation on termination of the agency agreement (**reg 17**), if Homes terminates Polly's agency contract as a result of her taking a bribe, **reg 18** will preclude her from making such a claim.[8]

(III) LATVIAN MANUFACTURER

Polly has actual authority to purchase furniture on behalf of Homes, so Homes are bound in contract with the Latvian manufacturer. However, the table lamps cannot be sold in England. Homes have two possible actions: first against the Latvian manufacturer and, secondly, against Polly.

Assuming the sales contract is governed by English law, the **Sale of Goods Act 1979** requires goods sold by a seller in the course of business to be of satisfactory quality (**s 14(2)**) and fit for their purpose (**s 14(3)**). Since Homes resell the goods in the course of their business, the sales contract is not a consumer transaction (*R and B Customs Brokers v United Dominion Trust* (1988); *Feldaroll Foundry v Hermes Leasing* (2004)). This means that the court has a discretion where it is just to do so to treat the implied terms under **s 14** as giving the buyer a right to warranty damages only (**s 15A**).

By **s 14(2)**, goods are required to be of satisfactory quality. We are told that the table lamps do not conform to safety standards. If these standards were applicable worldwide, it is likely that the Latvian manufacturer would be in breach of **s 14(2)**, since no reasonable person would regard table lamps to be of satisfactory quality if they are not safe and do not meet a general level of safety.[9]

....

7   Considering ambiguities in the question ensures completeness of your answer and demonstrates your understanding.

8   As accuracy and clarity of expression are important, the use of clear, precise, technical language will help to gain a good mark.

9   Remember to relate your analysis to the issues raised / facts outlined by the question; it is the proper application of the relevant legal rules to the requirements of the question upon which your assessed not the abstract discussion of the law.

It may be, however, that although the table lamps supplied by the Latvian manufacturer are in general satisfactory but merely do not meet the standards for resale in England, then whether or not Homes has an action against the manufacturer would depend on whether there is a breach of s14(3). Certainly, if the Latvian manufacturer knows that Polly is contracting on behalf of an English company and that the goods are to be delivered to England, this will be sufficient to impliedly make it known to the Latvian manufacturer that the goods are required to be fit for resale in England. However, there will be no breach of s14(3) if either the buyer does not rely on the skill and judgement of the seller, or it is unreasonable to rely on the seller to supply suitable goods. In *ST Belton v Teheran Europe* (1968), air compressors were sold to a Persian buyer. The Persian buyer complained that the goods were unfit for their purpose because the air compressors did not meet the safety regulations and could not be resold in Persia. The court held that there was no breach of s14(3), since it was unreasonable for the buyer to rely on the seller's knowledge of the safety regulations in Persia.[10] Following this case, therefore, it may be that Homes has no action against the Latvian manufacturer. If the court finds otherwise, and Homes has an action for breach of s14(3). this would normally entitle Homes to reject the entire consignment of lamps and claim damages under the *Hadley v Baxendale* (1854) principles. However, as discussed, since Homes are business buyers, the court has a direction under s15A to make an award of damages only.

Homes's second possible action would be against Polly.[11] Although she has carried out her instructions in purchasing furniture within her credit limit, she is under a duty to act with due care and skill. If she is being paid for special skills as a purchasing agent, a greater degree of care and skill is expected of her. If she has failed in purchasing suitable furniture and this results in loss to Homes, she is in breach of her agency contract, entitling Homes to claim an indemnity from her for their loss either under the common law or under the **Commercial Agents (Council Directive) Regulations 1993**.

QUESTION 33

On 1 April, Serpentine, an art dealer in Manchester, appoints Annabel as his agent in Liverpool and that same day, he sends a letter to FineArt Ltd, a company dealing in paintings in Liverpool, confirming Annabel's appointment and her authority to buy and sell pictures on his behalf. In fact, Annabel is under an express instruction not to deal with any pictures alleged to have been painted by Rubinstein, because of the risk of forgery. On 10 May, Annabel, purporting to act on behalf of Serpentine, contracts with

---

10 A good answer does not merely refer to the provision of a particular Act; where possible, it substantiates and illustrates the application of an Act with case law examples.

11 The consideration of different options ensures completeness of your analysis and attracts additional marks.

FineArt to buy from it *The Damsel in Distress*, a genuine Rubinstein painting, for £17,000. On 12 May, Annabel visits the office of Princeton Galleries and, without mentioning Serpentine, contracts to sell it *The Damsel in Distress* for £23,000. Annabel intends to keep the profit from this transaction for herself. On 16 May, FineArt discovers what Annabel is trying to do, and tells Serpentine that it intends to withdraw from the contract and keep *The Damsel in Distress*. On 17 May, Serpentine purports to ratify Annabel's actions of 10 and 12 May.

▶ Consider the rights and liabilities of all parties.

How to Answer this Question

Part of this problem is concerned with an agent's authority and, in particular, apparent authority. This relates to the effect of Annabel's actions on 10 and 12 May, and whether they can be regarded as falling within the scope of her authority so as to bind Serpentine.

The second issue that should be looked at is Annabel's attempt to make a secret profit out of her position as Serpentine's agent. The duty of the agent to act in good faith and account for any secret profit (for example *De Bussche v Alt* (1878)) needs to be noted here. Annabel may also be said to have broken another duty of an agent in her failure to follow instructions.

Finally, there is Serpentine's attempt to ratify what Annabel has done. The general requirements of ratification should be stated, that is:

❖ the agent must purport to act for the principal (*Keighley Maxsted and Co v Durant* (1901));

❖ the principal must be in existence at the time of the contract (*Kelner v Baxter* (1866)); and

❖ the principal must have capacity at the time of contract and at the time of ratification (*Grover and Grover v Matthews* (1910)).

These should be applied to the problem, and you should also note the effects of ratification, in particular its retrospective nature (*Bolton Partners v Lambert* (1889)).

The answer could well conclude with a summary of the position of each of the parties.

Answer Structure

This diagram illustrates the development of key points that will be covered in this answer.

ANSWER

This question raises issues relating to the extent of an agent's authority, the duties of an agent and the power of a principal to ratify an agent's unauthorised acts. These will be looked at in turn in discussing the rights and liabilities of all the parties.[12]

In making the contracts of 10 and 12 May, Annabel is acting outside the actual authority given to her by Serpentine, in that she has been forbidden to deal in pictures by Rubenstein. This does not necessarily mean, however, that her actions cannot bind Serpentine. This is because she may have 'apparent' authority (also known as 'ostensible' authority or 'agency by estoppel'). The requirements for this, as set out by Slade J in *Rama Corp Ltd v Proved Tin and General Investment* (1952), are: (a) that there is a representation

---

12 In your introduction, you should clearly identify the legal issues raised by the question. This is a good way to convince the examiner that you have understood what is relevant and will make him to be positively inclined towards your answer.

of authority by the principal to the third party;[a] (b) that the third party relies on that representation; and (c) that the third party alters his position in reliance on the representation.[13] This approach was followed by the Court of Appeal in *Freeman and Lockyer v Buckhurst Park Properties (Mangal) Ltd* (1964), which made it clear that the representation could be by conduct, rather than by a statement. Here, however, as far as FineArt is concerned, there was a clear and apparently unequivocal representation as to Annabel's authority in Serpentine's letter of 1 April. Provided that FineArt could show that it was important to it that Annabel was Serpentine's agent – in other words, that it was relying on Serpentine's representation – then the apparent authority would seem to operate. This would mean that if, on 10 May, FineArt had sought the £17,000 from Serpentine, it would have had every chance of success. This does not mean, however, that Serpentine can necessarily enforce the contract against FineArt. The doctrine of apparent authority has developed to protect third parties. It is unlikely that the courts would allow it to be used against a third party in a situation such as this. That is why it will become important to look later at Serpentine's power to ratify Annabel's actions.[14]

In relation to the contract with Princeton Galleries, the position is different. We are not told of any letter being sent to it about Annabel's authority. Moreover, Annabel apparently purports to contract on her own behalf. Even if she had been acting for Serpentine, so that Serpentine was an undisclosed principal, this would not affect the position. There can be no apparent authority without a representation from the principal to the third party, and it is difficult to see how this could occur if the third party is unaware of the existence of the principal. The possibility of Serpentine's ratifying what Annabel has done will be considered later.

Turning to Annabel, what is her position? Her actions have involved breaches of two of the duties which an agent owes to a principal. Firstly, she has disobeyed an instruction not to deal with Rubenstein pictures.[b] She will be liable for any loss flowing from this. This rule has been applied strictly, even in cases where there was some doubt as to whether, even if the agent had carried out his instructions, the principal would have avoided the loss. An example of this is *Fraser v Furman* (1967),[15] where the agent failed to take out an insurance policy on the principal's behalf, but argued that even if he had taken it out, the insurer would have been able to avoid paying out because of a minor

---

13 You need to provide an explanation of the relevant legal rules; without such explanation, it is more difficult for you to properly apply the law to the requirements of the question and thus also more difficult to demonstrate your knowledge and understanding.

14 Pointing out that you are going to discuss / analyse something at a later stage in your answer is a good idea for two reasons: first, it gives you more time to focus on the relevant issues rather than having to constantly repeat yourself and thus wasting valuable time; second, it might also enhance the readability of your argument and shows a certain degree of planning ahead on your part.

15 Referring to examples supports and strengthens your analysis; it also demonstrates your knowledge.

omission on the part of the principal. The Court of Appeal refused to get involved in that argument, and held the agent liable.

Secondly, Annabel is in the process of breaching one of her fiduciary duties, that is, the duty not to make a secret profit out of her position as agent. If she does, she will be liable to account to the principal for the profit. This is what happened in *De Bussche v Alt* (1878), where an agent, engaged to sell a ship, bought it himself at the minimum price specified by the principal and shortly afterwards sold it at a substantial profit. This profit had to be handed over to the principal. Here, if Annabel completed her transactions as she planned, the £6,000 profit on the resale of the picture would have to be handed over to Serpentine. There is no suggestion in the facts that Annabel has taken any bribe.[16] This type of secret profit is dealt with even more severely, with the principal being entitled to dismiss the agent, and sue both the agent and the third party for any losses resulting (*Logicrose v Southend United Football Club* (1988)), but it does not appear to be relevant on these facts.

Although Annabel has been acting beyond her instructions, and has been trying to make a profit for herself, Serpentine has now apparently recognised that the contracts which Annabel has negotiated in relation to *The Damsel in Distress* amount to a good bargain. He is therefore trying to take the benefit of them himself by ratifying Annabel's actions of 10 and 12 March. Can he do this?

The power of a principal to ratify the unauthorised acts of an agent is well established. There are, however, certain limitations.[17] First, the agent must have purported to act for a principal. This was established in *Keighley Maxsted & Co v Durant* (1901). The agent was authorised by the principal to buy wheat for their joint account at a certain price. He made a contract with the third party (Durant) at a higher price. He intended this to be for the joint account, but did not tell Durant this. The next day, the principal ratified what the agent had done, but subsequently refused to take delivery. An action by Durant against the principal failed because the agent had not purported to act for the principal, and ratification was therefore impossible.[c] Provided that the agent says that the contract is on behalf of a principal, however, it does not matter that in fact the agent is acting on his own account. In *Re Tiedemann and Ledermann Freres* (1899), it was held that in these circumstances, the principal could still ratify.

The second limitation on the power to ratify is that the principal must have been in existence at the time of the contract between the agent and the third party. This problem

---

16 The proper application of the relevant legal principle to the requirements of the questions is what the examiner is looking for.

17 Pointing out any potential limitations of the application of a particular legal principle is a good way to demonstrate that you have understood the complexities of the rule in question.

arises where contracts are made on behalf of companies which have not yet been incorporated. In *Kelner v Baxter* (1866), the promoters of a company which had not yet been incorporated made a contract to buy stock for it. When the company was incorporated, there was an attempt to ratify this contract. It was held that this was ineffective, and the promoters remained personally liable.

The third requirement is that the principal must have been able to make the contract at the time of the contract and at the time of ratification. The first part of this will be a problem where, for example, a minor attempts to ratify a contract which the minor would not have had capacity to make. The second part will also apply where at the time of ratification the contract would simply not have been possible. In *Grover and Grover v Matthews* (1910), for example, there was an attempt to ratify a contract of fire insurance after a fire had destroyed the property that was the subject of the insurance. It was held that ratification was impossible, because at that stage, the principal would not have been able to make the insurance contract.[18]

How does all this apply to the facts of the problem and to Serpentine's attempts to ratify Annabel's actions? The second two requirements appear not to create a problem, so we must concentrate on the first – that is, that the agent must purport to act for a principal. In relation to the contract made on 10 May, this is no problem. Annabel clearly says that she is acting for Serpentine, and we have seen that the fact that she is in reality acting for her own benefit is irrelevant (*Re Tiedemann and Ledermann Freres*). When Annabel makes the contract with Princeton Galleries on 12 May, however, she makes no mention of Serpentine or any other principal. This contract cannot therefore be ratified by Serpentine. So, it seems that Serpentine can take over the contract to buy *The Damsel in Distress*, but not the contract to sell. What about FineArt's attempt to withdraw, which comes before the ratification? This does not matter, because ratification is retrospective; it was so held in *Bolton Partners v Lambert* (1889), where it was said that the contract, once ratified, had to be treated as if it had been made with proper authority from the start. Similarly, in *Re Tiedemann and Ledermann Freres*, the third party had tried to withdraw on the basis of the false pretence about whom he was contracting with (which is similar to the situation here), but was prevented from doing so by the subsequent ratification of the contract.

Where does all this leave the various parties?[19]

Serpentine has a contract to buy *The Damsel in Distress* at £17,000, but no contract for resale. He may also be able to take action against Annabel for her various breaches of duty.

....

18 The use of examples demonstrates that you have a good grasp of the subject matter as it shows your awareness of how the law works in practice.
19 Finishing your essay with a conclusion ensures completeness of your analysis; this should summarise your findings in a clear and succinct manner. Don't introduce new arguments here.

Annabel has a contract with Princeton Galleries to sell it *The Damsel in Distress*. She will have difficulties fulfilling this contract, since *The Damsel in Distress* now belongs to Serpentine. She is also likely to face action by Serpentine, as noted above.

FineArt is obliged to sell *The Damsel in Distress* at £17,000 to Serpentine, and seems to have no possibility of any action against anyone else. Serpentine's ratification of Annabel's actions prevents it from pursuing her. Princeton Galleries has a contract to purchase *The Damsel in Distress* from Annabel which, as we have noted, Annabel will have difficulty fulfilling. It will be able to sue her for breach of contract. Finally, the best outcome for all concerned, apart from FineArt, might be for Serpentine to get together with Princeton Galleries, and see if they can come to a similar arrangement to that negotiated by Annabel.

QUESTION 34

Maria, who owned a shop named 'Maria Fruits and Flowers', sold the business earlier this year to Chessington, which appointed Maria as manager and renamed the business 'Maria Flower Specialists'. A sign was put up stating 'Under new management, part of the Chessington group'. Maria knows that Chessington does not sell fruit at any of its business outlets.

Maria, however, continues to sell at the shop fruit grown in her own garden. Ronald, who bought some strawberries from her, is claiming that the fruit was infected, causing him severe stomach pains which prevented him from working for two weeks. Ronald is an architect and lost the opportunity to bid for a lucrative contract during that period. He is threatening to sue Chessington.

Kelvin, Maria's former landlord, accepts five bouquets of flowers in part-settlement of Maria's unpaid rent.

Maria is persuaded by Joanna on one occasion to sell some fairy cakes which she has baked. Joanna gives Maria £10 for doing this.

▶ **Advise Chessington.**

How to Answer this Question

Part of this question is concerned with the types of authority, in particular usual or apparent authority, and the extent to which a principal can be bound by contracts that the agent has made without authority. This relates to Maria selling fruit and the fact that it is unclear whether Chessington had given her any instructions in this respect. If Ronald does not have a claim against Chessington, Maria may be personally liable (*The Swan* (1968)). The amount of damages Ronald may recover will also need to be discussed.

As for Kelvin, Maria has used her position as manager to satisfy a personal debt. If Chessington sues Kelvin for the value of the five bouquets of flowers, set-off may offer a partial defence to such a claim. This will depend on whether Chessington is held to be a disclosed or undisclosed principal.

In accepting £10 from Joanna, Maria is in breach of one of her fiduciary duties, that is, the duty not to make a secret profit out of her position as agent. The consequences of such a breach need to be discussed.

Answer Structure

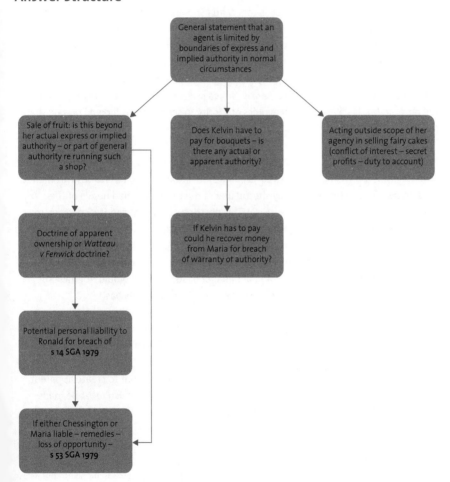

This diagram illustrates the progression of the main points that are covered in the answer.

ANSWER

This question concerns the issue of an agent's authority and, in particular, the extent to which a principal can be bound by contracts which the agent has made without authority.

As far as selling fruit is concerned, Chessington did not give any express instructions to Maria. The general rule is that where an agent is expressly appointed, the scope of his authority depends on the construction of the agreement.[20] If the terms of the agreement are ambiguous, the court will generally construe them in a way which is most favourable to the agent as long as the agent construes his instructions reasonably (*Weigall v Runciman* (1916)). Therefore, it could be argued that Maria was entitled to continue to sell fruit. The more likely view, however, is that Maria should have known that Chessington would not permit the selling of fruit, partly because of the renaming of the business to 'Maria Flower Specialists' with no mention of 'fruit', and partly because Maria knew that Chessington did not sell fruit at any of its outlets. Furthermore, it would be reasonable to expect Maria, faced with an ambiguity in her agency agreement, to seek clarification from Chessington (*European Asian Bank v Punjab and Sind Bank (No 2)* (1983)). Therefore, not only did Maria have no actual express authority to sell fruit, but it could be said that Maria should have known of the restriction not to sell fruit.

However, if it is usual for a flower shop manager such as Maria to have certain authority, then Chessington will be liable to a third party even if Maria knows that she is prohibited or restricted from acting in the way she did unless the third party had notice of the limitation (see *Watteau v Fenwick* (1893)). This doctrine of usual authority, however, may only be relied on by a third party where the agent makes a contract within the scope of the usual authority of an agent in that position.[21] Chessington may rely on the fact that a business named 'Maria Flower Specialists' does not imply that anything other than flowers would be sold in that shop, and a manager of such a shop would not have the authority to sell fruit. Chessington may thus escape liability on this basis.

The other possibility is that Ronald could argue for the existence of apparent authority (also known as 'ostensible' authority or 'agency by estoppel'). From the decisions in *Rama Corp v Proved Tin and General Investment Ltd* (1952) and *Freeman and Lockyer v Buckhurst Park Properties (Mangal) Ltd* (1964), the factors that must be present to create apparent authority include a representation that the agent has authority, which must be made by the principal. Such a representation must have been relied on by the third party claiming apparent authority.[22]

---

20 Use the general rule as a starting point for your analysis, then proceed to more specific points; this helps to structure your answer in a logical manner.

21 Showing an awareness of exceptions to the rule is a good way to attract additional marks as it demonstrates knowledge.

22 The explanation of a legal principle is an important factor for its successful application to the requirements of the question.

The essence of a principal's representation is that the agent is authorised to act on his behalf. It is an authority which 'apparently' exists, having regard to the conduct of the parties. The principal's representation need not depend on previous course of dealings, as in *Summers v Solomon* (1857), but could it be argued that simply by employing Maria as the manager, Chessington is representing that Maria has authority to do all the things that a flower shop manager would normally do, including selling fruit? The answer on the facts is likely to be in the negative, on the ground that a third party such as Ronald would not expect the manager of a well-known flower shop chain to have the authority to sell anything but flowers. Since the sign that was put up clearly states that 'Maria Flower Specialists' is part of the Chessington group, it is unreasonable for Ronald to believe that he is dealing with a manager who possesses the necessary authority to sell fruit.

Ronald does not seem to be on strong ground against Chessington. This does not mean, however, that Ronald has no claim at all. Maria may be personally liable to Ronald if the intention was that Maria should be personally liable. The intention is to be gathered from the nature and terms of the contract and the surrounding circumstances. An objective test is applied so that if Maria sells strawberries to Ronald in circumstances that make it reasonable to assume that Maria was contracting personally, Ronald will have an action against Maria.

In *The Swan* (1968), the defendant owned a boat called *The Swan* which was hired to a company of which he was a director. The company instructed the claimant to repair the ship on company notepaper which was signed by the defendant as director of the company. The company could not pay, and the question was whether the defendant was personally liable on the contract to repair the ship. The court held that the defendant contracted as agent for the company, but since it was reasonable for the repairer, who knew that the defendant owned the boat, to assume that the owner would accept personal liability for such repair, the defendant was personally liable on the contract. Applying this case to the question,[23] if Maria sold the strawberries in such a way that Ronald reasonably assumed that Maria was selling in her personal capacity, then Maria will be personally liable to Ronald in damages.

If, as is more likely, Maria is held not to have contracted personally but to have contracted as an agent, Maria cannot be made personally liable on the contract.[24] However, since Maria had no authority to sell fruit, Maria will be liable to Ronald who has contracted with her on the faith of her representation of authority. The nature of her liability depends on whether Maria had knowledge that she had no authority to sell fruit,[d] or

....

23 You need to go beyond mere description of the law; it is the proper application of the relevant legal rules that demonstrates your knowledge and understanding. Remember that it is this upon which you are assessed.

24 Considering different possibilities is a good way to attract marks as it shows that you have understood the potential implications of a particular legal rule.

whether she merely acted negligently or in good faith and under the honest but mistaken belief that she was contracting with Chessington's authority. The latter is the more likely, rendering Maria liable to Ronald for breach of the implied warranty of authority.

The amount of damages recoverable depends on the nature of the wrong committed. Essentially, the measure of damages will be either the loss that flowed directly as a natural or probable consequence, or the loss that was foreseeable by the parties as a probable consequence, of the breach of warranty. It seems, therefore, that Ronald will be able to sue Maria for damages. Whether or not Ronald can recover for the lost opportunity to bid for the 'lucrative' contract will depend on whether this opportunity was made known to Maria at the time the contract was made. This seems unlikely, in which event, Ronald will not be able to recover damages on the basis that the damage was too remote (*Victoria Laundry (Windsor) Ltd v Newman Industries Ltd* (1949)).

As far as Kelvin is concerned, can Chessington recover from Kelvin the price for the bouquets of flowers?[25] The right of a third party to set off a liability against a principal will only apply where the principal has induced the third party to believe that the agent is acting as a principal and not as an agent, that is, where the principal is undisclosed. Did Kelvin know of the existence of Chessington? Clearly, Kelvin knew that Maria had owned the business, but the question is really whether Kelvin had *actual* notice[e] of the existence of Chessington. This will depend on whether Kelvin noticed the sign which had been put up – that the business was now part of the Chessington group. If Kelvin had actual notice, then Kelvin has no right of set-off and Chessington is entitled to recover the price of the bouquets of flowers from Kelvin.

As far as accepting £10 for selling Joanna's fairy cakes is concerned, Maria is in breach of one of her fiduciary duties, that is, the duty not to make a secret profit out of her position as agent.[f] Unless Maria has revealed all the circumstances to Chessington and Chessington has consented to her retaining the profit, she will be liable to account to Chessington for the profit. If an agent takes a bribe, the principal is entitled to claim the amount of the bribe as money had and received (*Regier v Campbell-Stuart* (1939)).[g]

QUESTION 35

Brandon, the owner of a shop selling antique British goods, has several red telephone boxes for sale. Brandon is an eccentric and is well known for his dislike of Americans. Aaron, an American, knows that Brandon is unlikely to sell a telephone box to him and therefore asks his friend, Nancy, to visit Brandon's shop and to purchase one of the telephone boxes on his behalf, promising to buy it from Nancy for 10% more than she paid for it. Nancy takes Brandon out for lunch (the bill for which came to £30) and buys from him a telephone box for £300. She also agrees to buy an old chimney pot for £100.

....

25 Don't miss out on marks by not discussing more minor issues raised by the question.

Aaron is delighted with the telephone box and also wants to take up Nancy's offer to sell the chimney pot for £120. Brandon learns of Nancy's association with Aaron and purports to cancel both agreements.

▶ **Consider the rights and liabilities of all parties.**

How to Answer this Question

Part of this question is concerned with the problem of 'who is an agent?' It is not always easy to recognise an agent. It is the effect in *law* of the conduct of the parties that must be considered in order to determine whether the agency relationship has come into existence. This question requires you to analyse the nature of the relationship between Aaron and Nancy, and to consider whether Nancy is acting as an agent or buying in her own name and reselling to Aaron. If it is the latter, then the agreement is not one of agency (*Lamb v Goring Brick Co* (1932); *AMB Imballaggi Plastici SRL v Pacflex Ltd* (1999)).

If Nancy is an agent, she has acted on behalf of Aaron in such a way that the agency is wholly undisclosed. Many of the cases dealing with the effects of undisclosed agency are old, but will need to be discussed. There is a general right for the undisclosed principal to intervene on and enforce the contract made on his behalf, but there are restrictions on that right, as in *Said v Butt* (1920).

Answer Structure

This diagram shows the progression of key points in the answer.

ANSWER

This question raises issues relating to the nature of the relationship between a principal and his agent, the concept of the undisclosed principal and the right of an agent to be remunerated and indemnified for expenses in the performance of an agency agreement. These will be looked at in turn in discussing the rights and liabilities of Aaron, Nancy and Brandon.[26]

Aaron asks Nancy to buy a telephone box which Nancy does not own or possess at the time of the contract. It is a difficult question of fact whether this agreement between them involves Nancy as the 'seller' of goods acting for Aaron as the 'buyer', or as an agent acting for Aaron as the 'principal'.

If Nancy is held to be buying and reselling on her own account, then she is not a true agent in law (*Lamb v Goring Brick Company* (1932); *AMB Imballaggi Plastici SRL v Pacflex Ltd* (1999)). Accordingly, Brandon would be in breach of his agreement if he were to refuse subsequently to sell the telephone box to her. If the opposite is true, that is, Nancy is procuring the telephone box for Aaron as Aaron's true agent and Nancy is authorised to create privity between Aaron as principal and Brandon as the third party, Aaron may intervene and enforce the contract made on his behalf, subject to certain restrictions which will be discussed.

On the facts, it is likely that Nancy is acting as an agent. A particularly important factor in favour of this is the fact that Nancy's remuneration in carrying out Aaron's instructions has been fixed at 10% of the purchase price. Further, Nancy's duty to buy a telephone box on Aaron's behalf is not absolute, in the sense that she will not be liable to Aaron if she does not obtain the telephone box: her duty is to use her care and skill as an agent to endeavour to obtain what Aaron wants (*Anglo-African Shipping Co of New York Inc v J Mortner Ltd* (1962)).

The essence of an agency agreement is the agent's power to affect the principal's legal position *vis-à-vis* third parties. Nancy has been authorised by Aaron to buy a telephone box, but does not reveal the fact of agency to Brandon at all and purports to be acting on her own behalf. The general rule is that there is no need for an agent to identify his principal. Provided that an agent has his principal's actual authority for his actions, the undisclosed principal may enforce a contract made by his agent with a third party.[27,h] This rule may appear harsh, since its effect on this question is that Brandon deals with Nancy

---

26 A good introduction clearly identifies those legal rules which are raised by the question; this ensures a logical structure to your answer right from the start and puts your examiner in a positive frame of mind.

27 The explanation of a legal principle is an important factor for its successful application to the requirements of the question.

in ignorance of the presence of an American being interested in the contract. The doctrine does, however, carry certain restrictions to protect the position of the third party and, in some cases, the undisclosed principal is entirely prohibited from intervening on the contract.[28]

In *Said v Butt* (1920), the principal was a theatre critic who had been banned from a particular theatre after he had written an unfavourable review on a previous occasion.[29] He wanted to obtain a ticket for the opening night of a new play and, knowing that the theatre manager would not let him have one, employed an agent to obtain one for him. When he arrived at the theatre, he was refused entry. He then sued for breach of contract. The court held that he was not entitled to enforce the contract, on the basis that if the identity of the person with whom the third party is contracting is material to the making of the contract, the failure to disclose the fact that the agent is acting on behalf of a principal will deprive the principal of the right to sue on the contract. Applying this case to the question here, it would appear that Aaron will not be able to sue Brandon on the contract if Brandon refuses to sell the telephone box. Certainly, courts are likely to favour the interpretation of the situation which best protects the third party where third-party rights in goods are in issue.

However, there have been criticisms of the decision in *Said v Butt* on the basis that personal dislike of the undisclosed principal should not normally prevent him intervening on a contract.[30] In *Dyster v Randall & Sons* (1926), the agent, without revealing the fact that he was acting on behalf of a principal, entered into a contract for the sale of land. The court held that the identity of the person contracting with the third party was not material and, therefore, a valid contract was made with the principal who could sue for specific performance. Again, in *Nash v Dix* (1898), although the third party would not have sold the property concerned to the undisclosed principal, the court held that the identity of the contracting party was immaterial. Since Brandon's objection to the contract for the sale of the telephone box is not based on a particular dislike of Aaron, but on his dislike of Americans generally, this would not amount to personal reasons. Aaron will be entitled to intervene on the contract and sue Brandon for specific performance.

As far as the chimney pot is concerned, Aaron will be able to enforce the contract on the basis that Nancy was not acting as his agent at the time of her agreement to purchase it from Brandon (and is thus free to resell to whoever she wishes).[i]

....

28 Proceeding from the general rule to any existing limitations is a good way to structure your answer in a logical manner; it also demonstrates your knowledge and understanding.

29 It is important to refer to relevant authorities to substantiate your argument. Remember: it is the application of law upon which you are assessed.

30 The consideration of alternative views makes your answer stand out from the rest and demonstrates both deeper knowledge and understanding.

We are also told that Nancy takes Brandon out for lunch, presumably to conduct her negotiations for the purchase of the goods. The general rule is that all agents are entitled to be reimbursed expenses necessarily incurred in the course of performing their duties. This is so whether or not the agent is acting under a contract of agency. Nancy thus has the right to be indemnified for the expenses of lunch, such expenses having been incurred while acting within her actual authority to persuade Brandon to sell goods to her on Aaron's behalf.

If Nancy has taken possession of the goods, she is entitled to protect her rights to remuneration and indemnity by retaining the telephone box and the chimney pot until the amounts outstanding relating to the goods are discharged.[j]

To summarise the positions of the parties: Brandon has a contract with Aaron to sell him the telephone box and a contract with Nancy to sell her the chimney pot. If Brandon cancels either contract, he will be liable to damages to Aaron and Nancy, respectively. Nancy is entitled to her 10% commission *vis-à-vis* the telephone box, has agreed to resell the chimney pot to Aaron for a profit of £20 and has a lien over the goods in her possession until she is paid. Nancy is further entitled to be indemnified for the cost of lunch.[31]

> ## Aim Higher ★
> Before discussing the issues identified, a good answer needs to consider the question of whether Nancy is in fact an agent or just a reseller.

QUESTION 36

In January, Antonio appoints Marisa as the manager of his restaurant. He tells her not to buy dairy products from a new company, Celebrate & Co, because he has heard that its products are of poor quality. In February, Barnaby, a representative of Celebrate & Co, visits the restaurant and as a result, Marisa orders £100 worth of dairy products. Barnaby is unaware of Antonio's instructions to Marisa. When, later in the day, Antonio discovers what Marisa has done, they have an argument and Marisa resigns. The following day, Marisa goes to Balls Ltd, Antonio's regular supplier of wines and spirits, and purchases three cases of gin on credit in Antonio's name. She then absconds with the gin.

▶ Advise Antonio as to his liability to Celebrate & Co and Balls Ltd.

---

31 Ending your answer with a conclusion, i.e. a summary of the results of your analysis, ensures that you present a complete picture to the examiner.

How to Answer this Question

This question is concerned with the issue of an agent's authority, and in particular the extent to which a principal can be bound by contracts which the agent has made without authority.

The two contracts concerned here raise different points, though there is some possibility of overlap. In relation to the contract with Celebrate & Co, there is the possibility of Antonio being liable on the basis of 'usual' authority, as in *Watteau v Fenwick* (1893). This will involve looking at what is the usual authority of a restaurant manager.

The contract with Balls Ltd, on the other hand, will only be binding on Antonio if Marisa can be said to have 'apparent' authority. This is sometimes referred to as 'ostensible' authority or 'agency by estoppel'. It involves the principal having made a representation of the agent's authority which is then acted on by the third party. *Freeman and Lockyer v Buckhurst Park Properties (Mangal) Ltd* (1964), which is one of the leading authorities on this area, will need discussion, though the case of *Summers v Solomon* (1857) is closer to the facts in the problem.

The overlap arises from the fact that it might also be possible to treat the contract with Celebrate as being binding on the basis of apparent authority, if it can be established that there was some representation of authority by Antonio on which Celebrate & Co could rely.

Answer Structure

This diagram shows the progression of key points in the answer.

ANSWER

An agent frequently has the power to make contracts which are binding on his principal. Problems arise, however, where the agent exceeds the authority given. In what circumstances can the principal still be liable? There are two main ways. First, if it is customary for an agent of a particular type to have certain authority, then restrictions on that authority will be ineffective unless the third party knows about them. This is also referred to as 'usual' authority, or sometimes 'implied' authority.[k] An example of this type of authority which will be discussed below is the case of *Watteau v Fenwick* (1893). The second type of extended authority that we will need to consider is 'apparent' authority, which arises where the principal has made some representation of the agent's authority on which the third party has relied.[32] An example of this is the case of *Freeman and Lockyer v Buckhurst Park Properties (Mangal) Ltd* (1964). We will need to examine whether either type of authority will lead to Antonio being bound to either of the two contracts made by Marisa.

In relation to the contract with Celebrate & Co, the most obvious type of authority to consider is usual authority. In *Watteau v Fenwick* (1893), the defendants owned a beerhouse which was managed by a man named Humble.[33,l] Humble was under instructions not to buy cigars for the business from anyone other than the defendants. In breach of this instruction, Humble bought cigars on credit from the claimant. At the time of the contract, the claimant thought that Humble was the owner of the beerhouse. When he discovered the truth, however, he sought payment from the defendants. The defendants resisted on the basis that Humble had no authority to bind them to this contract. On the contrary, he was acting in breach of express instructions not to act in this way. The court nevertheless found the defendants liable. They said that it was within the usual authority of the manager of a beerhouse to be able to buy cigars from any source. The fact that Humble had been instructed not to do so was irrelevant, since the plaintiff was unaware of this restriction. He was entitled to rely on Humble's usual authority, and thus the defendants were obliged to pay for the cigars. The issue of what constitutes usual authority is a question of fact, which will have to be decided in each case. The decision in *Watteau v Fenwick* can, for example, be contrasted with the earlier case of *Daun v Simmins* (1879), where it was held that where a public house was 'tied' to a particular brewer, the third party should have realised that the freedom of the manager to purchase would be restricted.

---

32 Pointing out that you are going to discuss / analyse something at a later stage in your answer is a good idea for two reasons: first, it gives you more time to focus on the relevant issues rather than having to constantly repeat yourself and thus wasting valuable time; second, it also enhances the readability of your argument and shows a certain degree of planning ahead on your part.

33 Outlining the facts of a particular case is a good way to illustrate the relevant legal rules and thus supports your argument.

Watteau v Fenwick has been the subject of considerable criticism, in that it applied this approach to a situation where the third party was unaware that he was dealing with an agent. This, however, does not detract from the general principle. Even if it only applies where the principal is disclosed, it is still a type of authority that can bind the principal even where the agent has exceeded his actual authority.

Applying this to the problem, we find that Marisa, the manager of a restaurant, has, like Humble in *Watteau v Fenwick*, failed to follow an express limitation on the contracts she is entitled to make. It is not clear whether Barnaby knew that he was dealing with an agent. If he did not, it is possible that the court would refuse to apply *Watteau v Fenwick* on the basis that, despite what happened in the case itself, the concept of usual authority should not be applied to situations involving an undisclosed principal. It seems more likely, however, that Barnaby would have realised that he was dealing with a manager rather than the owner of the restaurant. In that case, the next issue to decide concerns the limits of the usual authority of the manager of a restaurant.[34]

As indicated above, this is a question of fact, not of law. In other words, it would be necessary to look at evidence as to what was normally accepted as being within the scope of the authority of someone like Marisa. If it was found that such managers usually had authority to purchase goods from suppliers chosen at their own discretion, then Antonio will be likely to be found liable for this contract. If the opposite is found, or if it is not possible to determine any particular usual authority for such managers, then Celebrate will probably have to pursue Marisa rather than Antonio. The only other possibility is if Celebrate could argue for the existence of apparent authority. Consideration of this point, however, will be left until after the discussion of the position as regards Balls Ltd

In respect of the contract for the gin, there is no possibility of using usual authority, because Marisa is no longer an agent when she makes the contract. The only possibility here will be for Balls to argue that Marisa had apparent authority to make this contract (the phrases 'ostensible authority' and 'agency by estoppel' are also used to describe this concept). As defined by Diplock LJ in *Freeman and Lockyer v Buckhurst Park Properties (Mangal) Ltd* (1964),[35] this requires a representation by the principal[m] intended to be acted on by the third party, and in fact acted on, that the agent does have authority to make the contract.[n] The representation need not be in the form of words: conduct will be sufficient. In *Freeman and Lockyer v Buckhurst*, a person had been allowed to act as managing director of a company by the other directors, although he had never been appointed as such in the manner required by the company's Articles of Association. It was

---

34 Drawing an interim conclusion is a good way of signposting the relevant issues and also helps you to structure your answer logically.

35 Stating by whom or how a particular legal principle was stated in a case (*obiter* or *ratio*) demonstrates a deeper knowledge and is likely to attract additional marks.

held that the directors' actions in allowing him to act in this way amounted to a representation to the outside world that he had authority to do so. The company was therefore bound by his actions. The case which is closest to the facts of the problem, however, is *Summers v Solomon* (1857).[36] Solomon owned a jeweller's shop and employed a manager to run it. Solomon regularly paid for jewellery that had been ordered by the manager from Summers. After the manager had left Solomon's employment, he ordered jewellery in Solomon's name from Summers and then absconded with it. It was held that Solomon was bound to pay for the jewellery. His previous conduct in paying for the jewellery had amounted to a representation of the manager's authority. That representation had not been contradicted or withdrawn, and so Summers was still entitled to rely on it.

At first sight, this decision would seem clearly to mean that Antonio will have to pay Balls for the gin. There are, however, two questions that need to be asked.[37] We are told that Balls is Antonio's regular supplier. What we do not know, however, is what the usual ordering procedures were. In particular, was it usual for goods to be ordered on credit? If so, did Marisa follow the usual procedures in placing this order and immediately taking the goods away? If the answer to either of these questions is no, Antonio may escape liability. If it was not usual for goods to be ordered on credit, then there is less in the way of a representation of authority for what Marisa has done in this case. Secondly, if Marisa has not followed the normal procedures, should Balls not have been put on notice that something unusual was happening, and therefore made some attempt to confirm that Marisa was acting with authority? If, however, these issues are not resolved in Antonio's favour, then it seems certain that he will be bound by Marisa's apparent authority and will have to pay for the gin.

The final point to consider is whether the contract with Celebrate could fall under the heading of apparent authority as well.[38] The problem here is that of finding a representation. We are told that Celebrate is a new company, and therefore there will have been no previous dealings. It might be argued, however, that simply by employing Marisa as a manager, Antonio is representing that she has authority to do all the things that a restaurant manager would normally do, including, perhaps, making contracts to buy dairy products. This was the kind of approach adopted in *United Bank of Kuwait v Hamoud; City Trust v Levy* (1988), where it was held that a firm that employed X as a solicitor was representing to the world that X had authority to engage in all transactions on the firm's behalf which came within the normal scope of a solicitor's responsibilities.[o]

---

36 When a problem scenario resembles what happened in a well-known case, don't automatically assume that you have found the answer to the problem; this assumption might lose you valuable marks as the finer points of the question set might make an important difference to the analysis.

37 Considering different options or implications demonstrates both understanding and knowledge of the legal area in question.

38 Signposting enhances clarity of expression.

If this was followed here, it would be another argument for making Antonio responsible for Marisa's contract with Celebrate.

The advice to Antonio in relation to these two contracts must be that he is on fairly weak ground.[39] The doctrines of usual and apparent authority taken together mean that it is very likely that he will have to meet the obligations under the contracts with both Celebrate & Co and Balls Ltd. His only remedy then will be to try to trace Marisa, and attempt to recover his losses from her.

Common Pitfalls ✗

If the difference between implied and apparent authority is not appreciated, it is impossible to answer this question correctly or to put forward a sensible argument for or against usual authority.

QUESTION 37

In October 2012, Xavier approached Lilian, New Business Manager of Experian Bank plc, seeking a loan of £200,000 to start up a business selling sportswear. Lilian told Xavier that approval was needed from Head Office for loans over £100,000. She sought approval for him, but Xavier's application was rejected.

In January 2013, Xavier, together with his wife, Judith, again approach Lilian, this time seeking a loan of £150,000 to set up an Internet business selling sportswear. On 10 January 2013, Xavier and Judith receive a letter from Lilian, addressed to them both, stating 'I am pleased to inform you that your loan can proceed' and asking them to call in to deal with the paperwork. In fact, the papers are made out in Xavier's name alone, since the loan is secured on property which is in his sole ownership. Judith resigns from her well-paid job as a lawyer so that she can devote her time to the new business.

Before the money is paid, however, Experian Bank informs Xavier that Lilian has agreed the loan without authorisation. Although they have in the recent past ratified some loans of more than £100,000 arranged by Lilian without authorisation, in this case they are not prepared to do so because of the risks involved in Internet businesses.

▶ **Advise Xavier and Judith.**

How to Answer this Question

There are two main issues to discuss in this question:

❖   Did Lilian have apparent authority to make the loan to Xavier?

❖   If she did not, what remedies might Xavier and Judith have against Lilian?

---

39 Concluding your analysis with tailored advice to the advisee will ensure completeness of your answer.

The first issue requires consideration of whether any representation has been made by Experian Bank plc to Xavier as to Lilian's authority, as required by *Freeman and Lockyer v Buckhurst Park Properties (Mangal) Ltd* (1964) and *Armagas v Mundogas* (1986). The case of *First Energy (UK) Ltd v Hungarian International Bank Ltd* (1993) on the extent to which an agent can represent his own authority will also need to be considered.

As regards the second issue, since there is no basis for making Lilian liable on the loan contract, this will involve consideration of the remedies available against her in tort, or for breach of the implied warranty of authority. As far as Judith's reliance on the implied warranty is concerned, the effect of the decision in *Penn v Bristol and West Building Society* (1997) will need to be considered.

Answer Structure

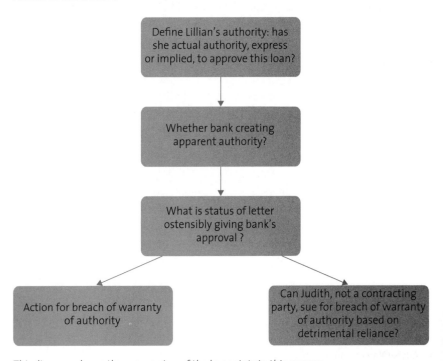

This diagram shows the progression of the key points in this answer.

ANSWER

This question concerns the extent to which agents may bind their principals even when acting outside their actual authority. It also raises the question of what remedies a third party will have if the agent has acted without authority, and this has led to loss.

The best outcome for Xavier and Judith in this situation would be for it to be found that Experian Bank plc was obliged to make Xavier the loan for the business, despite the fact that Lilian had not sought approval for it. If that is not possible, however, they may well wish to seek a remedy against Lilian personally.[40]

There is no doubt that Lilian has acted beyond her actual authority in arranging the loan to Xavier.[41] She did not have authority to approve loans of over £100,000, and Xavier was aware of this as a result of their previous dealings. Although Experian Bank has ratified some loans of over £100,000 made recently by Lilian, there is no suggestion that her actual authority has changed. Experian Bank is not obliged to ratify any contract, and is quite entitled to 'pick and choose' which ones it is prepared to accept. The fact that it does not wish to become involved in Xavier's Internet business is therefore a decision which it is free to take.

Xavier may argue, however, that Lilian has bound Experian Bank to the loan agreement on the basis of apparent authority. The requirements for apparent authority were established by *Freeman and Lockyer v Buckhurst Park Properties (Mangal) Ltd* (1964). There must be a representation (by words or conduct) from the principal to the third party, which is relied on by the third party and which leads to an alteration of position by the third party.[42] There is no doubt here that Xavier has relied on an assumption that Lilian had authority, and changed his position by entering into the loan contract. The more difficult question is whether the assumption has been created by any representation from Experian Bank to him. In some situations, it can be argued that by placing a person in a particular position (for example, New Business Manager) this in itself amounts to a representation of authority or, alternatively, that agents in such a position might be argued to have the 'usual' authority attaching to that position. That cannot apply here, however, since Xavier is aware of the limitation on Lilian's authority as a result of their dealings in October 2012. Nor can it be said that the ratification by Experian Bank of other loans of over £100,000 amounts to a representation, since there is no evidence that Xavier is aware of these.[43]

Could it be argued that the letter that Lilian wrote to Xavier is a representation that she has authority to agree the loan? It may well have this implication, but the problem is that it emanates from Lilian, rather than from Experian Bank. In *Armagas v Mundogas* (1986),

....

40 It is essential that your essay has a structure. By outlining the issues to be discussed in your introduction you take the first important step towards ensuring that you achieve this aim.
41 Keep your focus on what is relevant in light of the question, don't write down everything you know. Remember that relevancy is an important assessment criterion.
42 Dissecting the relevant legal principle into its constituent parts and considering these parts on a point-by-point basis ensures that your answer is structured logically.
43 Remember to draw conclusions from your analysis; this evidences your understanding of how to apply the law.

the House of Lords emphasised that, for apparent authority to exist, the representation must come from the principal, not from the agent. In this case, the vice president of a company had indicated that he had authority to agree a deal for the sale and charter-back of a ship. His plan was to make a secret profit out of the transactions. When his deceit came to light, the third party argued that the shipowners were bound by the agent's apparent authority. The House of Lords disagreed, holding that there was no representation of authority from the principal as opposed to the agent, and that therefore apparent authority could not arise.

This case would suggest that Xavier will not be able to rely on apparent authority, since he has only had dealings with Lilian, and there has been no direct representation from Experian Bank. The subsequent decision of the Court of Appeal in *First Energy (UK) Ltd v Hungarian International Bank Ltd* (1993) must, however, also be considered.[44] The facts of this case bear some similarity to those of the problem. A branch manager of a bank had, in contravention of limitations on his actual authority, agreed arrangements with a third party for the provision of credit facilities to customers of the third party's business. The third party knew that the manager had no personal authority to enter into such arrangements on behalf of his principal, but assumed from a letter written by the manager that the appropriate approvals had been obtained. Although this appeared to amount to a representation by the agent, and therefore to fall foul of the decision in *Armagas v Mundogas*, the Court of Appeal felt able to distinguish the earlier case. It held that an agent who does not have apparent authority to enter into a particular transaction may nevertheless have apparent authority to communicate to a third party that such a transaction has been approved. Part of the reason for this was a feeling that it would be unreasonable to expect a third party to have to check in such situations whether the Board, or whatever other body within the principal company was appropriate, had in fact given approval to the transaction. It may well be, therefore, that it would be held here that Lilian did have apparent authority to communicate to Xavier that the necessary approval for his loan had been obtained. If that is the case, then Xavier will be able to insist that the loan goes ahead, or claim compensation if it does not.[45]

What is the position, on the other hand, if the strict requirements as laid down in *Armagas v Mundogas* are held to apply in this situation, so that Lilian did not have apparent authority, even to the limited extent found to exist in *First Energy (UK) Ltd v Hungarian International Bank Ltd* (1993)? Xavier will then have to seek a remedy from Lilian herself. This is not a situation where Lilian would be liable for the loan contract itself. Xavier will rather be looking for compensation for any losses he may have suffered.

....

44 The consideration of more than one possible legal argument or an opposing view demonstrates wider knowledge and deeper understanding.

45 Drawing an interim conclusion is another way of signposting the relevant issues and also helps you to structure your answer logically.

There are two ways in which this might be possible.[46] First, there is the possibility of an action in tort for deceit or negligent misstatement under the *Hedley Byrne v Heller* (1964) principle, as modified in *Caparo v Dickman* (1990). If Lilian is found to have made a statement as to the fact that the transaction had been authorised, which she knew was false, or which she made without proper care, this could give an action for damages.

Alternatively, and this is particularly applicable if Lilian's misrepresentation was innocent (that is, neither deliberately deceitful nor negligent), Xavier may be able to sue for breach of the implied warranty of authority which is held to be given by agents (see, for example, *Collen v Wright* (1857)). This may enable him to recover all losses which have resulted from the fact that Lilian was in fact acting without authority.[P] It is possible to obtain either expectation or reliance damages under this action.

Finally, what is Judith's position? She was not a party to the purported contract with Experian Bank, but this does not necessarily mean that she would have no action against Lilian. In reliance on Lilian's letter, she has given up her job, and can therefore claim to have suffered loss. It is clear that she could bring an action in deceit, if it is clear that Lilian's misrepresentation was made to her and she acted on it. Similarly, an action for negligent misstatement would also be possible, provided that Judith could be said to be owed a duty of care by Lilian. This would not seem to be too difficult on the facts. Lilian's letter was addressed to both Xavier and Judith; Judith was therefore within the group whom Lilian could have expected to rely on the statements in the letter. The type of action she took (giving up her job) was reasonably foreseeable, and she could therefore claim for damages consequent upon this.

What about a claim under the breach of the implied warranty of authority? It might be thought that this would not be applicable, since Lilian was not in the end someone whom Judith was purporting to bring into a contractual relationship with her principal. The decision in *Penn v Bristol and West Building Society* (1997), however, suggests that this may not be an obstacle. In this case, a solicitor agent's innocent misrepresentation of authority to a building society was held to give rise to liability for breach of the implied warranty, even though the building society's loss resulted not from attempting to contract with the solicitor's principal, but from lending money to someone who was entering into such a contract. It was held to be sufficient that the representation of authority had been made to the building society and that it had acted on it to its detriment. Applying that to the situation in the problem, the representation of authority was clearly made to Judith, and she has acted on it to her detriment by giving up her job. On this basis, Judith, like Xavier, could also seek damages for breach of the implied warranty from Lilian.[47]

....

46 Credit is given for pointing out different possibilities as this makes your analysis more complete.
47 The proper application of the relevant legal principle to the requirements of the questions is what the examiner is looking for. This is a good example of how to achieve this aim.

In conclusion, therefore, it seems that either Lilian will be found to have apparent authority, so that the loan agreement with Experian Bank will be enforceable or, if she did not have such authority, both Xavier and Judith will be able to recover compensation from her on the basis of an action in tort or for breach of the implied warranty of authority.

QUESTION 38

On 21 March 2011, Wetstones Ltd employed Raymond as the manager of its new bookshop in Poole. The contract was for a fixed term of three years and stated that Raymond was to receive £15,000 per year and a 5% bonus if sales exceeded £50,000 in any one year. The contract forbade Raymond from selling books not supplied or ordered by Wetstones' head office.

Advise Wetstones in the following circumstances:

(a) Raymond sells a copy of *How to Pass Exams* by Hitchcock to Bertha, a student, who only agrees to buy it on Raymond's personal guarantee that Bertha will pass her exams if she follows the instructions in the book. She fails her exams.

(b) Raymond is out of stock of *Uncommon Law* by Cartwright and is told by Wetstones' head office that it would take four weeks before Raymond could expect fresh supplies of the book. Raymond approaches Middletons, who owns a bookshop, and obtains from Middletons 10 copies of *Uncommon Law* on credit.

(c) On 1 April 2012, Wetstones informs Raymond that the bookshop in Poole is to be closed down due to a restructure of the company. The sales for the Poole bookshop for 2011 were £55,000.

How to Answer this Question

This question concerns the issue of an agent's authority and, in particular, the extent to which a principal can be bound by contracts which the agent has made without authority. We have been asked to look at the agency contract from the principal's point of view.

We are concerned here with the two contracts which Raymond made with third parties. Although the contracts raise different points, there is some possibility of overlap. In relation to the contract with Bertha, Wetstones will only be bound if Raymond can be said to have had 'express' or 'usual' authority. This will involve looking at Raymond's express contractual obligations as well as his implied duties owed to his principal. As far as the contract with Middletons is concerned, Wetstones may be liable on the basis of 'usual' authority, as in *Watteau v Fenwick* (1893). We will need to look at what is the usual authority of a bookshop manager. The concept of 'apparent' authority will need to be discussed, as in *Summers v Solomon* (1857).

The final part of the question concerns Raymond's entitlement to claim remuneration where his employment contract is brought to an end earlier than the fixed term. Note that Raymond is not a 'commercial agent' because he is not self-employed.

Answer Structure

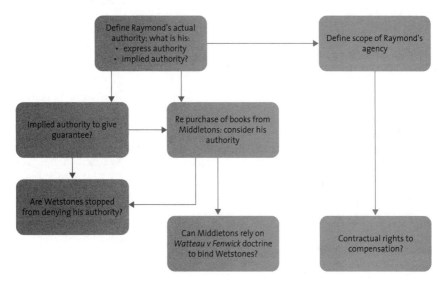

This flowchart shows the connection between key points in the answer.

ANSWER

The relationship between an agent and his principal is a contractual one and as such, it imposes upon both parties rights, duties and obligations. An agent frequently has the power to make contracts which are binding on his principal. Problems arise, however, where the agent exceeds the authority given when contracting with a third party. This question concerns two types of authority. Firstly, if it can be said that the nature and extent of Raymond's express contract with Wetstones Ltd includes the giving of a personal guarantee to customers, then Wetstones will be bound by the contract made with Bertha ('express' authority). Secondly, if it is customary for a bookshop manager such as Raymond to have certain authority, then restrictions on that authority will be ineffective unless the third party knows about them ('usual' authority). This is sometimes referred to as 'implied' authority.[9] We will need to examine whether either type of authority will lead to Wetstones being bound to either of the two contracts made by Raymond.[48]

....

48 Your introduction should clearly set out the relevant issues raised by the question; this demonstrates to the examiner that you have understood what the question requires. Remember that relevancy is an important assessment criterion.

(A) BERTHA

In relation to the contract with Bertha, it does not appear that Wetstones had in any way incorporated into the employment contract with Raymond a term that Raymond should have the right to give personal guarantees to customers. Certainly, Raymond is contractually bound to sell books and Wetstones has invested Raymond with actual express authority to act on Wetstones' behalf. Although Raymond may have express authority to promote Wetstones' books to customers,[49] the giving of a personal guarantee that, by using *How to Pass Exams*, a customer *will* pass exams seems likely to fall outside his express contract of agency.

It seems that Raymond's guarantee to Bertha is a personal one and will not bind Wetstones.

Furthermore, an agent has an implied duty, which is over and above his express contractual duties, to act in good faith in pursuance of the principal's interest. Raymond does not appear to be acting in the best interests of Wetstones. Even if Raymond expressly named Wetstones at the time of the contract with Bertha, Wetstones has the option of whether or not to ratify the guarantee.'

It seems unlikely that Wetstones will wish to ratify Raymond's guarantee even if Wetstones was named at the time of the contract, since this would clearly be to Wetstones' detriment. Accordingly, if Bertha decides to sue on the personal guarantee, Wetstones is entitled to hold Raymond personally liable. The guarantee that Raymond gave Bertha is a personal one and will not bind Wetstones.

(B) MIDDLETONS

In respect of the contract for the purchase of 10 copies of *Uncommon Law* from Middletons, the most obvious type of authority to consider here is usual authority. In *Watteau v Fenwick* (1893), the defendants owned a public house and had appointed a man named Humble as its manager.[50] The defendants forbade Humble from buying cigars for the business from anyone other than the defendants. In breach of this, Humble bought cigars on credit from the claimant. The claimant sought payment from the defendants, who resisted on the basis that Humble had no authority to bind them to this contract because Humble had acted in breach of express instructions not to buy cigars from anyone other than the defendants. The court nevertheless found the defendants

---

49 Don't state all you know about the area of law in question (here: authority), remember to focus on the relevant issues – it is as much your ability to apply the relevant legal rules to the question as your knowledge that is assessed.
50 Outlining the legal context of a particular case is a good way to provide your answer with a logical structure.

liable to pay for the cigars. The court considered that it was within the usual authority of the manager of a public house to be able to buy cigars from any source. Since the claimant was unaware of Humble's restriction to do so, the claimant was entitled to rely on Humble's usual authority.[5]

Watteau v Fenwick has been the subject of considerable criticism on the basis that the approach was applied to a situation where the third party was unaware that he was dealing with an agent.[t] It has been argued that the principle should only apply where the principal is disclosed. Even so, the general principle is clear. 'Usual' authority can bind the principal even where the agent has exceeded his actual authority.

How does all this apply to the facts of the problem? Raymond has, like Humble in *Watteau v Fenwick*, failed to follow an express restriction on the contracts he is entitled to make. It is not known whether Middletons knew that he was dealing with an agent. If he did not, it is possible that the court would refuse to apply *Watteau v Fenwick* on the basis that the concept of usual authority should not be applied to a situation involving an undisclosed principal, despite the facts of that case itself. It seems more likely, however, that Middletons would have realised that Raymond was dealing as a manager rather than as the owner of the bookshop. In that case, the issue that needs to be discussed is what constitutes the usual authority of a bookshop manager. This is a question of fact which will have to be decided in each case. If it is normally accepted that bookshop managers have the authority to purchase books from suppliers chosen at their own discretion, then Wetstones will be likely to be found liable for this contract. If it is not possible to determine that bookshop managers have this usual authority, then Middletons will probably have to pursue Raymond for payment rather than Wetstones.

The only other possibility is if Middletons could argue for the existence of apparent authority (also known as 'ostensible' authority or 'agency by estoppel'). This requires a representation by the principal which is intended to be acted on by the third party, and is in fact acted on, that the agent does have authority to make the contract (*per* Diplock LJ in *Freeman and Lockyer v Buckhurst Park Properties (Mangal) Ltd* (1964)). In *Summers v Solomon* (1857), Solomon owned a jewellery shop and employed a manager to run it. Solomon regularly paid for jewellery ordered by the manager from Summers. After the manager left Solomon's employment, he ordered jewellery from Summers and then absconded with it. The court held that Solomon was bound to pay for the jewellery on the basis that his previous conduct in paying for the jewellery had amounted to a representation of the manager's authority. Summers was entitled to rely on that representation since he was unaware that the manager's authority had been withdrawn.

Applying this to the contract with Middletons, the problem here is that of finding a representation.[51] We are told that the Poole bookshop is a new business and, therefore, there will have been no previous course of dealings. Could it be argued that simply by employing Raymond as the manager, Wetstones is representing that Raymond has authority to do all the things that a bookshop manager would normally do, including buying books from suppliers chosen at their own discretion? This approach was favoured by the court in *United Bank of Kuwait v Hamoud* (1988) and *Gurtner v Beaton* (1993). If followed here, it would make Wetstones liable for Raymond's contract with Middletons, and Wetstones will have to pay for the books.

(C) RAYMOND

The contract here is that Raymond is to receive £15,000 per year for three years and a 5% bonus payment if sales exceeded £50,000 in any one year. It would seem that Wetstones' decision to close down the Poole bookshop amounts to a breach of the agency contract by Wetstones. It is unlikely that either of the contracts made with Bertha or Middletons will render Raymond guilty of misconduct entitling Wetstones to dismiss him. In the circumstances, Raymond will be entitled to claim remuneration from Wetstones for the full period of three years, since it has been expressed in the contract that Raymond was to be employed for that period.[52]

The sales for 2011 exceeded £50,000 and it seems that Raymond will be entitled to his 5% bonus. Is Wetstones liable to pay compensation to Raymond for his removal of the opportunity to earn bonuses for 2012 and 2013?[53] One test is whether or not the agency contract is one of service. Phillimore J in *Northey v Trevillion* (1902) indicated that if the contract is one of service, then the agency contract cannot be terminated without compensation to the agent. In *Turner v Goldsmith* (1891), the agent was employed for a period of five years on a commission basis by the principal to sell shirts. The principal's factory which manufactured the shirts accidentally burnt down. The court held that the principal was still liable to pay the agent a reasonable sum representing what the agent would have been likely to earn by way of commission. Since Raymond's contract contains an express term about the length of service and duration of the liability to pay bonuses, it seems that Raymond will also be entitled to recover a reasonable sum for loss of bonus which Wetstones' decision to close down the Poole bookshop will prevent him from earning.

---

51 Remember to relate your analysis to the issues raised / facts outlined by the question; it is the proper application of the relevant legal rules to the requirements of the question upon which you are assessed not the abstract discussion of the law.

52 Providing an interim conclusion for each major issue considered is a good way to signpost.

53 Remember to aim for completeness in your answer. This means that you have to analyse the problems raised by a question in their entirety, whether you 'like' the potential outcome or not.

QUESTION 39

'In the great mass of contracts it is a matter of indifference to either party whether there is an undisclosed principal or not. If he exists it is, to say the least, extremely convenient that he should be able to sue and be sued as a principal, and he is only allowed to do so on terms which exclude injustice.'

(Lord Lindley in *Keighley Maxted & Co v Durant* (1901))

▶ Discuss.

How to Answer this Question

In most commercial contracts, it does not matter who the other contracting party is. So it does not matter to the third party at the time he contracts with an agent whether there is an undisclosed principal or not. This is the essence of Lord Lindley's statement, hence the general rule that the principal can intervene and enforce the contract. This is an exception to the doctrine of privity under the common law. The **Contracts (Rights of Third Parties) Act 1999** does not apply because an undisclosed principal is neither identified nor identifiable within the meaning of s 1 of that Act.

Answer Structure

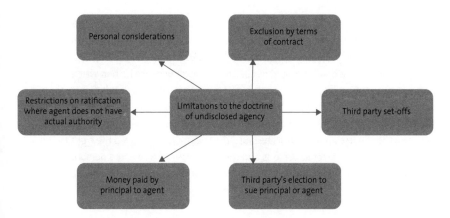

This mind map illustrates the main points that will be covered in the answer.

ANSWER

The justification for the doctrine of the undisclosed principal has been the subject of much discussion. It is generally accepted that although it runs against the fundamental principles of privity of contract (that is, there must be agreement between the parties), the undisclosed principal rules are justified on grounds of commercial convenience.[54] Generally, in commercial law, the assumption is that buyers and sellers are willing to buy/sell to anyone. Contracts are not personal and business people are not concerned about the identity of the other contracting party. As Lord Lloyd said in *Siu Yin Kwan v Eastern Insurance* (1994), an undisclosed principal can sue and be sued on a contract made by an agent on his behalf, if it was within the scope of the agent's actual authority, unless there are special circumstances.[u]

It is important to bear in mind that the initial contract is between the agent and the third party. The undisclosed principal intervenes in an existing contract. This contradicts the fundamental principle of contract law that there needs to be agreement between the parties. There are, therefore, limitations to the doctrine of the undisclosed principal. There needs to be, because it might be unfair to a third party who thought he was dealing only with the other party to then find out that that other party was in fact the agent of a principal.

(1) PERSONAL CONSIDERATIONS

The general rule is that an undisclosed principal cannot intervene if the agent's contract is of a personal nature, that is, where the third party relied on the skill, solvency or other personal characteristics of the agent and which cannot be vicariously performed.[55,v]

Difficulty has been caused by cases where the third party is not relying on the agent's positive attribute but is objecting to the undisclosed principal's negative attribute. *Said v Butt* (1920) involved a theatre critic who wanted tickets to attend the first night of a play. He knew the theatre owners would not sell him a ticket because he had written an unfavourable review on a previous occasion. He asked a friend to obtain tickets for him. When the critic arrived at the theatre, the manager would not permit him entry. The critic sued the manager for breach of contract. The court held that there was no contract between the theatre and the critic, because the theatre had reserved the right to sell first-night tickets to selected persons and the critic was not a selected person. McCardie J said that the critic could not assert the right as an undisclosed principal because he knew the theatre was not willing to contract with him.

Said v Butt has been severely criticised.[56] Whether an undisclosed principal should be allowed to intervene ought to depend on whether the third party felt the agent was the only person he wanted to deal with, that is, the agent has some positive attribute

---

54 As with every essay question, providing a brief outline of the issues you will analyse in the main part is the first essential step to ensure that your answer has a structure.

55 Use the general rule as a starting point for your analysis, then proceed to more specific points; this adds structure and logic to your answer.

56 You need to evaluate the law, especially when dealing with a question that asks you to 'critically analyse'. This means that you need to be prepared to challenge the statements made by the question.

important to the third party. The *Said v Butt* decision is allowing a third party to argue that although the agent's identity does not matter, the undisclosed principal's personality is detrimental. The court in *Said v Butt* clearly felt that the first-night performance at the theatre was a special case. Whatever happened on the first night would more or less determine the success or failure of the play, so the theatre had special reasons to restrict the audience to people who could influence the outcome of the first night in their favour. So the theatre would not wish to permit entry to antagonistic theatre critics.

The result in *Dyster v Randall* (1926) is preferred. A developer wanted to buy land from the owner, but he knew the owner mistrusted him. He therefore employed X to buy in X's name. The developer then said he intervened as an undisclosed principal. Specific performance was granted. The court held that there was a contract between the third party and the principal. Lawrence J agreed with some of what McCardie J said in *Said v Butt*. Perhaps the first night of a theatre performance was special. But in *Dyster*, the undisclosed principal could intervene because the third party did not rely on the personal attributes of the agent. It was a simple agreement for the sale of land. The benefit of such agreements is assignable and the assignee can enforce specific performance.[w]

Courts favour this approach, particularly where commercial parties are involved.[x] The principle seems clear: an undisclosed principal can intervene even if the third party would not have dealt with the agent if he had known the agent was an agent of the principal. The decision in *Said v Butt* is out on a limb, that is, the limitation on the undisclosed principal's right to intervene should only relate to the agent's personal attributes and not to the principal's negative attributes.

(2) EXCLUSION BY THE TERMS OF THE CONTRACT

The doctrine of the undisclosed principal can be excluded by the terms of the contract. In *Humble v Hunter* (1848), an agent chartered out a ship. He signed the charterparty as 'owner'. His mother was in fact the owner. His mother then revealed herself as the undisclosed principal and wanted to enforce the contract. The court held that the undisclosed principal cannot intervene. The description of the agent as 'owner' in the charterparty contract was inconsistent with the terms of that contract. It was a term of the contract that the agent was contracting as the owner of property. He cannot then show that someone else is in fact the owner. The agent impliedly contracted that there is no principal behind him.

Humble v Hunter has been criticised and is unlikely to be followed.[57] For example, in *Fred Drughorn v Rederiaktiebolaget Trans-Atlantic* (1919), the agent signed a charterparty as

---

57 Explaining why a particular course of action might be unsuccessful will attract additional marks.

'charterer'. The House of Lords held that the undisclosed principal can intervene in the contract. A charterparty is essentially a contract for the hire or use of a ship. It was a custom of the trade that charterers often contract as agents for undisclosed principals. *Humble v Hunter* was distinguished.

Only in exceptional cases will an undisclosed principal not be permitted to intervene on grounds that it is inconsistent with the terms of the contract. Possibly the only situation is if the agent signed as 'owner' or 'proprietor'.*y*

As Lord Lloyd said in *Siu Yin Kwan*,[58] 'If courts are too ready to construe written contracts as contradicting the right of the undisclosed principal to intervene, it would go far to destroy the beneficial assumption in commercial cases . . .'.

(3) SET-OFFS

The general rule where the principal is undisclosed is that a third party can set off against the principal any defences accrued against the agent up to point the principal intervenes. On the other hand, if the third party did not consider the other contracting party's identity as relevant or did not believe he was dealing with an agent (that is, the third party thought there might be an undisclosed principal involved), the third party cannot set off the agent's debts against the principal.*z*

(4) MONEY PAID

Armstrong v Stokes suggests that if an undisclosed principal gives money to his agent to pay a third party but the agent fails to do so, the principal is absolved from liability to the third party.*aa*

Armstrong v Stokes (1872) has been severely criticised and the Court of Appeal in *Irvine v Watson* (1880) suggested that *Armstrong* will probably not be followed.*bb*

In *Irvine v Watson*, the court said that the principal remained liable to the third party. Although the doctrine of the undisclosed principal exists for commercial convenience, it is important to protect the third party. In a situation where an agent fails to pass payment to the third party, either the principal or the third party will lose out. It is surely fairer to place the loss on the principal. It is submitted therefore that the better position is this: an undisclosed principal who pays his agent but whose agent does not pass the payment onto the third party, remains liable to the third party.[59]

---

58 Stating by whom or how a particular legal principle was stated in a case (*obiter* or *ratio*) demonstrates a deeper knowledge and is likely to attract additional marks.

59 The critical evaluation of a particular argument is what the examiner is looking for in an essay question.

ELECTION

In an undisclosed principal situation, the initial contract is between the agent and the third party, which is why Lord Lloyd in *Siu Yin Kwan* said that an agent can sue and be sued on the contract. Once the undisclosed principal intervenes, the agent loses his rights of action against the third party. The agent nevertheless remains liable to the third party until the third party elects whether to hold the principal or the agent liable.

The third party cannot sue both, because the third party only makes one contract with one person, that is, there is only one obligation. So, the right to sue the agent and the right to sue the principal are alternatives. The third party may lose his right to sue one of them if he has 'elected' to hold the other liable. The third party cannot change his mind who to sue once he has elected.[cc]

SUMMARY

As Lord Lindley's statement suggests, it is usually a matter of no importance to the contracting parties whether or not there is an undisclosed principal. The doctrine is justified on grounds of commercial convenience. Nevertheless, there needs to be some protection afforded to the third party so as to exclude injustice.[60]

Notes

a In *Armagas v Mundogas* (1986), the House of Lords emphasised that for apparent authority to exist, the representation must come from the principal, not from the agent. In this case, the vice president of a company had indicated that he had authority to agree a deal for the sale and charter-back of a ship. His plan was to make a secret profit out of the transactions. When his deceit came to light, the third party argued that the shipowners were bound by the agent's apparent authority. The House of Lords disagreed, holding that there was no representation of authority from the principal as opposed to the agent, and that therefore apparent authority could not arise.

b This assumes that Annabel has a contractual relationship with Serpentine.

c The lower courts disagreed on the result, but this was the unanimous decision of an eight-person House of Lords.

d In which event, Maria acted fraudulently and will be liable in the tort of deceit (*Polhill v Walter* (1832)). This will be the case if Maria knew Chessington's policy of restricting the types of goods sold at its outlets.

e It is clear from *Greer v Downs Supply Co* (1927) that in respect of the existence of an undisclosed principal, the kind of notice that is required in order to be effective is actual notice, and constructive notice will be insufficient to affect the position of the third party.

f The facts do not suggest that the £10 was a bribe. This type of secret profit is dealt with more severely, with the principal being entitled to summarily dismiss the agent and sue both the agent and the third party for any losses resulting. If an agent takes a bribe, the principal is entitled to claim the amount of the bribe as money had and received (*Logicrose v Southend United Football Club* (1988)).

g Maria holds the £10 on constructive trust (*Boardman v Phipps* (1966)). See also Question 28 on the duties owed by an agent.

---

60 A good conclusion summarises the findings made in the main body of your answer and relates these findings to the question set.

h   Similarly, the third party may enforce the contract made by an agent against his principal.
i   Ratification does not apply here, since one of the requirements is that an agent must purport to act for the principal at the time the contract was made (*Keighley Maxsted and Co v Durant* (1901)). Clearly, Nancy did not disclose the agency at the time she agreed to buy the goods from Brandon.
j   Nancy is entitled to a particular lien, that is, she may retain Aaron's property until debts relating to that property are discharged (cf a general lien exercised by certain types of agents, for example, bankers and solicitors).
k   Though it is probably preferable to restrict 'implied' authority to filling out the relationship between principal and agent, as in *Waugh v Clifford* (1982), rather than as indicating the extent to which the agent may bind the principal to a third party despite a clear breach of the authority given by the principal.
l   Humble had in fact previously been the owner of the beerhouse.
m   It was confirmed in *Armagas v Mundogas* (1986) that the representation must be by the principal. A representation by the agent will not be sufficient. But cf *First Energy (UK) Ltd v Hungarian International Bank* (1993) (discussed in Question 37).
n   Note also *Rama Corp Ltd v Proved Tin and General Investment* (1952), where Slade J identified the need for: (i) a representation; (ii) reliance on the representation by the third party; (iii) an alteration of position resulting from such reliance.
o   Cf also *Gurtner v Beaton* (1993). This approach if used widely would, of course, render the concept of usual authority virtually redundant.
p   The existence of the warranty does not depend on the agent's awareness of the lack of authority. This was established in *Collen v Wright* (1857) and taken to its logical extreme in *Yonge v Toynbee* (1910). In the latter case, the warranty was held to operate against a solicitor who had continued to act for a client who, unknown to the solicitor, had become mentally incapacitated (which had the automatic effect of terminating the solicitor's authority). The fact that the solicitor had acted in good faith throughout was regarded as irrelevant.
q   It is preferable to restrict the use of the type of authority here to 'usual' authority rather than using the phrase 'implied authority', since the latter should be regarded as merely filling out the relationship between principal and agent (see *Waugh v Clifford* (1982)).
r   If Wetstones decides to ratify Raymond's guarantee, Wetstones will have to adopt unequivocally all of Raymond's actions after his full disclosure (*Keighley Maxsted & Co v Durant* (1901)).
s   If a third party knew or should have known of the restriction on the freedom of the manager to purchase from any source, it is unlikely that the third party may rely on the manager's 'usual' authority (*Daun v Simmins* (1879)).
t   At the time of the contract, the claimant thought that Humble was the owner of the public house.
u   *Greer v Downs Supply* (1927) is an example of such a special circumstance. The third party bought timber from an agent who was acting for an undisclosed principal. One reason for the purchase was because the agent owed the third party a debt on a previous transaction. The agent agreed to set off his previous debt against the purchase price. The Court of Appeal did not permit the undisclosed principal to intervene in this transaction because the third party intended to contract only with the agent. The agent specifically agreed that the third party could set off his previous debt against the purchase price. No other party can intervene.
v   For example, if the third party and the agent enter into a contract whereby the agent is to paint the third party's portrait, the principal cannot intervene. This is because the third party is relying on the agent's positive attributes. These attributes need not be personal skills. It can be because of the agent's solvency or where the agent owes the third party money. We have already seen the case of *Greer v Downs Supply* (1927).
w   There was no direct misrepresentation in *Dyster*. If misrepresentation was involved, the undisclosed principal cannot intervene (*Archer v Stone* (1898)).

x See also the case of *Nash v Dix* (1898), referred to by Lawrence J in *Dyster*.

y In *Siu Yin Kwan v Eastern Insurance* (1994), an employer's liability insurance policy was taken out covering the crew on a ship. The agent's name was stated as the employer. In fact, the employers were the owners of the ship. The owners were negligent and the ship sank in a typhoon. Two crew members died. Because the owners were insolvent, the relatives of the dead crew members sued the insurers. The question was whether or not they could do so. The answer depended on whether the owners could themselves have enforced the policy. The insurers argued that the insurance policy included a term that benefits under the policy could not be assigned, so the undisclosed principal cannot intervene. The Privy Council held that the undisclosed principal (who was the true employer) can intervene. It was of no consequence to the insurance company who the employers were because all the information required was the same and thus nothing material to risk. The relatives were entitled to recover against the insurers.

z In *Cooke v Eshelby* (1887), the agents were cotton brokers. It was the practice of the Liverpool cotton market that brokers sometimes dealt on their own account and sometimes as agents. The agents sold cotton to a third party on behalf of an undisclosed principal. The third party did not enquire whether this transaction was on their own account or for an undisclosed principal. The third party had not paid when the undisclosed principal went into liquidation. The trustee in bankruptcy claimed the price from the third party. The third party argued that they should be allowed to set off what the agent owed them on a previous occasion. The House of Lords held that the third party had no right of set off. If it had really mattered to the third party that they dealt with the brokers on their own account (so they could set off previous debts), they should have enquired. The third party knew that the agents were either dealing on their own account or for an undisclosed principal. This was sufficient to put the third party on notice of the possible existence of a principal.

aa This case involved agents who were brokers. They dealt sometimes on their account and sometimes they acted for principals. The third party dealt with these agents many times. They never asked if the agents were acting for themselves or for principals. The agents bought shirts from the third party on behalf of an undisclosed principal. The shirts were delivered to the agents on credit. The principal paid the price of the shirts to the agent but the agent did not pay the third party. When the third party discovered the existence of a principal, the third party sued the principal for the unpaid shirts. The court held that the third party was not entitled to be paid. The principal had already made payment via its agents.

bb In *Irvine v Watson* (1880), a principal employed an agent to buy oil. The agent bought from a third party on payment terms 'cash on delivery'. The third party knew the agent was buying for a principal but the principal was unnamed. The third party delivered the oil to the agent without asking for cash payment. The principal was not aware that the agent had not yet paid the third party in accordance with the contract terms, and the principal paid the agent. The agent did not pass on the monies to the third party who now sued the principal for the price. The Court of Appeal held that the principal must pay the third party.

cc Commencing proceedings constitutes evidence of election, but this is not conclusive (*Clarkson, Booker v Andjel* (1964)).

Fob Contracts

INTRODUCTION

The central feature of an fob (free on board) contract is that the seller fulfils his obligations when he delivers goods conforming to the contract on board the ship. He must bear all the costs up to that point. Although he is not under a duty to insure the goods once he has delivered them, the seller is under a statutory duty to give notice to the buyer so that the buyer has an opportunity to insure. Examiners often set questions dealing with this duty under s 32(3) of the Sale of Goods Act 1979.

The primary duty of the fob buyer is to nominate an effective ship to carry the goods. Unless and until he does so, the seller is not obliged to deliver the goods. Examination questions often involve the buyer's inability to nominate an effective ship and the related problem of where there is a delay in the arrival of a ship which the buyer has nominated to carry the goods.

Questions on international sale of goods contracts invariably involve the financing arrangements between the parties, and the rules in relation to documentary credits are important. It should be remembered that the buyer in such transactions has two distinct rights of rejection: firstly, the right to reject documents arises when the documents are tendered; and, secondly, the right to reject the goods arises when they are landed and when, after examination, they are not found to be in conformity with the contract.

This chapter deals mainly with fob contracts, although it is usual to have parts of questions involving other types of international sale contracts (Question 40, for instance, deals with both an fob as well as a cif contract).

Chapter 11 deals mainly with cif contracts.

The following topics should be prepared in advance of tackling the questions:

❖ the duties of the parties to an fob contract;
❖ the requirements of proper shipping documents;
❖ the strict rules in relation to documentary finance.

QUESTION 40

Cornerstone plc, wholesalers based in London, enters into two separate contracts for the purchase of 5,000 (3,000 superior models and 2,000 standard models) video recorders cif London from Hoshi (Japan) Ltd, and the purchase of 1,000 dolls' houses fob Amsterdam from Cobus. Both contracts called for September/October shipment and payment by irrevocable letter of credit at Yoshi Bank on presentation of the shipping documents. The contract with Cobus contained a clause requiring the dolls' houses to be delivered in time to catch the Christmas trade.

An irrevocable letter of credit in favour of Hoshi (Japan) Ltd was opened on 5 September and the bank paid on presentation of a received for shipment bill of lading, an insurance policy and an invoice. When the video recorders arrived in London, the 2,000 standard models were immediately delivered to Precision Ltd, which had agreed to buy them from Cornerstone plc, and the superior models were transferred to Cornerstone's warehouse. Three weeks later, Precision returned all 2,000 video recorders on discovering that the electrical wiring was faulty.

A revocable letter of credit in favour of Cobus was opened on 27 August and the bank paid on presentation of the shipping documents, which included a bill of lading dated 31 October and a certificate of quality dated 1 November. The dolls' houses arrived in London on 28 November but, due to a shortage of staff at the docks, Cornerstone plc was not notified of this until 26 December.

Both contracts are governed by English law.
▶ Advise Cornerstone plc as to its remedies.

How to Answer this Question

Both parts of the question require you to discuss the opening of the documentary credit. Although the cases do not lay down a conclusive rule in the cases of either fob or of cif contracts, you will need to discuss the time at which documentary credit must be available to the seller.

The bank's position needs to be dealt with. Both Hoshi and Cobus have presented the shipping documents to Yoshi Bank, but neither set of shipping documents is in accordance with Cornerstone's instructions to the bank. The contractual nature of the bank's undertaking to Cornerstone and the bank's entitlement to reimbursement will need to be discussed.

It is not uncommon to find international sale questions involving certain provisions of the Sale of Goods Act 1979. In this question, you will need to discuss the buyer's remedy where there has been a breach of s 14(2) and (3) but where he may have accepted the goods under s 35.

The final part of the question involves stipulations as to time of delivery in fob contracts.

Answer Structure

ANSWER

The general rule is that the documentary credit must be opened in accordance with the contract of sale. The contracts with Hoshi and Cobus do not provide a date for the opening of the credit. They do, however, stipulate a period for the shipment of the goods. It is clear from *Pavia & Co SpA v Thurmann-Nielsen* (1952) that in these circumstances, the documentary credit must be opened at the very latest on the first day on which shipment may take place. The reason for this is that the seller is not bound to tell the buyer the precise date when is he going to ship, but whenever he does ship the goods, the seller must be able to draw on the credit.[a]

As far as Hoshi is concerned, the documentary credit was not opened until 5 September. Following the *Pavia* case, Hoshi is not obliged to ship the goods and may terminate the contract and claim damages.[1, b] However, we are told that Hoshi presents the shipping documents to the bank for payment. Thus, Hoshi must have shipped the goods, although the credit was not opened until 5 September, and may be taken to have waived the breach or at least agreed to a variation of the contract.[c]

The credit in favour of Cobus was opened on 27 August, and this appears to have allowed a reasonable time before the shipment date (*Sinason-Teicher Inter-American Grain Corp v Oilcakes and Oilseeds Trading Co Ltd* (1954)).

However, the contract stipulated that the credit to be opened is to be an irrevocable credit, whereas the credit that was actually made available is a revocable one, that is, one where the bank is free to revoke its undertaking to pay the beneficiary at any time before payment is due. In these circumstances, Cobus is entitled to claim damages for a breach of the terms of the contract, such a breach qualifying as a condition.[d] As with Hoshi, Cobus appears to have either waived the breach or agreed to a variation to the

---

1   Remember to relate your analysis to the issues raised / facts outlined by the question; it is the proper application of the relevant legal rules to the requirements of the question upon which you are assessed not the abstract discussion of the law.

contract, because he does ship the goods and presents the documents to the bank for payment.

We are told that the contracts are governed by English law. It is also assumed that, as is usual, the documentary credits expressly incorporated the **Uniform Customs and Practice for Documentary Credits (UCP)** published by the International Chamber of Commerce. It appears from the question that Hoshi has already been paid on presentation of the shipping documents and nothing turns on the fact that some of the goods are faulty.[2, e] However, it seems that the bank has paid against a received for shipment bill of lading. Such a bill of lading is not good tender under a cif contract because the buyer cannot confirm that the goods have been loaded within the shipment period. The bank's duty is to examine all documents with reasonable care to ascertain that they appear on their face to be in accordance with the terms of the credit. Yoshi Bank does not seem to have scrutinised the documents carefully. Therefore, Cornerstone is not bound to take the shipping documents from the bank.[f] However, we are told that Cornerstone has taken physical delivery of the goods. This in turn means that Cornerstone must have ratified the bank's actions (otherwise the bank would not release the shipping documents to Cornerstone), and such ratification prevents Cornerstone from treating the shipping documents as anything but regular as against the bank.

Precision returns the 2,000 standard model video recorders. Faulty electrical wiring renders the goods unsatisfactory and will give Cornerstone a remedy for breach of **s 14(2)** of the **Sale of Goods Act 1979** against Hoshi.[3] Furthermore, the use of video recorders is well known, so that faulty electrical wiring would render Hoshi in breach of the implied term under **s 14(3)** whereby goods should be reasonably fit for that use. The often sought remedy for breach of **s 14(2)** and **(3)** is rejection of the goods and damages. However, this is subject, of course, to **s 15A**, which provides that where the buyer is not a consumer and the breach is so slight that it would be unreasonable for him to reject the goods, the breach may be treated as a breach of warranty.

Faulty electrical wiring, even if easily put right, would hardly appear to be a slight breach. However, rejection will not be available for those goods which have been accepted. **Section 35** of the **Sale of Goods Act 1979** provides that the buyer may be deemed to have accepted the goods, thus losing the right to reject, where *inter alia* he does some act 'inconsistent with the seller's ownership' or where after a reasonable period he retains the goods without indicating that he rejects them. It is unclear whether before the delivery to Precision, Cornerstone had an opportunity to examine the standard model video recorders for the purpose of seeing whether they conformed to the

---

2   Be clear and precise in what you are saying. Don't use convoluted sentences as it distracts from your analysis; clarity of expression is another important assessment criterion. This is a good example.

3   Restrict yourself to what is relevant, don't write down everything you know. Remember that relevancy is an important assessment criterion.

contract.[4] If Cornerstone resells the goods, having inspected them, and Precision then rejects them, it might be argued that Cornerstone has lost the right to reject the goods, it being argued that it had retained them for more than a reasonable length of time before rejecting them. On the other hand, it has been held (*Truk (UK) Ltd v Tokmakidis* (2000)) that where goods are bought for resale, the reasonable period of time before the right to reject the goods is lost will normally last for the time it takes to resell the goods, plus a further period of time for the ultimate purchaser to test the goods.

Thus, in determining whether Cornerstone has accepted the goods, the important factor becomes one of whether Precision has accepted the goods *vis-à-vis* Cornerstone. This in turn depends upon whether the three weeks which it took Precision to reject the goods amounts to more than a reasonable period of time and, since s 35 was amended by the Sale and Supply of Goods Act 1994, one of the relevant factors is whether that period allowed Precision a reasonable opportunity to examine the goods for the purpose of ascertaining whether they complied with the contract. Whereas, prior to the 1994 amendment, a three-week period was held to amount to more than a reasonable period of time (*Bernstein v Pamson Motors*),[5] it seems likely that the court would now find that it does not. Thus, Precision, it is submitted, is not restricted to a claim for damages but was entitled to reject the goods, and Cornerstone was similarly entitled. If, as soon as Precision intimated to Cornerstone its rejection of the goods, Cornerstone immediately informed Hoshi that it was rejecting the goods, then Cornerstone will not have lost its right to reject the goods. If, on the other hand, Cornerstone failed for some time to inform Hoshi that it was rejecting the goods, that delay will have increased the chances of Cornerstone being held to have accepted the goods.[6]

Assuming that Precision validly rejected the goods, Precision will also have a claim for damages against Cornerstone. The *prima facie* measure of those damages will be the difference between the contract price of the goods and (if it is higher) the market price (of goods that comply with the contract) on the day of delivery. If Cornerstone has also validly rejected the goods, that will also be the *prima facie* measure of damages that Cornerstone can claim against Hoshi. If Cornerstone has not validly rejected the goods, then it is entitled only to damages. Those damages will, however, include any consequent losses which Cornerstone has incurred in relation to the sub-sale to Precision. In the case of a breach of term as to quality in a contract where goods are bought for resale, the courts are prepared to take into account the effect of a sub-sale upon the losses incurred by the buyer (*Bence Graphics v Fasson UK* (1997)).

....

4   Considering ambiguities in the question demonstrates understanding and will attract a higher mark.
5   Showing an awareness of the development of the area of law in question demonstrates both knowledge and understanding.
6   Pointing out different possibilities ensures completeness of your analysis and attracts additional marks.

As discussed above, the opening of the credit on 27 August was not too late.[7] However, Cornerstone is in breach of the contract in that the credit was not an irrevocable one, but Cobus ships the goods and is paid by the bank on presentation of the shipping documents.

Yoshi Bank is only entitled to be reimbursed sums it pays out if it pays on receipt of documents which strictly comply with Cornerstone's instructions. Yoshi Bank has paid against the bill of lading which is dated 31 October (and thus appears to fall within the shipment period) but also a certificate of quality dated 1 November. On the face of the documents, read together, the goods could not have been shipped on 31 October. The bank is thus liable to Cornerstone, since the documents do not comply with the terms of the credit which stipulate for a September/October shipment (*Soproma v Marine and Animal By-Products* (1966)). Because Cornerstone appears to have ratified the bank's wrongful act, does Cornerstone have a second right to reject, that is, to reject the goods themselves on the ground that they are not of contract description? The general rule is that where a buyer who accepts documents in ignorance of a defect in them and later discovers the defect and takes delivery of the goods, he will be taken to have waived his right to reject not only the documents, but also the goods on account of that defect (see *Panchaud Frères v Establissements General Grain* (1970)). However, since Yoshi Banks acts as principal when accepting the shipping documents, and not as Cornerstone's agents, Cornerstone can reject the goods on arrival on the ground that they are not of contract description (even if Yoshi Bank accepted the documents which showed they were defective on the face of them).

May Cornerstone reject the goods since they did not arrive in time to catch the Christmas trade? In *Frebold and Sturznickel (Trading as Panda OGH) v Circle Products Ltd* (1970), German sellers sold toys to English buyers under an fob contract on terms that the goods were to be delivered in time for the Christmas trade. The goods arrived at the destination on 13 November. Due to an oversight (for which the sellers were not responsible), the buyers were not notified of the arrival of the goods until 17 January. The court held that the sellers were not in breach, since they had delivered the goods in such a way that would normally have resulted in the goods arriving in time for the Christmas trade. Applying this case to the question,[8] the dolls' houses did in fact arrive in London on 28 November and therefore in time for the Christmas trade but, because of a shortage of staff at the docks, which could not have been the fault of Cobus, Cornerstone did not know of the arrival until some time after. It seems, therefore, that Cornerstone will have no remedy against Cobus, since Cobus had delivered the goods in accordance with the requirements of the contract. Cornerstone's remedies may be in suing the port authorities, the carriers or their agents or other parties responsible.

....

7   Build upon points you have raised previously; this gives your answer structure.
8   In order to attract a good mark you need to ensure that you don't merely describe the law; you need to explain and apply it to the requirements of the question.

QUESTION 41

Katniss enters into three separate contracts for the sale of 4,000 tons of broad beans to Effie, 5,000 tons of soybeans to Seneca and 1,500 tons of castor beans to Caesar. Each contract calls for shipment in May, fob Southampton, and contains a clause permitting the buyer, on giving reasonable notice, to call for delivery at any time within the shipment period.

On 5 May, Effie informs Katniss that he has nominated *The Polygon* to take delivery of the consignment, ready to load on 11 May. Katniss protests at the length of notice, and since she is not able to have the consignment packed in time, she purchases 4,000 tons of already-packed broad beans from a third party at 5% above the normal market price. Katniss is able to send the broad beans to the docks at Southampton on 11 May. *The Polygon* is not ready to load and Effie nominates *The Achilleas* to take the consignment on 28 May. By this time, the broad beans have deteriorated due to rain seeping through the packaging. Effie refuses to load the consignment.

On 8 May, Seneca nominates *The Sylvia* and asks Katniss to have the consignment ready to load on 20 May. The general market price of soybeans has unexpectedly dropped by half since the contract was made. Owing to a strike at the farm, Katniss is not able to send the soybeans to the docks at Southampton until 23 May, and Seneca uses this as a reason for refusing to load the consignment.

On 25 May, Caesar informs Katniss that *The Eurymedon* will be ready to load on 30 May. When Katniss tries to load the goods, she is informed that recent regulations require an export licence for the supply of castor beans in excess of 1,000 tons. Caesar refuses to accept a smaller quantity when asked by Katniss.

The contracts are governed by English law.

▶ Advise Katniss.

How to Answer this Question

This question requires a review of the duties of both parties to an fob contract. In particular, the part of the question regarding the broad beans involves the buyer's duty to nominate an effective ship and the seller's duty to ensure compliance with the implied terms as to quality under the **Sale of Goods Act 1979**. The situation with the soybeans concerns a seller's failure to load within time.

The part of the question dealing with the castor beans is a little unusual, since it involves a partial prohibition on the export of goods imposed *after* the contract of sale was concluded. The issue is whether the contract is brought to an end because of frustration or whether the contract subsists for that part of the contract where performance was possible. Please note that frustration and prohibition of export have separate origins and consequences.

Since there are three parts to the question, the amount of detail required will be restricted to the time available for answering all the parts.

Answer Structure

This diagram shows the main factors to consider in relation to FOB obligations when writing your answer. It will also be important to consider definitions and how the specific circumstances of this scenario affect the contract.

ANSWER

In the absence of further information regarding express terms in the contract, the basic duties of the parties depend on commercial practice as recognised by English law. Under a 'classic' fob contract, the primary duties of the buyer are to nominate an effective ship to carry the goods, to notify the seller of such nomination in time for him to load the goods and to pay the agreed price (*Pyrene & Co v Scindia Navigation Co Ltd* (1954); *The El Amria and El Minia* (1982)). Once the buyer has nominated a ship, the seller is required to deliver goods which comply with the terms of the contract to the port in time for loading to take place during the contract period.[9]

....

9   Your introduction should clearly set out the relevant issues raised by the question; this demonstrates to the examiner that you have understood what the question requires. Remember that relevancy is an important assessment criterion.

BROAD BEANS

Effie informs Katniss on 5 May that *The Polygon* has been nominated to take delivery of the consignment on 11 May. Although Katniss protests at the short notice, this is normally irrelevant since the buyer in an fob contract has the option of when to ship during the contract period. More particularly, there is an express term in the contract allowing the buyer to call for delivery at any time. It is clear, however, that if the buyer nominates a ship in such a way that the seller is not given reasonable time to have the goods ready for loading, the seller is entitled to claim damages[g] for the failure of the buyer to nominate a suitable ship. The question of whether Effie has given Katniss adequate notice is one of fact.[10]

In an fob contract, the timing of the nomination of an effective ship is normally of the essence, that is, it is a condition of the contract. If Effie's notice of nomination is unreasonable, Katniss is entitled to treat the contract as repudiated and will be entitled to damages (*Bunge & Co Ltd v Tradax England Ltd* (1975)).[h] However, by delivering to the docks on 11 May, Katniss has probably waived her right to treat the contract as repudiated.

Katniss has had to purchase the broad beans at 5% above the normal market price. This additional cost cannot be recovered from Effie since, under a 'classic' fob contract, the seller is responsible for all the expenses of getting the goods over the ship's rail (*AG v Leopold Walford (London) Ltd* (1923)).

Effie subsequently nominates *The Achilleas*. A buyer is entitled to substitute a fresh nomination provided there is time to do so in accordance with the contract. Effie's first nomination is not irrevocable (*Agricultores Federados Argentinos v Ampro SA* (1965)). Thus, Effie is entitled to nominate a second ship.

The broad beans deteriorate before loading and Effie refuses to load the consignment on this basis. The implied terms as to satisfactory quality and as to fitness for a particular purpose under ss 14(2) and (3) of the **Sale of Goods Act 1979** apply to an fob contract, and breach of either term may entitle the buyer to reject the goods and claim damages, provided the buyer is not a consumer and the breach is not so slight that it would be unreasonable for him to reject the goods (s 15A of the **Sale of Goods Act 1979**).[i] Since the seller is responsible for the goods prior to loading, it appears that Effie is *prima facie* entitled to refuse to accept delivery of the defective broad beans on 28 May.[11]

If the broad beans deteriorate due to unsuitable packaging, this would amount to a breach of s 14(3). Where the seller knows that goods are to be shipped, he is under an obligation to ensure that the goods are packaged in such a way that they can endure the

---

10 A logical structure is the first step towards gaining a good mark. You need to present your arguments in an organised manner; don't jump.

11 It is important to refer to relevant authorities to substantiate your argument – this might be case law or a statutory provision. Remember: it is the application of law upon which you are assessed.

sea transit (*Wills v Brown* (1922)). It seems, therefore, that Effie may be able to reject the broad beans and will be entitled to recover damages for non-delivery from Katniss.ʲ

SOYBEANS

Katniss is not able to send the consignment of soybeans to the docks until three days after *The Sylvia* is ready to load. In a 'classic' fob contract, it is the buyer who has the option of when to ship within the contract period (*Bowes v Shand* (1877)) and, once shipping instructions have been received, the seller must load within a reasonable time. It seems that 12 days' notice is reasonable in this question, since we are told that the delay in sending the soybeans to the docks was due to a strike at the farm. A failure to load on 20 May is a breach of a condition of the contract and is a ground for rejection (*The Mihalis Angelos* (1971)), because time is of the essence in commercial contracts.

Seneca could have chosen to affirm the contract and claim damages for the loss occasioned by the delay but, due to the drop in the market price of soybeans, it seems more likely that Seneca will wish to reject the goods. He will also have a claim against Katniss in damages for non-delivery.[12]

CASTOR BEANS

As for the consignment of castor beans, we are told that Katniss is only aware of the recent prohibition on the export of such goods without a licence when she tries to load the goods on 30 May. It appears that the prohibition was imposed after the conclusion of the contract. Such a prohibition does not make the contract illegal *ab initio*, but may discharge it under the doctrine of frustration. Since the contract specifically provides that the castor beans is to be exported from Southampton (and within the country which is imposing the prohibition), the contract between Katniss and Caesar may be frustrated (*Tsakiroglou v Noblee Thorl* (1962)). However, where the prohibition is qualified, as in this question (making a previously unrestricted export of goods subject to a licensing requirement), the contract is not automatically discharged.[13] The court may decide to impose a duty on one of the parties to make reasonable efforts to obtain the licence. In the absence of an express provision as to licence, there is no general rule putting the burden of obtaining a licence on one party or another, and each case would depend on the facts.ᵏ *Pagnan SpA v Tradax Ocean Transportation* (1986) provided that in such cases, the court will ask itself whether the duty imposed on the seller to obtain a licence is absolute or is only to use due diligence.[14] If the duty is to be imposed on Katniss, then Katniss will only be able to rely on the prohibition as a ground of discharge if she can show that reasonable efforts to procure the licence would have failed. Certainly, Katniss

···

12 Explaining why a course of action might be preferable will attract additional marks.
13 Proceeding from the general rule to the specific is a good way to structure your answer in a logical manner; it also demonstrates your knowledge and understanding.
14 Restrict yourself to what is relevant; don't write down everything you know about a particular case. Remember that relevancy is an important part of the assessment criteria.

only knew of the prohibition on 30 May, giving her only 24 hours to obtain the licence before the end of the shipment period.

The prohibition, however, is only partial, in that the regulations merely restrict the amount of castor beans a seller is allowed to export without a licence to 1,000 tons. In the circumstances, although in the normal course of events a buyer is not obliged to accept a smaller quantity of goods than that contracted for, the contract is not discharged but the prohibition may excuse partial performance. Katniss must supply 1,000 tons of castor beans but is excused from supplying the remaining 500 tons.[14] If Caesar refuses to accept delivery of 1,000 tons of castor beans, Katniss will be entitled to recover damages under s 50(3) of the Sale of Goods Act 1979.[15]

> **Common Pitfalls**
> Where a question involves various issues, do not waste time by writing out the facts of the question.

QUESTION 42

Bella agrees to sell to Renee in Bristol 1,000 kilograms of anchovies packed in boxes, 25 kilograms in each box, fob Hamburg, payment by letter of credit on tender of documents to Ganesh Bank. The contract called for October shipment. On 3 October, Renee nominates *The Ostrich* to take the goods and Bella arranges for the consignment to arrive at the docks shortly afterwards. Renee had not booked shipping space on *The Ostrich* but Bella finally manages to persuade the master to take the goods on 31 October. The following day, a fire breaks out on *The Ostrich* and the boxes containing the anchovies are wetted while the fire is being extinguished. The boxes are unloaded and repacked in boxes of 50 kilograms. They are reloaded on 2 November. The master of the ship issues a bill of lading for '20 × 50 kilograms anchovies shipped on 31 October'.

When Bella presents the documents to Ganesh Bank, she is refused payment on the ground that the bill of lading shows incorrect packaging. Bella takes the bill of lading back to the master of *The Ostrich*, who agrees to have the anchovies repacked on the voyage and issues a fresh bill of 40 boxes of 25 kilograms of anchovies.

When the boxes arrive in Bristol, Renee discovers that the anchovies had been infected with fungus, causing the anchovies to deteriorate.

▶ Advise the parties.

....

15 Remember to draw conclusions from your analysis; this evidences your understanding of how to apply the law.

How to Answer this Question

Although Renee nominates a ship, she has not booked shipping space. This is not a fundamental breach of the contract, since Bella does manage to load the goods on the ship nominated by Renee. The problem is that the goods are damaged and then unloaded and the question of risk will need to be addressed.

Shipping documents have always played a key role in international sale contracts and the second part of this question requires you to discuss whether the bank may refuse to pay against documents which indicate incorrect packaging. The issue of packaging falls squarely within the implied term as to description under s 13 of the **Sale of Goods Act 1979**. Because the anchovies deteriorate, s 14 of that Act will also need to be discussed.

Answer Structure

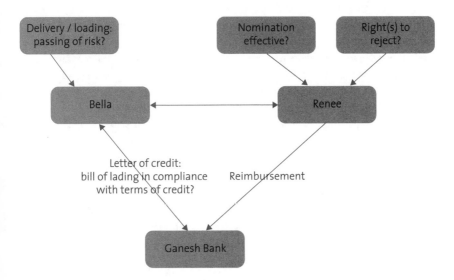

This diagram focuses on the parties involved in this scenario and the relationship between them. As well as issues of compliant and non-compliant documents the rights of rejection in relation to documents and goods must be dealt with separately.

ANSWER

In the absence of further information about the express terms, the contract between Bella and Renee is a 'classic' fob contract. The primary duties of the buyer are to nominate an effective ship to carry the goods, to notify the seller of such nomination in time for the seller to load goods and to pay the agreed price. The seller's primary duty is to deliver goods which comply with the terms of the contract once the seller has given his shipping instructions.

Where documentary credit is involved, the rule is that the letter of credit must be opened at the very latest before the first day of the shipment period. This is clear from *Pavia & Co SpA v Thurmann-Nielsen* (1952).[16] In this question, we are not told when Ganesh Bank advised Bella of the opening of the credit and, if this was on or after 1 October, Bella is entitled to refuse to ship the goods and may treat the contract as discharged and claim damages against Renee. We are told that Bella does in fact ship the goods, thus choosing not to treat the late opening of credit (if indeed it was opened on or after 1 October) as discharging the contract.

Although Renee nominates *The Ostrich*, she has not in fact booked shipping space for the goods. It is the prime duty of an fob buyer to give 'effective' shipping instructions, that is, it must be possible and lawful for the seller to comply with them (*Agricultores Federados Argentinos v Ampro SA* (1965)). The essential point is that the seller must be instructed as to the way in which he can perform his duty to put the goods on board. Bella, nevertheless, manages to persuade the master of *The Ostrich* to take the goods. Renee's nomination of *The Ostrich* is therefore adequate since the named ship can in fact take the goods, irrespective of her failure to make advance arrangements with the master. Nothing turns on this point, since if Renee had not reserved shipping space in advance, she runs the risk that her shipping instructions may be ineffective, but she does not commit any breach of contract as long as Bella is in fact able to ship the goods in accordance with the shipping instructions.[17] Despite the fact that Bella only managed to persuade the master of *The Ostrich* to take the goods on the last day stipulated within the contract shipment period, all the boxes were in fact loaded by the end of that day.

A fire breaks out on *The Ostrich* the next day, 1 November, and the boxes are unloaded. Once goods have been loaded, risk normally passes to the buyer because the seller has fulfilled his obligation to deliver the goods and nothing remains to be done by him under the contract except to tender the shipping documents for payment. Thus, Bella need not have involved herself with the events that occurred after 31 October, and it would have been Renee's decision whether or not to claim for any damage against the underwriters if she had taken out an insurance policy.[m] Because the goods are unloaded, a problem has arisen. For whatever reason, the anchovies have now been packed in boxes of 50 kilograms per box whereas the contract had stipulated for 25 kilograms per box. The bill of lading issued by the master states '20 x 50 kilograms anchovies shipped on 31 October'.

The requirement that goods must correspond to their description used to be a strict one, entitling the buyer to reject for quite trivial discrepancies, and to do so even though the

---

16   It is often not necessary to provide details of the cases you cite as you are merely using them as authorities (i.e. references) for the legal principles you have you explained / referred to.

17   This is a good example of how to achieve a logical structure. This is the first step towards gaining a good mark: you need to present your arguments in an organised manner; don't jump.

failure of the seller to deliver goods of the contract description does not in the least prejudice the buyer (*Arcos Ltd v Ronaasen & Son* (1933)).ᵗⁿ This is no longer the case due to s 15A of the **Sale of Goods Act 1979**.[18] The buyer who is a non-consumer can no longer reject where the breach is so slight that it would be unreasonable for him to do so.

Ganesh Bank was entitled to refuse to pay against the documents which Bella presented, since the bill of lading does not comply with the terms of the credit because it indicates incorrect packaging. This stems from the principle of strict compliance in documentary financing. As Lord Sumner said in *Equitable Trust Co of New York v Dawson Partners Ltd* (1927): 'There is no room for documents which are almost the same, or which will do just as well.'[19] Ganesh Bank has no discretion, in that it must comply strictly with the buyer's instructions as to payment.ᵒ The bank's right to reimbursement from Renee depends on it taking up a faultless set of documents and, since the bill of lading indicates incorrect packaging, Ganesh Bank was entitled to refuse to pay Bella, no matter how minor the discrepancy may appear.

Ganesh Bank's duty is to examine all the documents with reasonable care to ascertain whether they appear on their face to be in accordance with the terms of credit. It is not responsible for the genuineness or accuracy of the documents, merely whether they comply, and Ganesh Bank has rightly refused to pay Bella.

It appears that Ganesh Bank has notified Bella of the reason for rejection and Bella does have an opportunity to put right any defect and present the document again, provided that there is time to do so in accordance with the contract of sale and the credit. Bella therefore takes the bill of lading back to the master of *The Ostrich*, who issues a fresh bill now stipulating that the cargo is of 40 boxes each containing 25 kilograms of anchovies as was required under the contract.

We are not then told what the parties' actions were, but it is reasonable to assume that Bella then retenders the documents to Ganesh Bank which then pays against them, since the bill of lading now indicates the correct packaging. As far as the date of shipment is concerned, the bill of lading shows 31 October and thus the documents appear on their face in apparent good order and comply with the terms of the credit. In order for Renee to have taken possession of the goods on arrival, Renee will have reimbursed Ganesh Bank because a bank will not release the documents until payment by its principal. Once Ganesh Bank has taken reasonable care in scrutinising the documents, it will not be liable to Renee if the documents later turn out to be defective.

....

18 Showing an awareness of the development of a particular rule demonstrates your knowledge.

19 The inclusion of a direct quote by a judge or by a noted expert in the field is not only a good starting point for a wider discussion of the relevant issues but also serves as evidence of both your wider research efforts and your knowledge of the area in question.

Renee discovers that the anchovies have deteriorated due to fungus infection. Although she has previously accepted documents, Renee may be entitled to reject the goods. An fob buyer has two distinct rights of rejection. As Devlin J made clear in *Kwei Tek Chao v British Traders and Shippers* (1954), the right to reject documents arises when the documents are tendered, and the right to reject goods arises when they are landed and when, after examination, they are not found to be in conformity with the contract.[20]

This would be the case if the goods suffered from some qualitative defect not apparent on the face of the documents. In *Mash & Murrell v Joseph Emanuel* (1961), Cyprus horsebeans were sold cif Southampton. The horsebeans were sound when shipped but were found to be rotten on arrival. On the facts of the case, it was found that the deterioration was a result of fungus infection before or at the time of shipment. The court held that the seller was liable for the deterioration. As Diplock J said in that case:[21] '. . . when goods are sold under a contract such as a cif contract or fob contract which involves transit before use, there is an implied warranty not merely that they shall be [satisfactory] at the time they are put on the vessel, but that they shall be in such a state that they can endure the normal journey and be in a [satisfactory] condition on arrival . . .'

It therefore seems that because anchovies are normally capable of enduring a sea transit, Bella will be liable for any deterioration apparent on arrival.[22] This implied warranty is distinct from the implied term under s 14 of the **Sale of Goods Act 1979**, the former relating to an undertaking that the goods can endure sea transit as opposed to s 14(2) and (3), which are implied terms relating to satisfactory quality and fitness for purpose.

Renee may thus be entitled to reject the goods for breach of the implied terms as to satisfactory quality and fitness for purpose under s 14 of the **Sale of Goods Act 1979**, provided that the breach is not so slight so as to treat it as a breach of warranty (s 15A of the **Sale of Goods Act 1979**). If the anchovies no longer have commercial value, as it appears in this case, Renee is likely to be entitled to reject the goods despite the fact that Bella has already been paid against documents.

Furthermore, according to the House of Lords in *Bowes v Shand* (1877), stipulations as to the time of shipment form part of the description of the goods and breach of such

....

20 Remember to relate your analysis to the issues raised/facts outlined by the question; it is the proper application of the relevant legal rules to the requirements of the question upon which you are assessed not the abstract discussion of the law.

21 Stating by whom or how a particular legal principle was stated in a case (*obiter* or *ratio*) demonstrates a deeper knowledge and is likely to attract additional marks.

22 Remember to draw conclusions from your analysis; this evidences your understanding of how to apply the law.

stipulations entitles the buyer to reject.[23] Although *Bowes v Shand* was decided before the **Sale of Goods Act 1893**, subsequent cases have acknowledged that the time of shipment is part of the description of the goods and is within **s 13** of the **Sale of Goods Act** (*Avon & Co v Comptoir Wegimont* (1921)). Since the goods were not in fact shipped within the contract period, Renee may be able to reject the goods on the ground that they did not constitute an October shipment. However, it is arguable whether Renee can reject the goods, since **s 15A** of the **Sale of Goods Act 1979** provides that where the breach is so slight that it would be unreasonable for the buyer to reject the goods and the buyer does not deal as a consumer, the breach is to be treated as a breach of warranty and not as a breach of condition. Since time is of the essence in commercial contracts, it is submitted that the breach will not be perceived as so slight for it to be treated as a breach of warranty.

Notes

a   This principle applies to both cif and fob contracts. It has been argued that, since an fob buyer had the option as to the time of shipment, the documentary credit needs to be opened at a reasonable time before the date nominated by the buyer in the shipping instructions. Lord Diplock in *Ian Stach Ltd v Baker Bosley Ltd* (1958) thought that such a rule would lead to uncertainties and concluded that the *prima facie* rule is that the credit must be opened, at the latest, on the first day of the shipping period.

b   The measure of damages, it seems, is not limited by the market price rule in **s 50(3)** of the **Sale of Goods Act 1979**, but may extend to the seller's lost profits, provided that they are not too remote under the rule in *Hadley v Baxendale* (1854); *Trans Trust SPRL v Danubian Trading Co Ltd* (1952).

c   The difference between a waiver and an agreement to a variation is that the former entitles the seller to reinstate the requirement on giving the buyer reasonable notice, and the latter will prevent the seller unilaterally to reverting to the original position. The significance of the distinction does not arise in this question.

d   See note *b*, above.

e   Even if the bank knew that the goods were faulty at the time Hoshi presented the shipping documents, it is well established that the courts will not allow revocation at all where the credit is irrevocable.

f   The bank is also prevented from returning the documents to the seller.

g   The seller cannot claim the purchase price if the goods have not been shipped, even if non-shipment is the result of the buyer's failure to give effective shipment instruction: *Colley v Overseas Exporters* (1921).

h   The measure of damages will be that set out under **s 50(3)** of the **Sale of Goods Act 1979** for non-acceptance.

i   Damages will be for non-delivery of goods under **s 51(3)** of the **Sale of Goods Act 1979**.

j   If the question had not included a reason for the goods deteriorating, the issue would be whether a seller can recover damages for losses incurred because the buyer substitutes another ship (see *J&J Cunningham v Monroe* (1922), in particular Lord Heward's comments).

k   See *Brandt & Co v Morris & Co* (1917) (where the court held that the buyers were obliged to obtain the export licence on the basis that a ship which could not legally carry goods was not an effective ship) and *Pound & Co Ltd v Hardy & Co Inc* (1956) (where the court found

---

23   Pointing out an alternative course of action is a good way to attract marks as it demonstrates knowledge and understanding.

that the sellers were obliged to obtain the export licence since the licence could only be obtained by persons registered in the exporting country and as between the parties it was the sellers who were registered).

l   The effect of the partial prohibition is the same as that of physical impossibility caused by the failure of a specified crop.

m   An fob seller is not obliged to take out insurance cover for the goods, but s 32(3) of the Sale of Goods Act 1979 imposes on him an obligation to 'give such notice to the buyer as may enable him to insure [the goods] during their sea transit'. If the seller does not do so, the goods are deemed to be at the seller's risk. However, *Wimble Sons & Co v Rosenberg* (1913) established that in a classic fob contract, that is, where the buyer nominates the vessel and gives the shipping instructions, the buyer will normally have sufficient information to enable him to insure so that the seller need not give further notice under s 32(3).

n   In *Re Moore & Co and Landauer & Co* (1921), it was held that goods did not comply with their description when the contract called for 3,000 tins of fruit to be packed 30 tins to a case and the seller delivered the correct number of tins, but some were packed 24 tins to a case.

o   Lord Wilberforce in *Reardon Smith Line Ltd v Hansen Tangen* (1976) described some of the older cases as 'excessively technical', but that the need for certainty, particularly in international sales, outweighs the need for flexibility.

Cif Contracts

INTRODUCTION

Under a cif (cost, insurance and freight) contract, the seller is required to arrange the carriage of the goods and their insurance in transit, and all costs of such arrangements are included in the contract price. The essential duties of a cif seller are to obtain a bill of lading, a policy of insurance and any other document required by the contract, and to forward them to the buyer who pays on the invoice when he receives the shipping documents.

Shipping documents play a central role in cif contracts, particularly where documentary financing is concerned. Because the buyer in international sale contracts has two rights of rejection, he retains his right to reject the goods on arrival if they do not conform with the terms of the contract, even if he has paid against shipping documents.

Cif contracts are often concerned with the sale of unascertained goods, and issues concerning the passing of risk and property are often involved. A particular problem arises where unascertained goods are lost before the cif seller has appropriated the goods to the contract.

QUESTION 43

Pugwash agrees to buy 10,000 tons of garbanzo beans from Odessa out of the 15,000 tons of garbanzo beans currently in Odessa's warehouse in Swansea, cif Hong Kong. Shortly afterwards, Odessa sells to Flloyd the remaining 5,000 tons of garbanzo beans, fob Bristol, Odessa to make the shipping arrangements to Hong Kong. Payment is to be in cash against shipping documents on both contracts.

Odessa ships all 15,000 tons on board *The Wing On* and the cargo of garbanzo beans is put into two separate holds – 10,000 tons in hold No 1 and 5,000 tons in hold No 2. The master of *The Wing On* is hesitant in signing clean bills of lading because he knows of the rumour that the garbanzo beans were suspect, having been lying in Odessa's warehouse for some time. The gossip is that the garbanzo beans are unlikely to be usable by the time the cargo arrives in Hong Kong. Nevertheless, he is persuaded by Odessa and signs two clean bills of lading, one relating to hold No 1 and the other to hold No 2.

Before the ship sails, the garbanzo beans are severely wetted due to an exceptionally heavy storm. Water penetrates into both holds due to inadequate sealing of the hatch covers. The master notes on both bills of lading as follows: 'Cargo wetted by rain after shipment.'

After the ship sails, Odessa tenders the bill of lading relating to hold No 1, with the insurance policy and the invoice, to Pugwash who, having now heard about the rumours regarding the garbanzo beans, refuses to pay on the ground that the bill of lading is not 'clean'. Odessa tenders the bill of lading relating to hold No 2 to Flloyd, who also refuses to pay on the ground that because he had not been given any information about the shipping arrangements, he had not taken out an insurance policy covering the sea transit.

▶ Advise Pugwash and Flloyd as to their legal position.

How to Answer this Question

Shipping documents have always played a key role in international sale contracts, and the first part of this question requires you to discuss the time when the bill of lading must be 'clean'. The fact that Pugwash has heard of rumours concerning the cargo does not entitle him to reject the documents, but he does have the right to reject the goods on arrival. The cif buyer's two rights of rejection are separate and distinct.

As far as Flloyd is concerned, this is a straightforward question about the fob seller's statutory duty under s 32(3) of the **Sale of Goods Act 1979**.

Applying the Law

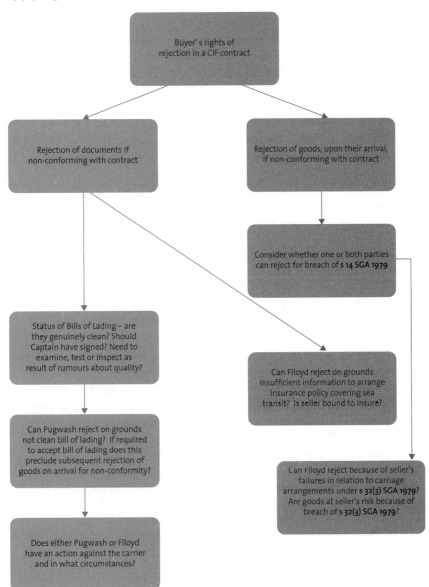

This diagram shows how the right of rejection can be understood in this scenario.

ANSWER

Both Pugwash and Flloyd are refusing to pay against shipping documents. If these documents conform to the contract, then Pugwash and Flloyd must accept them, otherwise they will be in breach of contract even if the goods themselves do not comply with the contract when they arrive (*Gill and Duffus SA v Berger & Co Inc* (1984)).[1]

Pugwash is refusing to pay on the ground that the bill of lading is not 'clean'. A clean bill of lading is one that does not contain any reservation as to the apparent good order or condition of the goods or the packing (*British Imex Industries Ltd v Midland Bank Ltd* (1958)). The time to which such a reservation must relate to prevent the bill of lading from being clean is that of shipment. In *The Galatia* (1980), a bill of lading was issued stating that the goods had been shipped in apparent good order and condition, but bore a notation that they had been subsequently damaged. The court held that the notation did not prevent the bill from being clean.[2]

Applying *The Galatia* to this question, Pugwash cannot reject the bill of lading on the ground that the bill is not clean. The master of *The Wing On* is neither bound to take samples of the garbanzo beans nor to have them analysed, nor otherwise investigate the cargo even if he is aware of rumours concerning the quality of the cargo. The master is justified in issuing a clean bill of lading. The note that was added referred to damage that occurred after loading. Thus, the bill of lading is still clean.

If Odessa has tendered the shipping documents (which, in a cif contract, will include an insurance policy and an invoice in addition to a bill of lading (*The Julia* (1949)) in accordance with the contract, Pugwash must pay against them. It seems that Pugwash has wrongfully refused to do so. It should be said, however, that a buyer in international sales contracts has two rights of rejection. For non-compliance with the contractual terms, he may have a right to reject documents, and a right to reject the goods on delivery where the breach is not slight (**ss 13, 14** and **15A** of the **Sale of Goods Act 1979**). These two rights of rejection are quite distinct (*Kwei Tek Chao v British Traders and Shippers* (1954)). A cif buyer to whom documents have been tendered is not entitled to refuse to pay until he has examined the goods for the purpose of determining whether the goods are of the contract quality. Even if Pugwash hears of the rumours and suspects that the garbanzo beans are not in accordance with the contract, he is nevertheless bound to pay on tender of documents which are in accordance with the contract.[3,a]

1   In your introduction, you should clearly identify the legal issues raised by the question. This is a good way to convince the examiner that you have understood what is relevant and will make him to be positively inclined towards your answer.
2   You need to provide an explanation of the relevant legal rules; without such explanation, it is more difficult for you to properly apply the law to the requirements of the question and thus also more difficult to demonstrate your knowledge and understanding.
3   Remember to draw conclusions from your analysis; this evidences your understanding of how to apply the law.

Pugwash is thus advised to pay against the shipping documents because by doing so, he retains his possible right to reject the goods on arrival provided that the breach is not so slight as to be treatable as a breach of warranty (s 15A of the **Sale of Goods Act 1979**). Certainly, even if the garbanzo beans are of satisfactory quality on shipment but are in such a state that they cannot endure a normal sea transit, Odessa will be in breach of an implied warranty entitling the buyer to claim damages (*Mash and Murrell Ltd v Joseph Emanuel* (1961)).[4] This implied warranty is distinct from the implied term under s 14 of the **Sale of Goods Act 1979**, the former relating to an undertaking that the goods can endure sea transit, as opposed to s 14(2) and (3) which are implied terms relating to satisfactory quality and fitness for purpose. If the garbanzo beans at the outset were of satisfactory quality and usable, then no action arises under s 14. But, because garbanzo beans are normally capable of enduring a sea transit, Odessa will be liable for any deterioration apparent on arrival.

Even if the garbanzo beans were of satisfactory quality at the time of shipment and were in such a state that they could have endured the sea transit, the cargo was damaged due to rain penetrating through improperly sealed hatches.[5] It may be that Pugwash will have an action against the carrier (but if, as we are informed, this is due to exceptionally heavy weather, perhaps the carrier might be covered by the excepted perils under the **Hague-Visby Rules**). It must be said, however, that in order to take the benefit of the contract of carriage, Pugwash must be the holder of the relevant documents and the only way Pugwash will be the holder of the documents is to have paid Odessa for them. If Pugwash does pay Odessa, Pugwash will have the right to sue the carrier for breach of his duty to take proper care of the goods, as is required under the contract of carriage.[b] Since Odessa is under a duty to make a reasonable contract of carriage (s 32(2) of the **Sale of Goods Act**), Pugwash will have a good action against the carriers.

Furthermore, once Pugwash has paid against the shipping documents, he will have the insurance policy assigned to him and he will be able to claim against the underwriter if he can show that the damage to the garbanzo beans by heavy storm conditions is a peril insured against.[c]

As for Flloyd, he is refusing to pay against the shipping documents because he did not receive information from Odessa as to the shipping arrangements and so he has not insured the cargo. In an fob contract, a seller is not obliged to obtain insurance cover for goods, but s 32(3) of the **Sale of Goods Act 1979** provides that the seller must give such notice to the buyer as may enable the buyer to insure the goods during the sea transit. If the seller fails to do so, the goods are at the seller's risk during sea transit. In a 'classic' fob

....

4   Providing an interim conclusion for each major issue considered is a good way to signpost.
5   The consideration of different options ensures completeness of your analysis and attracts additional marks.

contract, it is the buyer who makes the shipping arrangements and thus a seller need not give notice under s 32(3) where the buyer already has enough information to be able to insure (*Wimble Sons & Co v Rosenberg & Sons* (1913)).[6] The contract between Flloyd and Odessa appears to be an fob contract with additional services, obliging Odessa to make the necessary shipping arrangements. If Odessa has not given Flloyd notice to enable him to insure, then although the cargo will be at Odessa's risk during the sea transit, Flloyd is not entitled to refuse to pay against the shipping documents. Section 32(3) imposes a statutory duty and not a contractual duty. Thus, if the goods arrive safely, Flloyd has no cause of action because of the lack of insurance cover. As was discussed above, however, if the goods are not of satisfactory quality or unfit for their purpose, Flloyd may have a second right of rejection, that is, against the goods on arrival, provided he is a non-consumer and the breach is not so slight that it would be unreasonable to treat it as a breach of condition (s 15A of the Sale of Goods Act 1979).[7]

In order to have an action against the carrier for breach of the contract of carriage, Flloyd must, like Pugwash, have paid against the shipping documents. If Flloyd does not accept the documents but wishes to claim damages against the carrier in tort, the position following *Leigh and Sillivan v Aliakmon Shipping, The Aliakmon* (1986) is that he must show that at the time of the damage, he had legal ownership of the goods. Because he will not be able to do so (having refused to pay against the documents), Flloyd does not have a claim in tort and must pursue his claim in contract against Odessa. Flloyd is thus advised to pay against the documents and reserve the possibility of rejecting the goods on arrival. If the cargo is damaged during the sea transit, Flloyd will then have a claim against either the carrier for breach of the contract of carriage or Odessa for breach of s 32(3).

QUESTION 44

Discuss the rights of the parties in all of the following situations:

(a)   Warren bought a quantity of silk from Posner, a Belgian silk manufacturer, 'cif Southampton'. The contract did not stipulate the type of vessel to be used. Posner was unable to find a cargo ship, but knew that Warren needed the silk urgently, and so sent it on a canal barge, which was not designed for sea journeys. As a result, the silk was damaged by sea water.

(b)   A quantity of wool was bought by Warren from Traynor 'cif Bristol'. Traynor bought the wool from Browne, who claimed to have shipped it. Traynor tendered to Warren a bill of lading which recorded that the wool was on a ship called *Memphis*. When

---

6   Explaining a legal rule before applying it to the requirements of the question gives structure to your answer.

7   Considering different possibilities ensures that your analysis / advice is complete.

this ship arrived there was no wool on board, and it was discovered that no wool had ever been carried on the ship.

(c) Warren bought cotton from Hatchett Ltd, 'cif London'. Shortly afterwards, Warren found a cheaper supplier and so rejected the documents tendered by Hatchett. When Hatchett threatened to bring a claim, Warren responded by correctly stating that when the cotton arrived it was not of satisfactory quality.

How to Answer this Question

Part (a) requires a clear grasp of the fundamental principles of cif contracts and that contracts are subject to the express terms agreed between the parties.

Part (b) raises the time-honoured argument that a cif contract is more akin to a sale of documents than a sale of goods. The consensus, however, is that a cif contract is a genuine sale of goods contract which the seller performs using documents.

Part (c) raises the issue of whether a buyer who wrongfully rejects the documents may rely on a subsequent right to repudiate on the grounds that the goods are defective to justify his initial wrongful repudiation. The general rule set out in *Gill and Duffus v Berger* (1984) needs to be discussed.

Applying the Law

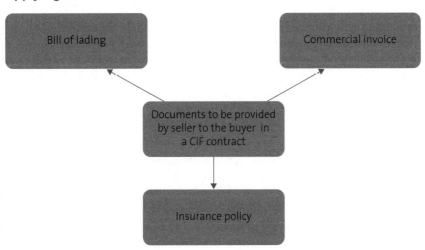

This mind map shows the main documents required. You will also have to consider the nature of the vessel on which goods were shipped and rejection issues in relation to first documents and then the goods.

ANSWER

(A) POSNER

According to the House of Lords in *Johnson v Taylor Bros* (1920), the duties of the cif seller are to ship the goods, to procure proper shipping documents and to tender the documents to the buyer. Thus, Posner fulfils its part of the bargain by tendering to Warren proper shipping documents.[8] Although the goods have been damaged by sea water, in cif contracts this is irrelevant. A buyer must still pay against the proper documents. Unless the contract stipulates otherwise, Posner must tender three documents: the bill of lading, the insurance policy and the commercial invoice. We are not told whether or not Posner has tendered these documents to Warren.

We know that Posner was unable to find a suitable cargo ship, hence a barge was used instead. Unless the contract between Warren and Posner specified what type of vessel was to be used, as long as Posner makes a reasonable contract of carriage, Posner is not in beach of its cif duties and Warren must pay against the documents (s 28 of the **Sale of Goods Act 1979**). However, Posner is the seller of silk, and ought to have been aware of the nature of the goods being shipped. It is therefore questionable whether shipping silk using a barge is a reasonable method of carriage. Certainly, Posner needs to tender a bill of lading. If the terms of the contract of carriage for barges are approximate to those for cargo ships, it may be that Posner has fulfilled its duties.

Warren needs to be assured of its rights against the carrier (under the contract of carriage) and the insurer (under the insurance policy). Therefore, if Posner makes a reasonable contract of carriage with the barge owners and the endorsement to Warren of the bill of lading provides Warren with rights under s 2(1) of the **Carriage of Goods by Sea Act** (that is, a lawful holder of the bill of lading can sue the carrier as if he were a party to the original contract of carriage) and satisfies all other requirements of the bill of lading (such as providing continuous documentary cover (*Hansson v Hamel and Horley* (1922)), and the insurance policy satisfies the terms of the cif contract, then Warren needs to pay Posner against the documents. Warren' claim will be against the carrier and/or the insurer.

On the other hand, if the contract of carriage is not a reasonable one, Warren can reject the documents at the time they are tendered to him for payment.[9] The goods in that situation remain at Posner's risk and Posner bears the loss of the silk being damaged by sea water.

---

8   Don't state all you know about the area of law in question. Remember to focus on the relevant issues – it is as much your ability to apply the relevant legal rules to the question as your knowledge that is assessed.

9   Considering possible options demonstrates both understanding and knowledge of the legal area in question.

(B) TRAYNOR

The cif seller has a choice. He either ships goods in accordance with the contract, or he buys goods afloat. We are told that, as between Warren and Traynor, Traynor has bought goods afloat, that is, the original shipper was Browne. If the cloth was lost in transit, Traynor is entitled to tender the proper shipping documents to Warren, and Warren must pay even though both parties know that the goods have been lost (*Manbre Saccharine v Corn Products* (1919)). If this was the case, Warren' remedy is against the carrier under contract of carriage or against the insurer under the insurance policy.[10]

However, it seems that no cloth had ever been shipped. Because a cif seller can demand payment against shipping documents, some argue that the cif contract is more akin to a sale of documents than a sale of goods. The consensus, however, is that a cif contract is a genuine sale of goods contract which the seller performs using documents. A seller who tenders a bill of lading showing goods have been shipped when this is not true has not performed his contractual duties. It makes no difference that Traynor is not the shipper but an intermediate seller in a chain of contracts. Professor Goode argues that a buyer can reject tender of documents in these circumstances.[11] This is because even a cif buyer is contracting primarily to buy goods, not claims. So, if goods are lost or damaged before the contract of sale is made, a cif buyer cannot be made to accept the tender of documents, because there were no goods conforming to contract at the time the contract was made. Thus, Warren can reject the documents against Traynor.

However, it sounds as though Warren has already paid against the documents. Although Warren cannot now reject the documents, he does have a second right of rejection. According to Lord Devlin in *Kwei Tek Chao v British Traders* (1954),[12] the buyer's right to reject goods arises when they are landed and when after examination are found to be not in conformity with the contract. Assuming the fact that no cloth was ever shipped was not apparent on the face of the shipping documents, Warren may rely on his second right to reject. There has been a total failure of consideration, and Warren will be entitled to the return of the purchase price he has paid and damages for non-delivery, which is assessed by reference to the difference between the market price and contract price at the due date for delivery (s 51). Alternatively, since, as against the indorsee, the bill of lading is conclusive evidence of the facts contained, Warren may wish to claim against the shipowner of *Memphis*, who is estopped from denying that the cloth was shipped. Similarly, Traynor can make his claim against Browne.

----

10 Providing an interim conclusion for each major issue considered is a good way to signpost.

11 The inclusion of academic references rather than the 'mere' consideration of case law shows not only that you have researched and read more widely but also adds to the criticality of your analysis.

12 It is important to refer to relevant authorities to substantiate your argument – this might be case law or a statutory provision. Remember: it is the application of law upon which you are assessed.

(C) HATCHETT

As discussed above, the cif buyer has two distinct rights of rejection (*Kwei Tek Chao v British Traders*).[13] We are told that Warren has rejected the shipping documents because it found a cheaper supplier. The courts do not question a party's motive for rejection. If Warren had the right to reject, then Warren had that right irrespective of market price movements. However, nothing in the question suggests that the documents were defective, so Warren should have accepted the documents and paid against them. Warren' wrongful rejection of conforming documents amounts to a repudiatory breach, entitling Hatchett to **s 50** of the **Sale of Goods Act 1979** damages for non-acceptance (since the bill of lading represents goods).

Warren, however, claims that the goods were defective. The question is whether Warren's wrongful rejection of the documents is justified on the ground that the goods are subsequently found to be defective. The general rule is set out in *Gill and Duffus v Berger* (1984). The House of Lords in that case made it clear that a buyer's rejection of conforming documents is a wrongful repudiation. This is true even if the buyer subsequently discovers that the goods themselves are not in accordance with the contract. As Lord Diplock said, the duties to ship goods and to present documents are separate and independent duties. Thus, Warren's wrongful rejection amounts to a repudiatory breach.[14d]

Aim Higher ★

It should be noted, however, that Professor Goode submits that this principle ('pay now, argue later') is open to serious objection. He argues that the idea that the buyer's remedy to pay against documents and then later reject goods on arrival and sue for the recovery of the purchase price lacks commercial realism. He questions the rationale of insisting that the buyer go through the exercise.

QUESTION 45

Augustus agreed to buy the following goods under separate contracts:

(a) 1,000 tons of oats cif Antwerp from Hadrian;

(b) 2,000 potatoes fob Yarmouth from Magnus;

(c) 3,000 staves of Latvian timber cif Mumbai from Ballista.

---

13 By referring to a previously drawn conclusion or explanation you link different stages of your analysis and thus present a more complete answer.

14 The proper application of the law is what the examiner is looking for in your answer.

Each contract stipulated for payment by irrevocable letter of credit at Jovian Bank on presentation of the shipping documents, and called for shipment in August/September.

The following events have occurred and you are asked to advise Augustus:

(i)   Hadrian has the oats ready to load by 10 September, but discovers that no credit has been opened and hence refuses to load. The credit was in fact opened on 28 September, and although Hadrian begins to load the oats, loading was not completed until 1 October. The bank refused to pay against the shipping documents, which included the bill of lading showing a shipment of 1 October.

(ii)   Jovian Bank informed Magnus that the credit was opened on 30 July. Augustus contacted Magnus to say that he wanted his local representative to inspect the potatoes before shipment, but Magnus refused to allow the representative to do so. The bank paid on presentation of the shipping documents. On arrival of the vessel, the potatoes were found to have been damaged due to severe storms during the voyage. The shipment date was 10 August, but Augustus knew nothing of this.

(iii) On 7 August, the Latvian authorities announced that the exportation of timber was prohibited as from 1 September. Since the market price for timber was rising, Ballista used the prohibition announcement as an excuse for not being able to ship the contract goods.

How to Answer this Question
Part (a) concerns the opening of credit, which comes too late to enable Hadrian to load the goods within the contract shipment period.

Part (b) involves a discussion as to an fob buyer's right to examine the goods. In relation to this, a comparison to domestic sale contracts must be made since in that situation, the point of delivery is the normal place of inspection, whereas in international sale contracts, there is no such rule. Was Augustus entitled to insist on an inspection at the point of shipment (which in international sale contracts is the point of delivery)? What are the effects of Magnus' refusal to allow Augustus's representative to inspect?

The answer should also deal with the fob seller's statutory duty under **s 32(3)** of the **Sale of Goods Act 1979**.

Part (c) asks you to discuss whether Ballista is entitled to rely on the prohibition of timber as justifying her refusal to deliver (for instance because the contract has been frustrated).

Applying the Law

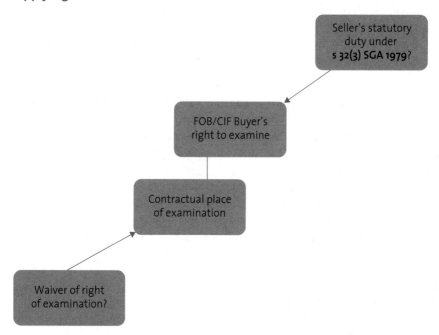

As well as position of the buyer and seller you will have to consider the legal position of the bank issuing the letter of credit.

ANSWER

(A) HADRIAN

The general rule is that documentary credit must be opened in accordance with the terms of the contract of sale. The contract between Augustus and Hadrian does not provide a date for the opening credit but it does, however, stipulate a period for the shipment of goods. It is clear from *Pavia & Co SpA v Thurmann-Nielsen* (1952) that in these circumstances, the documentary credit must be opened at the very latest on the first day on which shipment may take place. In a cif contract, the seller is not bound to tell the buyer the precise date on which he is going to ship, because it is the seller who has the option as to the time of shipment. Whenever the seller does ship, he must nevertheless be able to draw on the credit. Thus, Hadrian is entitled to refuse to load the goods if the credit has not been opened, and is entitled to treat the contract as discharged because of Augustus's breach. Furthermore, Hadrian will be entitled to claim damages.[15,e]

----

15 Clarity of expression and a logical structure are important assessment criteria. Don't use convoluted sentences as this is likely to interrupt the flow of your argument.

The credit is opened on 28 September and Hadrian begins to load. However, there is insufficient time before the end of the shipment period to complete the loading. *Bunge & Co Ltd v Tradax England Ltd* (1975) involved an fob contract where the buyer nominated a ship which was not ready to load until two hours before the end of the last working day of the shipment period; it was held that the seller could have rejected the nomination. Although Hadrian is a cif seller, and thus has the option of when to load, his option was restricted to that part of the shipment period when the letter of credit was open. By loading part of the goods within the available period, he has not waived his right to treat the contract as repudiated because of Augustus's failure to comply with the contractual stipulations as to payment.

When Hadrian tenders the shipping documents to Jovian Bank, the documents are rejected. Since the bill of lading gives the shipment as 1 October, as far as the bank is concerned, it is not obliged to pay the seller because the documents do not comply with the terms of credit (*Equitable Trust Company of New York v Dawson Partners Ltd* (1927)).[16] Jovian Bank's right of reimbursement depends on it taking up a faultless set of documents and since the bill of lading indicates a shipment date outside that permitted under the terms of credit, Jovian Bank is entitled to refuse to pay Hadrian. Hadrian's remedy is against Augustus for failure to have the documentary credit opened in his favour in time for him to load the goods before the end of the shipment period.

(B) MAGNUS

Magnus refuses Augustus's request for an inspection of the potatoes to be carried out before shipment. Under s 35(2) of the **Sale of Goods Act 1979**, there is no 'right' to inspect the goods before shipment, but if the buyer had not done so, there is no legal acceptance when the goods are shipped until the buyer has had a reasonable opportunity to inspect them upon delivery.

The fact that the buyer here was not afforded an opportunity to inspect the goods before shipment does not deprive him of his right to inspect at the contractual place of examination. This means that although Augustus was not given an opportunity to look at the goods when he asks to do so, he is nevertheless entitled to ask to inspect (and be allowed to do so) at the contractual place of examination.[17]

Where is this contractual place of examination in Augustus's case? **Section 35(2)** refers to the place of delivery and this reflects the rule at common law, where it was held in *Perkins v Bell* (1893) that there is a presumption that the place of examination is the contractual delivery point.

---

16 Focus on the issues which are raised by the question; don't simply write down everything you know about a particular legal rule.
17 The proper application of the relevant legal principle to the requirements of the questions is what the examiner is looking for.

'Delivery' in this instance is to be construed according to the terms of the fob contract. Where it is a classic or a strict fob case, namely, where the buyer acts as shipper of the goods, then the buyer is entitled to inspect the goods or have the local representative look at the goods before the ship sails. Where it is an fob contract with extended services, then the seller acts as the buyer's agent in shipping and hence the contractual (note: not necessarily coinciding with the statutory!) point of delivery for the purposes of s 35(2) would be at the point of arrival.[18] So, unless the contract provides otherwise, the assumption is that inspection and examination of the potatoes is postponed until the consignment arrives at the destination, and that is the place for examination. Even then, if Magnus knows that the potatoes are being resold to Augustus's sub-buyer, then the opportunity to examine goods is postponed until his sub-buyer has had an opportunity to examine.

We will need to inquire as to whether the buyer had waived the right to inspect.[19] If Augustus was requesting inspection at a non-contractual time, Magnus was acting within his rights not to let Augustus inspect the goods. If, however, Augustus did not purport to exercise his right to inspect at the contractual time, it is possible that such an omission might be construed as a waiver (especially in the case of a non-consumer transaction). In *B&P Wholesale Distributors v Marko* (1953), when the goods arrived, the buyer was given an opportunity to inspect the goods at the docks, but the buyer did not avail himself of the opportunity. Instead, the buyer transported the goods to his depot and then examined the goods. The court held that the buyer had not lost his right to reject. He would only be deemed to have waived his right to examine the goods if he had been given a genuine and practical opportunity to make a proper examination of the goods at the docks.

If Augustus had been offered a real and practical opportunity to inspect the goods, then he may not be able to quibble with any defects or deficiencies which that inspection could have revealed. However, where the goods deteriorated as in the present case and it is possible that an inspection could not have revealed the inherent vice in the goods, then the buyer retains his statutory and contractual right to damages for unfit goods as long as the deterioration was caused by the state of the goods as they were at shipment: *Mash & Murrell Ltd v Joseph Emanuel* (1961).[20] Deterioration caused by the sea passage shall naturally be borne by the buyer (as he is the shipper) and any claim (if any) would have to be brought against the carrier under the contract of carriage.

....

18 You need to provide an explanation of the relevant legal rules; without such explanation, it is more difficult for you to properly apply the law to the requirements of the question and thus also more difficult to demonstrate your knowledge and understanding.

19 Considering the implications of a particular action for the parties concerned shows an in-depth understanding and will attract additional marks.

20 It is not always necessary to provide details of the cases you cite as you are merely using them as authorities (i.e. references) for the legal principles you have you explained / referred to.

It is also possible that Augustus wished to inspect the potatoes in order to discover matters necessary for him to take out effective insurance. There is no information in the question leading to the suggestion that Magnus must have made the shipping arrangements. Unless the fob contract stipulated otherwise, Magnus is not obliged to obtain insurance cover for the goods. It is Augustus's responsibility to ensure that insurance cover was in place if he required it. We are told that the goods are damaged during the voyage, but we are not told whether or not Augustus had insured the potatoes.[21] Since Augustus only knew of the date of shipment after the damage occurred, it may be that under the contract, Magnus had the responsibility to make the shipping arrangements. Thus, if Augustus had not taken out effective insurance cover because he did not have sufficient information to insure, then **s 32(3)** of the **Sale of Goods Act 1979** places the risk of damage after shipment on the seller, Magnus. Although in a 'classic' fob contract, it is the buyer who makes all shipping arrangements (*Pyrene Co Ltd v Scindia Navigation Co Ltd* (1954)), it seems in this question that Magnus might have made them, otherwise Augustus would have had sufficient information on which to insure the goods.[22]

Thus, if Magnus is in breach of **s 32(3)** by failing to give notice to Augustus and Augustus has not insured the goods, although the risk in goods normally passes on shipment, Magnus bears the damage to the potatoes during the voyage.[23]

(C) BALLISTA

Once the contract has been concluded, a contract may be frustrated because of supervening governmental prohibition rendering the contract illegal. However, the prohibition operates as a frustrating event only if it is final and extends to the whole time still available for the performance of the contract. Ballista will not be able to rely on the prohibition of export to excuse performance, since the Latvian authorities had indicated in advance that the export of timber would only be prohibited from a future date within the shipment period.

In *Ross T Smyth & Co Ltd (Liverpool) v WN Lindsay Ltd* (1953), the contract provided for the shipment of horsebeans from a Sicilian port, cif Glasgow during October/November. On 20 October, the Italian authorities announced that the exportation of horsebeans was prohibited as from 1 November except under special licence. The sellers failed to ship. The court held that the buyers were entitled to claim damages, since the prohibition did not operate as a frustrating event.[24][f] Applying this case to the question, although Ballista has

---

21 Pointing out omissions in the information provided by the question and considering the impact these omissions might have on the outcome of your analysis will attract a higher mark as it demonstrates your understanding.
22 Simplicity and clarity of expression are more likely to attract a good mark than highly complex statements – be accurate in what you are saying, however.
23 Concluding your analysis with tailored advice to the advisee will ensure completeness of your answer.
24 Whilst demonstrating wider knowledge is a good way to attract extra marks, be sure that your answer remains focused on what is relevant. Remember: relevancy gains marks, irrelevancy loses marks.

the option of when to ship, she is not entitled to refuse to ship the goods before 1 September. The prohibition merely limited her option of when to ship from two months to one month and, when the announcement was made, Ballista should have shipped the goods between the date of the announcement and 31 August. Augustus is thus entitled to claim damages from Ballista.

QUESTION 46

Makro ships 10,000 tons of peanut oil from Southampton to Hamburg via Antwerp on board *Boniface*. While the goods are afloat, Makro enters into the following three separate contracts:

(a)   to sell 5,000 tons of peanut oil to Cathay cif Antwerp, payment to be made by letter of credit to be issued by Cathay's bank;

(b)   to sell 3,000 tons of peanut oil to Hassan cif Hamburg, payment by cash against documents;

(c)   to sell 2,000 tons of peanut oil to Penelope *ex Boniface*, payment in full in advance.

The voyage between Antwerp and Hamburg is beset with difficulties and the master of *Boniface* informs Makro that 1,000 tons of peanut oil have been lost. Cathay's bank accepts a bill of exchange on tender of documents which include a delivery order for 5,000 tons of peanut oil, but Cathay refuses to take delivery of the goods, claiming that the peanut oil is of inferior quality. Makro couriers the shipping documents to Hassan, who rejects them because they included a delivery order indicating that 500 tons of peanut oil have been lost. Penelope refuses to pay Makro because only 1,500 tons of peanut oil had been discharged at Hamburg.

❚   Advise Makro.

How to Answer this Question

Shipping documents have always played a key role in international sale contracts and normally shipping documents include the bill of lading. In all three parts to this question, however, a delivery order is tendered. In the absence of an express term in the contract, is the seller entitled to tender such a document where the sale involves a part of a bulk quantity?

Part (a) also involves s 14 of the **Sale of Goods Act 1979**. Part (b) requires you to discuss whether goods must be appropriated to the contract before loss. Part (c) involves a straightforward discussion of s 30 of the **Sale of Goods Act 1979**. Note, however, that the contract with Penelope is *ex* ship.

Applying the Law

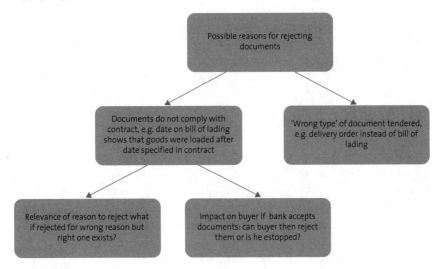

This diagram focuses on the two possible reasons for rejecting documents to be discussed in this answer. Important consideration in addition to this is which party bears the risk of any accidental loss or damage to the goods.

ANSWER

Neither the contract with Cathay nor the contract with Hassan requires Makro to supply goods from those on board *Boniface*. The contract with Penelope, however, does so require. When did the loss of the 500 tons occur? Was it before risk passed to the buyer? Risk will, however, have passed under the first two contracts (with Cathay and Hassan) when the goods are loaded on the ship. Thus, assuming (as seems to be implied by the question) that the loss occurred during the voyage, the risk falls upon the buyer under a cif contract. Of course, that is so provided that the buyer has taken up, or has no legitimate reason for not taking up, the documents.[25]

(A) CATHAY

As far as Cathay is concerned, his bank has taken up the documents and, it being his bank, Cathay is presumably bound by what his bank has done. Thus, Cathay – although he may have been entitled to reject the documents – cannot now resile from the acceptance of the documents by his bank. To put it another way, he is estopped from

---

25 In your introduction, you should clearly identify the legal issues raised by the question. This is a good way to convince the examiner that you have understood what is relevant and will make him to be positively inclined towards your answer.

rejecting the goods on any ground which would have entitled him to reject the documents (*Panchaud Frères v Etablissements General Grain* (1970)).[26] Thus, he is not entitled to reject the documents or the goods on the ground that he should not have been tendered a delivery order, but a bill of lading. In any case, it may be that the cif contract in this case expressly or impliedly provided for the tendering of a delivery order instead of the more normal bill of lading. This may be so especially if both buyer and seller (Makro and Cathay) contemplated that the contract would be performed by delivery of documents relating to goods consisting of an undivided part of a cargo.[g] As already indicated, however, even if Makro was not entitled to tender a delivery order, the documents tendered were accepted and Cathay is estopped from relying on that non-compliance. On the other hand, a buyer under a cif contract has two rights of rejection:[27] (i) to reject non-complying documents; and (ii) to reject goods which on arrival prove to be in breach of condition (except on any ground which would have entitled him to reject the documents) (*Kwei Tek Chao v British Traders and Shippers* (1954)). Thus, if the goods when tendered are in breach of condition, Cathay is entitled to reject them. It is possible that the peanut oil being 'of inferior quality' means that: (i) there is a breach of an express term of the contract; and/or (ii) there is a breach of one of the conditions implied by s14 of the **Sale of Goods Act 1979** (as to satisfactory quality or fitness for purpose).[h] In the case of (i), it is only if either: (a) the express term amounts to a condition; or (b) the breach is such as to deprive Cathay of substantially the whole of the benefit of the contract, that the buyer will have a right of rejection. From the facts given, it is impossible to determine whether the goods being of inferior quality amounts to a breach of condition, express or implied.

If, in fact, Cathay's bank has accepted documents which it was entitled to reject and which it ought to have rejected, then although Cathay is estopped as indicated above, he will have a remedy against his bank if the bank has acted contrary to his instructions in accepting the documents.

(B) HASSAN

Unlike Cathay, Hassan has rejected the documents. The reason that motivated him to reject the documents is irrelevant. What is relevant is whether he had a valid reason to reject the documents. He can rely on a valid reason, even if at the time of his rejection he relied upon an invalid reason, and he was unaware of the existence of the valid reason (*Glencore Grain Rotterdam BV v Lebanese Organisation for International Commerce* (1997)). There are two possibly valid reasons: firstly, that he was tendered a delivery order rather than a bill of lading – though, as seen above, it may be that the contract expressly or

---

26 Restrict yourself to what is relevant, don't write down everything you know about a particular case. Remember that relevancy is an important part of the assessment criteria.
27 Considering different possibilities is a good way to attract marks as it shows that you have understood the area of law in question.

impliedly allowed tender of a delivery order; secondly, that the delivery order showed less than the contract quantity. It is unclear whether Makro had appropriated[i] the lost 500 tons of peanut oil to Hassan's contract before the goods were in fact lost. Cases such as *Re Olympia Oil and Cake Co and Produce Brokers Ltd* (1915) indicate that a seller *can* appropriate lost cargo since, in a cif contract, the buyer has the benefit of a contract of carriage and a policy of insurance so that, in the event of loss, the buyer has a claim against either the carrier or the insurer, even though the loss or damage to the goods occurred before those documents were tendered (*Manbre Saccharine Co Ltd v Sugar Beet Products Co Ltd* (1919)).[28] There is academic opinion, however, that the seller *cannot* make a valid tender of documents after the loss of the goods unless, before the loss occurred, they had become fully identified as the contract goods.[29] In this case, they appear not to have been fully identified. Indeed, the problem does not even state that the goods supplied to Hassan must come from the cargo on *Boniface*. It would appear that Makro could have complied with the terms of his contract with Hassan by buying a cargo of peanut oil afloat (cif Hamburg) and using that cargo to fulfil his contract with Hassan. Thus, although the matter is not free from doubt, Makro is advised that his tender of documents to Hassan was not valid and that accordingly Hassan was entitled to reject them.

(C) PENELOPE

The difference between *ex* ship and cif contracts is that in the former, documents do not stand in the place of goods so that actual delivery of the goods must be made (*The Julia* (1949)). So far as Penelope is concerned, the risk in an *ex* ship contract, unless the contract specifically provides otherwise, passes upon delivery from the ship against payment. According to s 30(1) of the **Sale of Goods Act 1979**, where the seller delivers a quantity less than he has contracted to sell, the buyer has the option of either rejecting them or to accept the part-delivery and pay for them at the contract rate. However, according to s 30(2A), the buyer who does not deal as a consumer will not be able to reject the goods under s 30(1) if the shortfall is so slight that it would be unreasonable for him to do so. A shortfall of 500 tons, in the present instance, is not slight.[30] There is no question of Penelope getting her money back, since she has not yet paid the price. She has refused to pay. It seems, therefore, that Penelope is entitled to reject the goods and to refuse to pay (s 30(1) of the **Sale of Goods Act**).

....

28 Credit is given for pointing out different possibilities / possible solutions as this makes your analysis more complete.

29 The inclusion of academic references rather than the 'mere' consideration of case law shows not only that you have researched and read more widely but also adds to the criticality of your analysis.

30 Remember to relate your analysis to the issues raised / facts outlined by the question; it is the proper application of the relevant legal rules to the requirements of the question upon which you are assessed not the abstract discussion of the law.

> **Common Pitfalls** ✗
> Be careful not to spend too long on the first or the first two answers and run
> out of time for the last answer.

QUESTION 47

Sachin agrees to sell to Garfield 1,500 motor cycles, cif Buenos Aires, shipment by 31
January, payment by Sobers Bank's letter of credit, the bank to accept Garfield's bill of
exchange. Garfield arranges for the opening of the letter of credit and Sobers Bank
informs Sachin of this on 25 January. Sachin arranges for *The Storm* to ship the goods and
loading began on 30 January and finished on 1 February. During loading, 10 motor cycles
are dropped into the sea and five more are later damaged. The master signs three bills of
lading, the first being dated 30 January, the second 31 January and the third 1 February.
The total quantity shipped referred to in the bills of lading was 1,490 motor cycles and a
notation was made referring to 'five motor cycles damaged after loading'. Sachin tenders
the documents including an insurance policy covering the goods 'from warehouse to
warehouse' to Sobers Bank, which rejects them. Sachin then tenders the documents
to Garfield who, hearing that *The Storm* has been involved in a collision, also refuses
to pay.

▶ Advise Sachin.

How to Answer this Question

Much of the question is concerned with the passing of risk in cif contracts. Normally, risk
will pass to the buyer on shipment (that is, when the goods are delivered on board the
ship), but here the seller has obtained warehouse to warehouse insurance cover for the
benefit of the buyer. Does this fact alter the time at which risk normally passes to the
buyer?

When the buyer rejects documents, all rights of property (if transferred) and liabilities of
risk re-vest in the seller, and we will need to discuss whether Garfield was entitled to
reject the documents and/or the goods. If he was, the damage to the motor cycles which
has occurred will be at Sachin's risk.

Two further points need to be discussed: firstly, the effect of one of the three bills of
lading being dated outside the contractual date of shipment (are the goods therefore of
contract description?); secondly, the fact that a smaller quantity of goods was shipped
(is a buyer entitled to reject the smaller quantity of goods tendered?).

Applying the Law

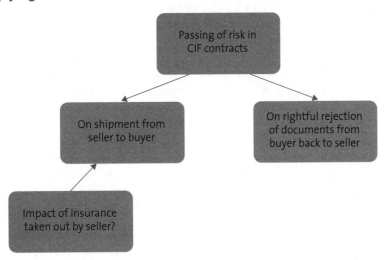

This diagram illustrates the passing of risk in this scenario.

ANSWER

Sachin's primary duties as a cif seller are to ship goods of the description contained in the contract, to procure the shipping documents and to tender those documents in the manner agreed (*The Julia* (1949)). Garfield's main obligation is to be ready and willing to pay the price.[31]

The contract between Sachin and Garfield does not provide a date for the opening of the credit. It does, however, stipulate a date by which shipment must take place: 31 January. Following *Pavia & Co SpA v Thurmann-Nielsen* (1952), Garfield must open the credit within a reasonable time to allow Sachin to arrange and make shipment by 31 January. We are told that Sobers Bank informs Sachin on 25 January that the letter of credit was opened.[32] If this does not allow Sachin sufficient time to make the necessary shipping arrangements and load the goods, Sachin is not obliged to ship the goods and is entitled to treat the contract as repudiated by Garfield and claim damages. However, Sachin has chosen not to accept Garfield's breach as discharging the contract because he ships the goods. The contract therefore remains open to the benefit of both parties.

31 A good introduction clearly identifies those legal rules which are raised by the question; this ensures a logical structure to your answer right from the start and puts your examiner in a positive frame of mind.

32 Dealing with the points raised in a question on a one-by-one basis adds structure and clarity to your analysis.

We are told that during the loading operation, 10 motor cycles are dropped into the sea. Normally, risk under a cif contract does not pass before shipment (*Law and Bonar Ltd v British American Tobacco Ltd* (1916)).[33] This is based on the assumption that goods are at the buyer's risk only once insurance cover begins. In a 'classic' cif contract, the seller takes out an insurance policy to cover the goods as from shipment. In this question, however, we are told that Sachin has effected 'from warehouse to warehouse' insurance cover.[k] It may be that since cover is available as from Sachin's warehouse, this excludes the general rule that risk in the goods does not pass before shipment. It is possible, therefore, that the goods are at Garfield's risk from the beginning of the insurance cover. It should be said, however, that such a variation of the general rule should be by express agreement, and there is nothing in the facts to indicate either that Garfield agreed to warehouse cover or that, if he did agree to such cover, that was indicative of the intention to place risk on him before shipment. If the general rule applies, then any damage prior to shipment is at the seller's risk and Sachin must bear the loss of the 10 motor cycles.

Once goods have been loaded on board the ship, risk passes to the buyer. This presupposes that the buyer does accept property in the goods, that is, by accepting the documents and/or the goods. If Garfield has the right to reject the documents and/or the goods and he does so, then even if property has passed to him (and therefore risk as well), all rights re-vest in the seller (*Kwei Tek Chao v British Traders and Shippers* (1954)). The only significance of the passing of risk on shipment, therefore, is that it prevents Garfield from claiming from Sachin for loss which occurs after shipment. If the whole contract is discharged, then property re-vests in Sachin and Garfield will not bear the risk during any part of the transit.[34]

As far as the five motor cycles are concerned, the damage appears to have occurred after they were loaded on board the ship. Thus, if Garfield does accept the contract, he must bear the loss, although he may have a claim against the underwriters of the insurance policy and/or against the carrier for breach of duty under the contract of carriage.

The master of the ship issues three bills of lading, indicating that 1,490 motor cycles were shipped in total. According to **s 30(1)** of the **Sale of Goods Act 1979**, where the seller delivers a quantity less than he has contracted to sell, the buyer has the option of either rejecting them or to accept the part-delivery and pay for them at the contract rate. However, by **s 30(2A)**, the buyer who does not deal as a consumer will not be able to reject the goods under **s 30(1)** if the shortfall is so slight that it would be unreasonable for him to do so.[35] A shortfall of 10 motor cycles, in the present instance, may be considered slight. Even if it was, Garfield is not deprived of his right to the full quantity sold merely because he accepts the smaller quantity shipped.

....

33 Proceeding from the general rule to more specific points adds structure and logic to your answer.
34 Remember to draw conclusions from your analysis; this evidences your understanding of how to apply the law.
35 Considering any potential limitation after outlining and applying the general legal rule to the requirements of the question ensures that your analysis proceeds in a logical way.

We are not told whether the Uniform Customs and Practice for Documentary Credits was incorporated into the contract. If it was, although Sobers Bank must ensure that the documents presented by Sachin comply strictly with the terms of the letter of credit, **Art 30(b)** does allow a plus or minus 5% in the quantity of goods. 10 motor cycles fewer than the contract quantity of 1,500 is within the permitted range. On this ground alone Sobers Bank does not have the right to reject the documents tendered by Sachin..[36] However, one of the bills of lading indicates a late shipment: 1 February. This is not merely a breach by Sachin of the duty to ship the goods by 31 January, but also means that the goods tendered did not match the description by which they were sold. The requirement that goods correspond to their description, until recently, entitled the buyer to reject for quite trivial discrepancies and to do so even though the failure of the seller to deliver goods of the contract description does not in the least prejudice the buyer (*Arcos Ltd v Ronaasen & Son* (1933)). *Bowes v Shand* (1877) established that the time of shipment is part of the description of goods. In that case, a contract for the sale of rice provided for shipment in March/April. Most of the rice[j] was loaded in February and the balance in March. Four bills of lading were issued, three bearing February dates and one a March date. The court held that this was a February shipment.[37] Applying this case to the question, since one-third of the goods was shipped too late, it is submitted that Sachin is in breach of **s 13** of the **Sale of Goods Act 1979** in not shipping goods complying with the contract description. However, it is arguable whether Garfield can reject the goods, since **s 15A** of the **Sale of Goods Act 1979** provides that, where the breach is so slight that it would be unreasonable for the buyer to reject the goods and the buyer does not deal as a consumer, the breach is to be treated as a breach of warranty and not as a breach of condition. Since time is of the essence in commercial contracts, it is submitted that the breach will not be perceived as so slight for it to be treated as a breach of warranty.

It seems that Sobers Bank has rightly rejected the shipping documents. Sachin then tenders the documents directly to Garfield for payment. Garfield is entitled to refuse to accept the documents, since the contract has provided for payment by letter of credit and that the only acceptable method of tender was to Sobers Bank (*Soproma SpA v Marine & Animal By-Products Corp* (1966)). The principle of short-circuiting credits prohibits direct presentation to the buyer where the documents have been rejected by the bank. This does not mean that Garfield must reject the documents, since he is always entitled to accept defective tender, but clearly he does not wish to do so. Garfield rejects the documents on the ground that the goods may have been damaged afloat due to a collision. This of itself is not a good reason for rejecting, because the seller is not in breach by tendering documents relating to goods damaged afloat, provided that the documents themselves are in order. The giving of an improper reason for rejecting documents does

....

36 Drawing an interim conclusion is a good way of signposting the relevant issues and also helps you to structure your answer logically.

37 Outlining the facts of a particular case is a good way to illustrate the relevant legal rules and thus strengthens your argument / conclusion.

not prevent Garfield from justifying his rejection, provided that there was good reason available at the time of rejection.[38]

Sachin is therefore advised that Sobers Bank was entitled to reject the documents because they revealed that the shipment was late. In addition to these reasons, Garfield was entitled to refuse the documents, since the contract had provided for payment by Sobers Bank. Sachin is liable in damages to Garfield for non-delivery.[39,m]

QUESTION 48

Describe the stages for the opening of a documentary credit and its operation. Why do commercial parties use documentary credits?

How to Answer this Question

This question requires you to demonstrate knowledge of how letters of credit operate in international commerce and an appreciation of the commercial reasons for their use.

You should approach the first part of the question as follows:

❖ explain the stages for the opening of a commercial credit pursuant to a term to that effect in an international sale contract;

❖ identify the main parties to the transaction (applicant, issuing bank, advising/confirming bank and beneficiary) and mention the different contracts between these parties;

❖ identify the two main principles underlying the system, namely the principle of autonomy and the principle of strict compliance.

For the second part of the question, you should discuss the main problems of dealing with foreign contracting parties and that the goods will be in transit for some time, with one or the other party being out of pocket during that time unless financing can be obtained from the banking system. Explain how these are addressed by the letter of credit system.

---

38 As accuracy and clarity of expression are important, the use of clear, precise, technical language will help to gain a good mark.
39 Concluding your analysis with tailored advice to the advisee will ensure completeness of your answer.

Applying the Law

This diagram illustrates how the law relating to letters of credit can be understood in this scenario.

ANSWER

If the contract of sale provides for payment by documentary credit, the credit opened in favour of the seller must comply in all respects with what was agreed in the contract of sale. The buyer must ensure that the letter of credit issued to the seller complies with what was agreed under the contract. For example, if the contract requires a confirmed credit, then the setting up of an unconfirmed credit is not sufficient. The buyer must open the credit as a condition precedent to the seller's duty to delivery: *Garcia v Page* (1936). The buyer's duty to furnish the documentary credit is absolute. If the credit is not in accordance with the contract, the seller can refuse to ship the goods.[40]

If the seller has the right to reject the letter of credit as non-conforming, the buyer may cure the defect if there is sufficient time. If the buyer does not cure or has no time to cure, he commits a repudiatory breach and the seller can treat the contract as discharged and claim damages.[n]

The letter of credit is considered as conditional payment so, whilst the credit is alive, the seller's right to sue for the price is suspended. If the credit is honoured, this constitutes payment under the contract of sale. If it is dishonoured (for example, if the Issuing Bank

---

40 Simplicity and clarity of expression are more likely to attract a good mark than highly complex statements – be accurate in what you are saying, however.

(IB) or Advising Bank (AB) does not pay on the presentation of conforming documents),[41] the seller's right to sue the buyer for price or damages revives.

The seller is entitled to a letter of credit within a reasonable time. The date when the seller is actually ready to ship is irrelevant because the seller usually has the option of when to ship within the full shipment period under the contract. The seller is not required to notify the buyer in advance of the date of shipment as a pre-condition of obtaining the letter of credit. Unless the contract says otherwise, this means that the letter of credit is to be made available to the seller no later than the earliest shipment date under the contract (*Pavia v Thurmann-Nielsen* (1952)).

STAGES FOR THE OPENING OF THE CREDIT

The stages for the opening of the credit are as follows:[42]

(a) The buyer applies to his bank, known as the Issuing Bank (IB), to open a credit in favour of the seller, undertaking the payment of the contract price against presentation of specified documents. The buyer must ensure his instructions are clear and conform to the contract of sale. The IB is not concerned with the contract of sale, so the IB is unlikely to see the contract of sale document. The IB will act on the buyer's instructions only. It will be most unusual for a bank these days not to include in its terms and conditions a clause incorporating the **Uniform Customs and Practice for Documentary Credits (UCP 600)**.[o] The **UCP 600** covers only irrevocable credits.[p]

(b) The IB can issue the letter of credit directly to the seller but almost always arranges for notification by another bank, called the Advising Bank (AB) (sometimes also called the Correspondent Bank) in the seller's country. Notification by the AB *is* the letter of credit. The IB is bound to the seller as soon as the seller receives the notification.[q]

(c) Unless the letter of credit says the credit is available only with IB, it must nominate a Nominated Bank which is authorised to pay. Unless the Nominated Bank is a confirming bank, it is not under an obligation to the seller to pay.

However if, which is usual, the contract of sale calls for a confirmed credit, the IB will ask the AB to add its own undertaking to honour the credit on presentation of the documents. This undertaking is known as 'confirmation', that is, IB's promise to pay is reinforced by a separate promise to pay by the Confirming Bank (which is usually the AB). **Article 8** of the **UCP 600** clearly states that confirmation by a confirming bank constitutes an undertaking to pay *in addition to* that of the IB.

The advantages for the seller to have the credit confirmed by the AB are obvious. The seller does not have to rely exclusively on a foreign bank (the seller may not know how reliable the foreign bank is and need not sue the bank in a foreign country

---

41 The provision of a practical example demonstrates understanding of the law and will attract a good mark.
42 Dissecting the relevant legal principle into its constituent parts and considering these parts on a point-by-point basis ensure that your answer is structured logically.

should it have cause to). If the AB does not add its confirmation, the credit is known as 'unconfirmed' credit.[43]

(d) After the goods have been dispatched, the seller must present the transport documents in accordance with the terms of the letter of credit. Usually the letter of credit will provide for the seller to present them to the AB (rather than the IB) because it is more convenient for the seller to present to a bank in his own country. Presentation is usually made by the seller's bank, not by the seller himself. The seller's bank acts as a collecting bank (in a similar way as if it were collecting a cheque). When the seller's bank presents the documents to the AB, it does so not in its own right but as the seller's agent.

If the documents are in order, then the AB pays in accordance with the letter of credit. AB then passes the documents to IB. The IB then releases them to the buyer.

CONTRACTUAL RIGHTS AND OBLIGATIONS

Once the credit is opened, each party's contractual relationship with each other has its own rules.[44]

(I) RELATIONSHIP BETWEEN THE BUYER AND THE IB

The relationship between the buyer and the IB is that of banker and customer. The terms of the contract are usually set out in the IB's standard form of application which invariably incorporates the UCP. The IB is responsible for ensuring that the letter of credit issued to the seller complies strictly with the instructions contained in the application for credit and that payment is made only on presentation of documents that fully comply with the terms of the credit (Art 14(b) of the UCP 600). This is one of the fundamental principles of documentary credit – the doctrine of strict compliance. The International Standard Banking Practice for the Examination of Documents under Documentary Credits (ISBP), which is a practical complement to the UCP, contains paragraphs of best banking practice, explaining in detail how the rules in the UCP are to be applied by banks on a day-to-day basis, particularly in relation to Art 14 of the UCP ('Standard for Examination of Documents').[45]

When the IB issues the letter of credit to the seller, the IB acts as principal and not as agent of the buyer. This means that the buyer cannot give instructions to the IB to withhold payment or to change the terms of the letter of credit (where the credit is irrevocable). The IB is entitled and obliged to ignore such instructions as long as the

---

43 The explanation of the law is an important factor for its successful application to the requirements of the question.

44 A logical structure is the first step towards gaining a good mark. You need to present your arguments in an organised manner, don't jump.

45 Whilst demonstrating wider knowledge is a good way to attract extra marks, be sure that your answer remains focused on what is relevant. Remember: relevancy gains marks, irrelevancy loses marks.

documents are presented within the shipment period and conform. This is known as the principle of the autonomy of credit. Article 4 of the UCP 600 makes it clear that the credit is separate from and independent of the underlying contract of sale. Banks deal with documents and not with goods.

(II) RELATIONSHIP BETWEEN THE IB AND THE AB

The relationship between the IB and the AB is that of principal and agent.[46] The AB must strictly comply with the instructions in the letter of credit.

(III) RELATIONSHIP BETWEEN THE IB AND THE SELLER

The IB undertakes to pay the seller on presentation of the documents. The undertaking will be honoured even if there is a breach of the underlying contract of sale. The IB's undertaking is given by it as principal and not as the buyer's agent. The doctrine of strict compliance applies. Each document presented by the seller needs to be consistent with each other and all the documents must appear on their face to relate to the same transaction. Each bank involved in the credit has a maximum of five banking days following receipt of the documents in which to examine the documents and decide whether to accept or reject, and inform the seller (Art 14(b) of the UCP 600).

(IV) RELATIONSHIP BETWEEN THE AB AND THE SELLER

By adding its confirmation, the AB is giving its undertaking that the credit will be honoured on presentation. This is given by the AB as principal, not as agent of the IB. This undertaking is completely distinct from that given by the IB. It is not a matter of the IB and the AB being jointly and severally liable. The IB's undertaking and the AB's undertaking are separate and self-contained.[47]

The AB as a confirming bank must honour the credit if the documents presented by the seller appear on their face to conform, and the AB is not concerned with the underlying contract of sale. Thus the doctrines of strict compliance and the autonomy of credit apply to the AB where it has confirmed the credit.

(V) THE RELATIONSHIP BETWEEN THE ABs AND THE BUYER

Because of privity of contract, English law does not recognise any relationship between the AB and the buyer as far as the credit is concerned. If the AB pays against non-conforming documents, the B's remedy is against the IB.[48]

---

46 Restrict yourself to what is relevant, don't write down everything you know about agency. Remember that relevancy is an important part of the assessment criteria.

47 Clarity of expression and a logical structure are important assessment criteria. Don't use convoluted sentences as this is likely to interrupt the flow of your argument.

48 As accuracy and clarity of expression are important, the use of clear, precise, technical language will help to gain a good mark.

PURPOSE OF DOCUMENTARY CREDITS

Because international sales often involve a long interval of time between the despatch of goods and their arrival, during this period the parties are exposed to financial risks. The seller invariably wants to be assured of payment and to be paid without delay while retaining an interest in the goods until he is paid. On the other hand, the buyer will not want to pay for goods until he has received them, or least something that represents the goods.[49] The documentary credit system is designed to alleviate the financial risks involved for the parties to an international sales contract.

Documentary credit provides the seller with security (if irrevocable) but it also costs money. Banks involved with issuing, advising and confirming charge for services. The cost is passed to the buyer. It may be that a buyer is reluctant to agree to payment via letter of credit. It depends on whether the seller is in a position to insist on letter of credit as the payment method without having to cover the cost, which in turn depends on the relative bargaining power of the parties. In practice, the seller usually only requires a letter of credit where he has not yet developed a sufficient relationship with the buyer to enable him to adopt a cheaper payment method. Documentary credit remains, however, the most common method of payment in international sales.

The advantages of payment using documentary credit to the seller clearly include an assurance of payment irrespective of the solvency of the buyer; an assurance of payment irrespective of any disputes with the buyer concerning the underlying goods (under the principle of autonomy of credit); if the credit is transferable, the seller can use it to finance his own acquisition of goods; and not have to pursue the buyer in a different country, with all the risks and cost that this carries.

The system has fewer obvious advantages for the buyer. However, without the credit system, the transaction would possibly never come about at all, as the seller might not be willing to trade with a foreign buyer unless he was assured of payment. Moreover, the doctrine of strict compliance benefits the buyer considerably in that he can insist on a perfect tender of documents if payment is to be made. In the light of a very high percentage of non-compliant/defective tenders,' the buyer effectively has a right to call off the transaction should the market have moved against it.

Common Pitfalls ✗

Students must not merely give a general description of the parties to letters of credit and how letters of credit worked without relating these descriptions to the question asked.

---

49 The consideration of different positions demonstrates wider knowledge and deeper understanding.

QUESTION 49

(a) Discuss the implications of the rule that risk passes on or as from shipment in cif contracts.

(b) In the case of unascertained goods, is the cif seller entitled to appropriate lost goods to the contract?

How to Answer this Question

Not an easy two-part question. In particular, part (a) involves the concept of risk passing 'as from' shipment⁵ and the retrospective effect of this rule gives rise to a number of difficulties.

As far as part (b) is concerned, the cases and academic opinion are divided. The general rule in domestic sales is clear – goods may not be appropriated once lost. But, what is the rule in international sale contracts?

Answer Structure

A. Risk passing 'as from' shipment → The retrospective effect of rule

B. Discussion of current academic opinion → Discussion of the rule in international sale

ANSWER

(A)

The general rule is that **s 20** of the **Sale of Goods Act 1979**, which links the passing of risk to the passing of property, is ousted in international sale contracts. In *The Julia* (1949), Lord Porter said that risk generally passes 'on shipment or as from shipment' in cif contracts, whereas property passes at the time the buyer pays and takes up the documents.⁵⁰ Lord Porter's statement contains two rules: where the seller ships goods for the buyer, risk passes at the time of shipment, that is, *on* shipment; where the contract is made after shipment, risk passes at the time of the contract but retrospectively, that is, *as from* shipment.

The implications of the rule might appear harsh on the buyer because, for instance, risk, unlike property, may pass to the buyer although the goods are unascertained goods

....

50 Stating by whom or how a particular legal principle was stated in a case (*obiter* or *ratio*) demonstrates a deeper knowledge and is likely to attract additional marks.

which have not been appropriated by the contract. Furthermore, a buyer to whom risk, but not property, is transferred by the seller is not entitled to sue the carrier in the tort of negligence (*Leigh and Sillivan v Aliakmon Shipping Co* (1986)).[51,t]

If goods are shipped and lost during the sea transit, the seller is still entitled to tender shipping documents to the buyer and to claim the purchase price. The buyer's remedy is normally a claim against the carrier or the insurer because, on taking up the documents, the buyer takes the benefit of the contract of carriage and policy of insurance and is, therefore, able to claim in respect of loss from the time of shipment. Thus, although the rule that risk passes on or as from shipment does at first seem harsh, the buyer is not without a remedy where goods are lost, as long as the buyer is not exposed to risks not covered by the contract of insurance or carriage (*Groom v Barber* (1915)).

There are situations where the buyer has to pay for the goods whilst receiving nothing. In *Manbre Saccharine v Corn Products* (1919), goods were lost when the ship was sunk during World War I. The insurance policy did not cover war risks but, because the terms of the policy were usual at the time the contract was made, the buyer had to bear the loss.[u] On the other hand, where the seller fails to make a proper contract of carriage as he is contractually bound to do under a cif contract, he will be in breach of the contract of sale[v] and the buyer will be entitled to reject and no question of risk arises.

A particular difficulty arises with the concept of risk passing to the buyer *as from* shipment.[52] Where goods are first shipped, then deteriorate and are subsequently sold, it is clear that the rule that risk passes with retrospective effect means that the buyer has to bear the risk of deterioration which had already occurred when the contract of sale was made. It should be noted, however, that although the cif seller's obligations as to quality relate to the time of shipment, the seller impliedly undertakes that the goods are in such a state as to be able to withstand a normal sea transit (*Mash and Murrell v Joseph Emanuel* (1961)), so that the seller remains liable for deterioration if the goods suffer from some defect before risk in them has passed to the buyer *as from* shipment.

It can be seen, therefore, that there are cases where goods are lost in transit in circumstances where the buyer has no claim against the carrier or insurer, and that this sometimes involves hardship for the buyer, because the buyer has to pay the purchase price to the seller on tender of the shipping documents or, if he has already paid, he cannot recover the price on the ground that there was a total failure of consideration.[53]

....

51 Showing an appreciation of the wider implications of a particular principle is a good way to attract marks. However, remember to focus on the relevant issues; don't simply write down all you know.
52 Point to existing difficulties. This demonstrates your awareness and will attract a higher mark.
53 Finishing your answer with a conclusion ensures completeness of your analysis; this should summarise your findings in a clear and succinct manner. Don't introduce new arguments here.

(B)

Cif contracts are often concerned with sale of unascertained goods, and problems arise where such goods are lost before the seller has appropriated the goods to the contract. The general rule in domestic sales is that a seller who has not actually appropriated any goods to the contract is not entitled to rely on the fact that he had *intended* to do so before the goods were lost. However, Aitkin J in *Groom v Barber* (1915) said that:

> 'The seller must be in a position to pass property by the bill of lading if the goods are in existence, but he need not have appropriated the particular goods in the particular bill of lading until the moment of tender.'[54]

Although the question of appropriation was not discussed, *Manbre Saccharine v Corn Products* (1919) suggests that a cif seller is entitled to tender documents relating to a cargo which he knows to be lost. 'Appropriation' in the sense that the seller is bound contractually to deliver the goods in question in order to pass property will hardly ever take place under a cif contract before tender of documents.

The decided cases and academic opinion do not provide a clear answer to the question.[55] Certainly, *Re Olympia Oil and Cake Co and Produce Brokers* (1915) suggests that a cif seller can appropriate lost cargo to the contract (and the buyer's remedy is, therefore, against the carrier or the insurer). Rowlatt J in that case pointed out, however, that to allow appropriation after loss might lead to unjust results: if the market price of the goods rose (or the insurance policy did not cover the loss), the seller would tender the documents relating to the lost cargo; whereas, if the market price fell, the seller could buy an alternative cargo to fulfil the contract and claim on the insurance policy in respect of the lost goods. Of course, if the seller is not entitled to appropriate lost goods, he may suffer hardship, for example where he is liable to his supplier for goods appropriated *before* loss without being able to pass on that appropriation to the buyer *after* loss.

In the absence of clear authority to the contrary, academic opinion suggests that a cif seller of unascertained goods cannot appropriate a lost cargo, that is, he is not entitled to tender documents relating to the goods which have been lost unless at the time of loss he had appropriated the particular goods to the contract by binding himself contractually to deliver those goods that have been lost.[56]

---

54 Stating limitations to a particular principle is a good way to show greater knowledge of the area in question.

55 The consideration of more than one possible legal argument or opposing views demonstrates wider knowledge and deeper understanding.

56 A good conclusion summarises the findings made in the main body of your answer and relates these findings to the question set.

Notes

a　There is a controversial decision of the High Court of Australia (*Henry Dean & Sons (Sydney) Ltd v O'Day Pty Ltd* (1927)) which suggests that a buyer may be entitled to reject documents where the documents are, but the goods themselves are not, in accordance with the contract. The sellers, when refusing to pay against documents, are taking a risk but one that was 'justified by the result'. This problem is yet unresolved in the English courts.

b　Under s 2(1) of the **Carriage of Goods by Sea Act 1992**, the lawful holder of a bill of lading has the right to sue the carrier under the contract of carriage 'as if he had been a party to that contract'.

c　Marine insurance is not usually found in undergraduate commercial law syllabuses and students will not be expected to discuss the implications of whether or not Odessa, who arranges the policy, has disclosed the rumours that surround the quality of the garbanzo beans. Remember that contracts of insurance are contracts *uberrimae fidei*, that is, of utmost good faith, so that even if a non-disclosure does not relate to the loss, an insurer may decline to pay against a claim.

d　See note *a* above

e　The measure of damages in these circumstances is not limited by the market price rule in s 50(3) of the **Sale of Goods Act 1979**, but may extend to the seller's loss of profits, provided that they are not too remote under the rule in *Hadley v Baxendale* (1854); *Trans Trust SPRL v Danubian Trading Co Ltd* (1952).

f　If the prohibition of export had been instantaneous, it would have operated as a frustrating event. If, on the other hand, the Latvian authorities indicated that an export embargo might be imposed, then Ballista would probably not be in breach if she did not ship between the time of that announcement and the subsequent date of the embargo: *Tradax Export v André & Cie* (1976).

g　Even if this were the case, the delivery order must be one issued by the ship so that the document should give the buyer some contractual rights against the ship. (Under the **Carriage of Goods by Sea Act 1992**, this has the same effect as a bill of lading in transferring property.)

h　It is unlikely to amount to breach of the condition implied by s 13, since the matter of quality is not normally regarded as part of the contract description (*Ashington Piggeries v Christopher Hill* (1972)).

i　'Appropriation' here is used in the sense that the seller has contractually bound himself to deliver certain goods. There can be appropriation in this sense even though the goods remain 'unascertained' because they form part of a larger bulk.

j　Under Incoterms 2010 (in force since 1 January 2011), the seller's obligation is to place goods 'on board the vessel', rather than over the ship's rail. If no specific loading point is indicated by the buyer, the new Incoterms make clear that the seller may select a point that best suits the seller.

k　Institute Cargo Clauses (on which most cif contracts are now covered) cover loss or damage from warehouse to warehouse plus 60 days after landing, and during loading and unloading.

l　8,150 bags of rice out of 8,200.

m　The measure of damages will be calculated in accordance with s 51(3) of the **Sale of Goods Act 1979**, that is, the difference between the contract price and the market value the goods would have had, had the documents and goods both been properly delivered.

n　The seller can of course waive the breach and accept a non-conforming letter of credit. If he waives, then he loses the right to complain of the breach later: *Alan v El Nasr Export* (1972).

o　The **UCP 600** is effective from 1 July 2007.

p　If parties want to use revocable credits, they will have to issue the credit subject to the **UCP 500** instead or incorporate their own terms of revocability.

q　Note that there is no consideration moving from the seller to Issuing Bank. It is generally accepted that a letter of credit is treated as a promise binding through mercantile usage, so that it is enforceable without consideration. Documentary credit therefore is an exception to the doctrine of consideration.

r   In *Bankers Trust v State Bank of India* (1991), there was expert evidence that discrepancies are found in nearly 50% of cases which may justify rejection of the documents presented by the seller.

s   Under Incoterms 2010 (in force since 1 January 2011), goods are shipped as between the seller and buyer once the goods are loaded 'on board the vessel', rather than over the ship's rail. If no specific loading point is indicated by the buyer, the new Incoterms make clear that the seller may select a point that best suits the seller.

t   There is now apparent contradiction between the **Carriage of Goods by Sea Act 1992** (which allows for the transfer of property irrespective of whether the goods are in bulk and unascertained goods) and which implemented *The Elafi* (1982) and **s 16** of the **Sale of Goods Act 1979** (which does not allow for the transfer of property in unascertained goods until the goods have become ascertained). The position is unclear. Note, however, under **s 20A** and **s 20B** of the **Sale of Goods Act 1979**, a pre-paying buyer of some or all of its goods of an identified bulk becomes an owner in common of the bulk (see Question 14).

u   In fact, the buyer escaped liability in this case because the seller did not tender the proper shipping documents.

v   **Section 32(2)** of the **Sale of Goods Act 1979**.

Index